BLEU 1

Discovering FRENCH Nouveau!

Jean-Paul Valette
Rebecca M. Valette

McDougal Littell
A HOUGHTON MIFFLIN COMPANY

Evanston, Illinois • Boston • Dallas

Cover photography

Background: Eiffel Tower, Paris, France; Inset: St. Louis, Senegal; Credits appear on page R52

McDougal Littell wishes to express its heartfelt appreciation to **Gail Smith**, Supervising Editor for DISCOVERING FRENCH. Her creativity, organizational skills, determination, and sheer hard work have been invaluable in all aspects of the program.

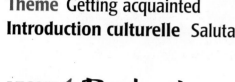

UNITÉ 1 Invitation au français
Faisons connaissance 12

Thème Getting acquainted
Introduction culturelle Salutations 13

LEÇON 1 Bonjour!

VIDÉO-SCÈNE A: La rentrée — 14

• **Notes culturelles**
  1. La rentrée 2. Les prénoms français **15**
• **Pour communiquer**
  Bonjour! Je m'appelle …, Comment t'appelles-tu? **15**
• **Petit commentaire** Astérix **16**
• L'alphabet **17**
• Les signes orthographiques **17**
• Les nombres de 0 à 10 . . . . **17**

VIDÉO-SCÈNE B: Tu es français? — 18

• **Note culturelle** En Bref: La Martinique **19**
• **Pour communiquer**
  Tu es de …?, Je suis de …; Les nationalités **19**
• **Petit commentaire**
  La statue de la Liberté et la tour Eiffel **20**
• Français, française **20**
• Les nombres de 10 à 20 . . . . **21**
• **Prononciation** Les lettres muettes **21**

VIDÉO-SCÈNE C: Salut! Ça va? — 22

• **Note culturelle** Bonjour ou Salut? **23**
• **Pour communiquer**
  Bonjour! Comment vas-tu? **23, 24**
• Les nombres de 20 à 60 . . . . **25**
• **Prononciation** Les consonnes finales **25**

LEÇON 2 Famille et copains

VIDÉO-SCÈNE A: Copain ou copine? — 26

• **Note culturelle** Amis et copains **27**
• **Pour communiquer** Qui est-ce?; les personnes **27**
• **Petit commentaire** Cycling **28**
• Un garçon, une fille **28**
• Les nombres de 60 à 79 . . . . **29**
• **Prononciation** La liaison **29**

VIDÉO-SCÈNE B: Une coïncidence — 30

• **Note culturelle** En Bref: La province de Québec **31**
• **Pour communiquer**
  Tu connais …?, Comment s'appelle …? **31**
• **Petit commentaire** The French and the U.S. **32**
• Le garçon, la fille **32**
• Les nombres de 80 à 1 000 . . . . **33**
• **Prononciation** La voyelle nasale /ɛ̃/ **33**

VIDÉO-SCÈNE C: Les photos d'Isabelle — 34

• **Note culturelle** La famille française **35**
• **Pour communiquer** La famille **35**
• **Petit commentaire** Pets **36**
• Mon cousin, ma cousine **36**
• **Pour communiquer** Quel âge as-tu? **37**
• **Prononciation** Les voyelles nasales /ã/ et /ɔ̃/ **37**

À VOTRE TOUR Communication/révision **38**
ENTRACTE 1 Lecture et culture **40**

UNITÉ 2 Invitation au français

La vie courante 42

Thème Everyday life in Paris
Introduction culturelle Bon appétit! 43

LEÇON 3 Bon appétit!

VIDÉO-SCÈNE A: Tu as faim? 44
- **Note culturelle** Les jeunes et la nourriture 45
- **Pour communiquer**
  Tu as faim? Tu veux …?; les nourritures 45
- **Petit commentaire** *Sandwichs* 46
- Un sandwich, une pizza 46
- Prononciation: L'intonation 47

VIDÉO-SCÈNE B: Au café 48
- **Note culturelle** Le café 49
- **Pour communiquer**
  Tu as soif? S'il vous plaît …; les boissons 49
- **Petit commentaire** *Favorite beverages* 50
- **Prononciation** L'accent final 51

VIDÉO-SCÈNE C: Ça fait combien? 52
- **Note culturelle** L'argent européen 52
- **Pour communiquer**
  C'est combien? Il/elle coûte …; Prête moi 53
- **Petit commentaire** Restaurants 54
- **Prononciation** La consonne «r» 55

LEÇON 4 De jour en jour

VIDÉO-SCÈNE A: L'heure 56
- **Pour communiquer A** Les heures 56
- **Pour communiquer B**
  Les quarts d'heure, les minutes 58

VIDÉO-SCÈNE B: Le jour et la date 60
- **Pour communiquer A** Les jours de la semaine 61
- **Pour communiquer B** Les mois de l'année; la date 62

VIDÉO-SCÈNE C: Le temps 64
- **Pour communiquer** Le temps; les saisons 65

À VOTRE TOUR Communication/révision 66
ENTRACTE 2 Lecture et culture 68

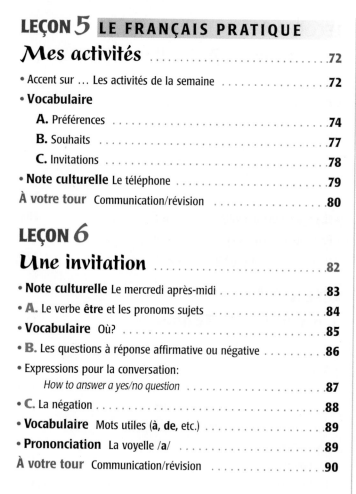

UNITÉ 3

Qu'est-ce qu'on fait? 70

Thème Daily activities

LEÇON 5   LE FRANÇAIS PRATIQUE

Mes activités 72

- Accent sur ... Les activités de la semaine 72
- Vocabulaire
  - **A.** Préférences 74
  - **B.** Souhaits 77
  - **C.** Invitations 78
- **Note culturelle** Le téléphone 79
- **À votre tour** Communication/révision 80

LEÇON 6

Une invitation 82

- **Note culturelle** Le mercredi après-midi 83
- **A.** Le verbe **être** et les pronoms sujets 84
- **Vocabulaire** Où? 85
- **B.** Les questions à réponse affirmative ou négative 86
- Expressions pour la conversation:
  - *How to answer a yes/no question* 87
- **C.** La négation 88
- **Vocabulaire** Mots utiles (**à**, **de**, etc.) 89
- **Prononciation** La voyelle /**a**/ 89
- **À votre tour** Communication/révision 90

LEÇON 7

Une boum 92

- **Note culturelle** Une boum 93
- **A.** Les verbes en **-er**: le singulier 94
- **Vocabulaire** Les verbes en **-er** 95
- **B.** Les verbes en **-er**: le pluriel 96
- **C.** Le présent des verbes en **-er**: affirmatif, négatif 98
- **Vocabulaire** Mots utiles (**bien**, **mal**, etc.) 100
- Expressions pour la conversation:
  - *How to express approval or regret* 100
- **D.** La construction: verbe + infinitif 101
- **Prononciation** Les voyelles /**i**/ et /**u**/ 101
- **À votre tour** Communication/révision 102

LEÇON 8

Un concert de musique africaine ..104

- **Note culturelle** En Bref: Le Sénégal 105
- **A.** Les questions d'information 106
- **Vocabulaire** Expressions interrogatives 106
- Expressions pour la conversation:
  - *How to express surprise or mild doubt* 107
- **B.** Les expressions interrogatives avec **qui** 108
- **C.** Qu'est-ce que? 109
- **D.** Le verbe **faire** 110
- **Vocabulaire** Expressions avec **faire** 110
- **E.** L'interrogation avec inversion 111
- **Prononciation** La voyelle /**y**/ 111
- **À votre tour** Communication/révision 112

TESTS DE CONTRÔLE 114
VOCABULAIRE 116
ENTRACTE 3 Lecture et culture 118

IMAGES À l'école en France 124

UNITÉ 4
Le monde personnel et familier 134

Thème People and possessions

LEÇON 9 LE FRANÇAIS PRATIQUE
Les personnes et les objets 136

- Accent sur … Les jeunes Français **136**
- **Vocabulaire**
  - **A.** La description des personnes **138**
  - **B.** Les objets **140**
  - **C.** Les affaires personnelles **142**
  - **D.** Ma chambre **144**
  - **E.** Mon ordinateur (Vocabulaire supplémentaire) . . .**147**
- **À votre tour** Communication/révision **148**

LEÇON 10
Vive la différence! **150**

- **Note culturelle** En Bref: Haïti **151**
- **A.** Le verbe **avoir** **152**
- **Vocabulaire** Expressions avec **avoir** **152**
- **B.** Les noms et les articles: masculin et féminin . . .**153**
- **C.** Les noms et les articles: le pluriel **154**
- **D.** L'article indéfini dans les phrases négatives **156**
- Expressions pour la conversation:
  How to contradict a negative statement or question **157**
- **E.** L'usage de l'article défini dans le sens général . . .**158**
- **F.** L'usage de l'article défini avec les jours de la semaine **159**
- **Prononciation** Les articles «le» et «les» **159**
- **À votre tour** Communication/révision **160**

LEÇON 11
Le copain de Mireille **162**

- **Note culturelle** L'amitié et la bande de copains **163**
- **A.** Les adjectifs: masculin et féminin **164**
- **Vocabulaire** La description **165**
- **B.** Les adjectifs: le pluriel **166**
- **Vocabulaire** Les adjectifs de nationalité **167**
- Expressions pour la conversation:
  How to introduce a conclusion **167**
- **C.** La place des adjectifs **168**
- **Prononciation** Les consonnes finales **169**
- **À votre tour** Communication/révision **170**

LEÇON 12
La voiture de Roger **172**

- **Note culturelle** Les Français et la voiture **173**
- **A.** Les couleurs **174**
- **Vocabulaire** Les couleurs **174**
- **B.** La place des adjectifs avant le nom **175**
- **Vocabulaire** Les adjectifs qui précèdent le nom **175**
- Expressions pour la conversation:
  How to get someone's attention **176**
- **C.** Il est ou c'est **177**
- **D.** Les expressions impersonnelles avec c'est **178**
- **Vocabulaire** Opinions **178**
- **Prononciation** Les lettres «ch» **179**
- **À votre tour** Communication/révision **180**

TESTS DE CONTRÔLE **182**

VOCABULAIRE **184**

ENTRACTE 4 Lecture et culture **186**

UNITÉ 5

En ville 192

Thème Visiting a French city

LEÇON 13 LE FRANÇAIS PRATIQUE
La ville et la maison 194

• **Accent sur … Les villes françaises** 194
• **Note culturelle** Le nom des rues 196
• **Vocabulaire**
   A. Où habites-tu? 196
   B. Ma ville 197
   C. Pour demander un renseignement 199
   D. Ma maison 200
• **À votre tour** Communication/révision 202

LEÇON 14
Week-end à Paris 204

• **Note culturelle** À Paris 205
• **A.** Le verbe **aller** 206
• **B.** La préposition **à; à** + l'article défini 208
• **Vocabulaire** En ville 210
• **C.** La préposition **chez** 211
• **D.** La construction: **aller** + l'infinitif 212
• **Prononciation** Les semi-voyelles /**w**/ et /**j**/ 213
• **À votre tour** Communication/révision 214

LEÇON 15
Au café de l'Univers 216

• **Note culturelle** Au café 217
• **A.** Le verbe **venir** 218
• **B.** La préposition **de; de** + l'article défini 219
• **Vocabulaire** Les sports, les jeux et la musique 220
• **C.** Les pronoms accentués 221
• **Expressions pour la conversation:**
   How to express surprise; How to contradict someone 222
• **D.** La construction: nom + **de** + nom 223
• **Prononciation** Les voyelles /ø/ et /œ/ 223
• **À votre tour** Communication/révision 224

LEÇON 16
Mes voisins 226

• **Note culturelle** Les animaux domestiques en France 227
• **A.** La possession avec **de** 228
• **Vocabulaire** La famille 229
• **B.** Les adjectifs possessifs: **mon, ton, son** 230
• **Expressions pour la conversation:**
   How to question a statement or express a doubt 231
• **C.** Les adjectifs possessifs: **notre, votre, leur** 232
• **D.** Les nombres ordinaux 233
• **Prononciation** Les voyelles /o/ et /ɔ/ 233
• **À votre tour** Communication/révision 234

TESTS DE CONTRÔLE 236
VOCABULAIRE 238
ENTRACTE 5 Lecture et culture 240

IMAGES À Paris 246

UNITÉ 6

Le shopping 254

Thème Buying clothes

LEÇON 17 LE FRANÇAIS PRATIQUE

L'achat des vêtements 256

• Accent sur ... L'élégance française 256
• Vocabulaire
   A. Les vêtements 258
   B. D'autres vêtements et accessoires 260
   C. Dans un magasin 262
• **Vocabulaire** Les nombres de 100 à 1 000 263
À votre tour Communication/révision 264

LEÇON 18

Rien n'est parfait! 266

• **Note culturelle** Le grand magasin 266
• **A.** Les verbes **acheter** et **préférer** 268
• **Vocabulaire** Verbes comme **acheter** et **préférer** 269
• **B.** L'adjectif démonstratif **ce** 270
• **C.** L'adjectif interrogatif **quel** 271
• **D.** Le verbe **mettre** 272
• **Prononciation** Les lettres «e» et «è» 273
À votre tour Communication/révision 274

LEÇON 19

Un choix difficile 276

• **Note culturelle** Les jeunes et la mode 276
• **A.** Les verbes réguliers en **-ir** 278
• **Vocabulaire** Verbes réguliers en **-ir** 278
• **B.** Les adjectifs **beau, nouveau** et **vieux** 279
• **C.** La comparaison avec les adjectifs 280
• Expressions pour la conversation:
   How to introduce a personal opinion 281
• **Prononciation** Les lettres «ill» 281
À votre tour Communication/révision 282

LEÇON 20

Alice a un job 284

• **Note culturelle** L'argent des jeunes 285
• **Vocabulaire** L'argent 286
• **A.** Le pronom **on** 288
• Expressions pour la conversation:
   How to indicate approval 289
• **B.** Les verbes réguliers en **-re** 290
• **Vocabulaire** Verbes réguliers en **-re** 290
• **C.** L'impératif 291
• **Prononciation** Les lettres «an» et «en» 293
À votre tour Communication/révision 294

TESTS DE CONTRÔLE	**296**
VOCABULAIRE	**298**
ENTRACTE 6 Lecture et culture	**300**

UNITÉ 7

Le temps libre 306

Thème Leisure time activities

LEÇON 21 LE FRANÇAIS PRATIQUE

Le week-end et les vacances 308

• Accent sur ... Les loisirs 308
• Vocabulaire
    A. Le week-end 310
    B. Les vacances 312
• Vocabulaire Les activités sportives 313
• Note culturelle Les sports d'hiver 313
À votre tour Communication/révision 316

LEÇON 22

Vive le week-end! 318

• Note culturelle Le week-end 319
• **A.** Les expressions avec **avoir** 320
• Vocabulaire Expressions avec **avoir** 320
• **B.** Le passé composé des verbes en **-er** 321
• Expressions pour la conversation:
    How to indicate the order in which actions take place 323
• **C.** Le passé composé: forme négative 324
• **D.** Les questions au passé composé 326
• Prononciation Les lettres «**ain**» et «**in**» 327
À votre tour Communication/révision 328

LEÇON 23

L'alibi 330

• Note culturelle Les jeunes Français et la télé 331
• **A.** Le verbe **voir** 332
• **B.** Le passé composé des verbes réguliers en **-ir** et **-re** 333
• **C.** Le passé composé des verbes **être**, **avoir**, **faire**, **mettre** et **voir** 335
• Vocabulaire Quand? 336
• Prononciation Les lettres «**gn**» 337
À votre tour Communication/révision 338

LEÇON 24

Qui a de la chance? 340

• Note culturelle Les jeunes Français et la musique 341
• **A.** Le passé composé avec **être** 342
• Vocabulaire Quelques verbes conjugués avec **être** au passé composé 344
• **B.** La construction négative **ne ... jamais** 346
• **C.** Les expressions **quelqu'un**, **quelque chose** et leurs contraires 347
• Prononciation Les lettres «**qu**» 347
À votre tour Communication/révision 348

TESTS DE CONTRÔLE	350
VOCABULAIRE	352
ENTRACTE 7 Lecture et culture	354

UNITÉ 8

Les repas 360

Thème Food and meals

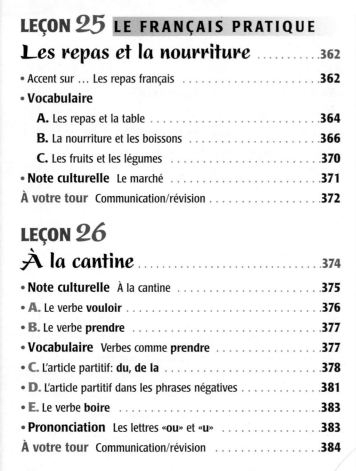

LEÇON 25 LE FRANÇAIS PRATIQUE
Les repas et la nourriture 362
- Accent sur … Les repas français 362
- Vocabulaire
  - **A.** Les repas et la table 364
  - **B.** La nourriture et les boissons 366
  - **C.** Les fruits et les légumes 370
- **Note culturelle** Le marché 371
- **À votre tour** Communication/révision 372

LEÇON 26
À la cantine 374
- **Note culturelle** À la cantine 375
- **A.** Le verbe **vouloir** 376
- **B.** Le verbe **prendre** 377
- **Vocabulaire** Verbes comme **prendre** 377
- **C.** L'article partitif: **du, de la** 378
- **D.** L'article partitif dans les phrases négatives 381
- **E.** Le verbe **boire** 383
- **Prononciation** Les lettres «ou» et «u» 383
- **À votre tour** Communication/révision 384

LEÇON 27
Un client difficile 386
- **Note culturelle** Les restaurants français et la cuisine française 387
- **A.** Les pronoms compléments **me, te, nous, vous** 388
- **Vocabulaire** Les services personnels 389
- **B.** Les pronoms compléments à l'impératif 390
- **C.** Les verbes **pouvoir** et **devoir** 392
- **Prononciation** Les lettres «s» et «ss» 393
- **À votre tour** Communication/révision 394

LEÇON 28
Pique-nique 396
- **Note culturelle** Un pique-nique français 397
- **A.** Le verbe **connaître** 398
- **B.** Les pronoms compléments **le, la, les** 399
- **C.** La place des pronoms à l'impératif 401
- **D.** Les pronoms compléments **lui, leur** 402
- **Vocabulaire** Verbes suivis d'un complément indirect 403
- **E.** Les verbes **dire** et **écrire** 404
- **Prononciation** Les lettres «on» et «om» 405
- **À votre tour** Communication/révision 406

TESTS DE CONTRÔLE 408
VOCABULAIRE 410
ENTRACTE 8 Lecture et culture 412

Reference Section R1

Appendix 1 Maps R2
Appendix 2 Sound/Spelling Correspondences R5
Appendix 3 Numbers R7
Appendix 4 Verbs R8
French-English Vocabulary R13
English-French Vocabulary R35
Index R49
Credits R52

Bienvenue . . . and welcome!

Chers amis,

Welcome to *Discovering French-Nouveau!* and congratulations on your choice of French as a foreign language! Perhaps someone in your family speaks French. Maybe you know people who are of French-speaking origin — from France or Canada or Louisiana or Haiti or western Africa — and you want to better appreciate their heritage. Or perhaps you are hoping to travel to Quebec or Martinique or Paris, and want to be able to get around easily on your own. Perhaps simply you were influenced by the fact that French is a beautiful language. Or maybe you have studied ballet and already know quite a few French expressions. Or you like to bicycle and enjoy watching the **Tour de France.** Or you love the Internet and want to explore the many exciting French sites. Or perhaps your friends have told you that French class is fun and opens doors to a whole new world. Whatever the reason or reasons, welcome and **bienvenue!**

By learning French, you will get to know and communicate with people who use French in their daily lives. These millions of French speakers or **francophones** come from a wide variety of ethnic and cultural backgrounds. As you will see, they live not only in France and other parts of Europe, but also in Africa, in North and South America, in Asia . . . in fact, on all continents.

By studying French, you will also develop a better understanding of your own language and how it works. And by exploring cultural similarities and differences, you will grow to appreciate your own culture and value the culture of others.

On the pages of this book and in the accompanying video, you will meet many young people who speak French. Listen carefully to what they say and how they express themselves. They will help you understand not only their language but also the way they live.

Bonne chance!

Jean-Paul Valette   Rebecca M. Valette

Pourquoi parler français?

WHY SPEAK FRENCH?

Here are ten good reasons.

▲ un cybercafé à Paris

1. ***French is an international language.***
   French is the first or second language in about fifty countries or regions in Europe, Africa, North and South America, Asia, and Oceania. It is spoken by over 100 million people around the world.

2. ***French is an important diplomatic language.***
   French is one of the five official languages of the United Nations and one of the two main languages of the European Union.

3. ***French is the second language on the Internet.***
   With French, you have immediate access to Internet sites in France and Quebec, as well as sites in Belgium, Switzerland, and French-speaking countries of Africa.

4. ***France is a technologically advanced country.***
   Historically, French inventors have contributed significantly to the advancement of science. Today, France is a leader in areas such as aero-space technology, high-speed transportation, automotive design, and medical research.

5. ***France is a leader in the world of art and literature.***
   Over the past 400 years, Paris has been an important cultural center, attracting artists and writers from around the world. France has won more Nobel Prizes in literature than any other country.

▲ l'Opéra National de Paris

le musée du Louvre ▶

le TGV (train à grande vitesse) ▶
high-speed train

6. ***France is a prime tourist destination.***
   If you like to travel, it will not surprise you to learn that millions of tourists visit France every year — and speaking French makes their vacations much more meaningful and more enjoyable.

7. ***For many people, France evokes style and elegance.***
   When people think of high fashion, beauty products, perfumes, or gourmet cuisine, they think of France . . . and rightly so.

8. ***Knowing French will enrich your English.***
   In 1066, William the Conqueror, a French nobleman, invaded England and became king, bringing with him his court and his language: French. Today over one-third of all English words are derived from French. As you study French, you will increase your English vocabulary.

9. ***Knowing French will help you with your university studies.***
   University admissions officers look for candidates who have foreign language skills. In addition, research by the College Board shows that the longer students study a foreign language, the higher their math and verbal SAT scores.

10. ***Knowing French will be useful for your career.***
    Many jobs require the knowledge of another language. France and Canada are major trading partners of the United States. In addition, about 1,000 French companies have subsidiaries in this country.

▲ l'Université Paris-Sorbonne

Et vous? *(And you?)*

Which three reasons for speaking French are most important to you? Take a class poll comparing your answers with those of your classmates. Which are the most popular reasons?

Bonjour, la France!

CONNAISSEZ-VOUS LA FRANCE? *(Do you know France?)*

- In area, France is the second-largest country in Western Europe. It is smaller than Texas, but bigger than California.

- Geographically, France is a very diversified country, with the highest mountains in Europe (**les Alpes** and **les Pyrénées**) and an extensive coastline along the Atlantic (**l'océan Atlantique**) and the Mediterranean (**la Méditerranée**).

- France consists of many different regions which have maintained their traditions, their culture, and — in some cases — their own language. Some of the traditional provinces are Normandy and Brittany (**la Normandie** and **la Bretagne**) in the west, Alsace (**l'Alsace**) in the east, Touraine (**la Touraine**) in the center, and Provence (**la Provence**) in the south.

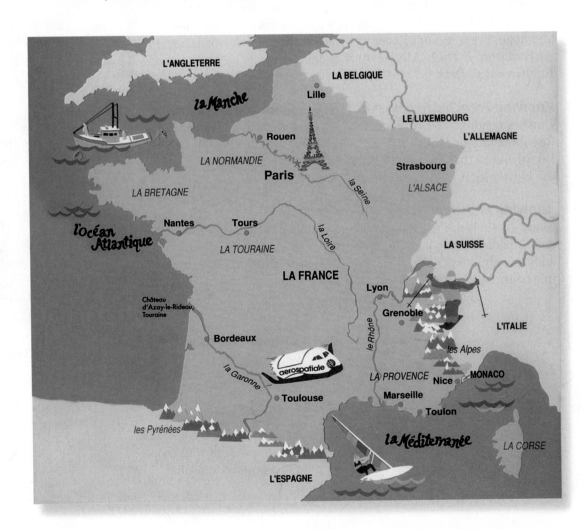

Paris: Montmartre

Paris, the capital of France, is also its economic, intellectual, and artistic center. For many people, Paris is the most beautiful city in the world.

Snowboarding in the Alps

During winter vacation, many French young people enjoy snowboarding or skiing. The most popular destinations are the Alps and the Pyrenees.

Château de Chenonceau

The long history of France is evident in its many castles and monuments. This chateau, built in the 16th century, attracts nearly one million visitors a year.

Home in Provence

The French love flowers and take pride in making their homes beautiful. This house is built in the traditional style of Provence, a region in southern France.

Bonjour, les Français!

Here are some facts about France and the French people.

LA FRANCE

Capitale: Paris

Population: 60 (soixante) millions d'habitants

Drapeau: bleu, blanc, rouge

Devise: Liberté, Égalité, Fraternité

Monnaie: l'euro

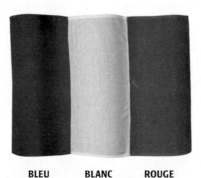

BLEU   BLANC   ROUGE

LE DRAPEAU FRANÇAIS

L'EURO

LA MONNAIE FRANÇAISE

LES FRANÇAIS

Origine de la population: multi-ethnique

• européenne (majorité)

• nord-africaine

• africaine

• asiatique

Principales religions pratiquées:

• catholique (majorité)

• musulmane

• juive

• protestante

STRATEGY Comparing Cultures

How does France compare to the United States or to your country of origin? Make a chart like the one above. Include the capital, the population, the flag, the motto, and the currency.

These are some of the young French people you will meet in the video.

Jean-Paul âge: 14 ans

Céline âge: 15 ans

Léa âge: 15 ans

François âge: 14 ans

Isabelle âge: 14 ans

Stéphanie âge: 14 ans

Philippe âge: 15 ans

Trinh âge: 14 ans

Antoine âge: 14 ans

Bonjour, le monde francophone!

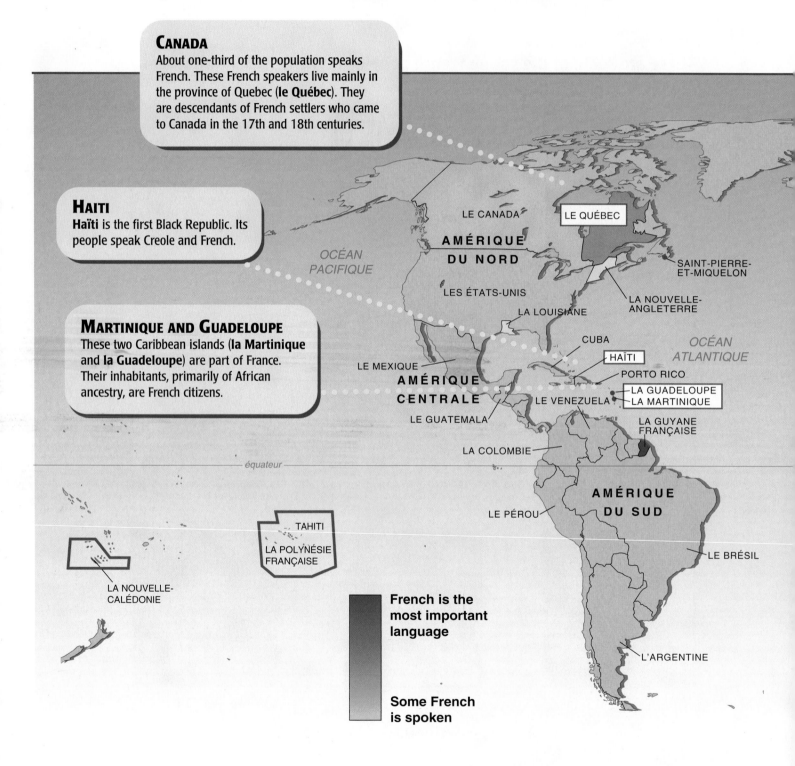

CANADA
About one-third of the population speaks French. These French speakers live mainly in the province of Quebec (**le Québec**). They are descendants of French settlers who came to Canada in the 17th and 18th centuries.

HAÏTI
Haïti is the first Black Republic. Its people speak Creole and French.

MARTINIQUE AND GUADELOUPE
These two Caribbean islands (**la Martinique** and **la Guadeloupe**) are part of France. Their inhabitants, primarily of African ancestry, are French citizens.

LE CANADA

LE QUÉBEC

AMÉRIQUE DU NORD

SAINT-PIERRE-ET-MIQUELON

OCÉAN PACIFIQUE

LES ÉTATS-UNIS

LA NOUVELLE-ANGLETERRE

LA LOUISIANE

CUBA

OCÉAN ATLANTIQUE

HAÏTI

LE MEXIQUE

PORTO RICO

AMÉRIQUE CENTRALE

LA GUADELOUPE
LA MARTINIQUE

LE VENEZUELA

LE GUATEMALA

LA GUYANE FRANÇAISE

LA COLOMBIE

équateur

AMÉRIQUE DU SUD

LE PÉROU

TAHITI

LA POLYNÉSIE FRANÇAISE

LE BRÉSIL

LA NOUVELLE-CALÉDONIE

French is the most important language

Some French is spoken

L'ARGENTINE

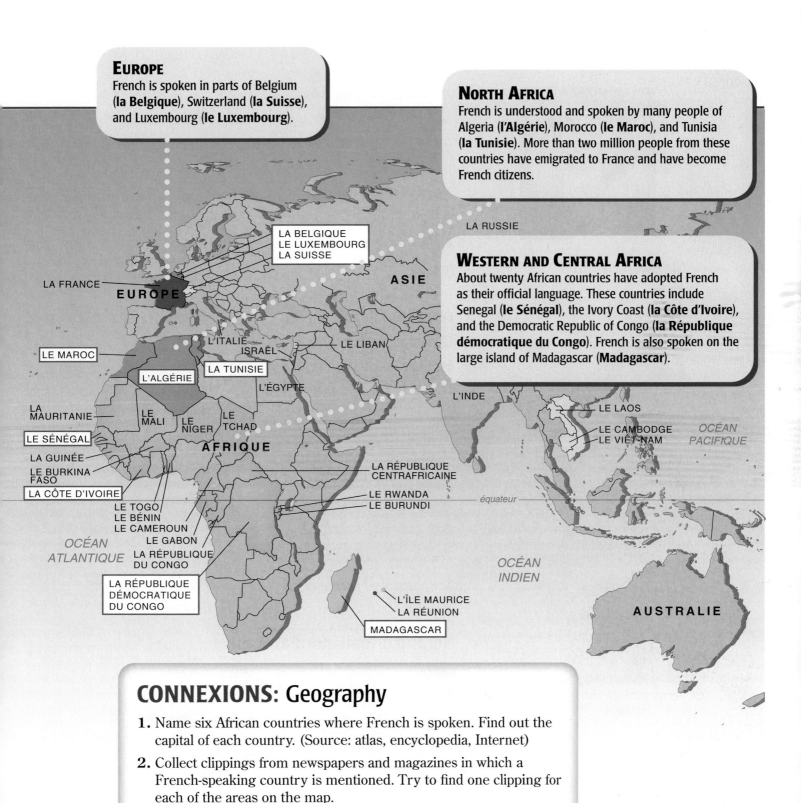

EUROPE
French is spoken in parts of Belgium (**la Belgique**), Switzerland (**la Suisse**), and Luxembourg (**le Luxembourg**).

NORTH AFRICA
French is understood and spoken by many people of Algeria (**l'Algérie**), Morocco (**le Maroc**), and Tunisia (**la Tunisie**). More than two million people from these countries have emigrated to France and have become French citizens.

WESTERN AND CENTRAL AFRICA
About twenty African countries have adopted French as their official language. These countries include Senegal (**le Sénégal**), the Ivory Coast (**la Côte d'Ivoire**), and the Democratic Republic of Congo (**la République démocratique du Congo**). French is also spoken on the large island of Madagascar (**Madagascar**).

LA RUSSIE

LA BELGIQUE
LE LUXEMBOURG
LA SUISSE

ASIE

LA FRANCE

EUROPE

L'ITALIE
ISRAËL

LE MAROC

LA TUNISIE

L'ALGÉRIE

L'ÉGYPTE

LE LIBAN

L'INDE

LE LAOS

LA MAURITANIE

LE MALI

LE NIGER

LE TCHAD

LE CAMBODGE
LE VIÊT-NAM

OCÉAN PACIFIQUE

LE SÉNÉGAL

AFRIQUE

LA GUINÉE

LE BURKINA FASO

LA CÔTE D'IVOIRE

LE TOGO
LE BÉNIN
LE CAMEROUN
LE GABON
LA RÉPUBLIQUE DU CONGO

LA RÉPUBLIQUE CENTRAFRICAINE

LE RWANDA
LE BURUNDI

équateur

OCÉAN ATLANTIQUE

LA RÉPUBLIQUE DÉMOCRATIQUE DU CONGO

OCÉAN INDIEN

L'ÎLE MAURICE
LA RÉUNION

MADAGASCAR

AUSTRALIE

CONNEXIONS: Geography

1. Name six African countries where French is spoken. Find out the capital of each country. (Source: atlas, encyclopedia, Internet)

2. Collect clippings from newspapers and magazines in which a French-speaking country is mentioned. Try to find one clipping for each of the areas on the map.

Bonjour, je m'appelle . . .

Antoine

Jérôme

Fatima

As you begin your study of French, you may want to "adopt" a French identity. Here is a list of some common French names.

Noms traditionnels (garçons):

Alain	Henri	Nicolas
André	Jacques	Olivier
Antoine	Jean	Patrick
Bernard	Jean-Louis	Paul
Christophe	Jean-Paul	Philippe
Clément	Jérôme	Pierre
Édouard	Joseph	Robert
Éric	Julien	Stéphane
François	Laurent	Thomas
Frédéric	Marc	Vincent
Georges	Mathieu	
Guillaume	Michel	

Some French people of North African or African descent have names that reflect their origin.

Noms d'origine nord-africaine

GARÇONS		FILLES	
Ali	Latif	Aïcha	Leila
Ahmed	Mustapha	Fatima	Yasmina
Habib	Youcef	Jamila	Zaïna

Aurélie

Léa

Noms traditionnels (filles):

Anne	Florence	Michèle
Anne-Marie	Françoise	Monique
Aurélie	Hélène	Nathalie
Béatrice	Isabelle	Nicole
Caroline	Jeanne	Pauline
Cécile	Julie	Sophie
Céline	Laure	Stéphanie
Charlotte	Léa	Suzanne
Christine	Louise	Sylvie
Claire	Marie	Thérèse
Élisabeth	Marie-Christine	Véronique
Élodie	Mathilde	Virginie
Émilie	Mélanie	

Mélanie

Noms d'origine africaine

GARÇONS		FILLES	
Abdou	Kouamé	Adjoua	Latifah
Amadou	Moussa	Asta	Malika
Koffi	Ousmane	Aya	Mariama

Ousmane

UNITÉ 1

Invitation au français

Faisons connaissance

LEÇON 1 Bonjour!

VIDÉO-SCÈNES

A La rentrée

B Tu es français?

C Salut! Ça va?

LEÇON 2 Famille et copains

VIDÉO-SCÈNES

A Copain ou copine?

B Une coïncidence

C Les photos d'Isabelle

THÈME ET OBJECTIFS

Getting acquainted

In this unit, you will be meeting French people.

You will learn ...

- to say hello and good-bye
- to introduce yourself and say where you are from
- to introduce friends, family, and relatives

You will also learn ...

- to count to 100
- to say how old you are and find out someone's age

WEBQUEST
CLASSZONE.COM

Introduction culturelle

Salutations *(Greetings)*

How do you greet people in the United States? You may nod or smile. With adults, you may shake hands when you are introduced for the first time.

In France, people shake hands with friends and acquaintances each time they see one another, and not only to say hello but also when they say good-bye. Among teenagers, boys shake hands with boys. Girls kiss each other on the cheeks two or three times. (This is called **une bise**). Boys and girls who are close friends also greet each other with **une bise.**

Bonjour!
A La rentrée

This is the first day of school. Students are greeting their friends and meeting new classmates.

> Bonjour! Je m'appelle Trinh.

Trinh: Bonjour! Je m'appelle Trinh.
Céline: Et moi, je m'appelle Céline.

> Et moi, je m'appelle Céline.

> Je m'appelle Marc. Et toi?

> Comment t'appelles-tu?

> Je m'appelle Nathalie.

> Moi, je m'appelle Isabelle.

Marc: Je m'appelle Marc. Et toi?
Isabelle: Moi, je m'appelle Isabelle.

Jean-Paul: Comment t'appelles-tu?
Nathalie: Je m'appelle Nathalie.
Jean-Paul: Bonjour.
Nathalie: Bonjour.

Invitation au français

POUR COMMUNIQUER

Bonjour!

▶ *How to say hello:*

Bonjour!	*Hello!*	—**Bonjour**, Nathalie!
		—**Bonjour**, Jean-Paul!

▶ *How to ask a classmate's name:*

Comment t'appelles-tu?	*What's your name?*	—**Comment t'appelles-tu?**
Je m'appelle …	*My name is …*	—**Je m'appelle** Céline.

Other Expressions

moi	*me*	**Moi**, je m'appelle Marc.
et toi?	*and you?*	**Et toi**, comment t'appelles-tu?

NOTES **culturelles**

1 La rentrée *(Back to school)*

French and American students have about the same number of days of summer vacation. In France, summer vacation usually begins at the end of June and classes resume in early September. The first day back to school in fall is called **la rentrée.**

2 Les prénoms français *(French first names)*

Many traditional French names have corresponding equivalents in English.

For boys:
- **Jean** *(John)*
- **Pierre** *(Peter)*
- **Marc** *(Mark)*
- **Philippe** *(Philip)*
- **Nicolas** *(Nicholas)*

For girls:
- **Marie** *(Mary)*
- **Monique** *(Monica)*
- **Cécile** *(Cecilia)*
- **Véronique** *(Veronica)*
- **Virginie** *(Virginia)*

Often the names **Jean** and **Marie** are combined in double names such as **Jean-Paul** and **Marie-Christine.** In recent years, names of foreign origin, like **Kevin** and **Laura,** have become quite popular.

R. GOSCINNY *Astérix* A. UDERZO
LE CADEAU DE
César
HACHETTE

PETIT COMMENTAIRE

Astérix le Gaulois is one of the best-loved cartoon characters in France. Small in size but extremely clever and courageous, he represents the "little man" defending his country Gaul (the ancient name of France) against the invading Roman legions led by Julius Caesar.

1 ### Bonjour!

PARLER Say hello to the student nearest to you.

Bonjour!

Bonjour!

Bonjour!

2 ### Je m'appelle …

PARLER Introduce yourself to your classmates.

▶ Je m'appelle (Paul).

▶ Je m'appelle (Denise).

3 ### Et toi?

PARLER Ask a classmate his or her name.

▶ —Comment t'appelles-tu?
  —Je m'appelle (Christine).

4 ### Bonjour, les amis! *(Hello everyone!)*

PARLER Say hello to the following students.

▶ **Bonjour, Marc!**

▶ **Marc**

1. **Céline**

2. **Jean-Paul**

3. **Isabelle**

François — 4.

5. **Stéphanie**

6. **Nathalie**

7. **Trinh**

L'alphabet

A	B	C	D	E	F	G	H	I	J	K	L	M
a	bé	cé	dé	e	effe	gé	hache	i	ji	ka	elle	emme

N	O	P	Q	R	S	T	U	V	W	X	Y	Z
enne	o	pé	ku	erre	esse	té	u	vé	double vé	ixe	i grec	zède

PRONONCIATION

Les signes orthographiques *(Spelling marks)*

French uses accents and spelling marks that do not exist in English. These marks are part of the spelling and cannot be left out.

In French, there are four accents that may appear on vowels.

´	**l'accent aigu** *(acute accent)*	Cécile, Stéphanie
`	**l'accent grave** *(grave accent)*	Michèle, Hélène
^	**l'accent circonflexe** *(circumflex)*	Jérôme
••	**le tréma** *(diaeresis)*	Noël, Joëlle

There is only one spelling mark used with a consonant. It occurs under the letter "**c**."

¸	**la cédille** *(cedilla)*	François

5  *La rentrée*

PARLER It is the first day of class. The following students are introducing themselves. Act out the dialogues with your classmates.

▶ Hélène et Philippe —Je m'appelle Hélène. Et toi?
  —Moi, je m'appelle Philippe.

1. Stéphanie et Marc
2. Cécile et Frédéric
3. Michèle et François
4. Anaïs et Clément
5. Céline et Jérôme
6. Mélanie et Noël

Les nombres de 0 à 10

0	1	2	3
zéro	un	deux	trois

4	5	6	7
quatre	cinq	six	sept

8	9	10
huit	neuf	dix

6 *Numéros de téléphone*

PARLER Imagine you are visiting a family in Quebec. Give them your American phone number in French.

617-963-4028   six, un, sept —

neuf, six, trois —

quatre, zéro, deux, huit

B Tu es français?

It is the opening day of school and several of the students meet in the cafeteria (**la cafétéria** or **la cantine**) at lunchtime. Marc discovers that not everyone is French.

Tu es français?

Oui, je suis français.

Marc: Tu es français?
Jean-Paul: Oui, je suis français.

Non! Je suis américain.

Marc: Et toi, Patrick, tu es français aussi?
Patrick: Non! Je suis américain.
Je suis de Boston.

Je suis française.

Marc: Et toi, Stéphanie, tu es française ou américaine?
Stéphanie: Je suis française.
Marc: Tu es de Paris?
Stéphanie: Non, je suis de Fort-de-France.
Marc: Tu as de la chance! *You're lucky!*

POUR COMMUNIQUER

> Tu es de Nice?

▶ **How to talk about where people are from:**

Tu es de …?	*Are you from …?*	—**Tu es de** Nice?
Je suis de …	*I'm from …*	—Non, **je suis de** Paris.

▶ **How to talk about one's nationality:**

Tu es …?	*Are you …?*	—Pierre, **tu es** français?
Je suis …	*I am …*	—Oui, **je suis** français.

Les nationalités

	français	**française**
	anglais	**anglaise**
	américain	**américaine**
	canadien	**canadienne**

Other Expressions

oui	*yes*	Tu es français? **Oui**, je suis français.
non	*no*	Tu es canadien? **Non**, je suis américain.
et	*and*	Je suis de Paris. **Et** toi?
ou	*or*	Tu es français **ou** canadien?
aussi	*also, too*	Moi **aussi**, je suis française.

NOTE culturelle

La Martinique

★
Fort-de-France

La Martinique

Martinique is a small French island located in the Caribbean, southeast of Puerto Rico. Because Martinique is part of the French national territory, its inhabitants are French citizens. Most of them are of African origin. They speak French as well as a dialect called **créole**.

EN BREF

Capitale: Fort-de-France
Population: 400 000
Langues: créole, français

PETIT COMMENTAIRE
The Statue of Liberty (**la statue de la Liberté**) was a gift to the United States from the French people on the occasion of the 100th anniversary of American independence. The Eiffel Tower (**la tour Eiffel**) was built to celebrate the 100th anniversary of the French Revolution.

français, française

Names of nationalities may have two different forms, depending on whom they refer to:

	MASCULINE	FEMININE
je suis … tu es …	français américain	française américaine

Note In written French the feminine forms always end in **-e**.

❶ Et toi?

PARLER Give your name, your nationality, and your city of origin.

▼

Bonjour!
Je m'appelle Bob Jones.
Je suis américain.
Je suis de Providence.

Bonjour!
Je m'appelle Linda Carlson.
Je suis américaine.
Je suis de Boston.

❷ Français ou française?

PARLER You meet the following young people. Ask them if they are French. A classmate will answer you, as in the model. (Be sure to use **français** with boys and **française** with girls.)

▶ —Sophie, tu es française?
—Oui, je suis française. Je suis de Strasbourg.

3 **Quelle nationalité?** *(Which nationality?)*

PARLER Greet the following young people and find out each one's nationality. A classmate will answer you, according to the model.

▶ —Bonjour, Marc. Tu es canadien?
—Oui, je suis canadien.
   Je suis de Montréal.

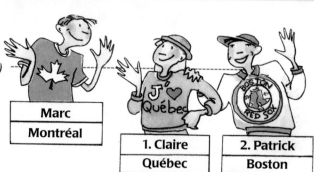

▶ | Marc |
| Montréal |

| 1. Claire | | 2. Patrick |
| Québec | | Boston |

| 3. Denise | 4. Donna | 5. Paul |
| Liverpool | Memphis | Cambridge |

Les nombres de 10 à 20

10	11	12	13	14	15
dix	onze	douze	treize	quatorze	quinze
16	**17**	**18**	**19**	**20**	
seize	dix-sept	dix-huit	dix-neuf	vingt	

4 **La fusée Ariane** *(The Ariane rocket)*

PARLER Give the countdown for the liftoff of the French rocket Ariane, from 20 to 0.

PRONONCIATION

Les lettres muettes *(Silent letters)*

In French, the last letter of a word is often not pronounced.

Paris

- Final "**e**" is always silent.
  Répétez: **Céline Philippe Stéphanie anglaise française
  onze douze treize quatorze quinze seize**

- Final "**s**" is almost always silent.
  Répétez: **Paris Nicolas Jacques anglais français trois**

- The letter "**h**" is always silent.
  Répétez: **Hélène Henri Thomas Nathalie Catherine Thérèse**

C Salut! Ça va?

On the way to school, François meets his friends.

Salut, Isabelle!

Salut! Ça va?

Ça va! Merci!

Salut, Nathalie! Ça va?

Ça va bien! Et toi?

Moi aussi!

Ça va, Philippe?

Ah non! Zut! Ça va mal.

François also meets his teachers.

Bonjour, monsieur.

Bonjour, François.

Monsieur Masson

Bonjour, madame.

Bonjour, François.

Madame Chollet

Bonjour, mademoiselle.

Bonjour, François.

Mademoiselle Lacour

After class, François says good-bye to his teacher and his friends.

Au revoir, mademoiselle.

Au revoir, François.

Au revoir, Nathalie!

Au revoir, François.

POUR COMMUNIQUER

Salut!

▶ *How to greet a friend or classmate:*

Salut!   *Hi!*

▶ *How to greet a teacher or another adult:*

Bonjour!   *Hello!*   **Bonjour, monsieur.**
                          Bonjour, madame.
                          Bonjour, mademoiselle.

▶ *How to say good-bye:*

Au revoir!   *Good-bye!*   **Au revoir, Philippe.**
                            Au revoir, monsieur.

➔ In written French, the following abbreviations are commonly used:

M. Masson	Monsieur Masson
Mme Chollet	Madame Chollet
Mlle Lacour	Mademoiselle Lacour

➔ Young people often use **Salut!** to say good-bye to each other.

NOTE *culturelle*

Bonjour ou Salut?

French young people may greet one another with **Bonjour,** but they often prefer the less formal **Salut.** When they meet their teachers, however, they always use **Bonjour.** French young people are generally much more formal with adults than with their friends. This is especially true in their relationships with teachers, whom they treat with respect.

Have you noticed that in France adults are addressed as **monsieur, madame,** or **mademoiselle?** The last name is usually not used in greeting people.

① Bonjour ou salut?

PARLER You are enrolled in a French school. Greet your friends and teachers.

Valérie

▶ Salut, Valérie!

Mademoiselle Pinot

▶ Bonjour, mademoiselle!

1. Céline

2. Monsieur Masson

3. Nathalie

4. Marc

5. Madame Albert

6. Mademoiselle Boucher

POUR COMMUNIQUER

▶ *How to ask people how they feel:*

—**Ça va?**   *How are you? How are things going? How's everything?*
—**Ça va!**   *(I'm) fine. (I'm) okay. Everything's all right.*

Ça va …   **très bien**   **bien**   **comme ci, comme ça**   **mal**   **très mal**

▶ *How to express one's feelings of frustration and appreciation:*

Zut! *Darn!*   **Zut!** Ça va mal!   **Merci!** *Thanks!*   Ça va, **merci.**

→ **Ça va?** *(How are you?)* is an informal greeting that corresponds to the following expressions:

Comment vas-tu? (when addressing a friend)
    Bonjour, Paul. Comment vas-tu?
Comment allez-vous? (when addressing an adult)
    Bonjour, madame. Comment allez-vous?

② Dialogue

PARLER Exchange greetings with your classmates and ask how they are doing.

▶ —Salut, (Thomas)! Ça va?
  —Ça va! Et toi?
  —Ça va bien. Merci.

③   Situations

PARLER Sometimes we feel good and sometimes we don't.
How would you respond in the following situations?

▶ You have the flu.
—Ça va?
—Ça va mal!

1. You just received an "A" in French.
2. You lost your wallet.
3. Your uncle gave you five dollars.
4. Your grandparents sent you a check for 100 dollars.
5. You bent the front wheel of your bicycle.
6. Your parents bought you a new video game.

7. Your little brother broke your cell phone.
8. It's your birthday.
9. You have a headache.
10. You just had an argument with your best friend.
11. Your French teacher has just canceled a quiz.

④ Ça va?

PARLER How would the following people answer the question **Ça va?**

Les nombres de 20 à 60

20 vingt	**30** trente	**40** quarante	**50** cinquante	**60** soixante
vingt et un	trente et un	quarante et un	cinquante et un	
vingt-deux	trente-deux	quarante-deux	cinquante-deux	
vingt-trois	trente-trois	quarante-trois	cinquante-trois	
...	...	...	...	
vingt-neuf	trente-neuf	quarante-neuf	cinquante-neuf	

Note Use **et** before **un: vingt et un.**

⑤ Séries

PARLER Read the following number series out loud.

13 21 37 42 55 60

16 20 29 31 48 56

PRONONCIATION

Les consonnes finales (Final consonants)

In French, the last consonant of a word is often not pronounced.

un deux trois

• Remember: Final "**s**" is usually silent.
Répétez: **trois français anglais**

• Most other final consonants are usually silent.
Répétez: **Richard Albert Robert salut américain canadien bien deux**

EXCEPTION: The following final consonants are usually pronounced: "**c**," "**f**," "**l**," and sometimes "**r**."
Répétez: **Éric Daniel Lebeuf Pascal Victor**

However, the ending **-er** is usually pronounced /e/.
Répétez: **Roger Olivier**

LEÇON 2

Famille et copains
A Copain ou copine?

In French, there are certain girls' and boys' names that sound the same. Occasionally this can be confusing.

SCÈNE 1   **Philippe et Jean-Paul**
Philippe is at home with his friend Jean-Paul. He seems to be expecting someone. Who could it be … ? The doorbell rings.

Philippe: Tiens! Voilà Dominique!
Jean-Paul: Dominique? Qui est-ce?
Un copain ou une copine?
Philippe: C'est une copine.

SCÈNE 2   **Philippe, Jean-Paul, Dominique**

Philippe: Salut, Dominique! Ça va?
Dominique: Oui, ça va! Et toi?
Jean-Paul: *(thinking)* <u>C'est vrai!</u>   *It's true!*
C'est une copine!

Unité 1   *Invitation au français*

Tiens! Voilà Caroline! C'est une copine!

POUR COMMUNIQUER

▶ **How to introduce or point out someone:**

Voici ...	*This is ..., Here come(s) ...*	**Voici** Jean-Paul.
		Voici Nathalie et François.
Voilà ...	*This (That) is ..., There's ...*	**Voilà** Isabelle.
		Voilà Philippe et Dominique.

▶ **How to find out who someone is:**

Qui est-ce?	*Who's that? Who is it?*	—**Qui est-ce?**
C'est ...	*It's ..., That's ..., He's ..., She's ...*	—**C'est** Patrick. **C'est** un copain.

▶ **How to get someone's attention or to express surprise:**

Tiens!	*Look! Hey!*	**Tiens**, voilà Dominique!

Les personnes

un garçon	*boy*	**une fille**	*girl*
un ami	*friend (male)*	**une amie**	*friend (female)*
un copain	*friend (male)*	**une copine**	*friend (female)*
un monsieur	*gentleman*	**une dame**	*lady*
un prof	*teacher*	**une prof**	*teacher*

NOTE culturelle

Amis et copains

French young people, like their American counterparts, enjoy spending time with their friends. They refer to their friends as **un ami** (for a boy) and **une amie** (for a girl) or — more commonly — as **un copain** or **une copine.** Note that the words **copain, copine** can also have special meanings. When a boy talks about **une copine**, he is referring to a friend who is a girl. However, when he says **ma** (*my*) **copine**, he may be referring to his girlfriend. Similarly, a girl would call her boyfriend **mon copain.**

PETIT COMMENTAIRE
Cycling is a popular competitive sport throughout France. The most popular races are the **Tour de France** for men and the **Grande Boucle Féminine Internationale** for women. French women cyclists have won many titles.

un garçon, une fille

In French, all NOUNS are either MASCULINE or FEMININE.
Nouns referring to boys or men are almost always MASCULINE.
    They are introduced by **un** *(a, an).*
Nouns referring to girls or women are almost always FEMININE.
    They are introduced by **une** *(a, an).*

MASCULINE		FEMININE	
un garçon / **un** ami	*a boy* / *a friend (male)*	**une** fille / **une** amie	*a girl* / *a friend (female)*

1 Copain ou copine?

PARLER Say that the following people are your friends. Use **un copain** or **une copine,** as appropriate.

▶ Élodie est une copine.

Élodie

1. Alice

2. Cécile

3. Trinh

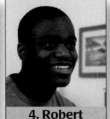

4. Robert

5. Céline

2 Les amis

PARLER The same young people are visiting your school. Point them out to your classmates, using **un ami** or **une amie,** as appropriate.

▶ —Tiens, voilà Élodie!
   —Qui est-ce?
   —C'est une amie.

3 Un ou une?

PARLER Identify the people below by completing the sentences with **un** or **une.**

1. Voici … fille.
2. Voilà … garçon.
3. Voici … dame.
4. C'est … amie.
5. Nicolas est … ami.
6. Jean-Paul est … copain.
7. Cécile est … copine.
8. Voici Mlle Lacour. C'est … prof.
9. Voici M. Masson. C'est … prof.
10. Voici Mme Chollet. C'est … prof.

4   **À la fenêtre** *(At the window)*

PARLER You and a friend are walking down the street and you see the following people at their windows. Identify them in short dialogues.

▶ —Tiens, voilà un monsieur!
—Qui est-ce?
—C'est Monsieur Mercier.

▶
Monsieur Mercier

1. Nicole

2. Mademoiselle Lasalle

3. Éric

4. Madame Albert

5. Monsieur Lavie

6. Alain

Les nombres de 60 à 79

60 soixante

61 soixante et un
62 soixante-deux
63 soixante-trois
64 soixante-quatre
65 soixante-cinq

66 soixante-six
67 soixante-sept
68 soixante-huit
69 soixante-neuf

70 soixante-dix

71 soixante et onze
72 soixante-douze
73 soixante-treize
74 soixante-quatorze
75 soixante-quinze

76 soixante-seize
77 soixante-dix-sept
78 soixante-dix-huit
79 soixante-dix-neuf

---

5 *Numéros de téléphone*

PARLER Read aloud the phone numbers of Jean-Paul's friends in Paris.

▶ Philippe — zéro un, quarante-deux, soixante et un, dix-neuf, soixante-quinze

▶ Philippe   01.42.61.19.75
Martine   01.41.33.64.79
Michèle   01.42.56.76.62
Stéphanie   01.45.68.77.35
François   01.49.78.13.62

PRONONCIATION

La liaison

un ami

Pronounce the following words:

un ami   un Américain   un Anglais   un artiste

In general, the "**n**" of **un** is silent. However, in the above words, the "**n**" of **un** is pronounced as if it were the *first* letter of the next word. This is called LIAISON.

Liaison occurs between two words when the second one begins with a VOWEL SOUND, that is, with "**a**", "**e**", "**i**", "**o**", "**u**", and sometimes "**h**" and "**y**".

➔ Although liaison is not marked in written French, it will be indicated in your book by the symbol ‿ where appropriate.

Contrastez et répétez:

LIAISON: **un ami   un Américain
un Italien   un artiste**

NO LIAISON: **un copain   un Français
un Canadien   un prof**

 VIDÉO DVD AUDIO

B Une coïncidence

Isabelle is at a party with her new Canadian friend Marc. She wants him to meet some of the other guests.

Tu connais la fille là-bas?

Non. Qui est-ce?

C'est une copine. Elle s'appelle Juliette Savard.

Isabelle:	Tu connais la fille <u>là-bas</u>?	*over there*
Marc:	Non. Qui est-ce?	
Isabelle:	C'est une copine. Elle s'appelle Juliette Savard.	
Marc:	Elle est française?	
Isabelle:	Non, elle est canadienne. Elle est de Montréal.	
Marc:	Moi aussi!	
Isabelle:	<u>Quelle coïncidence!</u>	*What a coincidence!*

Elle est française?

Non, elle est canadienne. Elle est de Montréal.

Moi aussi!

Quelle coïncidence!

Invitation au français

POUR COMMUNIQUER

Tu connais la dame?

Oui, elle s'appelle Madame Leblanc.

▶ *How to inquire about people:*

Tu connais …?	*Do you know …?*	**Tu connais** Jean-Paul?

▶ *How to describe people and give their nationalities:*

Il est …	*He is …*	**Il est** canadien.
Elle est …	*She is …*	**Elle est** canadienne.

▶ *How to find out another person's name:*

Comment s'appelle …?	*What's the name of …?*	**Comment s'appelle** le garçon?
		Comment s'appelle la fille?
Il s'appelle …	*His name is …*	**Il s'appelle** Marc.
Elle s'appelle …	*Her name is …*	**Elle s'appelle** Juliette.

NOTE culturelle

La province de Québec

Québec (City)
★
Montréal

EN BREF

Capitale: Québec *(Quebec City)*
Population: 7 500 000
Langues: français, anglais

La province de Québec

The province of **Québec** is located in the eastern part of Canada. French speakers represent about 75% of its population. Most of them are descendants of French settlers who came to Canada in the 17th and 18th centuries. There are also a large number of Haitian immigrants who are of African origin.

Montréal (population 2 million) is the largest city in the province of Quebec. In population, it is the second-largest French-speaking city in the world after Paris.

le garçon, la fille

The French equivalent of *the* has two basic forms: **le** and **la**.

MASCULINE			FEMININE		
le garçon	*the boy*		**la** fille	*the girl*	
le copain	*the friend*		**la** copine	*the friend*	

Note Both **le** and **la** become **l'** before a vowel sound.

un copain	→	le copain		une copine	→	la copine
un ami	→	**l'**ami		une amie	→	**l'**amie

---

1 Qui est-ce?

PARLER Ask who the following people are, using **le**, **la**, or **l'**.

▶ une prof
Qui est la prof?

1. un monsieur
2. une dame
3. une fille
4. un garçon
5. un prof
6. un ami
7. une amie
8. une copine

---

2 **Tu connais ... ?**

PARLER Ask your classmates if they know the following people. They will answer that they do.

▶ une dame / Madame Vallée

1. un prof / Monsieur Simon
2. un garçon / Christophe
3. une fille / Charlotte
4. une dame / Mademoiselle Lenoir
5. une prof / Madame Boucher
6. un monsieur / Monsieur Duval

---

3 **Comment s'appelle ... ?**

PARLER Ask the names of the following people, using the words **le garçon, la fille.** A classmate will respond.

▶ —Comment s'appelle la fille?
▼ —Elle s'appelle Stéphanie.

| **Stéphanie** | **1. Marc** | **2. Céline** | **3. François** |

| **4. Jean-Paul** | **5. Nathalie** | **6. Trinh** | **7. Isabelle** |

4 Français, anglais, canadien ou américain?

PARLER Give the nationalities of the following people.

▶ Julia Roberts?
  Elle est américaine.

1. le prince Charles?
2. Céline Dion?
3. Juliette Binoche?

4. Catherine Deneuve?
5. Pierre Cardin?
6. Matt Damon?

7. Oprah Winfrey?
8. Brad Pitt?
9. Elton John?

Les nombres de 80 à 1000

80 quatre-vingts
81 quatre-vingt-un
82 quatre-vingt-deux
83 quatre-vingt-trois
84 quatre-vingt-quatre
85 quatre-vingt-cinq

86 quatre-vingt-six
87 quatre-vingt-sept
88 quatre-vingt-huit
89 quatre-vingt-neuf

90 quatre-vingt-dix
91 quatre-vingt-onze
92 quatre-vingt-douze
93 quatre-vingt-treize
94 quatre-vingt-quatorze
95 quatre-vingt-quinze

96 quatre-vingt-seize
97 quatre-vingt-dix-sept
98 quatre-vingt-dix-huit
99 quatre-vingt-dix-neuf

100 cent   **1000** mille

→ Note that in counting from 80 to 99, the French add numbers to the base of **quatre-vingts** *(fourscore):*

$$80 = 4 \times 20 \qquad 90 = 4 \times 20 + 10$$
$$85 = 4 \times 20 + 5 \qquad 99 = 4 \times 20 + 19$$

---

5 Au téléphone

PARLER In France, the telephone area code (**l'indicatif**) is always a four-digit number. Your teacher will name a city (**une ville**) from the chart. Give the area code.

▶ Nice?   **C'est le zéro quatre quatre-vingt-treize.**

VILLE ☎	INDICATIF
Albi	05-63
Avignon	04-90
Dijon	03-80
Marseille	04-91
Montpellier	04-67
Nancy	03-83
Nice	04-93
Nîmes	04-66
Rennes	02-99
Saint-Tropez	04-94
Strasbourg	03-88
Vichy	04-70

PRONONCIATION   /ɛ̃/

La voyelle nasale /ɛ̃/

In French, there are three nasal vowel sounds:

/ɛ̃/ **cinq** (5)   /ɔ̃/ **onze** (11)   /ɑ̃/ **trente** (30)

Practice the sound /ɛ̃/ in the following words.

→ Be sure not to pronounce an "n" or "m" after the nasal vowel.

Répétez: "in"   cinq quinze vingt vingt-cinq quatre-vingt-quinze

"ain"   américain Alain copain

"(i)en"   bien canadien tiens!

"un"   un

Tiens! Voilà Alain. Il est américain. Et Julien? Il est canadien.

5
cinq

C Les photos d'Isabelle

Isabelle is showing her family photo album to her friend Jean-Paul.

Isabelle:	Voici ma mère.	
Jean-Paul:	Et <u>le monsieur</u>, c'est <u>ton</u> père?	*the man / your*
Isabelle:	Non, c'est mon oncle Thomas.	
Jean-Paul:	Et la fille, c'est <u>ta</u> cousine?	*your*
Isabelle:	Oui, c'est ma cousine Béatrice. <u>Elle a seize ans.</u>	*She's sixteen.*
Jean-Paul:	Et le garçon, c'est ton cousin?	
Isabelle:	Non, c'est un copain.	
Jean-Paul:	Un copain ou ton copain?	
Isabelle:	<u>Dis donc, Jean-Paul, tu es vraiment trop curieux!</u>	*Hey there, Jean-Paul, you are really too curious!*

ma mère

mon oncle
Thomas

ma cousine
Béatrice

? ?

Voici mon chien Malice.

POUR COMMUNIQUER

▶ *How to introduce your family:*

| Voici mon père. | This is my father. |
| Et voici ma mère. | And this is my mother. |

La famille *(Family)*

un frère	brother		une soeur	sister
un cousin	cousin		une cousine	cousin
un père	father		une mère	mother
un oncle	uncle		une tante	aunt
un grand-père	grandfather		une grand-mère	grandmother

Les animaux domestiques *(Pets)*

 **un chat**   **un chien**

NOTE *culturelle*

La famille française

When you and your friends talk about your families, you usually are referring to your brothers, sisters, and parents. In French, however, **la famille** refers not only to parents and children but also to grandparents, aunts, uncles, cousins, as well as a whole array of more distant relatives related by blood and marriage.

Since the various members of a family often live in the same region, French teenagers see their grandparents and cousins fairly frequently. Even when relatives do not live close by, the family finds many occasions to get together: for weekend visits, during school and summer vacations, on holidays, as well as on special occasions such as weddings and anniversaries.

PETIT COMMENTAIRE

The French people love pets, especially cats and dogs. What is important is the animal's personality and friendliness rather than its pedigree. Some common names given to animals are:

Minou, Pompon, Fifi (cats)
Titus, Milou, Azor (dogs)

mon cousin, ma cousine

The French equivalents of *my* and *your* have the following forms:

MASCULINE		
mon cousin	*my cousin (male)*	
mon frère	*my brother*	
ton cousin	*your cousin (male)*	
ton frère	*your brother*	

FEMININE		
ma cousine	*my cousin (female)*	
ma soeur	*my sister*	
ta cousine	*your cousin (female)*	
ta soeur	*your sister*	

→ Note that the feminine **ma** becomes **mon** and the feminine **ta** becomes **ton** before a vowel sound. Liaison is required.

une amie → **mon** amie **ton** amie

1 L'album de photos

PARLER You are showing a friend your photo album. Identify the following people, using **mon** and **ma,** as appropriate.

▶ cousine Jacqueline **Voici ma cousine Jacqueline.**

1. frère	**5.** père	**9.** copine Pauline	**13.** chien Toto
2. soeur	**6.** mère	**10.** amie Florence	**14.** chat Minou
3. tante Monique	**7.** copain Nicolas	**11.** grand-mère Michèle	**15.** cousine Émilie
4. oncle Pierre	**8.** ami Jérôme	**12.** grand-père Robert	**16.** cousin Marc

2 Comment s'appelle … ?

PARLER Ask your classmates to name some of their friends, relatives, and pets. They can invent names if they wish.

▶ le copain —**Comment s'appelle ton copain?**
—**Mon copain s'appelle Bob.**

1. l'oncle	**3.** le cousin	**5.** la copine	**7.** le grand-père	**9.** le chien
2. la tante	**4.** la cousine	**6.** l'ami	**8.** la grand-mère	**10.** le chat

POUR COMMUNIQUER

Quel âge as-tu?

How to find out how old a friend is:

Quel âge as-tu?	*How old are you?*	**—Quel âge as-tu?**
J'ai … ans.	*I'm … (years old).*	**—J'ai quinze ans.**

J'ai quinze ans.

How to ask about how old others are:

—Quel âge a ton père?	*How old is your father?*
—Il a quarante-deux ans.	*He is 42 (years old).*
—Quel âge a ta mère?	*How old is your mother?*
—Elle a trente-neuf ans.	*She is 39 (years old).*

➔ Although *years old* may be left out in English, the word **ans** must be used in French when talking about someone's age.

    Il a vingt ans.   *He's twenty. (He's twenty years old.)*

---

3 *Quel âge as-tu?*

PARLER Ask your classmates how old they are.

▶ —Quel âge as-tu?
   —J'ai (treize) ans.

4 *Joyeux anniversaire!*
(Happy birthday!)

PARLER Ask your classmates how old the following people are.

▶ —Quel âge a Stéphanie?
   —Elle a quatorze ans.

 Stéphanie

1. Éric   2. Mademoiselle Doucette   3. Monsieur Boucher

4. Madame Dupont   5. Monsieur Camus   6. Madame Simon

---

5 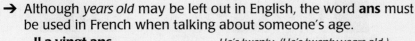 *Curiosité*

PARLER Find out the ages of your classmates' friends and relatives. If they are not sure, they can guess or invent an answer.

▶ la copine —Quel âge a ta copine?
         —Ma copine a (treize) ans.

1. le père	**4.** la tante	**7.** le grand-père
2. la mère	**5.** le cousin	**8.** la grand-mère
3. l'oncle	**6.** la cousine	

PRONONCIATION /ã/ /ɔ̃/

Les voyelles nasales /ã/ et /ɔ̃/

  tante **oncle**

The letters "**an**" and "**en**" usually represent the nasal vowel /ã/. Be sure not to pronounce an "**n**" after the nasal vowel.

Répétez: ans tante français quarante
            trente comment Henri Laurent

The letters "**on**" represent the nasal vowel /ɔ̃/. Be sure not to pronounce an "**n**" after the nasal vowel.

Répétez: non bonjour oncle garçon

Contrastez: an–on tante–ton onze–ans
          Mon oncle François a trente ans.

À votre tour!

OBJECTIFS

Now you can...
• greet people and say where you are from
• introduce friends and relatives
• give your age and ask how old people are
• understand and use numbers up to 100

1 🎧 Écoutez bien!

ÉCOUTER Loto is a French version of Bingo. You will hear a series of numbers. If the number is on Card A, raise your left hand. If it is on Card B, raise your right hand.

A

3		25	61	82
8	12		72	
	17	42		93

B

5		48	67	
	19	55		89
15	33		70	98

2 🎧 Et toi?

ÉCOUTER ET PARLER You and Nathalie meet at a sidewalk café. Respond to her greetings and questions.

1. Salut! Ça va?
2. Comment t'appelles-tu?
3. Tu es canadien (canadienne)?
4. Quel âge as-tu?
5. Comment s'appelle ton copain (ta copine)?
6. Quel âge a ton copain (ta copine)?

3 🎧 Conversation dirigée

ÉCOUTER ET PARLER Two students, Jean-Pierre and Janet, meet on the Paris-Lyon train. With a partner, compose and act out their dialogue according to the suggested script.

Jean-Pierre

Janet

Jean-Pierre		Janet
says hello	→ ↙	responds and asks how things are
says things are fine	↗	asks him what his name is
says his name is Jean-Pierre ... asks her name	→ ↙	says her name is Janet
asks her if she is English	→ ↙	says no and responds that she is American
asks her if she is from New York	→	replies that she is from San Francisco

4 Ma famille (My family)

PARLER You are showing your friends pictures of your family. Introduce everyone, giving their ages. If you prefer, show your classmates a picture of your own family and give each person's age.

▶ **Voici ma soeur. Elle a douze ans.**

1

2

3

4

5

6

5 En scène

PARLER With a classmate, act out the following scene.

CHARACTERS:

You and a French guest

SITUATION:

You are in France. Your French friends have invited you to a picnic. You meet one of the guests and have a conversation.

- Greet the guest.
- Ask how things are.
- Tell the guest that you are American and ask the guest if he/she is French.
- Tell the guest how old you are and ask his/her age.
- *(The guest waves to a friend.)* Ask the guest the name of his/her friend.
- *(It is the end of the picnic.)* Say good-bye.

6 Les nombres

PARLER

1. Select any number between 0 and 15 and give the next five numbers in sequence.
2. Select a number between 1 and 9. Use that number as a starting point and count by tens to 100.

▶ deux...
douze, vingt-deux, trente-deux, etc.

LESSON REVIEW
CLASSZONE.COM

Les Couleurs

rouge	orange	jaune	vert	bleu	violet	blanc	noir

Le drapeau des pays francophones

In the following countries, many people use French in their daily lives. Locate each country on the map on pages 8–9 and then describe the colors of its flag.

▶ La Belgique: **Le drapeau est noir, jaune et rouge.**

Europe

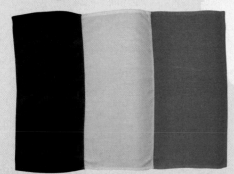

LA BELGIQUE
Population: 10 millions
Capitale: Bruxelles

LE LUXEMBOURG
Population: 0,5 million
Capitale: Luxembourg

LA SUISSE
Population: 7 millions
Capitale: Berne

Amérique

LE CANADA
Population: 31 millions
Capitale: Ottawa

HAÏTI
Population: 8 millions
Capitale: Port-au-Prince

rouge   orange   jaune   vert   bleu   violet   blanc   noir

Afrique

LE CAMEROUN
Population: 15 millions
Capitale: Yaoundé

LA CÔTE D'IVOIRE
Population: 16 millions
Capitale: Yamoussoukro

LE MAROC
Population: 28 millions
Capitale: Rabat

LE MALI
Population: 10 millions
Capitale: Bamako

LA RÉPUBLIQUE DÉMOCRATIQUE DU CONGO
Population: 42 millions
Capitale: Kinshasa

LE SÉNÉGAL
Population: 9 millions
Capitale: Dakar

CONNEXIONS World Geography

Increase your awareness of the francophone world. Select one of the countries mentioned and make a poster which includes the flag and a map showing the capital city. Complete the poster with pictures or other information of interest (sources: atlas, encyclopedia, Internet, travel ads, newspapers, and magazines).

La vie courante

LEÇON 3 Bon appétit!

VIDÉO-SCÈNES

A Tu as faim?

B Au café

C Ça fait combien?

LEÇON 4 De jour en jour

VIDÉO-SCÈNES

A L'heure

B Le jour et la date

C Le temps

THÈME ET OBJECTIFS

Everyday life in France

In this unit, you will learn how to get along in France. In particular, you may want to know how to buy something to eat or drink.

You will learn ...

- to order snacks and beverages in a café
- to ask about prices and pay for your food/drink
- to use French money

You will also learn ...

- to tell time
- to give the date and the day of the week
- to talk about the weather

WEBQUEST
CLASSZONE.COM

STEAK-FRITES 2.50
OMELETTE-FRITES 2.50
HOT-DOG 2.30
OMELETTE 2.30
PIZZA 2.30

THÉ 1.10
Jus de fruits 1.10

Introduction culturelle

Bon appétit!

Where do you go when you want something to eat or drink? Maybe to a fast-food restaurant or an ice cream place?

French teenagers also have a large choice of places to go when they are hungry or thirsty. Some go to a bakery **(une boulangerie)** or a pastry shop **(une pâtisserie)** to buy **croissants**, **éclairs,** or other small pastries. Some may buy pizzas, **crêpes,** hot dogs, or ice-cream cones from street vendors. Still others may go to a fast-food restaurant **(un fast-food).** But the favorite place to get something to eat or drink is the **café.** There are **cafés** practically everywhere in France. As you will see, the **café** plays an important role in the social life of all French people.

Bon appétit!
A Tu as faim?

Pierre, Philippe, and Nathalie are on their way home from school. They stop by a street vendor who sells sandwiches and pizza. Today it is Pierre's turn to treat his friends.

SCÈNE 1 Pierre et Nathalie

Pierre: Tu as faim?
Nathalie: Oui, j'ai faim.
Pierre: Tu veux un sandwich ou une pizza?
Nathalie: Donne-moi une pizza, s'il te plaît.
Pierre: Voilà.
Nathalie: Merci.

SCÈNE 2 Pierre et Philippe

Pierre: Et toi, Philippe, tu as faim?
Philippe: Oh là là, oui, j'ai faim.
Pierre: Qu'est-ce que tu veux? Un sandwich ou une pizza?
Philippe: Je voudrais un sandwich … <u>euh</u> … et donne-moi aussi une pizza.   *er …*
Pierre: C'est vrai! Tu as <u>vraiment</u> faim!   *really*

POUR COMMUNIQUER

> J'ai faim!
> Tu as faim?

▶ *How to say that you are hungry:*

J'ai faim.	*I'm hungry.*
Tu as faim?	*Are you hungry?*

▶ *How to offer a friend something:*

Tu veux … ?	*Do you want …?*	**Tu veux** un sandwich?
Qu'est-ce que tu veux?	*What do you want?*	**Qu'est-ce que tu veux?**
		Un sandwich ou une pizza?

▶ *How to ask a friend for something:*

Je voudrais …	*I would like …*	**Je voudrais** un sandwich.
Donne-moi …	*Give me …*	**Donne-moi** une pizza.
S'il te plaît …	*Please …*	**S'il te plaît,** François, donne-moi une pizza.

Les nourritures *(Foods)*

un croissant   un sandwich   un steak   un steak-frites   un hamburger   un hot dog

une salade   une pizza   une omelette   une crêpe   une glace

NOTE culturelle

Les jeunes et la nourriture

In general, French teenagers eat their main meals at home with their families. On weekends or after school, however, when they are with friends, they often stop at a fast-food restaurant or a café for something to eat.

At fast-food restaurants, French teenagers order pretty much the same types of foods as Americans: hamburgers, hot dogs, and pizza.

At a café, teenagers may order a croissant, a sandwich, or a dish of ice cream. Some favorite sandwiches are ham (**un sandwich au jambon**), Swiss cheese (**un sandwich au fromage**), or salami (**un sandwich au saucisson**). And, of course, they are made with French bread, which has a crunchy crust. Another traditional quick café meal is a small steak with French fries (**un steak-frites).**

PETIT COMMENTAIRE

In France, sandwiches are traditionally very simple: a piece of French bread with a slice of ham or cheese. However, nowadays one can buy fancier sandwiches made with different breads, such as "panini", and a variety of ingredients.

un sandwich, une pizza

You may have noted that the names of some foods are masculine and others are feminine. In French, ALL NOUNS, whether they designate people or things, are either MASCULINE or FEMININE.

MASCULINE NOUNS		FEMININE NOUNS	
un sandwich	**le** sandwich	**une** pizza	**la** pizza
un croissant	**le** croissant	**une** salade	**la** salade

1 ***Au choix*** (Your choice)

PARLER Offer your classmates a choice between the following items. They will decide which one they would like.

▶ une pizza ou un sandwich?

1. un hamburger ou un steak?
2. un hot dog ou un sandwich?
3. une salade ou une omelette?
4. un steak-frites ou une pizza?
5. une crêpe ou un croissant?
6. une glace à la vanille ou une glace au chocolat?

2 ***Au café***

PARLER You are in a French café. Ask for the following dishes.

▶

▶ Je voudrais un croissant.

 1

 2

 3

 4

 5

6

3 **Tu as faim?**

PARLER You have invited French friends to your home. Ask if they are hungry and offer them the following foods.

▶ —Tu as faim?
—Oui, j'ai faim.
—Tu veux un hamburger?
—Oui, merci.

▶

1

2

3

4

5

6

4 **Qu'est-ce que tu veux?**

PARLER Say which foods you would like to have in the following circumstances.

▶ You are very hungry.

Je voudrais un steak-frites.

1. You are at an Italian restaurant.
2. You are on a diet.
3. You are a vegetarian.
4. You are having breakfast.
5. You would like a dessert.
6. You want to eat something light for supper.

PRONONCIATION

L'intonation

When you speak, your voice rises and falls. This is called INTONATION. In French, as in English, your voice goes down at the end of a statement. However, in French, your voice rises after each group of words in the middle of a sentence. (This is the opposite of English, where your voice drops a little when you pause in the middle of a sentence.)

Voici un steak . . . et une salade.

Répétez: **Je voudrais une pizza.**

Je voudrais une pizza et un sandwich.

Je voudrais une pizza, un sandwich et un hamburger.

Voici un steak.

Voici un steak et une salade.

Voici un steak, une salade et une glace.

B Au café

This afternoon Trinh and Céline went shopping. They are now tired and thirsty. Trinh invites Céline to a café.

Tu as soif?

SCÈNE 1 **Trinh, Céline**

Trinh:	Tu as soif?	
Céline:	Oui, j'ai soif.	
Trinh:	<u>On va dans un café?</u>	*Shall we go to a café?*
	<u>Je t'invite.</u>	*I'm treating (inviting).*
Céline:	<u>D'accord!</u>	*Okay!*

Vous désirez, mademoiselle?

SCÈNE 2 **Le garçon, Céline, Trinh**

Le garçon:	Vous désirez, mademoiselle?	
Céline:	Un jus d'orange, s'il vous plaît.	
Le garçon:	Et <u>pour</u> vous, monsieur?	*for*
Trinh:	Donnez-moi une limonade,* s'il vous plaît.	

C'est pour vous, mademoiselle?

SCÈNE 3 **Le garçon, Céline, Trinh**

Le garçon:	*(à Céline)* La limonade, c'est pour vous, mademoiselle?	
Trinh:	Non, c'est pour moi.	
Le garçon:	<u>Ah, excusez-moi.</u>	*Oh, excuse me.*
	Voici le jus d'orange, mademoiselle.	
Céline:	Merci.	

*Une limonade is a popular inexpensive soft drink with a slight lemon flavor.

POUR COMMUNIQUER

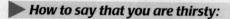

> Donnez-moi une limonade, s'il vous plaît!

▶ **How to say that you are thirsty:**

J'ai soif.	*I'm thirsty.*
Tu as soif?	*Are you thirsty?*

▶ **How to order in a café:**

Vous désirez?	*May I help you?*	—**Vous désirez?**
Je voudrais …	*I would like …*	—**Je voudrais** un jus d'orange.

▶ **How to request something …**

from a friend:	*from an adult:*	
S'il te plaît, donne-moi …	**S'il vous plaît, donnez-moi …**	*Please, give me …*

→ Note that French people have two ways of saying please. They use
s'il te plaît with friends, and
s'il vous plaît with adults.
As we will see later, young people address their friends as **tu** and
adults that they do not know very well as **vous.**

Les boissons *(Beverages)*

un soda	un jus d'orange	un jus de pomme	un jus de tomate	un jus de raisin*	une limonade	un café	un thé	un chocolat

NOTE **culturelle**

Le café

The café is a favorite gathering place for French young people. They go there not only when they are hungry or thirsty but also to meet their friends. They can sit at a table and talk for hours over a cup of coffee or a glass of juice. French young people also enjoy mineral water and soft drinks. In a French café, a 15% service charge is included in the check. However, most people also leave some small change as an added tip.

__Jus de raisin__ is a golden-colored juice made from grapes.

PETIT COMMENTAIRE
At a café, French young people often order carbonated soft drinks. They also enjoy natural beverages, such as flavored mineral water or juice. In the larger cities, one can find inviting juice bars that offer a wide selection of freshly blended fruit drinks.

1 🙍 **Tu as soif?**

PARLER You have invited a French friend to your house. You offer a choice of beverages and your friend (played by a classmate) responds.

▶ un thé ou un chocolat?
  —Tu veux un thé ou un chocolat?
  —Donne-moi un chocolat, s'il te plaît.

1. un thé ou un café?
2. une limonade ou un soda?
3. un jus de pomme ou un jus d'orange?   **4.** un jus de raisin ou un jus de tomate?

2 🙍 **Au café**

PARLER You are in a French café. Get the attention of the waiter (**Monsieur**) or the waitress (**Mademoiselle**) and place your order. Act out the dialogue with a classmate.

Que choisir? *(What to choose?)*

PARLER You are in a French café. Decide what beverage you are going to order in each of the following circumstances.

▶ You are very thirsty.
  S'il vous plaît, une limonade (un jus de pomme) …

1. It is very cold outside.
2. You do not want to spend much money.
3. You like juice but are allergic to citrus fruits.
4. It is breakfast time.
5. You have a sore throat.

4 **La faim et la soif** *(Hungry and thirsty)*

PARLER You are having a meal in a French café. Order the food suggested in the picture. Then order something to drink with that dish. A classmate will play the part of the waiter.

Note: **Et avec ça?** means *And with that?*

Vous désirez?

Je voudrais un steak-frites.

Et avec ça?

Un jus de tomate, s'il vous plaît!

1
2
3
4

PRONONCIATION

L'accent final

In French, the rhythm is very even and the accent always falls on the *last* syllable of a word or group of words.

Répétez: **Philippe   Thomas   Alice   Sophie   Dominique**

un ca**fé**	**Je voudrais un café.**
une sa**lade**	**Donnez-moi une salade.**
un choco**lat**	**Donne-moi un chocolat.**

un chocolat

C Ça fait combien?

At the café, Trinh and Céline have talked about many things.
It is now time to go. Trinh calls the waiter so he can pay the check.

> Dis, Céline, prête-moi 5 euros, s'il te plaît.

Trinh:	S'il vous plaît?
Le garçon:	Oui, monsieur.
Trinh:	Ça fait combien?
Le garçon:	Voyons, un jus d'orange, 2 euros 50, et une limonade, 1 euro 50. Ça fait 4 euros.
Trinh:	4 euros … Très bien … Mais, <u>euh</u> … *uh …*
	Zut! <u>Où est mon porte-monnaie …?</u> *Where is my wallet?*
	<u>Dis</u>, Céline, prête-moi *Hey*
	5 euros, s'il te plaît.

NOTE *culturelle*

L'argent européen (European money)

Since 2002, twelve European countries have been using a new currency: the euro (**l'euro**). These countries include France, as well as Germany, Ireland, Austria, Italy, Spain, Portugal, Greece, Finland, Belgium, Luxembourg, and the Netherlands. The euro has the same value in all of these countries. It is also very convenient since you do not need to change money when you travel from one country to another.

The euro is divided into 100 cents or **centimes**. The euro currency consists of 7 different bills and 8 different coins. The euro bills are of different colors and different sizes. The largest is worth 500 euros and the smallest 5 euros.

POUR COMMUNIQUER

> *C'est combien?*

▶ **How to ask how much something costs:**

C'est combien?	*How much is it?*	—**C'est combien?**
Ça fait combien?	*How much does that come to (make)?*	—**Ça fait combien?**
Ça fait ...	*That's ..., That comes to ...*	—**Ça fait** 10 euros.
Combien coûte ...?	*How much does ... cost?*	—**Combien coûte** le sandwich?
Il/Elle coûte ...	*It costs ...*	—**Il coûte** 5 euros.

▶ **How to ask a friend to lend you something:**

Prête-moi ...	*Lend me ..., Loan me ...*	**Prête-moi** 30 euros, s'il te plaît.

→ Note that masculine nouns can be replaced by **il** and feminine nouns can be replaced by **elle.**

| Voici **une glace.** | **Elle** coûte 2 euros. | *It costs 2 euros.* |
| Voici **un sandwich.** | **Il** coûte 5 euros. | *It costs 5 euros.* |

STRATEGY Speaking

Linking words When counting in euros, be sure to use the proper liaisons and elisions.

un euro	trois euros	cinq euros	sept euros	neuf euros
n	z	k	t	

deux euros	quatre euros	six euros	huit euros	dix euros
z		z	t	z

ÇA FAIT COMBIEN?

PETIT COMMENTAIRE

French people of all ages love to eat out, and French restaurants have the reputation of offering the best cuisine in the world. Of course, there are all kinds of restaurants for all kinds of budgets, ranging from the simple country inn (**l'auberge de campagne**) with its hearty regional food to the elegant three-star restaurant (**restaurant trois étoiles**) with its exquisite—and expensive—menu.

1 S'il te plaît ...

PARLER You have been shopping in Paris and discover that you did not exchange enough money. Ask a friend to loan you the following sums.

▶ 5 euros
    S'il te plaît, prête-moi cinq euros.

1. 2 euros	**4.** 20 euros	**7.** 25 euros
2. 3 euros	**5.** 30 euros	**8.** 15 euros
3. 10 euros	**6.** 40 euros	**9.** 50 euros

2 Décision

PARLER Before ordering at a café, Charlotte and Fatima are checking the prices. Act out the dialogues.

▶ le chocolat

Combien coûte le chocolat?

Il coûte deux euros cinquante.

1. le thé
2. le jus d'orange
3. la salade de tomates
4. la glace à la vanille
5. le café
6. le steak-frites
7. le hot dog
8. l'omelette
9. la salade mixte
10. le jus de raisin

LE SELECT
CAFÉ RESTAURANT

_____ *BOISSONS* _____

café	1€50
chocolat	2€50
thé	2€
limonade	2€50
jus d'orange	2€70
jus de raisin	2€70

_____ *GLACES* _____

glace au chocolat	2€50
glace à la vanille	2€50

_____ *SANDWICHS* _____

sandwich au jambon	3€50
sandwich au fromage	3€50

_____ *ET AUSSI . . .* _____

steak-frites	8€
salade mixte	3€50
salade de tomates	4€
omelette	4€25
hot dog	4€
croissant	1€40
pizza	8€

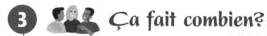 **Ça fait combien?**

PARLER You have gone to Le Select with your friends and have ordered the following items. Now you are ready to leave the café, and each one wants to pay. Check the prices on the menu for Le Select, and act out the dialogue.

▶ —Ça fait combien, s'il vous plaît?
▶ —Ça fait deux euros cinquante.
—Voici deux euros cinquante.
—Merci.

1   2

3

4   5

4 **Au «Select»**

PARLER You are at Le Select. Order something to eat and drink. Since you are in a hurry, ask for the check right away. Act out the dialogue with a classmate who will play the part of the waiter/waitress.

Monsieur, s'il vous plaît!

Vous désirez?

Je voudrais un sandwich au jambon et un café. Ça fait combien?

Ça fait 5 euros.

PRONONCIATION   /r/

La consonne «r»

The French consonant "**r**" is not at all like the English "**r.**" It is pronounced at the back of the throat. In fact, it is similar to the Spanish "jota" sound of José.

Répétez: **Marie   Paris   orange   Henri
franc   très   croissant   fromage
bonjour   pour   Pierre   quart
Robert   Richard   Renée   Raoul**

Marie, prête-moi trente euros.

Marie

De jour en jour
A L'heure

1. Un rendez-vous

Jean-Paul and Stéphanie are sitting in a café.
Stéphanie seems to be in a hurry to leave.

Stéphanie:	Quelle heure est-il?
Jean-Paul:	Il est trois heures.
Stéphanie:	Trois heures?
Jean-Paul:	Oui, trois heures.
Stéphanie:	Oh là là. <u>J'ai un rendez-vous avec</u> David dans vingt minutes. Au revoir, Jean-Paul.
Jean-Paul:	Au revoir, Stéphanie. <u>À bientôt!</u>

I have a date with

See you soon!

Il est huit heures!

POUR COMMUNIQUER

▶ *How to talk about the time:*

Quelle heure est-il?	*What time is it?*
Il est ...	*It's ...*

une heure	deux heures	trois heures	quatre heures	cinq heures	six heures

sept heures	huit heures	neuf heures	dix heures	onze heures	midi	minuit

1 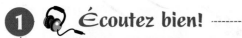 Écoutez bien!

ÉCOUTER Listen as people talk about the time. For each dialog, indicate which of the watches below corresponds to the time you hear.

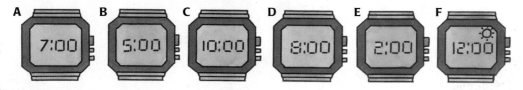

A 7:00   B 5:00   C 10:00   D 8:00   E 2:00   F 12:00

2 Quelle heure est-il?

PARLER Ask your classmates what time it is.

> Quelle heure est-il?
>
> Il est quatre heures.

 1
 2
 3
 4
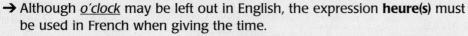 5
 6
 7

→ Although *o'clock* may be left out in English, the expression **heure(s)** must be used in French when giving the time.

It's ten. (It's ten o'clock.)   **Il est dix heures.**

→ To distinguish between A.M. and P.M., the French use the following expressions:

du matin	*in the morning*	Il est dix heures **du matin.**
de l'après-midi	*in the afternoon*	Il est deux heures **de l'après-midi.**
du soir	*in the evening*	Il est huit heures **du soir.**

NOTE DE PRONONCIATION: In telling time, the NUMBER and the word **heure(s)** are linked together. Remember, in French the letter "**h**" is always silent.

une heure   deux heures   trois heures   quatre heures   cinq heures   six heures
       z   z   k   z

sept heures   huit heures   neuf heures   dix heures   onze heures
     t   t   v   z

2. À quelle heure est le film?

Stéphanie and David have decided to go to a movie.

Stéphanie: Quelle heure est-il?

David: Il est trois heures et demie.

Stéphanie: Et à quelle heure est le film?

David: À quatre heures et quart.

Stéphanie: <u>Ça va.</u> <u>Nous avons le temps.</u>

That's okay. / We have time.

> À quelle heure est le dîner?

POUR COMMUNIQUER

▶ *How to ask at what time something is scheduled:*

À quelle heure est …?	*At what time is …?*
—À quelle heure est le concert?	*At what time is the concert?*
—Le concert est à huit heures.	*The concert is at eight.*

▶ *How to say that you have an appointment or a date:*

J'ai un rendez-vous à …	*I have an appointment (a date) at …*	**J'ai un rendez-vous à deux heures.**

▶ *How to indicate the minutes:*

 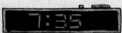 

Il est …	dix heures dix	six heures vingt-cinq	sept heures trente-cinq	deux heures cinquante-deux

▶ *How to indicate the half hour and the quarter hours:*

 et quart **et demie** **moins le quart**

 Il est une heure **et quart.** Il est deux heures **et demie.** Il est trois heures **moins le quart.**

③ L'heure

PARLER Give the times according to the clocks.

▶ **Il est une heure et quart.**

④ À quelle heure?

PARLER Ask your classmates at what time certain activities are scheduled. They will answer according to the information below.

▶ 8h 50   le film

—**À quelle heure est le film?**
—**Le film est à huit heures cinquante.**

1. 7h 15   le concert
2. 2h 30   le match de football *(soccer)*
3. 3h 45   le match de tennis
4. 5h 10   le récital
5. 7h 45   le dîner

⑤ Rendez-vous

PARLER Isabelle has appointments with various classmates and teachers. Look at her notebook and act out her dialogues with Philippe.

▶ ISABELLE: **J'ai un rendez-vous avec Marc.**
PHILIPPE: **À quelle heure?**
ISABELLE: **À onze heures et demie.**

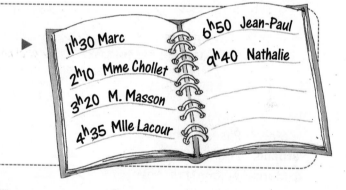

11h30 Marc
2h10 Mme Chollet
3h20 M. Masson
4h35 Mlle Lacour
6h50 Jean-Paul
9h40 Nathalie

⑥ À la gare *(At the train station)*

PARLER You are at the information desk of a French train station. Travelers ask you the departure times for the following trains. Answer them according to the posted schedule.

▶ le train pour Nice

À quelle heure est le train pour Nice?

Le train pour Nice est à six heures dix.

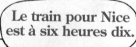
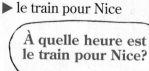

DÉPARTS			
NICE	◆ 6h 10	TOULON	◆ 9h 35
LYON	◆ 7h 15	COLMAR	◆ 10h 40
CANNES	◆ 7h 30	TOULOUSE	◆ 10h 45
TOURS	◆ 8h 12	MARSEILLE	◆ 10h 50
DIJON	◆ 8h 25	BORDEAUX	◆ 10h 55

B Le jour et la date

1. Quel jour est-ce?

For many people, the days of the week are not all alike.

DIALOGUE 1 Vendredi

Philippe: Quel jour est-ce?
Stéphanie: C'est vendredi.
Philippe: Super! Demain, c'est samedi!

DIALOGUE 2 Mercredi

Nathalie:	Ça va?	
Marc:	Pas très bien.	
Nathalie:	<u>Pourquoi?</u>	*Why?*
Marc:	Aujourd'hui, c'est mercredi.	
Nathalie:	<u>Et alors?</u>	*So?*
Marc:	Demain, c'est jeudi! Le jour de l'examen.	
Nathalie:	<u>Zut!</u> <u>C'est vrai!</u> Au revoir, Marc.	*Darn! /That's right!*
Marc:	Au revoir, Nathalie. À demain!	

Invitation au français

POUR COMMUNIQUER

À samedi!

▶ **How to talk about days of the week:**

Quel jour est-ce?	*What day is it?*
Aujourd'hui, c'est mercredi.	*Today is Wednesday.*
Demain, c'est jeudi.	*Tomorrow is Thursday.*

▶ **How to tell people when you will see them again:**

À samedi!	*See you Saturday!*
À demain!	*See you tomorrow!*

Les jours de la semaine *(Days of the week)*

lundi	*Monday*	**vendredi**	*Friday*	**aujourd'hui**	*today*
mardi	*Tuesday*	**samedi**	*Saturday*	**demain**	*tomorrow*
mercredi	*Wednesday*	**dimanche**	*Sunday*		
jeudi	*Thursday*				

---

1 Questions

PARLER

1. Quel jour est-ce aujourd'hui?
2. Et demain, quel jour est-ce?

Aujourd'hui, c'est samedi?

Non, aujourd'hui, c'est dimanche!

---

2 Un jour de retard *(One day behind)*

PARLER Georges has trouble keeping track of the date. He is always one day behind. Monique corrects him.

▶ samedi

1. lundi
2. mardi
3. jeudi
4. vendredi
5. dimanche
6. mercredi

---

3 Au revoir!

PARLER You are on the phone with the following friends. Say good-bye and tell them when you will see them.

▶ Christine/lundi
Au revoir, Christine. À lundi.

1. David/dimanche
2. Nicolas/samedi
3. Céline/mercredi
4. Julie/vendredi
5. Thomas/mardi
6. Pierre/jeudi

LUNDI	MARDI	MERCREDI	JEUDI	VENDREDI	SAMEDI	DIMANCHE
					1	2
3	4	5	6	7	8	9
10	11	12	13	14	15	16
17	18	19	20	21	22	23
24	25	26	27	28	29	30
31						

2. Anniversaire

François and Isabelle are on their way to Nathalie's birthday party. As they are talking, François wants to know when Isabelle's birthday is.

François:	C'est quand, ton anniversaire?
Isabelle:	C'est le 18 mars!
François:	Le 18 mars? Pas possible! *That's not possible!*
Isabelle:	Si! Pourquoi? *Yes, it is! Why?*
François:	C'est aussi mon anniversaire.
Isabelle:	Quelle coïncidence! *What a coincidence!*

POUR COMMUNIQUER

Quelle est la date?

▶ *How to talk about the date:*

Quelle est la date?	*What's the date?*
C'est le 12 (douze) octobre.	*It's October 12.*
C'est le premier juin.	*It's June first.*

▶ *How to talk about birthdays:*

—C'est quand, ton anniversaire?	*When is your birthday?*
—Mon anniversaire est le 2 (deux) mars.	*My birthday is March 2.*

Les mois de l'année *(Months of the year)*

janvier ✓	**avril** ✓	**juillet**	**octobre** ✓
février	**mai** ✓	**août**	**novembre** ✓
mars ✓	**juin**	**septembre** ✓	**décembre**

La date

To express a date in French, the pattern is:

L'ÉVÉNEMENT MUSICAL DE L'ANNÉE
LE 19 JANVIER

le	+	NUMBER	+	MONTH
le		11 (onze)		novembre
le		20 (vingt)		mai

EXCEPTION: The first of the month is **le premier.**

➔ In front of numbers, the French use **le** (and never **l´**): **le onze, le huit.**

➔ Note that when dates are abbreviated in French, the day always comes first.

2/8 **le deux août**   1/11 **le premier novembre**

4  🎵 *Anniversaires*

PARLER Ask your classmates when their birthdays are.

C'est quand, ton anniversaire?

Mon anniversaire est le 3 février.

5 *Quelle est la date?*

PARLER Ask what the date is.

▶ —Quelle est la date?
—C'est le douze septembre.

6 *Dates importantes*

PARLER Give the following dates in French.

▶ Noël *(Christmas)*: 25/12   C'est le **vingt-cinq décembre.**

1. le jour de l'An *(New Year's Day)*: 1/1
2. la fête *(holiday)* de Martin Luther King: 15/1
3. la Saint-Valentin: 14/2
4. la Saint-Patrick: 17/3
5. la fête nationale américaine: 4/7
6. la fête nationale française: 14/7
7. la fête de Christophe Colomb: 12/10

LEÇON 4

VIDÉO-SCÈNE

VIDÉO   DVD   AUDIO

C Le temps

It is nine o'clock Sunday morning. Cécile and her brother Philippe have planned a picnic for the whole family. Cécile is asking about the weather.

Quel temps fait-il?

Il fait mauvais.

Zut, zut et zut!

Papa va nous inviter au restaurant.

Cécile:	Quel temps fait-il?	
Philippe:	Il fait mauvais!	
Cécile:	Il fait mauvais?	
Philippe:	Oui, il fait mauvais! <u>Regarde!</u> Il pleut!	*Look!*
Cécile:	Zut, zut et zut!	
Philippe:	!!!???	
Cécile:	Et le <u>pique-nique?</u>	*picnic*
Philippe:	Le pique-nique? Ah oui, le pique-nique! … <u>Écoute, ça n'a pas d'importance.</u>	*Listen, it doesn't matter. (It's not important.)*
Cécile:	<u>Pourquoi?</u>	*Why?*
Philippe:	Pourquoi? <u>Parce que Papa va nous inviter au restaurant.</u>	*Because Dad is going to take us out (invite us) to a restaurant.*
Cécile:	Super!	

Quel temps fait-il?

POUR COMMUNIQUER

▶ **How to talk about the weather:**

Quel temps fait-il?   *How's the weather?*

Il fait beau.

Il fait bon.

Il fait chaud.

Il fait frais.

Il fait froid.

Il fait mauvais.

Il pleut.

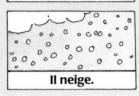

Il neige.

Les saisons *(Seasons)*

le printemps	*spring*	**au printemps**	*in (the) spring*
l'été	*summer*	**en été**	*in (the) summer*
l'automne	*fall, autumn*	**en automne**	*in (the) fall*
l'hiver	*winter*	**en hiver**	*in (the) winter*

① Ta région

PARLER Say what the weather is like in your part of the country.

▶ en juillet

En juillet, il fait chaud.

1. en août
2. en septembre
3. en novembre
4. en janvier
5. en mars
6. en mai

② Les quatre saisons

PARLER Describe what the weather is like in each of the four seasons in the following cities.

▶ à Miami

En été, il fait chaud. En automne, il fait chaud aussi. En hiver, il fait frais. Au printemps, il fait bon.

Miami

1. à Chicago   4. à Boston
2. à San Francisco 5. à Seattle
3. à Denver   6. à Dallas

À votre tour!

OBJECTIFS

Now you can...
- order snacks and beverages in a café
- ask about prices and pay for your food/drink
- tell time and give the date
- talk about the weather

1  **Écoutez bien!**

ÉCOUTER Isabelle is in a café talking to Jean-Paul. You will hear Isabelle asking questions. For each of Isabelle's questions, select Jean-Paul's response from the suggested answers.

a. Deux euros cinquante.
b. Quatre heures et demie.
c. Oui, j'ai soif.
d. C'est le 3 novembre.
e. Oui, j'ai faim.
f. Il fait beau.

2 **Quelle heure est-il?**

PARLER Give the times indicated on the following clocks.

1	2	3	4	5	6
	3:15			4:45	8:05

3 **Conversation dirigée**

ÉCOUTER ET PARLER Stéphanie is in a café called Le Select. The waiter is taking her order. With a partner, compose and act out a dialogue according to the script suggested below.

le garçon		Stéphanie
greets client and asks if he may help her →	says that she would like a croissant and asks how much an orange juice costs	
answers 2 euros →	asks for an orange juice... calls the waiter and asks how much she owes	
says 4 euros cinquante →	gives waiter 5 euros **(Voici...)**	
says thank you		

4  Au café

PARLER You are in a French café. Call the waiter/waitress and order the following items. A classmate will play the part of the waiter/waitress.

▶ —Monsieur (Mademoiselle), s'il vous plaît!
—Vous désirez?
—Un croissant, s'il vous plaît!
(Donnez-moi un croissant, s'il vous plaît!)
(Je voudrais un croissant, s'il vous plaît!)

5  En scène

STRATEGY Speaking

Sounding French If you want French people to understand you, the most important thing is to speak with an even rhythm and to stress the last syllable in each group of words. (Try speaking English this way: people will think you have a French accent!)

PARLER With two other classmates, act out the following scene.

CHARACTERS:
You, a French friend, and the waiter in the café

SITUATION:
A French friend has been showing you around Paris. You invite your friend to a café and discover too late that you have not changed enough money. Your friend will respond to your questions.

- Ask your friend if he/she is thirsty.

- Ask if he/she wants a soft drink.

- Ask if he/she is hungry.

- Ask if he/she wants a sandwich.

- When the waiter comes, your friend orders and you ask for a croissant and a cup of hot chocolate.

- Ask the waiter how much everything is.

- Ask your friend to please lend you 20 euros.

6 La date, la saison et le temps

PARLER Look at the calendar days. For each one, give the day and the date, the season, and the weather.

▶ C'est mardi, le dix avril.
C'est le printemps.
Il pleut.

Les parties du corps

(Parts of the body)

la tête

les cheveux

l'oeil (les yeux)

l'oreille

le nez

la bouche

le cou

la main

le bras

le ventre

le dos

la jambe

le pied

Un jeu: Jacques a dit

The French sometimes play a game called **Jacques a dit** *(Jim said)*. The rules are the same as the English game of *Simon Says.* Everyone stands up to play.

The game leader says: **Jacques a dit: Les mains sur la tête!** placing her hands on her head. The other players also place their hands on their heads.

Then the game leader may say: **Les mains sur le dos!** placing her hands on her back. This time, however, the other players should not move, because the game leader did not first say **Jacques a dit**. Any player that did move must sit down, but may continue playing.

The game continues until only one player is left standing.

Une chanson: Alouette

ALOUETTE *(The Lark)* is a popular folk song of French-Canadian origin. As the song leader names the various parts of the bird's anatomy, he points to his own body. The chorus repeats the refrain with enthusiasm.

Alouette

A - lou - et - te, gen - tille a - lou - et - te,
a - lou - et - te, je te plu - me - rai.
Je te plu - me - rai la tête, je te plu - me - rai la tête.
Et la tête, et la tête, a - lou - ett', a - lou - ett', oh!

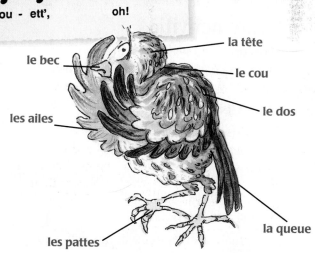

la tête
le cou
le dos
le bec
les ailes
la queue
les pattes

1. Alouette, gentille alouette,
   Alouette, je te plumerai.

   Je te plumerai la tête,
   Je te plumerai la tête.

   Et la tête—et la tête
   Alouette—Alouette
   Oh oh oh oh

2. Alouette, gentille alouette
   Alouette, je te plumerai.

   Je te plumerai le bec,
   Je te plumerai le bec.

   Et le bec—et le bec
   Et la tête—et la tête
   Alouette—Alouette
   Oh oh oh oh

3. Je te plumerai le cou ...

4. Je te plumerai les ailes ...

5. Je te plumerai le dos ...

6. Je te plumerai les pattes ...

7. Je te plumerai la queue ...

COMMUNAUTÉS: French song

As a class project, you might want to memorize *Alouette* and perform it at a senior center or teach the song to a local grade school class.

UNITÉ 3

Qu'est-ce qu'on fait?

LEÇON 5 **LE FRANÇAIS PRATIQUE:** Mes activités

LEÇON 6 **Une invitation**

LEÇON 7 **Une boum**

LEÇON 8 **Un concert de musique africaine**

THÈME ET OBJECTIFS

Daily activities

In this unit, you will be talking about the things you do every day, such as working and studying, as well as watching TV or playing sports.

You will learn ...

- to describe some of your daily activities
- to say what you like and do not like to do
- to ask and answer questions about where others are and what they are doing

You will also learn ...

- to invite friends to do things with you
- to politely accept or turn down an invitation

WEBQUEST
CLASSZONE.COM

Mes activités

Accent sur … Les activités de la semaine

French teenagers spend a great deal of time on their studies since they and their families consider it important to do well in school. They have a longer class day than American students and are given more homework.

However, French teenagers do not study all the time. They also enjoy listening to music, watching TV, and playing computer games. Many participate in various sports activities, but to a lesser extent than American students. On weekends, they like to go out with their friends to shop or see a movie. They also go to parties and love dancing.

*Mélanie est à la maison.
Elle écoute un CD.*

Mélanie: J'aime le rock anglais.

Marc, Élodie et David sont au stade. Ils jouent au foot.

Marc: Nous jouons au foot.

Élodie: Nous jouons aussi au basket.

David: Nous aimons les sports.

Olivier est en ville. Il téléphone.

Olivier: J'aime téléphoner.
Je téléphone à une copine.

Zaïna joue aux jeux vidéo.

Zaïna: J'aime jouer aux jeux vidéo.
J'aime aussi regarder la télé.

A VOCABULAIRE Préférences

Est-ce que tu aimes parler français?

▶ **How to talk about what you like and don't like to do:**

Est-ce que tu aimes …?	*Do you like …?*	**Est-ce que tu aimes** parler *(to speak)* **français?**
J'aime …	*I like …*	Oui, **j'aime** parler français.
Je n'aime pas …	*I don't like …*	Non, **je n'aime pas** parler français.
Je préfère …	*I prefer …*	**Je préfère** parler anglais.

J'aime …

téléphoner
to phone

parler français
to talk, speak French

parler anglais
to speak English

parler espagnol
to speak Spanish

manger
to eat

chanter
to sing

danser
to dance

nager
to swim

---

1 **Et toi?**

PARLER/ÉCRIRE Indicate what you like to do in the following situations by completing each sentence with two of the suggested activities.

1 En classe, j'aime … mais je préfère …
étudier • écouter le professeur • parler avec *(with)* **un copain • parler avec une copine**

2. En été, j'aime … mais je préfère …
travailler • nager • voyager • jouer au volley *(volleyball)*

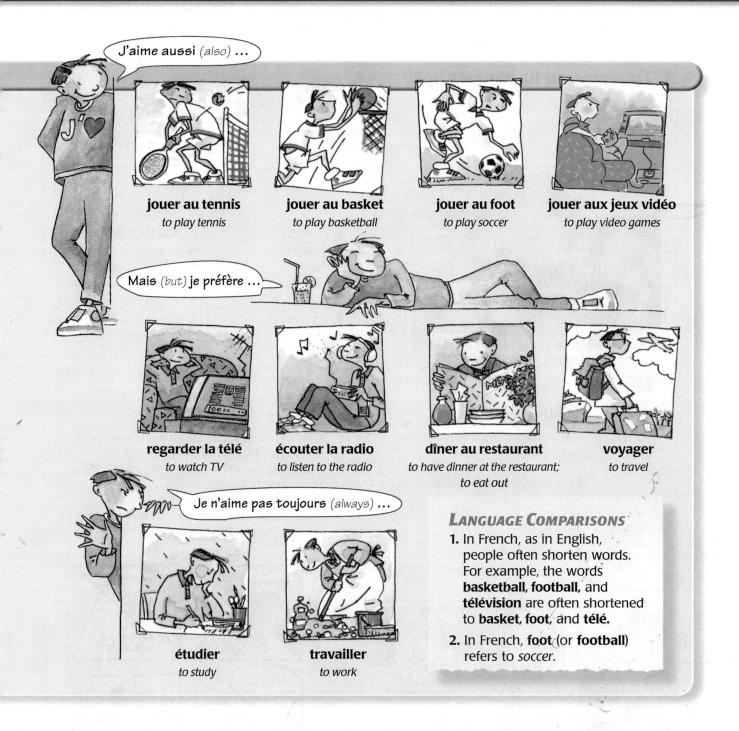

J'aime aussi *(also)* …

jouer au tennis
to play tennis

jouer au basket
to play basketball

jouer au foot
to play soccer

jouer aux jeux vidéo
to play video games

Mais *(but)* **je préfère** …

regarder la télé
to watch TV

écouter la radio
to listen to the radio

dîner au restaurant
*to have dinner at the restaurant;
to eat out*

voyager
to travel

Je n'aime pas toujours *(always)* …

étudier
to study

travailler
to work

LANGUAGE COMPARISONS

1. In French, as in English, people often shorten words. For example, the words **basketball, football,** and **télévision** are often shortened to **basket, foot,** and **télé.**

2. In French, **foot** (or **football**) refers to *soccer.*

---

3. Avec mes *(my)* copains, j'aime … mais je préfère …
chanter • **manger** • **écouter la radio** • **jouer au basket**

4. Avec ma famille, j'aime … mais je préfère …
voyager • **regarder la télé** • **jouer aux jeux vidéo** • **dîner au restaurant**

5. À la maison *(At home)*, j'aime … mais je préfère …
étudier • **téléphoner** • **manger** • **écouter mes CD**

2 Tu aimes ou tu n'aimes pas?

PARLER/ÉCRIRE Say whether or not you like to do the following things.

▶ chanter?

J'aime chanter.

Je n'aime pas chanter.

1. manger?
2. étudier?
3. danser?
4. téléphoner?
5. voyager?
6. travailler?
7. regarder la télé?
8. dîner au restaurant?
9. jouer au basket?
10. jouer aux jeux vidéo?
11. écouter la radio?
12. parler français?

3 Préférences

PARLER Ask your classmates if they like to do the following things.

▶ —Est-ce que tu aimes téléphoner?
—Oui, j'aime téléphoner.
(Non, je n'aime pas téléphoner.)

 1
 2
 3

 4
 5
 6

 7
 8
 9

4 Dialogue

PARLER Marc is asking Léa if she likes to do certain things. She replies that she prefers to do other things. Play both roles. Note: "??" means you can invent an answer.

▶ MARC: **Est-ce que tu aimes nager?**
LÉA: **Oui, mais je préfère jouer au tennis.**

▶

 1

 2
 3

 4
 5

B   VOCABULAIRE   Souhaits *(Wishes)*

Je voudrais voyager en France.

▶ **How to talk about what you want, would like, and do not want to do:**

Je veux …	*I want …*	**Je veux** parler français.
Je voudrais …	*I would like …*	**Je voudrais** voyager en France.
Je ne veux pas …	*I don't want …*	**Je ne veux pas** étudier aujourd'hui.

---

5 **Ce soir** *(Tonight)*

PARLER/ÉCRIRE Say whether or not you want to do the following things tonight.

▶ étudier?
  Oui, je veux étudier.
  (Non, je ne veux pas étudier.)

1. parler français?
2. travailler?
3. jouer aux jeux vidéo?
4. chanter?
5. danser?
6. regarder la télé?
7. écouter la radio?
8. dîner avec une copine?
9. manger une pizza?
10. téléphoner à mon cousin?

6 **Week-end**

PARLER/ÉCRIRE Léa and her friends are discussing their weekend plans. What do they say they would like to do?

▶ LÉA: **Je voudrais jouer au tennis.**

Léa
1. Jérôme
2. Monique
3. Jean-Louis
4. Caroline
5. Patrick

---

7 **Trois souhaits** *(Three wishes)*

ÉCRIRE Read the list of suggested activities and select the three that you would like to do most.

parler français	voyager avec ma cousine
parler espagnol	voyager en France
parler avec *(with)* Oprah Winfrey	chanter comme *(like)* Britney Spears
dîner avec le Président	jouer au tennis comme Venus Williams
dîner avec Matt Damon	jouer au basket comme Shaquille O'Neal

▶ **Je voudrais parler espagnol.**
  Je voudrais chanter comme Britney Spears.
  Je voudrais voyager en France.

C VOCABULAIRE Invitations

> Est-ce que tu veux jouer au tennis?

▶ How to invite a friend:

Est-ce que tu veux …?	*Do you want to …?*	**Est-ce que tu veux** jouer au tennis?
Est-ce que tu peux …?	*Can you …?*	**Est-ce que tu peux** parler à mon copain?
avec moi/toi	*with me/you*	Est-ce que tu veux dîner **avec moi?**

▶ How to accept an invitation:

Oui, bien sûr …	*Yes, of course …*	
Oui, merci …	*Yes, thanks …*	
Oui, d'accord …	*Yes, all right, okay …*	
je veux bien.	*I'd love to.*	**Oui, bien sûr, je veux bien.**
je veux bien …	*I'd love to …*	**Oui, merci, je veux bien** dîner avec toi.

▶ How to turn down an invitation:

Je regrette, mais	*I'm sorry, but*	**Je regrette, mais je ne peux pas**
je ne peux pas …	*I can't …*	dîner avec toi.
Je dois …	*I have to, I must …*	**Je dois** étudier.

---

8  *Oui, d'accord*

PARLER Invite the following French students (played by your classmates) to do things with you. They will accept.

▶ Monique / dîner

> Monique, est-ce que tu veux dîner avec moi?

> Oui, d'accord, je veux bien dîner avec toi.

1. Thomas / parler français
2. Simon / étudier
3. Céline / jouer au tennis
4. Anne / manger une pizza
5. Jean-Claude / chanter
6. Caroline / danser

9 Conversation

PARLER Ask your classmates if they want to do the following things. They will answer that they cannot and explain why.

▶ jouer au basket?
(étudier)
— Est-ce que tu veux jouer au basket?
— Non, je ne peux pas. Je dois étudier.

1. jouer aux jeux vidéo?
(travailler)
2. jouer au ping-pong?
(téléphoner à ma cousine)
3. étudier avec moi?
(étudier avec ma copine)
4. dîner avec moi?
(dîner avec ma famille)
5. nager?
(jouer au foot à deux heures)

NOTE **culturelle**

Le téléphone

French teenagers, like their American counterparts, love to talk with their friends on the phone. At home, they can use the family phone, but now more and more young people also have a cell phone which is called **un téléphone portable** or simply **un portable** for short. (**Portable** comes from the French verb **porter**, which means *to carry*.)

Europeans have been ahead of Americans in the use of mobile phones. In France, for instance, almost half of the people own a cell phone. This proportion is higher with teenagers and college students. Cell phones have many advantages. You can call your friends from wherever you are and whenever you want, and if you are going to be late for dinner, you can call and let your parents know. Cell phones, however, can be annoying and even distracting. In France, it is illegal to make cell phone calls while driving a car. Moreover, students are not allowed to bring cell phones to class. It is also considered impolite to use them in restaurants, cinemas, and concert halls.

COMPARAISONS CULTURELLES

Compare the French and American attitudes toward the use of cell phones.

How do you feel about people using cell phones in the following circumstances? Indicate whether you think it is appropriate or not by saying: **C'est acceptable.** or **Ce n'est pas acceptable.**

- au café
- au cinéma
- au restaurant
- pendant *(during)* la classe de français
- pendant un concert de rock
- en conduisant *(while driving)*

L'étiquette téléphonique

- to introduce yourself when phoning a friend, you say:

  Allô … Ici Thomas. Bonjour. Ça va?

- if your friend is not home and if a parent answers, you say:

  Allô … Ici Thomas Rémi. Bonjour, monsieur (madame).

  Est-ce que je pourrais *(May I)* parler à Mélanie?

- if you would like to leave a message, you ask:

  Est-ce que je peux *(Can I)* laisser un message?

- before hanging up, you say:

  Merci, monsieur (madame). Au revoir.

10  **Allô!**

PARLER Céline is phoning Trinh to ask him if he wants to go to a movie. Trinh's mother says that he is not home. Céline asks her to take a message. Act out the conversation between Céline and Trinh's mother.

À votre tour!

OBJECTIFS

Now you can …
• talk about activities you like and do not like
• extend and accept invitations
• give an excuse when you cannot accept

1 Écoutez bien!

ÉCOUTER You will hear French young people telling you what they like to do.
Listen carefully to each activity. If it is illustrated in the picture on the left,
mark A. If it is illustrated in the picture on the right, mark B.

A

B

	A	B
1.		
2.		
3.		
4.		
5.		
6.		

2 Communication

ÉCOUTER You have invited a French friend to spend the weekend at your house.
Ask your friend …

• if he/she likes to watch TV
• if he/she wants to play video games
• if he/she likes to listen to the radio
• if he/she wants to eat a pizza

A classmate will play the role of your French friend and answer your questions.

3 Conversation dirigée

PARLER Trinh is phoning Céline. Write out their conversation according to
the directions. You may want to act out the dialogue with a classmate.

Trinh

Céline

Trinh		Céline
asks Céline how she is	→ ↙	answers that she is fine
asks her if she wants to eat out	→ ↙	asks at what time
says at 8 o'clock	→ ↙	says that she is sorry but that she has to study
says it is too bad (**Dommage!**)		

4 **Créa-dialogue**

PARLER Ask your classmates if they want to do the following things with you. They will answer that they cannot and will give one of the excuses below.

▶ jouer au tennis

1. jouer au basket
2. manger une pizza
3. regarder la télé
4. jouer au ping-pong
5. dîner au restaurant
6. jouer aux jeux vidéo

Est-ce que tu veux jouer au tennis avec moi?

Non, je ne peux pas. Je dois travailler.

EXCUSES:

téléphoner à une copine

étudier   travailler

parler avec ma mère

dîner avec ma cousine

chanter avec la chorale (choir)

5 **Expression personnelle** ---

PARLER/ÉCRIRE What we like to do often depends on the circumstances. Complete the sentences below saying what you like and don't like to do in the following situations.

▶ En hiver ...
   En hiver, j'aime regarder la télé.
   J'aime aussi jouer au basket.
   Je n'aime pas nager.

1. En été ...
2. En automne ...
3. Le samedi (On Saturdays) ...
4. Le dimanche ...

5. Le soir (In the evening) ...
6. En classe ...
7. Avec mes (my) amis ...
8. Avec ma famille ...

6 **Correspondance** ---

ÉCRIRE This summer you are going to spend two weeks in France. Your e-mail correspondent Vincent has written asking what you like and don't like to do on vacation (en vacances). Respond with a short e-mail, answering his questions.

STRATEGY Writing

1. Make a list of activities you like and do not like. Use only vocabulary that you know.

   :) _____
       _____
       _____

   :(_____
       _____
       _____

2. Write your e-mail.   *Cher Vincent,*
                         En vacances, j'aime ...

3. Read over your letter to be sure you have used the right verb forms.

Une invitation

VIDÉO   DVD   AUDIO

It is Wednesday afternoon. Antoine is looking for his friends but cannot find anyone. Finally he sees Céline at the Café Le Bercy and asks her where everyone is.

Antoine:	<u>Où</u> est Léa?	*Where*
Céline:	Elle est <u>à la maison</u>.	*at home*
Antoine:	Et Mathieu? Il est <u>là</u>?	*here*
Céline:	Non, il n'est pas là.	
Antoine:	Où est-il?	
Céline:	Il est <u>en ville</u> avec une copine.	*in town*
Antoine:	Et Julie et Stéphanie? Est-ce qu'elles sont <u>ici</u>?	*here*
Céline:	Non, elles sont au restaurant.	
Antoine:	<u>Alors</u>, qui est là?	*So*
Céline:	Moi, je suis ici.	
Antoine:	C'est <u>vrai</u>, tu es ici! Eh bien, <u>puisque</u> tu es là, <u>je t'invite au cinéma</u>. D'accord?	*true / since* *I'll invite you to the movies.*
Céline:	Super! Antoine, tu es un <u>vrai</u> copain!	*real*

Compréhension

Indicate where the following people are by selecting the appropriate completions.

en ville

1. Léa est …   3. Julie et Stéphanie sont …   *au café*

2. Mathieu est …   4. Antoine et Céline sont …   *à la maison*   *au restaurant*

NOTE culturelle

Le mercredi après-midi

French middle school students do not usually have classes on Wednesday afternoons. Some young people use this free time to go out with their friends or to catch up on their homework. For other students, Wednesday afternoon is also the time for music and dance lessons as well as sports activities. Many students play soccer with their school team or with their local sports club. Other popular activities include tennis, skateboarding, and in-line skating.

COMPARAISONS CULTURELLES

- How does the school week in France compare to the school week in the United States?

- Do you see any differences in the ways French and American teenagers spend their free time? Explain.

- Do American and French teenagers like the same sports? Explain.

A   Le verbe *être* et les pronoms sujets

Être *(to be)* is the most frequently used verb in French. Note the forms of **être** in the chart below.

	être	*to be*	
SINGULAR	je **suis**	*I am*	Je **suis** américain.
	tu **es**	*you are*	Tu **es** canadienne.
	il/elle **est**	*he/she is*	Il **est** anglais.
PLURAL	nous **sommes**	*we are*	Nous **sommes** à Paris.
	vous **êtes**	*you are*	Vous **êtes** à San Francisco.
	ils/elles **sont**	*they are*	Ils **sont** à Genève.

→ Note the liaison in the **vous** form:

Vous êtes français?

→ Note the expression **être d'accord** *(to agree)*:

—Tu **es d'accord**   *Do you agree*
  avec moi?   *with me?*
—Oui, je **suis d'accord!**   *Yes, I agree!*

TU or VOUS?

When talking to ONE person, the French have two ways of saying *you*:

- **tu** ("familiar *you*") is used to talk to someone your own age (or younger) or to a member of your family
- **vous** ("formal *you*") is used when talking to anyone else

When talking to TWO or more people, the French use **vous.**

 RAPPEL You should use …
- **vous** to address your teacher
- **tu** to address a classmate

ILS or ELLES?

The French have two ways of saying *they*:

- **ils** refers to two or more males or to a mixed group of males and females
- **elles** refers to two or more females

Ils sont à Paris.   Ils sont à Bordeaux.

Ils sont à Lyon.   Elles sont à Nice.

---

1 En France

PARLER/ÉCRIRE The following students are on vacation in France. Which cities are they in?

▶ Sophie … à Nice.   **Sophie est à Nice.**

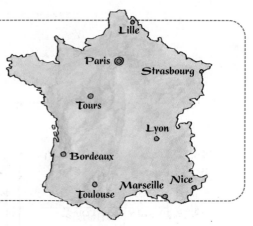

1. Antoine … à Tours.
2. Nous … à Toulouse.
3. Vous … à Marseille.
4. Je … à Strasbourg.

5. Julie et Marie … à Lille.
6. Éric et Vincent … à Lyon.
7. Ma cousine … à Paris.
8. Tu … à Bordeaux.

VOCABULAIRE Où?

Où est Cécile?	*Where is Cécile?*		
Elle est …	**ici** *(here)*	**là** *(here, there)*	**là-bas** *(over there)*
	à Paris *(in Paris)*	**à Boston**	**à Québec**
	en classe *(in class)*	**en ville** *(in town)*	
	en vacances *(on vacation)*	**en France** *(in France)*	
	au café *(at the café)*	**au restaurant**	**au cinéma** *(at the movies)*
	à la maison *(at home)*		

---

2 À Tours

PARLER/ÉCRIRE You are spending your summer vacation in Tours at the home of your friend Léa. Ask the following people questions using **Tu es** or **Vous êtes** as appropriate.

▶ *(the mailman)* … français?   **Vous êtes français?**

1. *(Léa's mother)* … de Tours?
2. *(Léa's best friend)* … française?
3. *(Léa's brother)* … en vacances?
4. *(a lady in the park)* … française?

5. *(Léa's cousin)* … de Paris?
6. *(a little girl)* … avec ta mère?
7. *(Léa's teacher)* … strict?
8. *(a tourist)* … américain?

3 *Où sont-ils?*

PARLER Corinne is wondering if some of the people she knows are in certain places. Tell her she is right, using **il, elle, ils,** or **elles** in your answers.

▶ Ta cousine est à Chicago?   **Oui, elle est à Chicago.**

1. Stéphanie est à Lyon?
2. Monsieur Thomas est à San Francisco?
3. Léa et Céline sont à la maison?
4. Cécile et Charlotte sont au café?

5. Ta soeur est en ville?
6. Ton cousin est en vacances?
7. Claire, Alice et Éric sont au cinéma?
8. Monsieur et Madame Joli sont à Montréal?

4 *Où?*

PARLER You want to know where certain people are. A classmate will answer you.

▶ —Où est Céline?
—Elle est à New York.

▶ Céline

1. Daniel

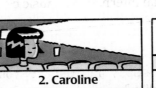
2. Caroline

3. Jean-Louis

4. Robert

5. Florence

6. Hélène

7. Julien

B Les questions à réponse affirmative ou négative

The sentences on the left are statements. The sentences on the right are questions. These questions are called YES/NO QUESTIONS because they can be answered by *yes* or *no*. Note how the French questions begin with **est-ce que.**

STATEMENTS   YES/NO QUESTIONS

Stéphanie est ici.   **Est-ce que** Stéphanie est ici?   *Is Stéphanie here?*
Tu es français.   **Est-ce que** tu es français?   *Are you French?*
Paul et Marc sont au café. **Est-ce qu'**ils sont au café?   *Are they at the café?*
Tu veux jouer au foot.   **Est-ce que** tu veux jouer au foot?   *Do you want to play soccer?*

Yes/no questions can be formed according to the pattern:

est-ce que + STATEMENT?	**Est-ce que** Pierre est ici?
↓ **est-ce qu'** (+ VOWEL SOUND)	**Est-ce qu'**il est en ville?

→ In yes/no questions, the voice goes up at the end of the sentence.

Est-ce que Paul et Florence sont au café?

→ In casual conversation, yes/no questions can be formed without **est-ce que** simply by letting your voice rise at the end of the sentence.

Tu es français?   Cécile est en ville?

Observation When you expect someone to agree with you, another way to form a yes/no question is to add the tag **n'est-ce pas** at the end of the sentence.

Tu es américain, **n'est-ce pas?**   *You are American, **aren't you?***
Tu aimes parler français, **n'est-ce pas?**   *You like to speak French, **don't you?***
Vous êtes d'accord, **n'est-ce pas?**   *You agree, **don't you?***

5 *Nationalités*

PARLER/ÉCRIRE You are attending an international music camp.
Ask about other people's nationalities.

▶ Marc/canadien?   **Est-ce que Marc est canadien?**

1. Jim / américain?
2. Luisa / mexicaine?
3. Paul et Philippe / français?
4. tu / canadien?
5. vous / anglais?
6. Anne / française?
7. Ellen et Carol / américaines?

VOCABULAIRE **Expressions pour la conversation**

How to answer a yes/no question:

Oui!	*Yes!*	**Peut-être ...**	*Maybe ...*	**Non!**	*No!*
Mais oui!	*Sure!*			**Mais non!**	*Of course not!*
Bien sûr!	*Of course!*				

6 *Conversation*

PARLER Ask your classmates the following questions. They will answer, using an expression from **Expressions pour la conversation**.

▶ Ton cousin est français?

1. Ta mère est à la maison?
2. Ta cousine est en France?
3. Ton copain est en classe?
4. Tu veux manger une pizza avec moi?
5. Tu veux jouer aux jeux vidéo avec moi?

Alice, est-ce que ton cousin est français?

Mais oui!
(Mais non!)

C La négation

Compare the affirmative and negative sentences below:

AFFIRMATIVE	NEGATIVE	
Je **suis** américain.	Je **ne suis pas** français.	*I'm not French.*
Nous **sommes** en classe.	Nous **ne sommes pas** en vacances.	*We are not on vacation.*
Claire **est** là-bas.	Elle **n'est pas** ici.	*She is not here.*
Tu **es** d'accord avec moi.	Tu **n'es pas** d'accord avec Marc.	*You do not agree with Marc.*

Negative sentences are formed as follows:

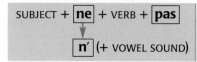

SUBJECT + ⎢**ne**⎥ + VERB + ⎢**pas**⎥   Éric et Anne **ne** sont **pas** là.

⎢**n'**⎥ (+ VOWEL SOUND)   Michèle **n'**est **pas** avec moi.

Nous sommes en ville.
Nous **ne** sommes **pas** à la maison.

7 *Non!*

PARLER Answer the following questions negatively.

▶ —Est-ce que tu es français (française)?
  —Non, je ne suis pas français (française).

1. Est-ce que tu es canadien (canadienne)?
2. Est-ce que tu es à Québec?
3. Est-ce que tu es à la maison?
4. Est-ce que tu es au café?
5. Est-ce que tu es en vacances?
6. Est-ce que tu es au cinéma?

8 *D'accord*

PARLER It is raining. François suggests to his friends that they go to the movies. Say who agrees and who does not, using the expression **être d'accord.**

▶ Philippe

Philippe n'est pas d'accord.

▶ Hélène

Hélène est d'accord.

1. ☺ nous   3. ☹ tu   5. ☺ Patrick et Marc   7. ☺ ma copine
2. ☺ je   4. ☹ vous   6. ☹ Claire et Stéphanie   8. ☹ mon frère

VOCABULAIRE **Mots utiles** *(Useful words)*

à	*at*	Je suis **à** la maison **à** dix heures.
	in	Nous sommes **à** Paris.
de	*from*	Vous êtes **de** San Francisco.
	of	Voici une photo **de** Paris.
et	*and*	Anne **et** Sophie sont en vacances.
ou	*or*	Qui est-ce? Juliette **ou** Sophie?
avec	*with*	Philippe est **avec** Pauline.
pour	*for*	Je veux travailler **pour** Monsieur Martin.
mais	*but*	Je ne suis pas français, **mais** j'aime parler français.

Fête Nationale
mardi 14 juillet
à 22h
P A R I S

→ **De** becomes **d'** before a vowel sound:
  Patrick est **de** Lyon.   François est **d'**Annecy.

---

9 **Le mot juste** *(The right word)*

PARLER/ÉCRIRE Complete each sentence with the word in parentheses that fits logically.

1. Monsieur Moreau est en France.
   Aujourd'hui, il est … Lyon. (à/de)
2. Martine est canadienne.
   Elle est … Montréal. (de/et)
3. Florence n'est pas ici.
   Elle est … Jean-Claude. (et/avec)
4. Léa … Paul sont en ville. (avec/et)
5. Jean-Pierre n'est pas à la maison.
   Il est au café … au cinéma. (ou/et)
6. J'aime jouer au tennis … je ne veux pas jouer avec toi. (ou/mais)
7. Je travaille … mon père. (pour/à)

10 **Être ou ne pas être**

PARLER/ÉCRIRE We cannot be in different places at the same time. Express this according to the model.

▶ Aline est en ville. (ici)
  Aline n'est pas ici.

1. Frédéric est là-bas. (à la maison)
2. Nous sommes en classe.
   (au restaurant)
3. Tu es à Nice. (à Tours)
4. Vous êtes au café. (au cinéma)
5. Jean est avec Sylvie. (avec Julie)
6. Juliette et Sophie sont avec Éric.
   (avec Marc)

PRONONCIATION /a/

La voyelle /a/

The letter "**a**" alone always represents the sound /a/ as in the English word *ah*. It never has the sound of "*a*" as in English words like *cl<u>a</u>ss, d<u>a</u>te,* or *cinem<u>a</u>.*

chat

Répétez: **ch<u>a</u>t   ç<u>a</u> v<u>a</u>   <u>à</u>   l<u>a</u>   l<u>à</u>-b<u>a</u>s   <u>a</u>vec   <u>a</u>mi   voil<u>à</u>**
        cl<u>a</u>sse   c<u>a</u>fé   s<u>a</u>lade   d<u>a</u>me   d<u>a</u>te   M<u>a</u>d<u>a</u>me   C<u>a</u>n<u>a</u>da

        <u>A</u>nne est au C<u>a</u>n<u>a</u>d<u>a</u> <u>a</u>vec M<u>a</u>d<u>a</u>me L<u>a</u>v<u>a</u>l.

À votre tour!

OBJECTIFS

Now you can …
• say where people are
• ask and answer simple yes/no questions

1  Allô!

PARLER Jacques is phoning some friends. Match his questions on the left with his friends' answers on the right.

1. Où es-tu?

2. Où est ta soeur?

3. Est-ce que ton frère est à la maison?

4. Tes parents sont en vacances, n'est-ce pas?

5. Ta soeur est avec une copine?

a. Non, il est au cinéma.

b. Oui, elles sont au restaurant.

c. Je suis à la maison.

d. Elle est en classe.

e. Oui! Ils sont à Paris.

2 Où sont-ils?

LIRE Read what the following people are saying and decide where they are.

▶ Anne et Éric sont au café.

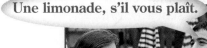

Une limonade, s'il vous plaît.

▶ **Anne et Éric**

Le film est génial (great).

1. nous

Où est le musée (museum)?

2. les touristes

Une pizza, s'il vous plaît.

3. vous

Bonjour, maman.

4. tu

Aujourd'hui, c'est le jour de l'examen!

5. Valérie

3 Créa-dialogue

PARLER You are working for a student magazine in France. Your assignment is to interview tourists who are visiting Paris. Ask them where they are from. (Make sure to address the people appropriately as **tu** or **vous**.) Remember: The symbol "??" means you may invent your own responses.

Nationalité	Villes *(Cities)*	
▶ anglaise	Londres? *(London)* Liverpool	

▶ —Bonjour. <u>Vous êtes anglaise</u>?
—Oui, je suis <u>anglaise</u>.
—Est-ce que <u>vous êtes</u> de <u>Londres</u>?
—Mais non, je ne suis pas de <u>Londres</u>.
    Je suis de <u>Liverpool</u>.

Nationalité	Villes	
1 américaine	New York? Washington	
2 canadien	Québec? Montréal	
3 française	Paris? Nice	
4 mexicain	Mexico? Puebla	
5 ??	?? ??	
6 ??	?? ??	

4 Composition: Personnellement

ÉCRIRE On a separate piece of paper, or on a computer, write where you are and where you are not at each of the following times. Use only words you know.

▶ à 9 heures du matin

- à 4 heures
- à 7 heures du soir
- samedi
- dimanche
- en juillet

À neuf heures du matin, je suis en classe. Je ne suis pas à la maison.

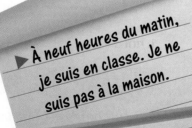

▶ À neuf heures du matin, je suis en classe. Je ne suis pas à la maison.

LEÇON 7

Une boum

AUDIO

Jean-Marc has been invited to a party. He is trying to decide whether to bring Béatrice or Valérie.

Jean-Marc:	<u>Dis</u>, Béatrice, tu aimes danser?	*Hey*
Béatrice:	Oui, j'adore danser. Je danse très, <u>très bien</u>.	*very well*
Jean-Marc:	Et toi, Valérie, tu danses bien?	
Valérie:	Non, je ne danse pas très bien.	
Jean-Marc:	Est-ce que tu veux <u>aller</u> à une boum avec moi samedi?	*to go*
Valérie:	Oui, d'accord, mais <u>pourquoi</u> est-ce que tu n'invites pas Béatrice? Elle adore danser …	*why*
Jean-Marc:	Oui, mais moi, <u>je ne sais pas</u> danser et je ne veux pas être <u>ridicule</u> …	*don't know how* *ridiculous*
Béatrice:	Écoute. <u>Entre</u> copains, <u>on n'est jamais</u> ridicule.	*Among / one is never*
Jean-Marc:	C'est vrai! <u>Alors</u>, je <u>vous invite toutes les deux</u>!	*Then / invite both of you*
Béatrice:	Super!	

Compréhension: Vrai ou faux?

Say whether the following statements are true (**C'est vrai!**) or false (**C'est faux!**).

1. Béatrice aime danser.
2. Elle danse bien.
3. Valérie danse très bien.

4. Jean-Marc adore danser.
5. Jean-Marc ne veut pas être ridicule.
6. Jean-Marc invite Béatrice et Valérie.

NOTE culturelle

Une boum

On weekends, French teenagers like to go to parties that are organized at a friend's home. These informal parties have different names according to the age group of the participants. For students at a **collège** (middle school), a party is sometimes known as **une boum** or **une fête.** For older students at a **lycée** (high school), it is called **une soirée.**

At a **boum**, parents are usually around to help out and set up a buffet which often features items contributed by the guests. Pizza and chips are very popular. There may also be homemade sandwiches or Chinese food. Preferred beverages are sodas and mineral waters.

Most of the young people like to dance and listen to their favorite music. Some may get drawn into the latest video games. Others simply enjoy getting together to talk about the week's events. For everyone, it is a way to spend a relaxing evening with friends.

COMPARAISONS CULTURELLES

How do French parties compare to parties that you and your friends organize? Explain.

Les verbes en *-er:* le singulier

The basic form of a verb is called the infinitive. Many French infinitives end in **-er.**
Most of these verbs are conjugated like **parler** *(to speak)* and **habiter** *(to live)*.
Note the forms of the present tense of these verbs in the singular. Pay attention
to their endings.

INFINITIVE	parler	habiter	ENDINGS
STEM	parl-	habit-	
PRESENT TENSE (SINGULAR)	Je **parle** français.	J' **habite** à Paris.	-e
	Tu **parles** anglais.	Tu **habites** à Boston.	-es
	Il/Elle **parle** espagnol.	Il/Elle **habite** à Madrid.	-e

The present tense forms of **-er** verbs consist of two parts:

STEM + ENDING

- The STEM does not change. It is the infinitive minus **-er**:

  parler **parl-**   habiter **habit-**

- The ENDINGS change with the subject:

  je → **-e**   **tu** → **-es**   **il/elle** → **-e**

→ The above endings are silent.
→ **Je** becomes **j'** before a vowel sound.
  je parle   **j'**habite

LEARNING ABOUT LANGUAGE
Verbs conjugated like **parler**
and **habiter** follow a *predictable
pattern*.

They are called REGULAR VERBS.

1 *Curiosité*

PARLER At the party, Olivier wants to learn more about Isabelle.
She answers his questions affirmatively. Play both roles.

Tu parles anglais? Oui, je parle anglais.

▶ parler anglais?

1. parler espagnol?
2. habiter à Paris?
3. danser bien?
4. jouer aux jeux vidéo?
5. jouer au basket?
6. chanter?
7. téléphoner à ton copain?
8. travailler en été?

VOCABULAIRE Les verbes en -er

▶ **Verbs you already know:**

chanter	to sing	**nager**	to swim
danser	to dance	**parler**	to speak, talk
dîner	to have dinner	**regarder**	to watch, look at
écouter	to listen (to)	**téléphoner (à)**	to phone, call
étudier	to study	**travailler**	to work
jouer	to play	**voyager**	to travel
manger	to eat		

▶ **New verbs:**

aimer	to like	Tu **aimes** Paris?
habiter (à)	to live (in + city)	Philippe **habite** à Toulouse?
inviter	to invite	J'**invite** un copain.
organiser	to organize	Sophie **organise** une **boum**/ une **soirée**/une **fête** (party).
visiter	to visit (places)	Céline **visite** Québec.

→ **Regarder** has two meanings:

to look (at)	Paul **regarde** Cécile.
to watch	Cécile **regarde** la télé.

→ Note the construction **téléphoner à:**

Céline **téléphone**	à	Marc.
Céline calls	...	Marc.

→ Note the constructions with **regarder** (to look at) and **écouter** (to listen to):

Philippe **regarde**	...	Alice.
Philippe looks	at	Alice.

Alice **écoute**	...	le professeur.
Alice listens	to	the teacher.

2 Quelle activité?

PARLER/ÉCRIRE Describe what the following people are doing by completing the sentences with one of the verbs below. Be logical.

chanter   écouter   parler   travailler   manger   voyager   inviter   regarder   habiter

1. Je ... un sandwich. Tu ... une pizza.
2. Tu ... anglais. Je ... français.
3. Éric ... la radio. Claire ... un CD.
4. Jean-Paul ... la télé. Tu ... un match de tennis.
5. M. Simon ... en (by) bus. Mme Dupont ... en train.
6. Nicolas ... Marie à la boum. Tu ... Alain.
7. Mlle Thomas ... dans (in) un hôpital. Je ... dans un supermarché (supermarket).
8. La chorale (choir) ... bien. Est-ce que tu ... bien?
9. Tu ... en France. Aya ... en Afrique.

3 Les voisins *(The neighbors)*

PARLER/ÉCRIRE Simon is explaining what his neighbors are doing. Describe each person's activity.

▶ **Madame Dumas téléphone.**

4 Où sont-ils?

PARLER You want to know where the following people are. A classmate tells you and says what they are doing.

▶ Jacques? (en classe/étudier)

Où est Jacques?

Il est en classe. Il étudie.

1. Pauline? (au restaurant/dîner)
2. Véronique? (à la maison/téléphoner)
3. Mme Dupont? (en ville/travailler)
4. M. Lemaire? (en France/voyager)
5. Léa? (à Paris/visiter la tour Eiffel)
6. André? (au stade/jouer au foot)
7. Alice? (à l'Olympic Club/nager)

B Les verbes en *-er:* le pluriel

Note the plural forms of **parler** and **habiter**, paying attention to the endings.

INFINITIVE	parler	habiter	ENDINGS
STEM	parl-	habit-	
PRESENT TENSE (PLURAL)	Nous **parlons** français.	Nous **habitons** à Québec.	-ons
	Vous **parlez** anglais.	Vous **habitez** à Chicago.	-ez
	Ils/Elles **parlent** espagnol.	Ils/Elles **habitent** à Caracas.	-ent

→ In the present tense, the plural endings of **-er** verbs are:

nous → **-ons**   vous → **-ez**   ils / elles → **-ent**

→ The **-ent** ending is silent.

→ Note the liaison when the verb begins with a vowel sound:

Nous étudions.   Vous invitez Thomas.   Ils habitent en France.   Elles aiment Paris.

Observation When the infinitive of the verb ends in **-ger**, the **nous** form ends in **-geons**.

nager: nous nageons   **manger:** nous mangeons   **voyager:** nous voyageons

5 Qui?

PARLER/ÉCRIRE Élodie is speaking to or about her friends. Complete her sentences with **tu, elle, vous,** or **ils.**

▶ … étudient à Toulouse.
  Ils étudient à Toulouse.

1. … habitez à Tours.
2. … joue aux jeux vidéo.
3. … étudiez à Bordeaux.
4. … aiment danser.
5. … organisent une boum.
6. … parlez espagnol.
7. … téléphone à Jean-Pierre.
8. … invites un copain.
9. … dîne avec Cécile.
10. … invitent Monique.

6 À la boum

PARLER At a party, Olivier is talking to two Canadian students, Monique and her friend. Monique answers yes to his questions.

▶ parler français?

Vous parlez français, n'est-ce pas?
Oui, nous parlons français.

1. parler anglais?
2. habiter à Québec?
3. étudier à Montréal?
4. voyager en France?
5. voyager en train?
6. visiter Paris?
7. aimer Paris?
8. aimer la France?

7 En colonie de vacances (At summer camp)

PARLER/ÉCRIRE Describe the activities of the following campers by completing the sentences.

▶ À cinq heures, Alice et Marc …   **À cinq heures, Alice et Marc jouent au foot.**

▶

1. À neuf heures, nous …
2. À quatre heures, vous …
3. À huit heures, Véronique et Pierre …
4. À sept heures, nous …
5. À trois heures, Thomas et François …
6. À six heures, vous …

8 Un voyage à Paris

PARLER/ÉCRIRE A group of American students is visiting Paris. During their stay, they do all of the following things:

| voyager en bus | téléphoner à un copain | inviter une copine |
| visiter la tour Eiffel | dîner au restaurant | parler français |

Describe the trips of the following people.

▶ Jim   **Il voyage en bus, il visite la tour Eiffel …**

1. Linda   2. Paul et Louise   3. nous   4. vous   5. Jen et Sarah

C **Le présent des verbes en *-er:* forme affirmative et forme négative**

Compare the affirmative and negative forms of **parler.**

AFFIRMATIVE	NEGATIVE
je **parle**	je **ne parle pas**
tu **parles**	tu **ne parles pas**
il/elle **parle**	il/elle **ne parle pas**
nous **parlons**	nous **ne parlons pas**
vous **parlez**	vous **ne parlez pas**
ils/elles **parlent**	ils/elles **ne parlent pas**

♻ **RAPPEL** The negative form of the verb follows the pattern:

subject + **ne** + VERB + **pas**	Il **ne** travaille **pas** ici.
→ **n'** (+ VOWEL SOUND)	Je **n'**invite **pas** Pierre.

Il **ne** travaille **pas**.

Ils **n'**écoutent **pas**.

Elle **ne** chante **pas** bien.

LANGUAGE COMPARISONS

English has several verb forms for expressing actions in the present.
In French there is only one form. Compare:

Je **joue** au tennis.
{ *I **play** tennis.*
*I **do play** tennis.*
*I **am playing** tennis.*

Je **ne joue pas** au tennis.
{ *I **do not play** tennis. (I **don't play** tennis.)*
*I **am not playing** tennis. (I**'m not playing** tennis.)*

9 Non!

PARLER One cannot do everything. From the following list of activities, select at least three that you do *not* do.

▶ **Je ne joue pas au bridge.**

parler espagnol

parler italien

danser le tango

jouer au hockey

jouer au water-polo

jouer au bridge

étudier à Paris

habiter à Québec

étudier le japonais

nager en hiver

dîner avec le prof

travailler dans un restaurant

10 Écoutez bien!

ÉCOUTER You will hear French young people tell you what they do and do not do. Listen carefully to what they each say and determine if they do the following activities.

▶ Marc: jouer au foot?
Non. Marc ne joue pas au foot.

1. Sophie: parler espagnol?
2. Vincent: habiter à Tours?
3. Mélanie: dîner à la maison?
4. Nicolas: téléphoner à un copain?
5. Julie: manger une pizza?
6. Jean: étudier l'anglais?
7. Marie: écouter un CD?

11 Un jeu: Week-end!

PARLER/ÉCRIRE On weekends, people like to do different things. For each person, pick an activity and say what that person does. Select another activity and say what that person does not do.

▶ Antoine et Isabelle
Antoine et Isabelle dansent.
Ils ne regardent pas la télé.

1. je
2. tu
3. ma cousine
4. nous
5. Nicolas et Élodie
6. Madame Jolivet
7. vous
8. le professeur

VOCABULAIRE Mots utiles

bien	*well*	Je joue **bien** au tennis.
très bien	*very well*	Je ne chante pas **très bien.**
mal	*badly, poorly*	Tu joues **mal** au volley.
beaucoup	*a lot, much, very much*	Paul aime **beaucoup** voyager.
un peu	*a little, a little bit*	Nous parlons **un peu** français.
souvent	*often*	Thomas joue **souvent** aux jeux vidéo.
toujours	*always*	Charlotte travaille **toujours** en été.
aussi	*also, too*	Je téléphone à Marc. Je téléphone **aussi** à Véronique.
maintenant	*now*	J'étudie **maintenant.**
rarement	*rarely, seldom*	Vous voyagez **rarement.**

→ In French, the above expressions *never* come *between* the subject and the verb.
They usually come *after* the verb. Compare their positions in French and English.

Nous parlons **toujours** français.   We *always* speak French.
Tu joues **bien** au tennis.   You play tennis *well*.

12 *Expression personnelle* ---

PARLER/ÉCRIRE Complete the following sentences with one of the suggested expressions.

bien   mal   très bien   toujours   souvent   rarement   un peu   beaucoup

1. Je chante …
2. Je nage …
3. Je regarde … la télé.
4. Je mange …
5. Je voyage … en bus.
6. Le prof parle … français.
7. Mes copains surfent … sur l'Internet.
8. Mon ami joue … aux jeux vidéo.
9. Les Yankees jouent … au baseball.

VOCABULAIRE Expressions pour la conversation

How to express approval or regret:

Super!   *Terrific!*   Tu parles français? **Super!**
Dommage!   *Too bad!*   Tu ne joues pas au tennis? **Dommage!**

13 *Conversation* -----------------------------

PARLER Ask your classmates if they do the following things. Then express approval or regret.

▶ parler français?

1. parler espagnol?
2. jouer au basket?
3. chanter bien?
4. voyager beaucoup?
5. dîner souvent au restaurant?
6. inviter souvent ton copain?

Est-ce que tu parles français?

Oui, je parle français.
(Non, je ne parle pas français.)

Super! (Dommage!)

D La construction: verbe + infinitif

Note the use of the infinitive in the following French sentences.

J'aime **parler** français.	*I like* **to speak** *French. I like* **speaking** *French.*
Ils n'aiment pas **danser.**	*They don't like* **to dance.** *They don't like* **dancing.**

To express what they like and don't like to do, the French use these constructions:

SUBJECT + PRESENT TENSE + INFINITIVE ... of **aimer**		SUBJECT + **n'** + PRESENT TENSE + **pas** + INFINITIVE ... of **aimer**		
Nous	**aimons** **voyager.**	Nous	**n'aimons pas**	**voyager.**

Note that in this construction, the verb **aimer** may be affirmative or negative:

AFFIRMATIVE: Jacques **aime** voyager.   NEGATIVE: Philippe **n'aime pas** voyager.

→ The infinitive is also used after the following expressions:

Je préfère ...	*I prefer ...*	**Je préfère travailler.**
Je voudrais ...	*I would like ...*	**Je voudrais voyager.**
Je (ne) veux (pas) ...	*I (don't) want ...*	**Je veux jouer** au foot.
Est-ce que tu veux ...	*Do you want ...*	**Est-ce que tu veux danser?**
Je (ne) peux (pas) ...	*I can (I can't) ...*	**Je ne peux pas dîner** avec toi.
Je dois ...	*I have to ...*	**Je dois étudier.**

14 Dialogue

PARLER Ask your friends if they like to do these things.

▶ nager?
—Est-ce que tu aimes nager?
—Oui, j'aime nager. (Non, je n'aime pas nager.)

1. étudier?   4. téléphoner?   7. jouer au foot?
2. voyager?   5. manger?   8. jouer au basket?
3. chanter?   6. danser?   9. travailler en été?

15 Une excellente raison (An excellent reason)

PARLER/ÉCRIRE The following people are doing certain things. Say that they like these activities.

▶ Thomas joue au tennis. **Il aime jouer au tennis.**

1. Alice chante.   6. Julie et Paul dansent.
2. Pierre voyage.   7. Nous jouons au frisbee.
3. Céline joue au foot.   8. Éric et Lise nagent.
4. Tu téléphones.   9. Vous surfez sur l'Internet.
5. Nous travaillons.   10. Léa organise la boum.

PRONONCIATION

Les voyelles /i/ et /u/

/u/ **où?**   /i/ **ici!**

Be sure to pronounce the French "**i**" as in **Mimi.**

Répétez:

/i/ **ici Philippe il Mimi Sylvie visite**
Alice visite Paris avec Sylvie.

/u/ **où nous vous écoute joue toujours**
Vous jouez au foot avec nous?

À votre tour!

OBJECTIFS

Now you can ...
- describe what you and other people are doing and not doing
- talk about what you and other people like and don't like to do

1 🎧 Allô!

PARLER Sophie is phoning some friends. Match her questions on the left with her friends' answers on the right.

1. Est-ce que Marc est canadien?

2. Est-ce que tu joues au tennis?

3. Ton frère est à la maison?

4. Ta mère est en vacances?

5. Tu invites Christine et Juliette à la boum?

a. Non, elle travaille.

b. Oui, mais pas très bien.

c. Bien sûr! Elles aiment beaucoup danser.

d. Oui, il habite à Montréal.

e. Non, il dîne au restaurant avec un copain.

2 🎧 Créa-dialogue

PARLER Find out how frequently your classmates do the following activities. They will respond using one of the expressions on the scale.

NON	OUI		
	rarement → un peu → souvent → beaucoup		

▶ —<u>Robert</u>, est-ce que tu <u>joues au tennis</u>?
—Non, je <u>ne joue pas au tennis</u>.
—Est-ce que tu <u>écoutes la radio</u>?
—Oui, j'<u>écoute souvent la radio</u>.

❸ Qu'est-ce qu'ils font?
(What do they do?)

PARLER/ÉCRIRE Look at what the following students have put in their lockers and say what they like to do.

Éric aime jouer au tennis.
Il aime aussi ...

❹ Message illustré

ÉCRIRE Marc wrote about certain activities, using pictures. On a separate sheet, write out his description replacing these pictures with the missing words.

Après *After*   **mes** *my*   **Parfois** *Sometimes*

❺ Point de vue personnel

ÉCRIRE Write a short composition in which you describe some of the activities you do and don't do in different situations: at home, in class, on vacation, with your friends, and with your family. If appropriate, you may indicate how frequently you engage in certain activities.

STRATEGY Writing

- First list the activities you want to mention, using infinitives.
- Write out your paragraph describing your activities and those that you do not do.
- Check your composition to be sure all verb forms are correct.

☺		☹
• à la maison	_____	_____
• en classe	_____	_____
• en vacances	_____	_____
• avec mes copains	_____	_____
• avec ma famille	_____	_____

LESSON REVIEW
CLASSZONE.COM

LEÇON

8

Un concert de musique africaine

VIDÉO DVD AUDIO

Nicolas is at a café with his new friend Fatou. He is interviewing her for an article in his school newspaper.

Nicolas: Bonjour, Fatou. Ça va?

Fatou: Oui, ça va.

Nicolas: Tu es <u>sénégalaise</u>, n'est-ce pas?   *from Senegal*

Fatou: Oui, je suis sénégalaise.

Nicolas: Où est-ce que tu habites?

Fatou: Je suis de Dakar, mais maintenant j'habite à Paris avec ma famille.

Nicolas: Est-ce que tu aimes Paris?

Fatou: J'adore Paris.

Nicolas: Qu'est-ce que tu fais le week-end?

Fatou: <u>Ça</u> dépend. En général, je regarde la télé ou je <u>sors</u> avec mes   *That / go out*
copains. Dis, Nicolas! Est-ce que je peux <u>te poser</u> une question?   *ask you*

Nicolas: Oui, bien sûr!

Fatou: Qu'est-ce que tu fais <u>ce</u> week-end?   *this*

Nicolas: Euh, … <u>je ne sais pas</u>.   *I don't know*

Fatou: Est-ce que tu veux aller avec nous à un concert de
Youssou N'Dour, le musicien sénégalais?

Nicolas: Oui, bien sûr! <u>Où</u>? <u>Quand</u>? Et à quelle heure?   *Where? / When?*

Compréhension:

1. Est-ce que Fatou est française?

2. Où est-ce qu'elle habite maintenant?

3. Qu'est-ce que *(What)* Fatou aime faire *(to do)* le week-end?

4. Qui est-ce qu'elle invite au concert de musique africaine?

NOTE *culturelle*

EN BREF: Le Sénégal
Capitale: Dakar
Population: 10 000 000
Langue officielle: français

A former French colony, Senegal became an independent republic in 1960. Its population is divided into about a dozen ethnic groups, each with its own language, the most important being **wolof** and **pulaar.**

Dakar, Sénégal

Des jeunes Sénégalais

Youssou N'Dour

Youssou N'Dour is an internationally known musician from Senegal who combines traditional African music with pop, rock, and jazz. He sings in French and English, as well as in three Senegalese dialects. His lyrics promote African unity and human dignity. In many of his songs, he also plays the **tama**, a traditional Senegalese drum covered with reptile skins.

Le tama

CONNEXIONS Senegal and African Music

• As a class project, make a display board on Senegal, using information and pictures from travel brochures or from the Internet.

• Obtain a CD of Youssou N'Dour or of music from another French-African country and play your favorite selection for the class.

Les questions d'information

The questions below ask for specific information and are called INFORMATION QUESTIONS. The INTERROGATIVE EXPRESSIONS in heavy print indicate what kind of information is requested.

—**Où** est-ce que tu habites?	*Where do you live?*
—J'habite **à Nice**.	*I live **in Nice**.*
—**À quelle heure** est-ce que vous dînez?	*At what time do you eat dinner?*
—Nous dînons **à sept heures**.	*We eat **at seven**.*

→ In French, information questions may be formed according to the pattern:

INTERROGATIVE EXPRESSION	+ **est-ce que** +	SUBJECT +	VERB ... ?
À quelle heure	**est-ce que**	vous	travaillez?

→ **Est-ce que** becomes **est-ce qu'** before a vowel sound.

Quand **est-ce qu'**Alice et Roger dînent?

→ In information questions, your voice rises on the interrogative expression and then falls until the last syllable.

Quand est-ce que tu travailles?   **À quelle heure** est-ce que vous dînez?

Observation In casual conversation, French speakers frequently form information questions by placing the interrogative expression at the end of the sentence. The voice rises on the interrogative expression.

Vous habitez **où?**   Vous dînez **à quelle heure?**

VOCABULAIRE Expressions interrogatives

où	*where?*	**Où** est-ce que vous travaillez?
quand?	*when?*	**Quand** est-ce que ton copain organise une boum?
à quelle heure?	*at what time?*	**À quelle heure** est-ce que tu regardes la télé?
comment?	*how?*	**Comment** est-ce que tu chantes? Bien ou mal?
pourquoi?	*why?*	—**Pourquoi** est-ce que tu étudies le français?
parce que	*because*	—**Parce que** je veux voyager en France.

→ **Parce que** becomes **parce qu'** before a vowel sound.

Juliette invite Olivier **parce qu'**il danse bien.

1  *Écoutez bien!*

STRATEGY Listening

Understanding questions Pay attention to the interrogative expression. It tells what type of information is asked for.

ÉCOUTER The questions that you will hear can be logically answered by only one of the following options. Listen carefully to each question and select the logical answer.

a. à sept heures   **c.** en octobre
b. à Paris   **d.** assez bien

2 *Curiosité*

PARLER At a party in Paris, Nicolas meets Béatrice, a Canadian student. He wants to know more about her. Play both roles.

▶ où / habiter? (à Québec)

NICOLAS: **Où est-ce que tu habites?**
BÉATRICE: **J'habite à Québec.**

1. où/étudier? (à Montréal)
2. où/travailler? (dans [in] une pharmacie)
3. quand/parler français? (toujours)
4. quand/parler anglais? (souvent)
5. comment/jouer au tennis? (bien)
6. comment/danser? (très bien)
7. pourquoi/être en France? (parce que j'aime voyager)
8. pourquoi/être à Paris? (parce que j'étudie ici)

VOCABULAIRE Expressions pour la conversation

How to express surprise or mild doubt:

Ah bon?   *Oh? Really?*   —Stéphanie organise une soirée.
—**Ah bon?** Quand?

3 *Au téléphone*

PARLER Jacques calls Élodie to tell her about his plans.

▶ organiser une soirée (quand? samedi)

1. organiser un pique-nique (quand? dimanche)
2. dîner avec Pauline (quand? lundi)
3. dîner avec Caroline (où? au restaurant Belcour)
4. regarder «Batman» (à quelle heure? à 9 heures)
5. inviter Brigitte (où? à un concert)

J'organise une soirée.

Samedi.

Ah bon? Quand est-ce que tu organises une soirée?

6. parler espagnol (comment? assez bien)
7. étudier l'italien (pourquoi? je veux voyager en Italie)

4 *Questions personnelles* **PARLER/ÉCRIRE**

1. Où est-ce que tu habites? *(name of your city)*
2. Où est-ce que tu étudies? *(name of your school)*
3. À quelle heure est-ce que tu dînes?
4. À quelle heure est-ce que tu regardes la télé?
5. Quand est-ce que tu nages? (en été? en hiver?)
6. Quand est-ce que tu joues au volley? (en mai? en juillet?)
7. Comment est-ce que tu chantes? (bien? très bien? mal?)
8. Comment est-ce que tu nages?

B Les expressions interrogatives avec *qui*

To ask about PEOPLE, French speakers use the following interrogative expressions:

qui?	*who(m)?*	**Qui** est-ce que tu invites au concert?
à qui?	*to who(m)?*	**À qui** est-ce que tu téléphones?
de qui?	*about who(m)?*	**De qui** est-ce que vous parlez?
avec qui?	*with who(m)?*	**Avec qui** est-ce que Pierre étudie?
pour qui?	*for who(m)?*	**Pour qui** est-ce que Laure organise la boum?

To ask *who is doing something,* French speakers use the construction:

qui + VERB … ?

Qui habite ici? **Who** *lives here?*
Qui organise la boum? **Who** *is organizing the party?*

5 *Curiosité*

PARLER Anne is telling Élodie what certain people are doing. Élodie asks for more details. Play both roles.

▶ Alice dîne. (avec qui? avec une copine)

1. Jean-Pierre téléphone. (à qui? à Sylvie)
2. Frédéric étudie. (avec qui? avec un copain)
3. Madame Masson parle. (à qui? à Madame Bonnot)
4. Monsieur Lambert travaille. (avec qui? avec Monsieur Dumont)
5. Juliette danse. (avec qui? avec Georges)
6. François parle à Michèle. (de qui? de toi)

Alice dîne.
Elle dîne avec une copine.
Ah bon? Avec qui est-ce qu'elle dîne?

6  *Un sondage* (A poll)

PARLER Take a survey to find out how your classmates spend their free time. Ask who does the following things.

▶ écouter la radio
Qui écoute la radio?

1. voyager souvent
2. aimer chanter
3. nager
4. aimer danser
5. regarder la télé
6. jouer au tennis
7. parler italien
8. travailler
9. regarder les clips (*music videos*)
10. jouer aux jeux vidéo
11. étudier beaucoup
12. visiter souvent New York

7 **Questions**

PARLER/ÉCRIRE For each illustration, prepare a short dialogue with a classmate using the suggested cues.

où?

à la maison

▶ —Où est-ce que tu dînes?
—Je dîne à la maison.

1. à quelle heure?

à 8 heures

2. quand?

en septembre

3. comment?

BONJOUR!

très bien

4. avec qui?

avec Denise

5. à qui?

à mon cousin

6. de qui?

BLA BLA BLA...

de toi

7. pour qui?

pour M. Lambert

C **Qu'est-ce que?**

Note the use of the interrogative expression **qu'est-ce que** *(what)* in the questions below.

Qu'est-ce que tu regardes?   Je regarde un match de tennis.

Qu'est-ce qu'Alice mange?   Elle mange une pizza.

To ask *what people are doing,* the French use the following construction:

qu'est-ce que + SUBJECT + VERB + ...?	**Qu'est-ce que** tu regardes?
↓	
qu'est-ce qu' (+ VOWEL SOUND)	**Qu'est-ce qu'**elle mange?

8 **À la FNAC**

PARLER People in Column A are at the FNAC, a store that sells books and recordings. Use a verb from Column B to ask what they are listening to or looking at. A classmate will answer you, using an item from Column C.

A	**B**	**C**
tu	écouter?	un livre de photos
vous	regarder?	un poster
Alice		un CD de rock
Éric		un CD de jazz
Antoine et Claire		un album de
		Youssou N'Dour

Qu'est-ce qu'Éric écoute?

Il écoute un album de Youssou N'Dour.

D Le verbe *faire*

Faire *(to do, make)* is an IRREGULAR verb. It is used in many French expressions. Note the forms of **faire** in the present tense.

faire *(to do, make)*	
je **fais**	Je **fais** un sandwich.
tu **fais**	Qu'est-ce que tu **fais** maintenant?
il/elle **fait**	Qu'est-ce que ton copain **fait** samedi?
nous **faisons**	Nous **faisons** une pizza.
vous **faites**	Qu'est-ce que vous **faites** ici?
ils/elles **font**	Qu'est-ce qu'elles **font** pour la boum?

VOCABULAIRE Expressions avec *faire*

faire un match	*to play a game (match)*	Mes cousins **font un match** de tennis.
faire une promenade	*to go for a walk*	Caroline **fait une promenade** avec Olivier.
faire un voyage	*to take a trip*	Ma copine **fait un voyage** en France.
faire attention	*to pay attention*	Je **fais attention** quand le prof parle.

9 La boum de Léa

PARLER/ÉCRIRE Léa's friends are helping her prepare food for a party. Use the verb **faire** to say what everyone is doing.

▶ Je … une crêpe.

Je fais une crêpe.

1. Nous … une salade.
2. Tu … une salade de fruits.
3. Vous … une tarte *(pie)*.
4. Cécile et Marina … un gâteau *(cake)*.
5. Christine … une pizza.
6. Marc … un sandwich.
7. Patrick et Thomas … une omelette.
8. Pierre et Karine … une quiche.

10 Qu'est-ce qu'ils font?

PARLER/LIRE Read the descriptions below and say what the people are doing. Use the verb **faire** and an expression from the list.

> un voyage
> une promenade
> une pizza
> un match
> attention

▶ Madame Dumont est en Chine. **Elle fait un voyage.**

1. Léa travaille dans *(in)* un restaurant.
2. Nous sommes en ville.
3. Céline et Jean-Paul jouent au tennis.
4. Je suis dans la cuisine *(kitchen)*.
5. Marc est dans le train Paris-Nice.
6. Vous jouez au volley.
7. Je suis dans le parc.
8. Monsieur Lambert visite Tokyo.
9. Nous écoutons le prof.

L'interrogation avec inversion

LEARNING ABOUT LANGUAGE

In conversational French, questions are usually formed with **est-ce que.** However, when the subject of the sentence is a pronoun, French speakers often use inversion, that is, they invert or reverse the order of the subject pronoun and the verb.

REGULAR ORDER: **Vous parlez** français.   INVERSION: **Parlez-vous** anglais?
SUBJECT   VERB   VERB   SUBJECT

The pairs of questions below ask the same thing. Compare the position of the subject pronouns.

Est-ce que **tu** parles anglais?	Parles-**tu** anglais?	*Do you speak English?*
Est-ce que **vous** habitez ici?	Habitez-**vous** ici?	*Do you live here?*
Où est-ce que **nous** dînons?	Où dînons-**nous**?	*Where are we having dinner?*
Où est-ce qu'**il** est?	Où est-**il**?	*Where is he?*

Inverted questions are formed according to the patterns:

YES/NO QUESTION	VERB / SUBJECT PRONOUN	...?	
	Voyagez-vous	souvent?	
INFORMATION QUESTION	INTERROGATIVE EXPRESSION + VERB / SUBJECT PRONOUN		...?
	Avec qui	**travaillez-vous**	demain?

→ In inversion, the verb and the subject pronoun are connected by a hyphen.

Observation In inversion, liaison is required before **il/elle** and **ils/elles**. If a verb in the singular ends on a vowel, the letter **"t"** is inserted after the verb so that liaison can occur:

Où travaille-t-il?   Où travaille-t-elle?   Avec qui dîne-t-il?   Avec qui dîne-t-elle?

---

11 *Conversation*

PARLER Ask your classmates a few questions, using inversion.

▶ où / habiter? —**Où habites-tu?**
               —**J'habite à (Boston).**

1. à quelle heure / dîner?
2. à quelle heure / regarder la télé?
3. avec qui / parler français?
4. à qui / téléphoner souvent?
5. comment / nager?
6. avec qui / étudier?
7. où / jouer aux jeux vidéo?
8. comment / chanter?

PRONONCIATION /y/

La voyelle /y/

Super!

The vowel sound /y/ — represented by the letter "**u**" — does not exist in English.

To say **super**, first say the French word **si.** Then round your lips as if to whistle and say **si** with rounded lips: /sy/. Now say **si-per.** Then round your lips as you say the first syllable: **super!**

Répétez: /y/   **super** **tu** **étudie** **bien sûr**
              Lucie **Luc**
              Tu étudies avec Lucie.

À votre tour!

OBJECTIFS

Now you can …
• ask and answer information questions
• ask about what people are doing

1 Allô!

PARLER Fatou is phoning some friends. Match her questions on the left with her friends' answers on the right.

1 Qu'est-ce que tu fais?

2 Qu'est-ce que vous faites samedi?

3 Où est ton père?

4 Quand est-ce que tu veux jouer au tennis avec moi?

5 Qui est-ce que tu invites au cinéma?

6 Pourquoi est-ce que tu étudies l'anglais?

a Il fait une promenade.

b Ma cousine Alice.

c Dimanche. D'accord?

d J'étudie.

e Nous faisons un match de tennis.

f Parce que je voudrais habiter à New York.

2 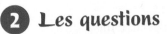 Les questions

LIRE/PARLER The following people are answering questions. Read what they say and figure out what questions they were asked.

Je chante très mal.

► Comment est-ce que tu chantes?

1 J'habite à Québec.

2 Je dîne à sept heures.

3  Nous dînons à l'Hippopotame.

4 Je mange une pizza.

5 Je regarde un film.

6 J'invite Catherine.

③ Créa-dialogue

PARLER Ask your classmates what they do on different days of the week. Carry out conversations similar to the model. Note: "??" means you can invent your own answers.

▶ —Qu'est-ce que tu fais <u>lundi</u>?
—Je <u>joue au tennis</u>.
—Ah bon? À quelle heure est-ce que tu <u>joues</u>?
—<u>À deux heures</u>.
—Et avec qui?
—Avec <u>Anne-Marie</u>.

	lundi	mardi	mercredi	jeudi	vendredi	samedi	dimanche
ACTIVITÉ						??	??
À QUELLE HEURE?	2 heures	6 heures	??	??	??	??	??
AVEC QUI?	avec Anne-Marie	avec un copain	??	??	??	??	??

④ Faisons connaissance! *(Let's get acquainted!)*

PARLER/ÉCRIRE Get better acquainted with a classmate. Ask five or six questions in French. Then write a summary of your conversation and give it to the friend you have interviewed.

▶ Mon ami(e) s'appelle …
 Il/elle habite …

You might ask questions like:

• Where does he/she live?

• Does he/she speak French at home? With whom?

• Does he/she watch TV? When? What programs (**quelles émissions**)?

• Does he/she play video games? When? With whom?

• Does he/she play soccer (or another sport)? Where? When?

• Does he/she like to swim? When? Where?

• What does he/she like to do on weekends? When? Where? With whom?

⑤ Curiosité

ÉCRIRE Imagine that a French friend has just made the following statements. For each one, write down three or four related questions you could ask him or her.

Je joue au tennis.

Je dîne avec un copain.

Je fais une promenade.

J'organise une soirée.

Je joue au foot demain.

• Avec qui est-ce que tu joues?
• Où est-ce que vous jouez?
• À quelle heure est-ce que vous jouez?
• Pourquoi est-ce que vous jouez au foot?

LESSON REVIEW
CLASSZONE.COM

Tests de contrôle

By taking the following tests, you can check your progress in French and also prepare for the unit test. Write your answers on a separate sheet of paper.

① The right activity

Review ...
• the uses and forms of -er verbs: pp. 94, 95, 96, and 98

Complete each of the following sentences by filling in the blank with the appropriate form of one of the verbs in the box. Be logical in your choice of verbs.

chanter	manger	écouter	habiter
jouer	parler	regarder	travailler

1. Jean-Paul — une pizza.
2. Vous — aux jeux vidéo.
3. Isabelle — un CD de rock.
4. Monsieur Mercier — pour une banque (*bank*).
5. Mon cousin — à Chicago.
6. Ils — dans une chorale (*choir*).
7. Nous — une comédie à la télé.
8. Est-ce que tu — français ou anglais?

② Être and faire

Review ...
• être and faire: pp. 84 and 110

For each item, fill in the first blank with the appropriate form of **être** and the second blank with the appropriate form of **faire.**

1. Je — en classe. Je — attention.
2. Léa — dans la cuisine (*kitchen*). Elle — un sandwich.
3. Nous — en ville. Nous — une promenade.
4. Les touristes — en France. Ils — un voyage.
5. Vous — au stade (*stadium*). Vous — un match de foot.

③ Non!

Review ...
• negative sentences: pp. 88 and 98

Rewrite the following sentences in the negative, replacing the underlined words with the words in parentheses.

▶ Thomas parle <u>français</u>. **(anglais)**   **Thomas ne parle pas anglais.**

1. Léa est <u>française</u>. **(américaine)**
2. Nous jouons <u>au foot</u>. **(au basket)**
3. Vous dînez <u>au restaurant</u>. **(à la maison)**
4. Tu invites <u>Céline</u>. **(Isabelle)**
5. Ils habitent <u>à Québec</u>. **(à Montréal)**

4 The right question

Write out the questions that correspond to the answers below. Make sure to begin your sentences with the question words that correspond to the underlined information. Use **tu** in your questions.

> ▶ J'habite <u>à Paris.</u>   **Où est-ce que tu habites?**

1. Je téléphone <u>à Marc.</u>

2. Je dîne <u>à sept heures.</u>

3. Je mange <u>une pizza.</u>

4. Je voyage <u>en juillet.</u>

5. J'écoute <u>un CD.</u>

6. Je joue <u>très bien</u> au foot.

Review …
• information questions: pp. 106 and 108

5 The right choice

Choose the word or expression in parentheses which logically completes each of the following sentences.

1. François habite — France. **(à, au, en)**

2. Isabelle est au café — Céline. **(et, avec, pour)**

3. Nicolas parle français, — il ne parle pas espagnol. **(pourquoi, mal, mais)**

4. Pierre écoute — radio. **(à, la, à la)**

5. Je n'habite pas ici. J'habite —. **(où, aussi, là-bas)**

6. Tu ne chantes pas bien. Tu chantes —. **(mal, souvent, beaucoup)**

7. Philippe aime beaucoup jouer au foot. Il joue —. **(pour, mais non, souvent)**

8. Je ne peux pas dîner avec toi. Je — étudier pour l'examen. **(dois, veux, n'aime pas)**

9. J'étudie l'espagnol — je voudrais visiter Madrid. **(où, comment, parce que)**

10. Qui est-ce? Jérôme — Patrick? **(pour, ou, aussi)**

Review …
• vocabulary: pp. 77, 78, 85, 89, 95, 100, 106

6 Composition: Les vacances

Write a short paragraph of five or six sentences saying what you and your friends do and don't do during summer vacation. Use only vocabulary and expressions that you know in French.

STRATEGY Writing

a Make a list of activities that you do and a second list of things that you don't do. Use infinitives.

b Organize your ideas and write your paragraph, using **je** or **nous.**

c Check each sentence to be sure that the verb endings agree with the subject.

oui	non
• *nager*	•
•	•
•	•
•	•
•	•

Vocabulaire

POUR COMMUNIQUER

Talking about likes and preferences

Est-ce que tu aimes	parler anglais?	Do you like	to speak English?
J'aime		I like	
Je n'aime pas		I don't like	
Je préfère	parler français.	I prefer	to speak French.
Je veux		I want	
Je voudrais		I would like	
Je ne veux pas		I don't want	

Inviting a friend

Est-ce que tu veux [jouer au tennis]?	Do you want to [play tennis]?
Est-ce que tu peux [jouer au foot] avec moi?	Can you [play soccer] with me?

Accepting or declining an invitation

Oui, bien sûr.	Yes, of course.	Je regrette, mais je ne peux pas.	I'm sorry, but I can't.
Oui, merci.	Yes, thanks.	Je dois [travailler].	I have to, I must [work].
Oui, d'accord.	Yes, all right, okay.		
Oui, je veux bien.	Yes, I'd love to.		

Expressing approval, regret, or surprise

Super!	Terrific!
Dommage!	Too bad!
Ah bon?	Oh? Really?

Answering a yes/no question

Oui!	Yes!	Non!	No!
Mais oui!	Sure!	Mais non!	Of course not!
Bien sûr!	Of course!	Peut-être …	Maybe …

Asking for information

où?	where?	qu'est-ce que …?	what?
quand?	when?	qui?	who, whom?
à quelle heure?	at what time?	à qui?	to who(m)?
comment?	how?	de qui?	about who(m)?
pourquoi?	why?	avec qui?	with who(m)?
parce que …	because	pour qui?	for who(m)?

Saying where people are

Pierre est …					
ici	here	à la maison	at home	en classe	in class
là	here, there	au café	at the café	en France	in France
là-bas	over there	au cinéma	at the movies	en vacances	on vacation
à [Paris]	in [Paris]	au restaurant	at the restaurant	en ville	in town

Saying how well, how often, and when

bien	well	beaucoup	a lot, much, very much	maintenant	now
très bien	very well	un peu	a little, a little bit	souvent	often
mal	badly, poorly	rarement	rarely, seldom	toujours	always

MOTS ET EXPRESSIONS

Verbes réguliers en *-er*

aimer	to like	jouer aux jeux vidéo	to play video games
chanter	to sing	manger	to eat
danser	to dance	nager	to swim
dîner	to have dinner	organiser une boum	to organize a party
dîner au restaurant	to eat out	parler anglais	to speak English
écouter	to listen, to listen to	parler espagnol	to speak Spanish
écouter la radio	to listen to the radio	parler français	to speak French
étudier	to study	regarder	to watch, to look at
habiter (à Paris)	to live (in Paris)	regarder la télé	to watch TV
inviter	to invite	téléphoner (à Céline)	to phone (Céline)
jouer au basket	to play basketball	travailler	to work
jouer au foot	to play soccer	visiter (Paris)	to visit (Paris)
jouer au tennis	to play tennis	voyager	to travel

Verbes irréguliers

être	to be	faire	to do, make
être d'accord	to agree	faire un match	to play a game (match)
		faire une promenade	to go for a walk
		faire un voyage	to take a trip
		faire attention	to pay attention

Mots utiles

à	at, in	et	and
aussi	also	mais	but
avec	with	ou	or
de	from, of	pour	for

TEST PREP
CLASSZONE.COM

FLASHCARDS
AND MORE!

Ce week-end, à la télé

Le week-end, les jeunes Français regardent souvent la télé. Ils aiment regarder les films et le sport. Ils regardent aussi les jeux et les séries américaines et françaises. Les principales chaînes° sont TF1, France 2, France 3, Cinquième Arte, M6 et Canal Plus. Voici le programme de télévision pour ce week-end.

chaînes *channels*

Note In French TV listings, times are expressed using a 24-hour clock. In this system, 8 p.m. is 20.00 **(vingt heures)**, 9 p.m. is 21.00 **(vingt et une heures)**, 10 p.m. is 22 heures **(vingt-deux heures)**, etc.

SÉLECTION DE LA SEMAINE	VENDREDI	SAMEDI
TF1	**20.50** Magazine **SUCCÈS** Émission présentée par Julien Courbet et Anne Magnien **23.15** MAGAZINE • **Célébrités**	**20.50** Jeu **QUI VEUT GAGNER DES MILLIONS?** avec Jean-Pierre Foucault **21.50** SÉRIE • **Les Soprano**
 **2** *France*	**20.55** Série **HÔTEL DE POLICE** **Le gentil Monsieur** de Claude Barrois avec Cécile Magnet **23.20** DOCUMENTAIRE • **Histoires Naturelles**	**21.00** Variétés **CHAMPS-ÉLYSÉES** Invités: Ricky Martin, Juliette Binoche, Ben Affleck **22.35** SÉRIE • **Buffy contre les Vampires**
france 3	**21.00** Film **LE CINQUIÈME ÉLÉMENT** de Luc Besson avec Bruce Willis et Milla Jovovich **22.15** CONCERT • **Viva Latino**	**20.40** Série **INSPECTEUR BARNABY** avec Daniel Casey **22.50** SPORT • **Grand Prix d'Italie** Motocyclisme
france 5 arte	**20.45** Documentaire **CATHÉDRALES** de Jean-François Delassus **22.20** FILM • **Quasimodo, le bossu de Notre Dame**	**20.50** Documentaire **ARCHITECTURES** La Tour Eiffel **20.05** CONCERT • **Le Philharmonique de Vienne**
 **M6**	**20.50** Variétés **GRAINES DE STAR** émission présentée par Laurent Boyer **22.20** THÉÂTRE • **Rhinocéros**	**20.35** Film **LE MARIAGE DE MON MEILLEUR AMI** avec Julia Roberts **22.15** SÉRIE • **Police District**
 **CANAL+**	**20.50** Football **MARSEILLE-NICE** Championnat de France **22.50** FILM • **Air Force One** avec Harrison Ford	**20.45** Film **MON PÈRE, CE HÉROS** avec Gérard Depardieu **23.15** RUGBY • **Toulouse-Biarritz**

COMPARAISONS CULTURELLES

The TV schedule on the opposite page presents the featured programs which are broadcast after the evening news on the major French channels. (As in the United States, French viewers also have access to numerous cable and satellite channels.) What similarities and differences do you see between French and American prime time TV?

- number of major channels
- starting times of the shows
- variety of programming
- importance of movies in programming

Samedi sport

Compréhension

1. À quelle heure est le match de foot vendredi? Sur quelle chaîne? Qui joue?
2. Comment s'appelle le programme de variétés sur France 2? Qui sont les invités?
3. Comment s'appelle le jeu télévisé sur TF1 samedi? À quelle heure est-ce? Comment s'appelle le jeu américain équivalent?
4. Comment s'appelle le film sur M6 samedi? Qui joue dans le film? À quelle heure commence le film? Comment s'appelle le film en anglais?

Et vous?

Vous êtes en France et vous aimez les films. Quel film est-ce que vous voudriez *(would like)* regarder à la télé ce week-end? Sur quelle chaîne? À quelle heure? Est-ce que c'est un film français ou américain?

L'INTERNET, c'est cool!

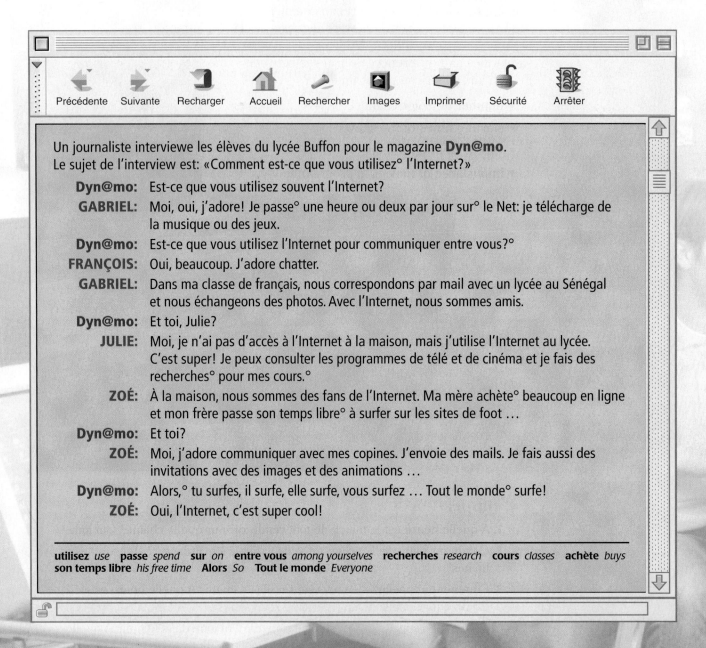

Un journaliste interviewe les élèves du lycée Buffon pour le magazine **Dyn@mo**.
Le sujet de l'interview est: «Comment est-ce que vous utilisez° l'Internet?»

Dyn@mo: Est-ce que vous utilisez souvent l'Internet?

GABRIEL: Moi, oui, j'adore! Je passe° une heure ou deux par jour sur° le Net: je télécharge de la musique ou des jeux.

Dyn@mo: Est-ce que vous utilisez l'Internet pour communiquer entre vous?°

FRANÇOIS: Oui, beaucoup. J'adore chatter.

GABRIEL: Dans ma classe de français, nous correspondons par mail avec un lycée au Sénégal et nous échangeons des photos. Avec l'Internet, nous sommes amis.

Dyn@mo: Et toi, Julie?

JULIE: Moi, je n'ai pas d'accès à l'Internet à la maison, mais j'utilise l'Internet au lycée. C'est super! Je peux consulter les programmes de télé et de cinéma et je fais des recherches° pour mes cours.°

ZOÉ: À la maison, nous sommes des fans de l'Internet. Ma mère achète° beaucoup en ligne et mon frère passe son temps libre° à surfer sur les sites de foot …

Dyn@mo: Et toi?

ZOÉ: Moi, j'adore communiquer avec mes copines. J'envoie des mails. Je fais aussi des invitations avec des images et des animations …

Dyn@mo: Alors,° tu surfes, il surfe, elle surfe, vous surfez … Tout le monde° surfe!

ZOÉ: Oui, l'Internet, c'est super cool!

---

utilisez *use* **passe** *spend* **sur** *on* **entre vous** *among yourselves* **recherches** *research* **cours** *classes* **achète** *buys*
son temps libre *his free time* **Alors** *So* **Tout le monde** *Everyone*

NOTE culturelle

Les jeunes Français et l'Internet

French people are technologically very sophisticated. They developed the **Minitel**, a precursor of the Internet, many years before this newer system of transmitting information became universally adopted.

At school, French students learn how to use the Internet in their computer science classes (**les cours d'informatique**). Many have Internet connections at home. Those who do not can go to a **cybercafé** where they can surf the Net while having a sandwich or a soda.

PETIT DICTIONNAIRE DE L'INTERNET

@ → Télérama
le site internet

- **chatter** = *to chat*
- **envoyer un mail (un mél)** = *to send an e-mail*
- **surfer sur l'Internet (le Net)** = *to surf the Internet*
- **télécharger** = *to download*
- **être en ligne** = *to be online*

COMPARAISONS CULTURELLES

Read the **Dyn@mo** interview again and make a list of the different ways students at the lycée Buffon use the Internet. Then list the ways in which you use the Internet. Do you engage in some of the same activities as the French teenagers?

les jeunes Français
-
-
-

moi
-
-
-

Bonjour, Trinh!

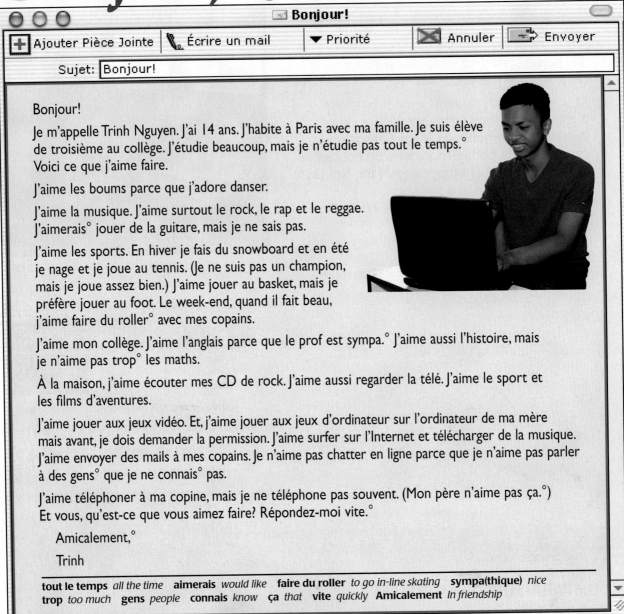

Bonjour!

Sujet: Bonjour!

Bonjour!

Je m'appelle Trinh Nguyen. J'ai 14 ans. J'habite à Paris avec ma famille. Je suis élève de troisième au collège. J'étudie beaucoup, mais je n'étudie pas tout le temps.° Voici ce que j'aime faire.

J'aime les boums parce que j'adore danser.

J'aime la musique. J'aime surtout le rock, le rap et le reggae. J'aimerais° jouer de la guitare, mais je ne sais pas.

J'aime les sports. En hiver je fais du snowboard et en été je nage et je joue au tennis. (Je ne suis pas un champion, mais je joue assez bien.) J'aime jouer au basket, mais je préfère jouer au foot. Le week-end, quand il fait beau, j'aime faire du roller° avec mes copains.

J'aime mon collège. J'aime l'anglais parce que le prof est sympa.° J'aime aussi l'histoire, mais je n'aime pas trop° les maths.

À la maison, j'aime écouter mes CD de rock. J'aime aussi regarder la télé. J'aime le sport et les films d'aventures.

J'aime jouer aux jeux vidéo. Et, j'aime jouer aux jeux d'ordinateur sur l'ordinateur de ma mère mais avant, je dois demander la permission. J'aime surfer sur l'Internet et télécharger de la musique. J'aime envoyer des mails à mes copains. Je n'aime pas chatter en ligne parce que je n'aime pas parler à des gens° que je ne connais° pas.

J'aime téléphoner à ma copine, mais je ne téléphone pas souvent. (Mon père n'aime pas ça.°) Et vous, qu'est-ce que vous aimez faire? Répondez-moi vite.°

Amicalement,°

Trinh

---

tout le temps *all the time* **aimerais** *would like* **faire du roller** *to go in-line skating* **sympa(thique)** *nice*
trop *too much* **gens** *people* **connais** *know* **ça** *that* **vite** *quickly* **Amicalement** *In friendship*

STRATEGY Reading

Cognates You have already discovered that there are many words in French that look like English words and have similar meanings. These are called cognates. Cognates let you increase your reading comprehension effortlessly. Be sure to pronounce them the French way!

• Sometimes the spelling is the same, or almost the same:

un champion	*champion*
la permission	*permission*

• Sometimes the spelling is a little different:

les maths	*math*

Activité écrite: Une lettre à Trinh

You are writing an e-mail to Trinh in which you introduce yourself and explain what you like to do. Be sure to use only vocabulary that you know in French. You may tell him:

- if you like music (and what kind)
- what sports you like to do in fall or winter
- what sports you like to do in spring or summer
- which school subjects you like and which you do not like
- what you like to do at home
- which programs you like to watch on TV
- what you like to do on the Internet and what you do not like to do

Writing Hint Use Trinh's letter as a model.

NOTE culturelle

Les Vietnamiens en France

Vietnam and other Southeast Asian countries like Laos and Cambodia have a long civilization. For a period of about eighty years until the mid-1950s, these countries were occupied and administered by France which established schools and promoted the use of the French language among their populations.

In recent years, many Vietnamese people like Trinh's family have emigrated to France. Vietnamese restaurants are very popular with French students because of their fine yet inexpensive cuisine.

À l'école en France

Bonjour, Nathalie!

Bonjour!
Je m'appelle Nathalie Aubin.
J'ai 15 ans et j'habite à Savigny-sur-Orge
avec ma famille. (Savigny est
une petite° ville à 20 kilomètres
au sud° de Paris.)
J'ai un frère, Christophe, 17 ans,
et deux soeurs, Céline, 13 ans,
et Florence, 7 ans.
Mon père est programmeur.
(Il travaille à Paris.)
Ma mère est dentiste.
(Elle travaille à Savigny.)
Je vais au lycée Jean-Baptiste
Corot.
Je suis élève° de seconde°
Et vous?

Nathalie

---

petite *small* **sud** *south* **élève** *student* **seconde** *tenth grade*

Les photos de Nathalie

Voici ma famille.

ma mère

ma sœur Céline

moi

mon père

mon frère Christophe et ma sœur Florence

Voici ma maison. (C'est une maison confortable, mais ce n'est pas un château!)

Voici mon école.°
Le lycée Jean-Baptiste Corot
est dans° un château!°

école *school* dans *in* château *castle*

Le lycée Jean-Baptiste Corot

Jean-Baptiste Corot

The lycée Jean-Baptiste Corot is located in Savigny-sur-Orge, a small town about 12 miles south of Paris. Like many French schools, it is named after a famous French person. Jean-Baptiste Corot was a 19th century painter, remembered especially for his landscapes.

The lycée Jean-Baptiste Corot is both old and modern. It was created in the 1950s on the grounds of a historical castle dating from the 12th century. The castle, which serves as the administrative center, is still surrounded by a moat. The lycée itself has many modern facilities which include:

- **les salles de classe** *(classrooms)*
- **la cantine** *(cafeteria)*
- **le stade** *(stadium)* **et le terrain de sport** *(playing field)*

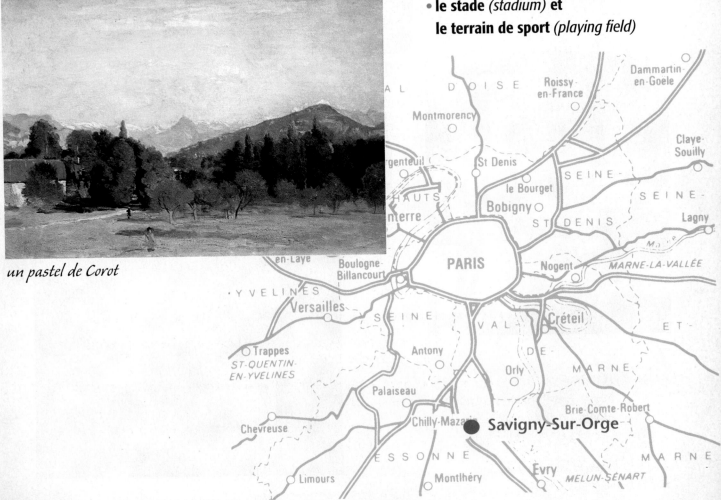

un pastel de Corot

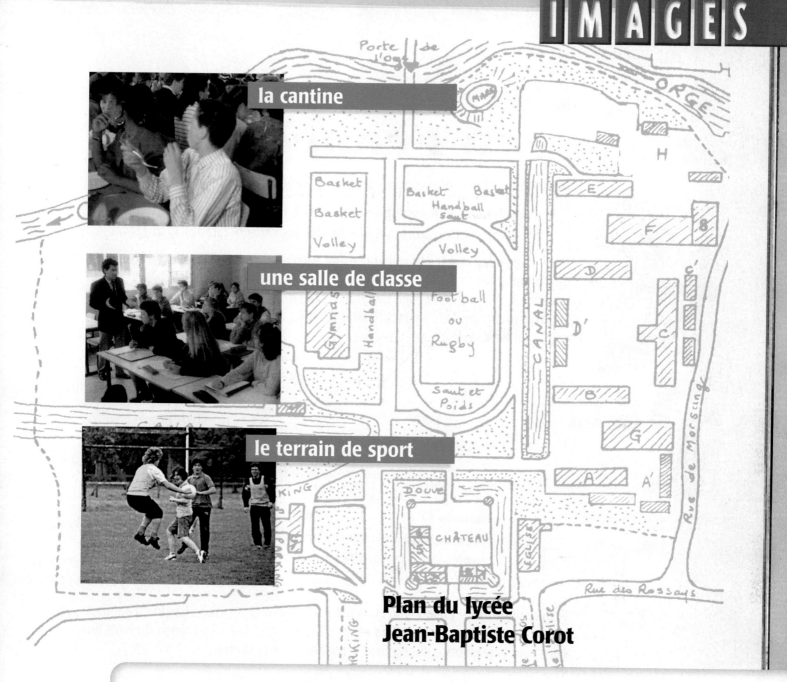

la cantine

une salle de classe

le terrain de sport

**Plan du lycée
Jean-Baptiste Corot**

Comparaisons Culturelles

1. Compare your school to the lycée Jean-Baptiste Corot.

- Is your school named after somebody? If so, why is this person famous?

- Is your school older or more modern than the lycée Jean-Baptiste Corot? When was it built (approximately)?

- Does your school have the same facilities as the lycée Jean-Baptiste Corot? Does it have other facilities?

2. Make a map of your school, giving French names to its facilities. (Ask for your teacher's help for words you do not know.)

L'école secondaire en France

There are two types of secondary schools in France:

- **le collège,** which corresponds to the U.S. middle school (grades 6 to 9)
- **le lycée,** which corresponds to the U.S. high school (grades 10 to 12)

On the following chart, you will notice that each grade **(une classe)** is designated by a number (as in the United States): **sixième (6ᵉ), cinquième (5ᵉ), quatrième (4ᵉ),** etc. However, the progression from grade to grade is the opposite in France. The secondary school begins in France with **sixième** and ends with **terminale.**

École	Classe	Âge des élèves	Équivalent américain
Le collège	sixième (6ᵉ)	11–12 ans	*sixth grade*
	cinquième (5ᵉ)	12–13 ans	*seventh grade*
	quatrième (4ᵉ)	13–14 ans	*eighth grade*
	troisième (3ᵉ)	14–15 ans	*ninth grade*
Le lycée	seconde (2ᵉ)	15–16 ans	*tenth grade*
	première (1ʳᵉ)	16–17 ans	*eleventh grade*
	terminale	17–18 ans	*twelfth grade*

A student **(un/une élève)** who does not do well in a given grade has to repeat that grade the next year. This is called **redoubler.** About 50% of the French students are kept back at least once during their secondary school studies.

At the end of high school, French students take a two-part national examination called **le baccalauréat,** or **le bac** for short, which they have to pass in order to enter the university.

- The first part, which focuses on the French language, is administered at the end of **première.**
- The second part, which is given at the end of **terminale,** offers students over twenty options reflecting their area of specialization.

Only 75% of the students who take the **bac** in a given year pass the exam. Of those who are successful, about 85% continue their studies either at the university or at a specialized professional school. Since education in France is considered a responsibility of the government, tuition is free at all public universities.

Des élèves vous parlent

David Souliac, 14 ans

J'habite à Bergerac, une petite ville
dans le sud-ouest° de la France.   *southwest*
Je suis élève de 4ᵉ au collège Jacques Prévert.
Là, j'étudie l'anglais et l'espagnol.

Antoine Restaut, 14 ans

J'habite à Paris.
Je suis élève au collège Jeannine Manuel.
C'est un collège international.
J'aime les maths et les sciences.
Je voudrais être pilote comme° mon père.   *like*

Pauline Lescure, 16 ans

Je suis élève de première au lycée Schoelcher
à Fort-de-France en Martinique.
J'étudie les sciences.
Je veux être médecin.°   *doctor*
Je voudrais aller° à l'université à Paris.   *to go*
Mais d'abord,° je dois être reçue° au bac.   *first/pass*

Le programme scolaire *(School curriculum)*

At the middle school **(au collège)**, all French students take certain required subjects **(des matières obligatoires)**. In **quatrième,** for instance, these subjects include French, math, one foreign language, history and geography, science **(sciences de la vie et de la terre** – life and earth sciences), and art. Depending on their preferences and career plans, they can also choose among a certain number of electives **(des matières facultatives)**. Many opt for a second foreign language **(une langue)**.

Here is a list of subjects taught in French middle schools. (Note that no school offers all the languages listed, but most schools offer three or four.) How many of the subjects can you identify?

Matières obligatoires	Matières facultatives	Langues modernes
français	latin	allemand
maths	grec	anglais
1ère langue moderne	2ème langue moderne	arabe
histoire		espagnol
géographie		hébreu
physique-chimie		italien
sciences de la vie et de la terre		portugais
technologie		russe
éducation civique		
éducation physique et sportive		
arts plastiques		
éducation musicale		

Comparaisons Culturelles

Compare the curriculum of an eighth grader in the United States with that of a French teenager in the equivalent grade **(quatrième).** You may first want to list the subjects offered in your school system for grades six through nine.

    a) Matières obligatoires

    b) Matières facultatives

    c) Langues modernes

Do you prefer the French or the American curriculum? Explain.

L'emploi du temps de Nathalie

Nathalie Aubin est en seconde au lycée Jean-Baptiste Corot. Voici son emploi du temps.

LYCÉE JEAN-BAPTISTE COROT

Étudiante: AUBIN, Nathalie

	LUNDI	MARDI	MERCREDI	JEUDI	VENDREDI	SAMEDI
8h30 à 9h30	Histoire	Allemand				
9h30 à 10h30	Anglais	Français		Informatique°		Français
10h30 à 11h30	Sport	Français	Anglais	Physique	Allemand	Français
11h30 à 12h30	Français	Latin	Informatique	Maths	Latin	Latin
13h00 à 14h00			Maths		Sciences vie et terre	Histoire ou civilisation
14h00 à 15h00	Sciences vie et terre	Maths				
15h00 à 16h00	Géographie	Maths		Allemand		
16h00 à 17h00	Physique	Anglais		Sport		

informatique *computer science*

Comparaisons Culturelles

Compare Nathalie's schedule with that of an American student in the same grade (tenth grade). You may want to make a chart:

	France	United States
number of classes per week		
number of foreign languages		
number of hours per week for sports		
other differences		

On the basis of your comparisons, do you prefer the French system or the American system? Explain.

Mon emploi du temps
Write out your own school schedule in French.

Expressions pour la classe

Le professeur dit ...

Écoutez!

à une élève   à un élève   à la classe

Regarde! *(Look!)*
   Regarde la vidéo.
Écoute! *(Listen!)*
   Écoute la cassette *(tape)*.

Parle! *(Speak!)*
   Parle plus fort *(louder)*.
Réponds! *(Answer!)*
   Réponds à la question.
Répète! *(Repeat!)*
   Répète la phrase *(sentence)*.

Lis! *(Read!)*
   Lis l'exercice.
Écris! *(Write!)*
   Écris dans ton cahier.

Prends *(Take)*	une feuille de papier.
	un crayon
Ouvre *(Open)*	ton livre.
	la porte
Ferme *(Close)*	ton cahier.
	la fenêtre

Viens! *(Come!)*
   Viens ici.
Va! *(Go!)*
   Va au tableau.
Lève-toi! *(Stand up!)*
Assieds-toi! *(Sit down!)*

Apporte-moi *(Bring me)*	
Donne-moi *(Give me)*	ton devoir.
Montre-moi *(Show me)*	

Regardez!
   Regardez la vidéo.
Écoutez!
   Écoutez la cassette.

Parlez!
   Parlez plus fort.
Répondez!
   Répondez à la question.
Répétez!
   Répétez la phrase.

Lisez!
   Lisez l'exercice.
Écrivez!
   Écrivez dans vos cahiers.

Prenez	une feuille de papier.
	un crayon
Ouvrez	vos livres.
	la porte
Fermez	vos cahiers.
	la fenêtre

Venez!
   Venez ici.
Allez!
   Allez au tableau.
Levez-vous!
Asseyez-vous!

Apportez-moi	
Donnez-moi	vos devoirs.
Montrez-moi	

Quelques objets

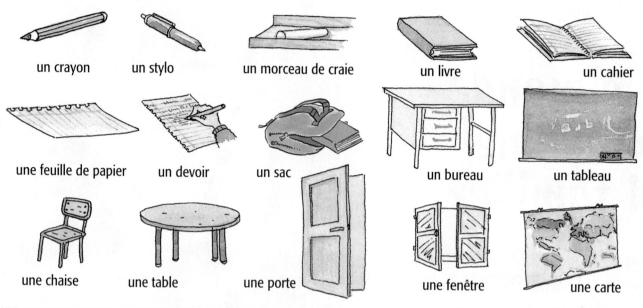

un crayon   un stylo   un morceau de craie   un livre   un cahier

une feuille de papier   un devoir   un sac   un bureau   un tableau

une chaise   une table   une porte   une fenêtre   une carte

Tu dis ...

Je sais.	*I know.*
Je ne sais pas.	*I don't know.*
Je ne comprends pas.	*I don't understand.*
Que veut dire ... ?	*What does ... mean?*
Comment dit-on ... en français?	*How does one say ... in French?*

🎧 Écoutez bien!

Imagine you are in a school in France. Listen carefully to what different French teachers ask you to do and carry out their instructions. If you have trouble understanding the commands, your teacher will mime the actions for you.

UNITÉ 4

Le monde personnel et familier

LEÇON 9 LE FRANÇAIS PRATIQUE: Les personnes et les objets

LEÇON 10 Vive la différence!

LEÇON 11 Le copain de Mireille

LEÇON 12 La voiture de Roger

THÈME ET OBJECTIFS

People and possessions

When you meet French teenagers, you will want to share information about yourself, your friends, and your possessions.

In this unit, you will learn ...

- to talk about yourself: your personality and what you look like
- to describe your friends and how old they are
- to describe your room
- to talk about everyday objects that you own or use
- to describe these objects: their size and color

WEBQUEST
CLASSZONE.COM

Les personnes et les objets

Accent sur … les jeunes Français

France is a young country. One quarter of the population is under the age of twenty. In their daily lives outside school, young people in France are not that different from their counterparts in the United States. They enjoy listening to music and going to the movies. On weekends, they go to the mall or into the city to check out the newest teen fashions and the latest in video games and sound equipment. As computers become more and more widespread, French young people often spend their free time surfing the Internet and participating in chat rooms and forums.

Since almost everyone studies English in school, French teenagers are very much aware of the American way of life. They have a generally positive attitude towards the United States and many would like to visit our country.

Thomas a un vélo. C'est un vélo anglais.
Michèle n'a pas de vélo. Elle a un scooter.

Élodie et Paul font une promenade en ville.
Paul a un baladeur. Il écoute un CD. Élodie a
un portable. Elle téléphone à une copine.

Jean-Marc et Valérie sont devant un magasin d'équipement hi-fi. Ils regardent des mini-chaînes.

Zaïna a un ordinateur. Elle surfe sur l'Internet. Elle aime aussi jouer aux jeux d'ordinateur avec Ousmane.

A **VOCABULAIRE** **La description des personnes**

Qui est-ce?

C'est un copain.

▶ *How to describe someone:*

Qui est-ce?
C'est un copain.

Comment s'appelle-t-il?
Il s'appelle Marc.

Quel âge a-t-il?
Il a seize ans.

Comment est-il?
Il est petit.
Il est blond.

Qui est-ce?
C'est une copine.

Comment s'appelle-t-elle?
Elle s'appelle Sophie.

Quel âge a-t-elle?
Elle a quinze ans.

Comment est-elle?
Elle est grande.
Elle est brune.

Les personnes

une **personne**

un **étudiant**	*student*
un **élève**	*pupil*
un **camarade**	*classmate*
un **homme**	*man*
un **professeur**, un **prof**	*teacher*
un **voisin**	*neighbor*

une **personne**

une **étudiante**
une **élève**
une **camarade**
une **femme**   *woman*
un **professeur**, une **prof**
une **voisine**

- -

→ **Une personne** is always feminine whether it refers to a male or female person.

→ **Un professeur** is always masculine whether it refers to a male or female teacher. However, in casual French, one distinguishes between **un prof** (male) and **une prof** (female).

La description physique

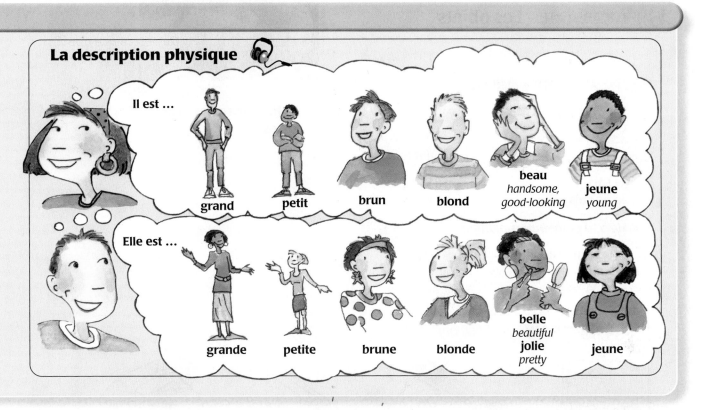

Il est …

grand | petit | brun | blond | **beau** *handsome, good-looking* | **jeune** *young*

Elle est …

grande | petite | brune | blonde | **belle** *beautiful* **jolie** *pretty* | jeune

---

1 Oui ou non?

PARLER Describe the people below in affirmative or negative sentences.

▶ Frankenstein / beau?
Frankenstein n'est pas beau.

1. Shaquille O'Neal / grand?
2. Brad Pitt / brun?
3. Dracula / beau?
4. mon copain / blond?
5. mon père / petit?
6. mon voisin / jeune?
7. Britney Spears / belle?
8. le président / jeune?
9. Oprah Winfrey / grande?
10. ma copine / petite?
11. ma mère / brune?
12. ma voisine / jolie?

2 Vacances à Québec

PARLER/ÉCRIRE You spent last summer in Quebec and have just had your photographs developed. Describe each of the people, giving name, approximate age, and two or three characteristics.

Alain

blond(e)   petit(e)
brun(e)   beau (belle)
grand(e)   jeune

▶ Il s'appelle Alain.
Il est blond.
Il a seize ans.
Il n'est pas grand.
Il est petit.

1. Anne-Marie

2. Jean-Pierre

3. Claire

4. Mademoiselle Lévêque

5. Madame Paquette

6. Monsieur Beliveau

Qu'est-ce que c'est?

B VOCABULAIRE Les objets

▶ *How to identify something:*

Qu'est-ce que c'est?	*What is it? What's that?*
C'est ...	*It's ..., That's ...*

—**Qu'est-ce que c'est?**
—**C'est** un livre.

▶ *How to say that you know or do not know:*

Je sais.	*I know.*
Je ne sais pas.	*I don't know.*

▶ *How to point out something:*

—**Regarde ça.**	*Look at that.*
—**Quoi?**	*What?*
—**Ça**, là-bas.	*That, over there.*

Quelques objets *(A few objects)*

un objet   **un stylo**   **un crayon**   **un téléphone**

un livre   **un cahier**   **un sac**

une chose *(thing)*   **une montre**   **une raquette**   **une guitare**

une affiche *(un poster)*   **une calculatrice**

♻ **RAPPEL**

In French, the names of objects are MASCULINE or FEMININE.

Masculine objects can be introduced by **un** or **le (l')**: **un stylo, le stylo, l'objet.**

Feminine objects can be introduced by **une** or **la (l')**: **une montre, la montre, l'affiche.**

—QU'EST-CE QUE C'EST QUE ÇA?
—QUOI?
—ÇA, LÀ-BAS!
—C'EST UNE TÉLÉ.

—OH LÀ LÀ, NON! REGARDE! C'EST UN EXTRA-TERRESTRE!

3 *Qu'est-ce que c'est?*

PARLER Ask a classmate to identify the following objects.

▶ **Qu'est-ce que c'est?**
  C'est un stylo.

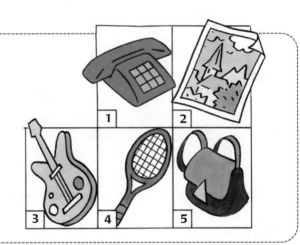

4 *S'il te plaît*

PARLER Ask a classmate to give you the following objects.

▶ **—S'il te plaît, donne-moi le livre.**
  —Voilà le livre.
  —Merci.

Est-ce que
tu as une moto?

Oui, j'ai une moto.

C VOCABULAIRE **Les affaires personnelles** *(personal belongings)*

▶ **How to talk about things you have:**

Est-ce que tu as … ? *Do you have … ?*
Oui, j'ai … *Yes, I have …*

—**Est-ce que tu as** une moto?
—**Oui, j'ai** une moto.

Quelques objets

un portable

un appareil-photo

un baladeur

un CD

une télé

un DVD

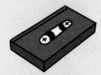

une cassette vidéo

un ordinateur

une radio

une radiocassette

**une chaîne hi-fi
(une mini-chaîne)**

**une voiture
(une auto)**

**un vélo
(une bicyclette)**

une mobylette

un scooter

une moto

▶ **How to ask if an object works:**

—Est-ce que la radio **marche?** *Does the radio work?*
—Oui, elle **marche.** *Yes, it works.*

➜ The verb **marcher** has two meanings:

for people: *to walk* Nous **marchons.**

for things: *to work, to run* Le scooter ne **marche** pas bien.

♻ **RAPPEL**

Masculine nouns can be
replaced by **il.**
 Le vélo marche.
 Il marche bien.
Feminine nouns can be
replaced by **elle.**
 La voiture marche.
 Elle marche bien.

5 **Et toi?**

PARLER

1. J'ai … *(Name 3 objects you own.)*
2. Je voudrais … *(Name 3 things you would like to have.)*
3. Pour Noël / Hanoukka, je voudrais … *(Name 2 gifts you would like to receive.)*

6 **Joyeux anniversaire** *(Happy birthday)*

PARLER/ÉCRIRE For your birthday, a rich aunt is giving you the choice between different possible gifts. Indicate your preferences.

▶ vélo ou scooter?

1. mobylette ou moto?
2. portable ou baladeur?
3. appareil-photo ou radio?
4. radiocassette ou chaîne hi-fi?
5. télé ou ordinateur?
6. DVD ou cassette vidéo?

Je préfère le vélo.

Je préfère le scooter.

7 **Qu'est-ce que tu as?**

PARLER Éric asks Léa if she has the following objects. She says that she does. Play both roles.

▶ ÉRIC: **Est-ce que tu as une guitare?**
LÉA: **Oui, j'ai une guitare.**

8 **Est-ce qu'il marche bien?**

PARLER Tell your classmates that you own the following objects. They will ask you if the objects are working. Answer according to the illustrations.

▶ —J'ai un vélo.
—Est-ce qu'il marche bien?
—Non, il ne marche pas bien.

▶ —J'ai une télé.
—Est-ce qu'elle marche bien?
—Oui, elle marche très bien.

D **VOCABULAIRE** **Ma chambre** *(My room)*

Dans ma chambre il y a une télé.

▶ *How to talk about what there is in a place:*

il y a	*there is*	Dans *(In)* ma chambre, **il y a** une télé.
	there are	Dans le garage, **il y a** deux voitures.
est-ce qu'il y a … ?	*is/are there … ?*	**Est-ce qu'il y a** un ordinateur dans la classe?
qu'est-ce qu'il y a … ?	*what is there … ?*	**Qu'est-ce qu'il y a** dans le garage?

Dans ma chambre

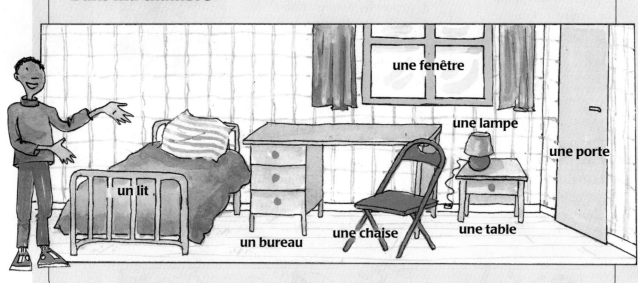

une fenêtre

une lampe

une porte

un lit

un bureau

une chaise

une table

▶ *How to say where something or someone is:*

Où est Félix?
Félix est …

dans le lit

sur le lit

sous le lit

devant le lit

derrière le lit

9 **Qu'est-ce qu'il y a?**

PARLER Describe the various objects that are in the pictures.

1. Sur la table, il y a … **2.** Sous le lit, il y a … **3.** Dans le garage, il y a …

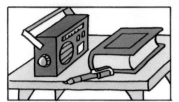  

10 **Ma chambre**

PARLER/ÉCRIRE Describe the various objects (pieces of furniture and personal belongings) that are in your room.

▶ **Dans ma chambre, il y a une radio, …**
Il y a aussi …

11 **Où est le téléphone?**

PARLER Michèle is looking for the telephone. Jean-Claude tells her where it is.

▶ MICHÈLE: **Où est le téléphone?**
JEAN-CLAUDE: **Il est sur la table.**

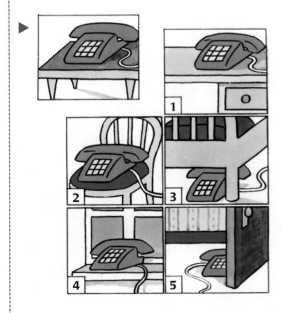

12 **C'est étrange!** *(It's strange!)*

PARLER/ÉCRIRE Funny things sometimes happen. Describe these curious happenings by selecting an item from Column A and putting it in one of the places listed in Column B.

▶ Il y a …

A	B
un rhinocéros	dans la classe
un éléphant	sur le bureau
une girafe	sous la table
un crabe	sous le lit
une souris *(mouse)*	derrière la porte
un ami de King Kong	sur la tour Eiffel
un extra-terrestre	dans le jardin *(garden)*
	devant le restaurant

13 *La chambre de Nicole*

PARLER Florence wants to borrow a few things from Nicole's room. Nicole tells her where each object is.

▶ la télé

FLORENCE: **Où est la télé?**

NICOLE: **Elle est sur la table.**

1. la raquette
2. la guitare
3. le livre

4. le vélo
5. l'ordinateur
6. le sac

7. la radio
8. le CD
9. le portable

14 **Pauvre Monsieur Vénard** *(Poor Mr. Vénard)*

PARLER/ÉCRIRE Today Monsieur Vénard left on vacation, but he soon ran out of luck. Describe the four cartoons by completing the sentences below.

Le voyage de Monsieur Vénard

1. M. Vénard est _____ la voiture.

2. M. Vénard est _____ la voiture.

3. M. Vénard est _____ la voiture.

4. La contractuelle° est _____ la voiture.

la contractuelle *meter maid*

E VOCABULAIRE Mon ordinateur

Vocabulaire supplémentaire
un ordinateur (un PC)

une imprimante

un écran

un jeu d'ordinateur

le clavier

la souris

un cédérom
(un CD-ROM)

un ordinateur portable
(un PC portable)

envoyer un mail (un mél)	*to send an e-mail*
surfer sur l'Internet (sur le Net)	*to surf the Internet*
chatter	*to chat (online)*
télécharger	*to download*

COMPARAISONS INTERPERSONNELLES

Here is a list of various activities that you can do with a computer. List the four activities you like to do best, ranking them in order of preference. Compare your lists with your classmates.

- chatter
- faire mes devoirs *(homework)*
- écouter de la musique
- envoyer un mail à un copain / une copine
- surfer sur le Net

- regarder les nouvelles *(news)*
- télécharger de la musique
- faire des recherches *(research)* pour la classe de français
- jouer aux jeux d'ordinateur

UN SONDAGE

Conduct a poll in your class to determine which two of the above computer activities students like the best and which two they like the least.

À votre tour!

OBJECTIFS
Now you can …
• describe your belongings
• talk about people and give their ages

1 🎧 Écoutez bien!

ÉCOUTER You will hear a series of sentences. In each one an object is mentioned. If you see the object only in Léa's room, mark A. If you see the object only in Pierre's room, mark B. If you see the object in the two rooms, mark both A and B.

A. La chambre de Léa

B. La chambre de Pierre

	A Léa	B Pierre
1.		
2.		
3.		
4.		
5.		
6.		
7.		
8.		
9.		
10.		
11.		
12.		
13.		
14.		
15.		
16.		
17.		
18.		

2 🎧 Conversation dirigée

PARLER André is visiting his cousin Marie. Act out the dialogue according to the instructions.

André

André		Marie
asks Marie if she has a computer	→ ←	answers affirmatively
asks her if it works well	→ ←	says that it works very well and asks why
says he would like to send an e-mail to a friend	→	says that the computer is on the desk in her room

Marie

3  **Créa-dialogue** --

PARLER Daniel is showing Nathalie his recent photographs, and she is asking questions about the various people. Create similar dialogues and act them out in class.

▶ **un copain**

Éric/14

▶ —Qui est-ce?
—C'est <u>un copain</u>.
—Comment s'appelle-t-<u>il</u>?
—<u>Il</u> s'appelle <u>Éric</u>.
—Quel âge a-t-<u>il</u>?
—<u>Il</u> a <u>quatorze</u> ans.

1. une cousine	2. un camarade	3. une camarade	4. un voisin	5. une voisine	6. un professeur
Valérie/20	Philippe Boucher/13	Nathalie Masson/15	Monsieur Dumas/70	Madame Smith/51	Monsieur Laval/35

4 **Mes affaires** --------------------

ÉCRIRE Imagine that your family is going to move to another city. Prepare for the move by making a checklist of your things. Write out your list by hand or on a computer.

```
Mes affaires:
· un lit
·
·
```

5 **Ma chambre** ---------------------------

ÉCRIRE A French student is going to spend two weeks at your house. Write him/her a short e-mail describing your room. In your note, mention …

- at least 3 pieces of furniture
- at least 3 school-related objects
- 4 personal belongings

If you wish, you can add some descriptive comments.

6 **Un ordinateur** ------------------------------------

ÉCRIRE Imagine that you have just won a brand new computer in a contest at your school. Write a short paragraph in which you …

- describe its various components
- mention 3 ways in which you want to use it

LESSON REVIEW
CLASSZONE.COM

cent quarante-neuf 149
Leçon 9

Vive la différence! _{AUDIO}

We are not necessarily like our friends. Léa describes herself and her best friend Céline. Both of them live in Paris and are quite different.

Léa

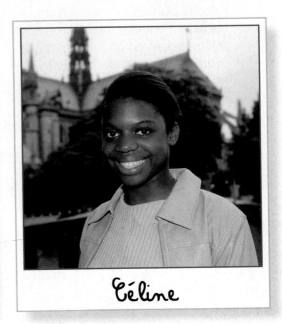

Céline

Je m'appelle Léa.

Je suis française.

J'ai des frères, mais je n'ai pas de soeur.

J'ai un chien.

J'ai un scooter.

J'aime la musique classique.

J'aime le basket et le tennis.

Elle s'appelle Céline.

Elle est haïtienne.

Elle n'a pas de frère, mais elle a deux soeurs.

Elle n'a pas de chien, mais elle a un chat très mignon.

Elle a un vélo.

Elle préfère le compas.

Elle préfère le foot.

Céline et moi, nous sommes très différentes … mais nous sommes copines. C'est l'essentiel, non?

Compréhension

Answer the questions below with the appropriate names: **Léa, Céline,** or **Léa et Céline.**

1. Qui habite en France?
2. Qui a deux soeurs?
3. Qui n'a pas de frère?
4. Qui a un vélo?
5. Qui aime la musique classique?
6. Qui aime les sports?

NOTE **culturelle**

Haïti
★
Port-au-Prince

EN BREF: Haïti

Capitale: Port-au-Prince
Population: 8 millions d'habitants
Langues: créole, français

Un marché à Pétionville (près de Port-au-Prince)

Une peinture haïtienne

Haiti occupies the western part of the large Caribbean island on which the Dominican Republic is also located. Its inhabitants are of African origin. Their enslaved ancestors revolted against their French masters in 1805 and established the first independent Black nation in modern history. Today many Haitians have emigrated to France, Canada, and especially to the United States. There are sizable Haitian communities in Florida and in cities along the northeastern seaboard.

Haitians are friendly, industrious, and artistic people. In the twentieth century, Haitian painters developed their own widely appreciated folk art style and Haitian paintings are now in collections around the world. The Haitians also love music, especially **compas** or **kompas** which highlights a variety of instruments including conga drums, guitar, and keyboard. Its creole lyrics are expressed against a background of African, Caribbean, reggae, and rock rhythms.

Haitian creole cuisine, which features rice dishes, pork, and shellfish, is often quite spicy. Typical Haitian dishes include **griots** (fried pork), **riz djon-djon** (rice with mushrooms), and **pain patate** (sweet potato cake).

CONNEXIONS Haïti

Learn more about Haiti. Divide the class into several groups, each with a different assignment. For example:

• Create a bulletin board display with pictures, maps, and newspaper clippings about Haiti.

• Find books on Haitian paintings and Haitian artists and make a presentation to the class.

• Find examples of **compas** music and play a selection for the class.

A **Le verbe *avoir***

The verb **avoir** *(to have, to own)* is irregular. Note the forms of this verb in the present tense.

avoir	to have	
j' **ai**	*I have*	J'**ai** une copine à Québec.
tu **as**	*you have*	Est-ce que tu **as** un frère?
il/elle **a**	*he/she has*	Philippe **a** une cousine à Paris.
nous **avons**	*we have*	Nous **avons** un ordinateur.
vous **avez**	*you have*	Est-ce que vous **avez** une moto?
ils/elles **ont**	*they have*	Ils n'**ont** pas ton appareil-photo.

→ There is liaison in the forms: **nous ̮avons, vous ̮avez, ils ̮ont, elles ̮ont.**

VOCABULAIRE Expressions avec *avoir*

avoir faim	*to be hungry*	J'ai **faim.** Et toi, est-ce que tu **as faim?**
avoir soif	*to be thirsty*	Paul **a soif.** Sylvie n'**a** pas **soif.**
avoir … ans	*to be … (years old)*	J'**ai** 14 **ans.** Le prof **a** 35 **ans.**

1 *Qu'est-ce qu'ils ont?*

PARLER From what the people are doing, say which object in the box they have.

> un baladeur
> un ordinateur
> un portable
> une raquette
> une télé

▶ Léa regarde un film.
  Elle a une télé.

1. Tu joues au tennis.
2. Éric écoute du rock.
3. Je regarde un film.
4. Vous téléphonez.
5. Nous écoutons un CD.
6. Vous envoyez un mail.
7. Elles jouent au tennis.
8. Ils surfent sur le Net.

2 *Expression personnelle*

PARLER/ÉCRIRE How old are the following people? Complete the sentences below. If you don't know their ages, guess.

1. J'ai …
2. *(A classmate)* Tu as …
3. *(The teacher)* Vous …
4. Mon copain …
5. Ma copine …
6. La voisine …

3 *Faim ou soif?*

PARLER You are at a party with your classmates. Offer them the following foods and beverages. They will accept or refuse by saying whether they are hungry or thirsty.

Tu veux un sandwich?

Oui, merci! J'ai faim.
(Non, merci! Je n'ai pas faim.)

▶ un sandwich

1. une crêpe
2. un soda
3. un hamburger
4. un jus d'orange
5. un croissant
6. un jus de raisin
7. une pizza
8. une limonade

B Les noms et les articles: masculin et féminin

NOUNS

- Nouns designating PEOPLE

  Nouns that designate male persons are almost always *masculine:*

  un garçon   **un ami**

  Nouns that designate female persons are almost always *feminine:*

  une fille   **une amie**

  → EXCEPTIONS:

  une personne is always feminine (even when it refers to a male)

  un professeur is always masculine (even when it refers to a woman)

- Nouns designating ANIMALS, OBJECTS, and THINGS

  There is no systematic way to determine whether these nouns are masculine or feminine. Therefore, it is very important to learn these nouns with their articles.

MASCULINE:	**un** portable	**un** vélo	**un** ordinateur
FEMININE:	**une** chaîne hi-fi	**une** moto	**une** affiche

> **LEARNING ABOUT LANGUAGE**
>
> NOUNS are words that designate people, animals, objects, and things.
>
> In French, all nouns have GENDER: they are either MASCULINE or FEMININE.

ARTICLES

Note the forms of the articles in the chart below.

	MASCULINE		FEMININE			
INDEFINITE ARTICLE	**un**	*a, an*	**une**	*a, an*	**un** garçon	**une** fille
DEFINITE ARTICLE	**le**	*the*	**la**	*the*	**le** garçon	**la** fille

> **LEARNING ABOUT LANGUAGE**
>
> Nouns are often introduced by ARTICLES. In French, ARTICLES have the *same* gender as the nouns they introduce.

→ Both **le** and **la** become **l'** before a vowel sound:

le garçon   **l'ami**

la fille   **l'amie**

PRONOUNS

Note the forms of the pronouns in the chart below.

| MASCULINE | **il** | *he* / *it* | Où est **le** garçon? | **Il** est en classe. |
			Où est **le** portable?	**Il** est sur la table.
FEMININE	**elle**	*she* / *it*	Où est **la** fille?	**Elle** est en ville.
			Où est **la** voiture?	**Elle** est là-bas.

> **LEARNING ABOUT LANGUAGE**
>
> Nouns may be replaced by PRONOUNS. In French, PRONOUNS have the *same* gender as the nouns they replace.

4 **Les célébrités**

PARLER You and Jean-Pierre have been invited to a benefit attended by many American celebrities. Jean-Pierre asks you who each person is. Answer him using **un** or **une**, as appropriate.

1. Dan Rather/journaliste
2. Julia Roberts/actrice
3. Brad Pitt/acteur
4. Will Smith/chanteur *(singer)*
5. Britney Spears/chanteuse
6. Tiger Woods/athlète
7. Venus Williams/athlète
8. Whoopi Goldberg/comédienne

▶ Katie Couric/journaliste
—**Tiens, voilà Katie Couric!**
—**Qui est-ce?**
—**Une journaliste.**

  5 **Sur la table ou sous la table?**

PARLER Caroline is looking for the following objects. Cécile tells her where each one is: on or under the table.

▶ baladeur
CAROLINE: **Où est le baladeur?**
CÉCILE: **Le baladeur?**
Il est sur la table.

1. ordinateur
2. sac
3. affiche
4. calculatrice
5. raquette
6. appareil-photo
7. radiocassette
8. télé

 C **Les noms et les articles: le pluriel**

Compare the singular and plural forms of the articles and nouns in the sentences below.

SINGULAR	PLURAL
Tu as **le livre?**	Tu as **les livres?**
Qui est **la fille** là-bas?	Qui sont **les filles** là-bas?
Voici **un sac.**	Voici **des sacs.**
J'invite **une copine.**	J'invite **des copines.**

PLURAL NOUNS

In written French, the plural of most nouns is formed as follows:

SINGULAR NOUN + **s** = PLURAL NOUN

→ If the noun ends in -s in the singular, the singular and plural forms are the same.

Voici **un Français.** Voici **des Français.**

→ In spoken French, the final -**s** of the plural is always silent.

→ NOTE: **des gens** *(people)* is always plural. Compare:

| **une personne** | *person* | Qui est **la personne** là-bas? |
| **des gens** | *people* | Qui sont **les gens** là-bas? |

SINGULAR AND PLURAL ARTICLES

The forms of the articles are summarized in the chart below.

	SINGULAR		PLURAL			
DEFINITE ARTICLE	le (l') la (l')	*the*	**les**	*the*	**les** garçons **les** filles	**les** ordinateurs **les** affiches
INDEFINITE ARTICLE	un une	*a, an*	**des**	*some*	**des** garçons **des** filles	**des** ordinateurs **des** affiches

→ There is liaison after **les** and **des** when the next word begins with a vowel sound.

→ **Des** corresponds to the English article *some*. While *some* is often omitted in English, **des** MUST be expressed in French. Contrast:

Il y a	des	livres sur la table.
There are	*some*	*books on the table.*

Je dîne avec	des	amis.
I'm having dinner with	*…*	*friends.*

6 Pluriel, s'il vous plaît

PARLER/ÉCRIRE Give the plurals of the following nouns.

▶ une copine
des copines

▶ l'ami
les amis

1. un copain
2. une amie
3. un homme
4. une femme
5. un euro
6. une affiche

7. le voisin
8. l'élève
9. la cousine
10. le livre
11. l'ordinateur
12. la voiture

7 Shopping

PARLER You are in a department store looking for the following items. Ask the salesperson if he or she has these items. The salesperson will answer affirmatively.

▶ —Pardon, monsieur (madame).
   Est-ce que vous avez des sacs?
  —Bien sûr, nous avons des sacs. ▶

8 Qu'est-ce qu'il y a?

PARLER/ÉCRIRE Explain what there is in the following places. Complete the sentences with **il y a** and at least two nouns of your choice. Be sure to use the appropriate articles: **un, une, des.**

Dans le garage, il y a une moto (des voitures …).

▶ Dans le garage, …

1. Sur le bureau, …
2. À la boum, …
3. Dans la classe, …
4. Au café, sur la table, …
5. Dans ma chambre, …
6. Dans mon sac, …

D L'article indéfini dans les phrases négatives

Compare the forms of the indefinite article in affirmative and negative sentences.

AFFIRMATIVE	NEGATIVE	
Tu as **un** vélo?	Non, je n'ai **pas de** vélo.	*No, I don't have a bike.*
Est-ce que Paul a **une** radio?	Non, il n'a **pas de** radio.	*No, he doesn't have a radio.*
Vous invitez **des** copains demain?	Non, nous n'invitons **pas de** copains.	*No, we are not inviting any friends.*

After a NEGATIVE verb:

> **pas + un, une, des** becomes **pas de**

→ Note that **pas de** becomes **pas d'** before a vowel sound.
   Alice a un ordinateur.   Paul n'a **pas d'**ordinateur.
   J'ai des amis à Québec.   Je n'ai **pas d'**amis à Montréal.

→ The negative form of **il y a** is **il n'y a pas:**
   Dans ma chambre,
   il y a une radio.   **Il n'y a pas de** télé.   *There is no TV.*
   il y a des affiches.   **Il n'y a pas de** photos.   *There are no photographs.*

→ After **être,** the articles **un, une,** and **des** do NOT change.
   Philippe est un voisin.   Éric n'est **pas un** voisin.
   Ce sont des vélos.   Ce ne sont **pas des** mobylettes.

---

9 Possessions

PARLER Ask your classmates if they own the following.

▶ un ordinateur

> Est-ce que tu as un ordinateur?

> **Oui, j'ai un ordinateur.**
> (Non, je n'ai pas d'ordinateur.)

1. un appareil-photo
2. une moto
3. une mobylette
4. une clarinette
5. des jeux vidéo
6. des affiches
7. un boa
8. un alligator
9. des hamsters
10. un portable

10 Oui et non

PARLER/ÉCRIRE One cannot have everything. Say that the following people do not have what is indicated in parentheses.

▶ Paul a un vélo. (un scooter)
   Il n'a pas de scooter.

1. Julien a un scooter. (une voiture)
2. J'ai une radio. (une télé)
3. Vous avez un baladeur. (une chaîne hi-fi)
4. Léa a une calculatrice. (un ordinateur)
5. Vous avez des frères. (une soeur)
6. Nous avons un chien. (des chats)
7. Tu as des copains à Bordeaux. (des copains à Lyon)
8. Marc a un oncle à Québec. (un oncle à Montréal)
9. Nathalie a des cousins à Paris. (des cousins à Lille)

11 Le grenier *(The attic)*

PARLER Your friend is cleaning the attic. Ask if the following items are up there. Your friend (a classmate) will answer according to the illustration.

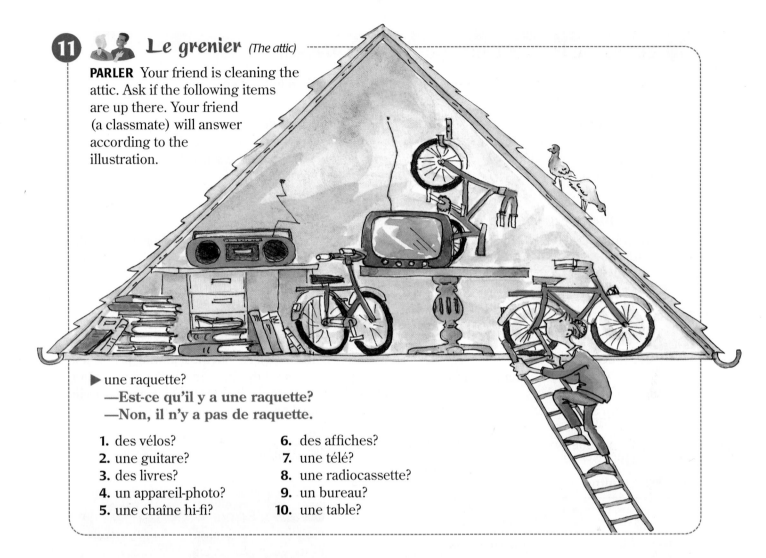

▶ une raquette?
—**Est-ce qu'il y a une raquette?**
—**Non, il n'y a pas de raquette.**

1. des vélos?
2. une guitare?
3. des livres?
4. un appareil-photo?
5. une chaîne hi-fi?
6. des affiches?
7. une télé?
8. une radiocassette?
9. un bureau?
10. une table?

VOCABULAIRE Expression pour la conversation

▶ *How to contradict a negative statement or question:*

Si! *Yes!*
—Tu n'as pas de chaîne hi-fi?
—**Si!** J'ai une chaîne hi-fi.

12 Contradictions!

PARLER/ÉCRIRE Contradict all of the following negative statements.

▶ Tu ne parles pas anglais! **Si, je parle anglais!**

1. Tu ne parles pas français!
2. Tu n'étudies pas!
3. Tu ne joues pas au basket!
4. Tu n'aimes pas les sports!
5. Tu n'aimes pas la musique!
6. Tu n'écoutes pas le professeur!

E L'usage de l'article défini dans le sens général

In French, the definite article **(le, la, les)** is used more often than in English.
Note its use in the following sentences.

J'aime **la musique.**	*(In general) I like* **music.**
Tu préfères **le tennis** ou **le golf?**	*(Generally) do you prefer* **tennis** *or* **golf?**
Julie aime **les jeux vidéo.**	*(In general) Julie likes* **video games.**
Nous aimons **la liberté.**	*(In general) we love* **liberty.**

LANGUAGE COMPARISONS

In contrast with English, French uses the definite article **(le, la, les)** to introduce ABSTRACT nouns, or nouns used in a GENERAL or COLLECTIVE sense.

J'♥ le français

13 Expression personnelle

PARLER/ÉCRIRE Say how you feel about the following things, using one of the suggested expressions.

Je n'aime pas …
J'aime un peu …
J'aime beaucoup …

▶ **Je n'aime pas la violence.**

la musique	le français	la violence	le théâtre
la nature	les maths	l'injustice	le cinéma
les sports	les sciences	la liberté	la danse
le camping			la photo
			(photography)

14 C'est évident! *(It's obvious!)*

PARLER Read about the following people and say what they like. Choose the appropriate item from the list. (Masculine nouns are in blue. Feminine nouns are in red.)

▶ Sophie écoute des CD.
Sophie aime la musique.

art	cinéma	**danse**	français
	musique	nature	tennis

1. Jean-Claude a une raquette.
2. Léa fait une promenade dans la forêt.
3. Nous visitons un musée *(museum)*.
4. Tu regardes un film.
5. Vous étudiez en classe de français.
6. Véronique et Roger sont dans une discothèque.

F L'usage de l'article défini avec les jours de la semaine

Compare the following sentences.

REPEATED EVENTS

Le samedi, je dîne avec des copains.
***(On) Saturdays** (in general), I have
dinner with friends.*

SINGLE EVENT

Samedi, je dîne avec mon cousin.
***(On) Saturday** (that is, this Saturday),
I am having dinner with my cousin.*

To indicate a repeated or habitual event, French uses the construction:

le + DAY OF THE WEEK

→ When an event happens only once, no article is used.

15 Questions personnelles   PARLER

1. Est-ce que tu étudies le samedi?
2. Est-ce que tu dînes au restaurant le dimanche? Si *(If)* oui, avec qui?
3. Est-ce que tu as une classe de français le lundi? le mercredi?
4. Est-ce que tu regardes les matchs de football américain le samedi? le dimanche?
5. Est-ce que tu travailles? Où? *(Name of place or store)* Quand?

16 L'emploi du temps

PARLER/ÉCRIRE

	LUNDI	MARDI	MERCREDI	JEUDI	VENDREDI
9 h	français	physique	sciences	biologie	
10 h		histoire		maths	anglais
11 h	maths	sciences	anglais		français

The following students all have the same morning
schedule. Complete the sentences accordingly.

▶ **Nous avons une classe de français
le lundi** ...

1. J'ai une classe de maths _____.
2. Tu as une classe de sciences _____.
3. Jacques a une classe de physique _____.
4. Thérèse a une classe d'histoire _____.
5. Vous avez une classe de biologie _____.
6. Les élèves ont une classe d'anglais _____.

PRONONCIATION   le/lə/   les/le/

Les articles *le* et *les*

Be sure to distinguish between the pronunciation of **le** and **les**.
In spoken French, that is often the only way to tell the difference
between a singular and a plural noun.

le sac   **les sacs**

Répétez: /lə/   **le**   le sac   le vélo   le portable   le copain   le voisin
          /le/   **les** les sacs les vélos les portables les copains les voisins

À votre tour!

OBJECTIFS

Now you can …
- talk about what you have and do not have
- describe in general what you like and do not like

①  Allô!

PARLER Jean-Marc is phoning some friends. Match his questions on the left with his friends' answers on the right.

1. Quel âge a ton copain?
2. Est-ce qu'Éric a un scooter?
3. Où est l'appareil-photo?
4. Tu as un baladeur?
5. Est-ce que tu aimes étudier l'anglais?
6. Tu as soif?

a. Oui, mais je n'ai pas de chaîne hi-fi.
b. Il est sur la table.
c. Quatorze ans.
d. Oui, je voudrais une limonade.
e. Oui, mais je préfère l'espagnol.
f. Non, mais il a une moto.

② Un sondage

PARLER/ÉCRIRE A French consumer research group wants to know what things American teenagers own. Conduct a survey in your class asking who has the objects on the list. Count the number of students who raise their hands for each object, and report your findings on a separate piece of paper.

► Qui a un portable? … Quinze élèves ont des portables.

UN SONDAGE

15

3 *Créa-dialogue*

PARLER Ask your classmates if they like the following things. Then ask if they own the corresponding object.

le tennis	1. la musique	2. le jogging	3. les maths	4. la photo	5. les matchs de baseball	6. l'exercice

▶ —Tu aimes le tennis?　　　　　—Tu as une raquette?
　—Oui, j'aime le tennis.　　　　—Oui, j'ai une raquette.
　　(Non, je n'aime pas le tennis.)　　(Non, je n'ai pas de raquette.)

4 *Quelle est la différence?*

PARLER/ÉCRIRE Sophie went away with her family for the weekend and she took some of her belongings with her. Describe what is in her room on Friday and what is missing on Saturday.

VENDREDI　　　　　　　　　　SAMEDI

▶ Il y a ...　　　　　　　　　▶ Il n'y a pas de ...

5 *Composition: Ma semaine*

ÉCRIRE In a short paragraph, describe what you do (or do not do) regularly on various days of the week. Select three days and two different activities for each day. Use only vocabulary that you know. Perhaps you might want to exchange paragraphs with a friend by e-mail.

Le lundi, j'ai une classe de français ...

LESSON REVIEW
CLASSZONE.COM

Le copain de Mireille

VIDÉO   DVD   AUDIO

Nicolas and Jean-Claude are having lunch at the school cafeteria. Nicolas is looking at the students seated at the other end of their table.

Nicolas:	Regarde la fille là-bas!
Jean-Claude:	La fille blonde?
Nicolas:	Oui! Qui est-ce?
Jean-Claude:	C'est Mireille Labé.
Nicolas:	Elle est <u>mignonne</u>!
Jean-Claude:	Elle est aussi <u>amusante</u>, intelligente et <u>sympathique</u>.
Nicolas:	Est-ce qu'elle a un copain?
Jean-Claude:	Oui, elle a un copain.
Nicolas:	Il est sympathique?
Jean-Claude:	Oui … Très sympathique!
Nicolas:	Et intelligent?
Jean-Claude:	Aussi!
Nicolas:	Dommage! … Qui est-ce?
Jean-Claude:	C'est moi!
Nicolas:	Euh … oh … Excuse-moi et <u>félicitations</u>!

cute

fun/nice

congratulations

Compréhension

1. Qui est-ce que Nicolas regarde?
2. Comment s'appelle la fille?
3. Est-ce qu'elle est jolie?
4. Est-ce qu'elle a d'autres *(other)* qualités?
5. Est-ce qu'elle a un copain?
6. Qui est le copain de Mireille *(Mireille's boyfriend)*?

NOTE *culturelle*

L'amitié et la bande de copains

French people believe in friendship (**l'amitié**) and family life and rank these values far above money, material comfort, and personal success. The friendships they establish at an early age tend to be durable. Since French people move much less frequently than Americans, and since distances are much smaller, they remain in close contact with their high school friends throughout their entire lives.

French teenagers, like their American counterparts, are very sociable. They have a close-knit group of friends, known as **la bande de copains,** with whom they share common interests. They go out together, especially to movies, concerts, and parties. This group may include classmates, cousins, other young people whom they have met during vacations, as well as the children of family friends. When young people invite their friends to the house, it is customary to introduce them to their parents.

COMPARAISONS CULTURELLES

What similarities and differences do you see between the French and American attitudes towards friendship?

- les similarités
- les différences

In your opinion, are these attitudes basically the same? Explain.

OPINION PERSONNELLE

Rank the following values mentioned in the text from 1 (the highest) to 5.

- l'amitié
- l'argent *(money)*
- le confort matériel
- la famille
- le succès personnel

Compare your rankings with your classmates.

A Les adjectifs: masculin et féminin

Compare the forms of the adjectives in heavy print as they describe masculine and feminine nouns.

MASCULINE	FEMININE
Le scooter est **petit.**	La voiture est **petite.**
Patrick est **intelligent.**	Caroline est **intelligente.**
L'ordinateur est **moderne.**	La télé est **moderne.**

> **LEARNING ABOUT LANGUAGE**
>
> ADJECTIVES are words that describe people, places, and things.
>
> In French, MASCULINE adjectives are used with masculine nouns, and FEMININE adjectives are used with feminine nouns. This is called NOUN-ADJECTIVE AGREEMENT.

In written French, feminine adjectives are usually formed as follows:

> MASCULINE ADJECTIVE + **-e** = FEMININE ADJECTIVE

→ If the masculine adjective ends in **-e,** there is no change in the feminine form.

Jérôme est **timide.**   Juliette est **timide.**

→ Adjectives that follow the above patterns are called REGULAR adjectives. Those that do not are called IRREGULAR adjectives. For example:

Marc est **beau.**   Sylvie est **belle.**
Paul est **canadien.**   Marie est **canadienne.**

NOTE French dictionaries list adjectives by their masculine forms. For irregular adjectives, the feminine form is indicated in parentheses.

NOTES DE PRONONCIATION:

- If the masculine form of an adjective ends in a silent consonant, that consonant is pronounced in the feminine form.

- If the masculine form of an adjective ends in a vowel or a pronounced consonant, the masculine and feminine forms sound the same.

DIFFERENT PRONUNCIATION		SAME PRONUNCIATION	
peti~~t~~	petite	timide	timide
blon~~d~~	blonde	joli	jolie
françai~~s~~	française	espagnol	espagnole

1 Vive la différence!

PARLER/ÉCRIRE People can be friends and yet be quite different. Describe the girls named in parentheses, indicating that they are not like their friends.

▶ Jean-Marc est blond. (Mélanie)   **Mélanie n'est pas blonde.**

1. Jean-Louis est blond. (Carole)
2. Paul est petit. (Mireille)
3. Éric est beau. (Marthe)
4. Jérôme est grand. (Louise)
5. Michel est riche. (Émilie)
6. André est français. (Lisa)
7. Antonio est espagnol. (Céline)
8. Bill est américain. (Julie)

VOCABULAIRE La description

Voici Olivier.

Voici Sophie.

ADJECTIFS

amusant	amusing, fun	Il est **amusant**.	Elle est **amusante**.
intelligent	intelligent	Il est **intelligent**.	Elle est **intelligente**.
intéressant	interesting	Il est **intéressant**.	Elle est **intéressante**.
méchant	mean, nasty	Il n'est pas **méchant**.	Elle n'est pas **méchante**.
bête	silly, dumb	Il n'est pas **bête**.	Elle n'est pas **bête**.
sympathique	nice, pleasant	Il est **sympathique**.	Elle est **sympathique**.
timide	timid	Il est **timide**.	Elle n'est pas **timide**.
gentil (gentille)	nice, kind	Il est **gentil**.	Elle est **gentille**.
mignon (mignonne)	cute	Il est **mignon**.	Elle est **mignonne**.
sportif (sportive)	athletic	Il est **sportif**.	Elle est **sportive**.

ADVERBES

assez	rather	Nous sommes **assez** intelligents.
très	very	Vous n'êtes pas **très** sportifs!

2 Oui ou non?

PARLER In your opinion, do the following people have the suggested traits? (Note: These traits are given in the masculine form only.)

▶ le prince William / intéressant?

> Il est intéressant.

> Il n'est pas intéressant.

1. le Président / sympathique?
2. Venus Williams / sportif?
3. ma copine / gentil?
4. Britney Spears / mignon?

5. Oprah Winfrey / intelligent?
6. Einstein / bête?
7. Jay Leno / amusant?
8. le prof / méchant?

3 Descriptions

PARLER Select one of the following characters. Using words from the **Vocabulaire,** describe this character in two affirmative or negative sentences.

▶ Frankenstein
   Il est très méchant.
   Il n'est pas très mignon.

1. Tarzan
2. King Kong
3. Big Bird
4. Batman
5. Miss Piggy
6. Wonder Woman
7. Charlie Brown
8. Blanche-Neige (*Snow White*)
9. Garfield
10. Snoopy

4 L'idéal

PARLER/ÉCRIRE Now you have the chance to describe your ideal people. Use two adjectives for each one.

1. Le copain idéal est … et …
2. La copine idéale est … et …
3. Le professeur idéal est … et …
4. L'étudiant idéal est … et …
5. L'étudiante idéale est … et …

B Les adjectifs: le pluriel

Compare the forms of the adjectives in heavy print as they describe singular and plural nouns.

SINGULAR

Paul est **intelligent** et **timide**.
Alice est **intelligente** et **timide**.

PLURAL

Paul et Éric sont **intelligents** et **timides**.
Alice et Claire sont **intelligentes** et **timides**.

In written French, plural adjectives are usually formed as follows:

> SINGULAR ADJECTIVE + **-s** = PLURAL ADJECTIVE

→ If the masculine singular adjective already ends in **-s**, there is no change in the plural form.

Patrick est **français**.

BUT: Anne est **française**.

Patrick et Daniel sont **français**.

Anne et Alice sont **françaises**.

NOTE DE PRONONCIATION: Because the final **-s** of plural adjectives is silent, singular and plural adjectives sound the same.

SUMMARY: Forms of regular adjectives

	MASCULINE	FEMININE	also:	
SINGULAR	**-** grand	**-e** grand**e**	timide	timide
PLURAL	**-s** grand**s**	**-es** grand**es**	français	français**es**

5 Une question de personnalité

PARLER/ÉCRIRE Indicate whether or not the following people exhibit the personality traits in parentheses. (These traits are given in the masculine singular form only. Make the necessary agreements.)

▶ Alice et Thérèse aiment parler en public. (timide?)

1. Claire et Valérie sont très populaires. (amusant?)
2. Robert et Jean-Luc n'aiment pas danser. (timide?)
3. Catherine et Martine aiment jouer au foot. (sportif?)
4. Laure et Léa ont un «A» en français. (intelligent?)
5. Thomas et Vincent n'aiment pas le jogging. (sportif?)
6. Les voisins n'aiment pas parler avec nous. (sympathique?)

Elles ne sont pas timides.

Vocabulaire **Les adjectifs de nationalité**

américain	*American*	**italien (italienne)**	*Italian*
mexicain	*Mexican*	**canadien (canadienne)**	*Canadian*
français	*French*	**japonais**	*Japanese*
anglais	*English*	**chinois**	*Chinese*
espagnol	*Spanish*		
suisse	*Swiss*		

→ Words that describe nationality are adjectives and take adjective endings.

Monsieur Katagiri est **japonais.**

Kumi et Michiko sont **japonaises.**

Vocabulaire **Expression pour la conversation**

> J'habite à Québec.

> Alors, tu es canadien.

▶ *How to introduce a conclusion:*

alors   *so, then*   —J'habite à Québec.
                               —**Alors,** tu es canadien!

6 *Quelle nationalité?*

PARLER Ask where the following people live and what their nationalities are. A friend will answer you.

> ▶ —Où habitent Lois et Kim?
> —Elles habitent à Miami.
> —Alors, elles sont américaines?
> —Mais oui, elles sont américaines.

▶ Lois et Kim	1. Jim et Bob	2. Léa et Aline
Miami	Liverpool	Toulouse
américain	anglais	français
3. Clara et Tere	4. Luc et Paul	5. ??
Madrid	Montréal	??
espagnol	??	??

7 **Les nationalités**

PARLER/ÉCRIRE Give the nationalities of the following people.

> ▶ Silvia et Maria sont de Rome.
> **Elles sont italiennes.**

1. Lise et Nathalie étudient à Québec.
2. Michael et Dennis sont de Liverpool.
3. Luis et Paco étudient à Madrid.
4. Isabel et Carmen travaillent à Acapulco.
5. Yoko et Kumi sont de Tokyo.
6. Monsieur et Madame Chen habitent à Beijing.
7. Jean-Pierre et Claude sont de Genève.
8. Françoise et Sylvie travaillent à Paris.

C La place des adjectifs

Note the position of the adjectives in the sentences on the right.

Philippe a une voiture.	Il a une voiture **anglaise.**
Denise invite des copains.	Elle invite des copains **américains.**
Voici un livre.	Voici un livre **intéressant.**
J'ai des amies.	J'ai des amies **sympathiques.**

In French, adjectives usually come AFTER the noun they modify, according to the pattern:

ARTICLE	+	NOUN	+	ADJECTIVE
une		voiture		**française**
des		copains		**intéressants**

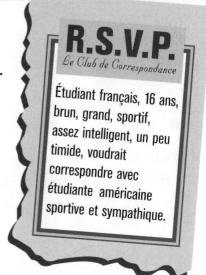

R.S.V.P.
Le Club de Correspondance

Étudiant français, 16 ans, brun, grand, sportif, assez intelligent, un peu timide, voudrait correspondre avec étudiante américaine sportive et sympathique.

8 Préférences personnelles

PARLER For each person or object below, choose among the characteristics in parentheses. Indicate your preference.

▶ avoir un copain (sympathique, intelligent, sportif)
Je préfère avoir un copain intelligent.

1. avoir une copine (amusante, mignonne, intelligente)
2. avoir un professeur (gentil, intelligent, amusant)
3. avoir des voisins (sympathiques, intéressants, riches)
4. avoir une voiture (moderne, confortable, rapide)
5. avoir une calculatrice (japonaise, américaine, française)
6. avoir une montre (suisse, japonaise, française)
7. dîner dans un restaurant (italien, chinois, français)
8. regarder un film (intéressant, amusant, intelligent)
9. travailler avec des personnes (gentilles, amusantes, sérieuses)
10. faire un voyage avec des gens (amusants, riches, sympathiques)

9 Qui se ressemble ...

(Birds of a feather ...)

PARLER Say that the following people have friends, relatives, or acquaintances with the same personality or nationality.

▶ Claire est anglaise. (un copain)
Elle a un copain anglais.

1. Jean-Pierre est sympathique. (des cousines)
2. La prof est intelligente. (des étudiants)
3. Madame Simon est intéressante. (des voisines)
4. Alice est américaine. (des copines)
5. Véronique est amusante. (un frère)
6. Michel est sportif. (une soeur)
7. Pedro est espagnol. (des camarades)
8. Antonio est mexicain. (une copine)
9. Bernard est sportif. (un voisin)

Qui se ressemble s'assemble.

Birds of a feather flock together.

⑩ Préférences internationales

PARLER/ÉCRIRE Choose an item from Column A and indicate your preference as to country of origin by choosing an adjective from Column B. Be sure to make the necessary agreement.

A	B
la musique	anglais
la cuisine	américain
les voitures	français
les ordinateurs	mexicain
les appareils-photo	chinois
les CD	japonais
les restaurants	italien

Je préfère …

> Je préfère les voitures italiennes.

PRONONCIATION

Les consonnes finales

/-/   /d/

blon**d**   blon**de**

As you know, when the last letter of a word is a consonant, that consonant is often silent. But when a word ends in "**e**," the consonant before it is pronounced. As you practice the following adjectives, be sure to distinguish between the masculine and the feminine forms.

MASCULINE ADJECTIVE *(no final consonant sound)*		FEMININE ADJECTIVE *(final consonant sound)*
Répétez: blon**d**	/d/	blon**de**
gran**d**		gran**de**
peti**t**	/t/	peti**te**
amusan**t**		amusan**te**
françai**s**	/z/	françai**se**
anglai**s**		anglai**se**
américai**n**	/n/	américai**ne**
canadie**n**		canadie**nne**

À votre tour!

OBJECTIFS

Now you can …
• describe your personality
• describe other people: their nationality, their physical appearance and their personality

1  Allô!

PARLER Valérie is phoning some friends. Match her questions on the left with her friends' answers on the right.

1. Ton frère aime jouer au foot?

2. Cécile et Sophie sont mignonnes, n'est-ce pas?

3. Pourquoi est-ce que tu invites Olivier?

4. Tu aimes la classe?

5. Tu as des cousins?

a. Oui, et intelligentes aussi!

b. Parce qu'il est amusant et sympathique.

c. Oui, j'ai un professeur très intéressant.

d. Oui, il est très sportif.

e. Oui, mais ils ne sont pas très sympathiques.

2 Créa-dialogue

PARLER With your classmates, talk about the people of different nationalities you may know or objects you may own.

des cousins

mignon?

▶ —J'ai des <u>cousins mexicains</u>.
—<u>Ils sont mignons?</u>
—<u>Oui, ils sont très mignons</u>.

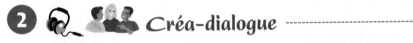

1. une voisine	2. un prof	3. des copines	4. un livre	5. une voiture
blond?	sympathique?	sportif?	intéressant?	grand?

③ Avis de recherche *(Missing person's bulletin)*

ÉCRIRE The two people in the pictures to the right have been reported missing. Describe each one as well as you can, using your imagination. Mention:

- the (approximate) age of the person
- the way he/she looks
- personality traits
- other features or characteristics

④ Descriptions

PARLER Give an oral presentation describing your favorite actor **(un acteur)** and actress **(une actrice).** In your descriptions, include:

- the person's name
- approximate age
- nationality
- physical appearance
- personality traits
- a film he/she plays in *(Il/elle joue dans …)*

You may wish to show photos of the two actors you have chosen to talk about.

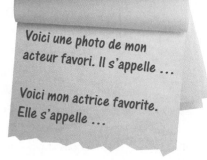

Voici une photo de mon acteur favori. Il s'appelle …

Voici mon actrice favorite. Elle s'appelle …

⑤ Composition: Fête d'anniversaire

ÉCRIRE You have invited Jean-Pierre, a French exchange student, to your upcoming birthday party. Write him an e-mail describing two of the guests that he will meet at the party: a boy and a girl. For each person (who may be real or imaginary), provide such information as name, age, nationality, physical appearance, and personality traits.

? Il y a un garçon qui s'appelle …

? Il y a une fille qui s'appelle …

LEÇON 12

La voiture de Roger

Dans la <u>rue</u>, il y a une voiture <u>rouge</u>. — *street/red*

C'est une petite voiture. C'est une voiture de sport.

Dans la rue, il y a aussi un café. Au café, il y a un jeune homme.

Il s'appelle Roger.

C'est le <u>propriétaire</u> de la voiture rouge. — *owner*

Une jeune fille <u>entre dans</u> le café. — *enters*

Elle s'appelle Véronique.

C'est <u>l'amie de Roger</u>. — *Roger's friend*

Véronique parle à Roger.

Véronique: Tu as une <u>nouvelle</u> voiture, n'est-ce pas? — *new*

Roger: Oui, j'ai une nouvelle voiture.

Véronique: Est-ce qu'elle est grande ou petite?

Roger: C'est une petite voiture.

Véronique: De quelle couleur est-elle?

Roger: C'est une voiture rouge.

Véronique: Est-ce que c'est une voiture italienne?

Roger: Oui, c'est une voiture italienne. Mais <u>dis donc</u>, — *hey there*
Véronique, tu es <u>vraiment</u> très curieuse! — *really*

Véronique: Et toi, tu n'es pas <u>assez curieux</u>! — *curious enough*

Roger: Ah bon? Pourquoi?

Véronique: Pourquoi?! … Regarde la <u>contractuelle</u> là-bas! — *meter maid*

Roger: Ah, zut alors!

Compréhension

1. Qu'est-ce qu'il y a dans la rue?
2. Est-ce que la voiture est grande?
3. Comment s'appelle le jeune homme?
4. Où est-il?
5. Comment s'appelle la jeune fille?
6. De quelle couleur est la voiture?

NOTE *culturelle*

Les Français et la voiture

France is one of the leading producers of automobiles in the world. The two automakers, **Renault** and **Peugeot-Citroën**, manufacture a variety of models ranging from sports cars to mini-vans and buses.

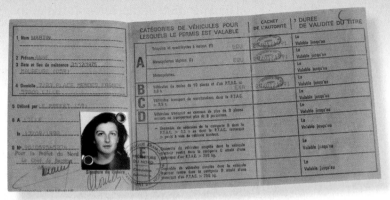

To obtain a driver's license (**un permis de conduire**) in France, you must be eighteen years old and pass a very difficult driving test. French teenagers can, however, begin to drive at the age of sixteen, as long as they take lessons at an accredited driving school (**auto-école**) and are accompanied by an adult. Lessons in these schools are expensive and it may cost you 300 euros before you pass the exam and get your official license.

The French driver's license is a **permis à points** (license with points). A new license carries with it 12 points. When a driver commits a traffic violation, such as speeding or not wearing a seat belt, a corresponding number of points is subtracted from the license. If a driver loses all 12 points, the license is revoked and that person can no longer drive.

OPINION PERSONNELLE

Do you think that the **permis à points** is a good idea? Explain your position.

A Les couleurs

Note the form and position of the color words in the following sentences:

Alice a un vélo **bleu.**   *Alice has a **blue** bicycle.*
Nous avons des chemises **bleues.**   *We have **blue** shirts.*

Names of colors are ADJECTIVES and take adjective ENDINGS. They come *after* the noun.

VOCABULAIRE Les couleurs

De quelle couleur ... ?   *What color ... ?*   **—De quelle couleur** est la moto?
                                                              —Elle est rouge.

blanc	noir	bleu	rouge	jaune	vert	gris	marron	orange	rose
(blanche)	(noire)	(bleue)	(rouge)	(jaune)	(verte)	(grise)	(marron)	(orange)	(rose)

→ The colors **orange** and **marron** are INVARIABLE. They do not take any endings.
  un sac **orange**   des sacs **orange**
  un tee-shirt **marron**   une chemise **marron**

(Purpil)
violet
violette

---

1 De quelle couleur?

PARLER Ask your classmates to name the colors of things they own. (They may invent answers.)

▶ ta chambre?

> De quelle couleur est ta chambre?

> Elle est blanche et bleue.

1. ta bicyclette?
2. ton tee-shirt?
3. ton appareil-photo?
4. ta montre?
5. ta raquette de tennis?
6. ton livre de français?
7. ton chien (chat)?

2 Possessions

PARLER Ask what objects or pets the following people own. A classmate will answer, giving the color.

▶ —Est-ce que Léa
   a un chat?
  —Oui, elle a
   un chat jaune.

▶ Léa

1. Mme Mercier

2. Marc

3. Delphine

4. Sophie

5. Éric

3 *L'arche de Noé*

PARLER/ÉCRIRE Noah's ark has just landed.
Give the colors of the animals as they get off the ship.

▶ le chien   **Le chien est blanc.**

1. le chat
2. l'éléphant *(m.)*
3. la panthère
4. le zèbre
5. le flamant
6. le cardinal
7. le lion
8. le perroquet

B La place des adjectifs avant le nom

Compare the position of the adjectives in the following sentences.

Voici une voiture **française.**   Voici une **petite** voiture.
Paul est un garçon **intelligent.**   Pierre est un **beau** garçon.

A few adjectives like **petit** and **beau** come BEFORE the noun they modify.

→ The article **des** often becomes **de** before an adjective. Compare:

      des voitures → **de** petites voitures

VOCABULAIRE Les adjectifs qui précèdent le nom

beau (belle)	*beautiful, handsome*	Regarde la **belle** voiture!
joli	*pretty*	Qui est la **jolie** fille avec André?
grand	*big, large, tall*	Nous habitons dans un **grand** appartement.
petit	*little, small, short*	Ma soeur a un **petit** ordinateur.
bon (bonne)	*good*	Tu es un **bon** copain.
mauvais	*bad*	Patrick est un **mauvais** élève.

→ There is a LIAISON after the above adjectives when the noun which follows
  begins with a vowel sound. Note that in liaison:
    • the "d" of **grand** is pronounced /t/: **un grand appartement**
    • **bon** is pronounced like **bonne: un bon élève**

④ Opinions personnelles

PARLER/ÉCRIRE Give your opinion about the following people and things, using the adjectives **bon** or **mauvais.**

▶ Julia Roberts est (une) actrice *(actress)*.
   Julia Roberts est une bonne actrice (une mauvaise actrice).

1. *Titanic* est un film.
2. «60 Minutes» est un programme de télé.
3. Britney Spears est (une) chanteuse.
4. Matt Damon est (un) acteur.
5. Dracula est une personne.
6. Les Yankees sont une équipe *(team)* de baseball.
7. Les Lakers sont une équipe de basket.
8. Je suis un(e) élève.
9. *Discovering French* est un livre.

VOCABULAIRE Expressions pour la conversation

▶ *How to get someone's attention:*

Dis!	*Say! Hey!*	**Dis**, Éric, est-ce que tu as une voiture?
Dis donc!	*Hey there!*	**Dis donc**, est-ce que tu veux faire une promenade avec moi?

⑤ Dialogue

PARLER Christine asks her cousin Thomas if he has certain things. He responds affirmatively, describing each one. Play both roles.

▶ une chaîne hi-fi (petite)   ▶ un scooter (italien)

1. une télé (petite)
2. une guitare (espagnole)
3. un vélo (rouge)
4. une calculatrice (petite)
5. un sac (grand)
6. des livres (intéressants)
7. une copine (amusante)
8. une mobylette (bleue)
9. une montre (belle)
10. un copain (bon)
11. une cousine (jolie)
12. une radio (japonaise)

C Il est ou c'est?

When describing a person or thing, French speakers use two different constructions,
il est (elle est) and **c'est.**

			Il est + ADJECTIVE **Elle est** + ADJECTIVE	**C'es**t + ARTICLE + NOUN (+ ADJECTIVE)
	Roger	*He is …*	**Il est** amusant.	**C'est** un copain. **C'est** un copain amusant.
	Véronique	*She is …*	**Elle est** sportive.	**C'est** une amie. **C'est** une bonne amie.
	un scooter	*It is …*	**Il est** joli.	**C'est** un scooter français. **C'est** un bon scooter.
	une voiture	*It is …*	**Elle est** petite.	**C'est** une voiture anglaise. **C'est** une petite voiture.

→ Note the corresponding plural forms:

(Pierre et Marc)	*They are …*	**Ils sont** amusants.	**Ce sont** des copains.
(Claire et Anne)	*They are …*	**Elles sont** timides.	**Ce sont** des copines.

→ In negative sentences, **c'est** becomes **ce n'est pas.**

Ce n'est pas un mauvais élève.   *He's not a bad student.*
Ce n'est pas une Peugeot.   *It's not a Peugeot.*

→ **C'est** is also used with names of people

C'est Véronique.   **C'est** Madame Lamblet.

SCOOTERS PEUGEOT

6 Descriptions

PARLER/ÉCRIRE Complete the following descriptions with **Il est, Elle est,**
or **C'est,** as appropriate.

Adj

A. Roger
Noun
1. _____ grand.
2. Il est brun.
3. C'est un garçon sympathique.
4. C'est un mauvais élève.

B. Véronique
5. _____ une fille brune.
6. _____ une amie sympathique.
7. _____ très amusante.
8. _____ assez grande.

C. La voiture de Roger
9. _____ une voiture moderne.
10. _____ une petite voiture.
11. _____ rouge.
12. _____ très rapide.

D. Le scooter de Véronique
13. Il est bleu et blanc.
14. _____ très économique.
15. _____ un joli scooter.
16. _____ assez confortable.

D Les expressions impersonnelles avec *c'est*

Note the use of **c'est** in the following sentences.

J'aime parler français.   **C'est** intéressant.   *It's interesting.*
Je n'aime pas travailler le week-end.   **Ce n'est pas** amusant.   *It's no(t) fun.*

To express an opinion on a general topic, French speakers use the construction:

C'est
Ce n'est pas } + MASCULINE ADJECTIVE

VOCABULAIRE Opinions

C'est …   *It's … , That's …*
Ce n'est pas …   *It's not … , That's not …*

vrai	*true*	**chouette**	*neat*
faux	*false*	**super**	*great*
		génial	*terrific*
facile	*easy*	**pénible**	*a pain, annoying*
difficile	*hard, difficult*	**drôle**	*funny*

→ To express an opinion, French speakers also use adverbs like **bien** and **mal**.

C'est bien.   *That's good.*   Tu étudies? **C'est bien.**
C'est mal.   *That's bad.*   Alain n'étudie pas. **C'est mal.**

H.W.

7   Vrai ou faux?

PARLER Imagine that your little sister is talking about where certain cities are located. Tell her whether her statements are right or wrong.

1. Paris est en Italie.
2. Los Angeles est en Californie.
3. Genève est en Italie.
4. Dakar est en Afrique.
5. Fort-de-France est au Canada.
6. Québec est en France.
7. Port-au-Prince est en Haïti.
8. Montréal est au Canada.

8  *Opinion personnelle*

PARLER Ask your classmates if they like to do the following things.
They will answer, using an expression from the **Vocabulaire.**

▶ nager

> **Tu aimes nager?**
>
> **Oui, c'est génial!**
> (Non, c'est difficile!)

1. téléphoner
2. parler en public
3. parler français
4. danser
5. voyager
6. dîner en ville
7. jouer aux jeux vidéo
8. étudier le week-end
9. écouter la musique classique
10. surfer sur l'Internet
11. télécharger de la musique

PRONONCIATION   **ch** /ʃ/

Les lettres «ch»

The letters "**ch**" are usually pronounced like the English "*sh.*"

Répétez: <u>ch</u>ien   <u>ch</u>at   <u>ch</u>ose   mar<u>ch</u>e
            <u>ch</u>ouette   <u>ch</u>ocolat   affi<u>ch</u>e
            Mi<u>ch</u>èle a un <u>ch</u>at et deux <u>ch</u>iens.

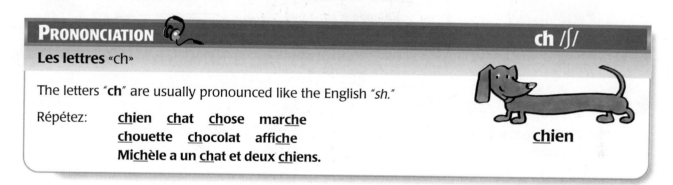

<u>ch</u>ien

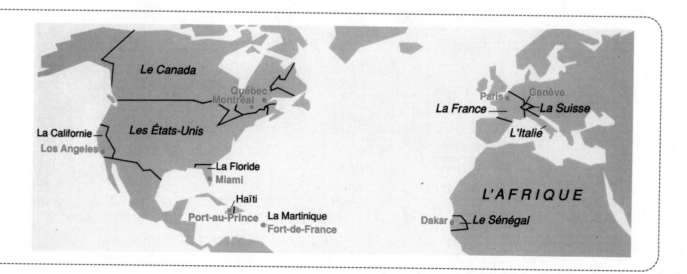

À votre tour!

OBJECTIFS

Now you can …
- express your opinions about people and activities
- describe everyday objects: their size and color

1 Allô!

PARLER Christophe is phoning some friends. Match his questions on the left with his friends' answers on the right.

1 De quelle couleur est ton vélo?

2 Ta raquette est bleue?

3 Tu aimes regarder la télé?

4 C'est un magazine français?

5 Philippe n'aime pas parler en public?

a Non, il est canadien.

b C'est vrai! Il est très timide.

c Non, elle est blanche.

d Oui, c'est amusant.

e Il est vert.

2 Créa-dialogue

PARLER There has been a burglary in the rue Saint-Pierre. By walkie-talkie, two detectives are describing what they see. Play both roles.

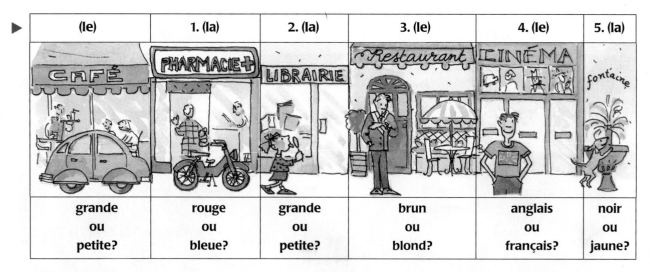

(le)	1. (la)	2. (la)	3. (le)	4. (le)	5. (la)
grande ou petite?	rouge ou bleue?	grande ou petite?	brun ou blond?	anglais ou français?	noir ou jaune?

▶ DÉTECTIVE 1: **Qu'est-ce qu'il y a devant <u>le café</u>?**
DÉTECTIVE 2: **Il y a <u>une voiture</u>.**

DÉTECTIVE 1: <u>**Elle**</u> **est <u>grande</u> ou <u>petite</u>?**
DÉTECTIVE 2: **C'est <u>une petite voiture</u>.**

3 Faisons connaissance! --------------------------------

PARLER Try to find out which students have the same interests you do. Select two activities you enjoy from Column A and ask a classmate if he/she likes to do them. Your classmate will answer yes or no, using an appropriate expression from Column B.

A	B
téléphoner	chouette
envoyer des mails	super
surfer sur l'Internet	génial
jouer aux jeux vidéo	amusant
jouer au foot	intéressant
voyager	pénible
organiser des boums	drôle
parler avec les voisins	difficile
parler français en classe	facile
étudier pour l'examen	
travailler dans le jardin	

Tu aimes voyager?

Oui, c'est amusant.

Tu aimes étudier pour l'examen?

Non, c'est difficile.

4 Dialogue: Un chien! --------------------------------

PARLER Imagine that your classmate has just received a dog for his/her birthday. You want to know more about this new pet. Ask your classmate ...

- what the dog's name is
- how old he is
- what color he is
- if he is a small dog or a big dog
- if he is cute
- if he is a mean dog (un chien méchant)

5 Composition: Une voiture --------------------------------

ÉCRIRE Describe your parents' car or any other car you have seen recently. Provide the following information, writing a sentence for each of these points.

- make/model
- color
- age
- country of origin
- size (petit? grand?)
- other characteristics (confortable? rapide? économique?)

LESSON REVIEW
CLASSZONE.COM

Tests de contrôle

By taking the following tests, you can check your progress in French and also prepare for the unit test. Write your answers on a separate sheet of paper.

Review...
• names of objects: pp. 140, 142, and 144

❶ The right object

Name the following objects. Make sure to use the appropriate article: **un** or **une.**

1.   2.   3.   4.   5.

6.   7.   8.   9.   10.

Review ...
• être and avoir: pp. 84 and 152

❷ Être and avoir

Complete the following sentences with the appropriate forms of **être** or **avoir.**

1. Tu — une chaîne hi-fi.

2. Tu — français.

3. Céline — quinze ans.

4. Nous — soif.

5. Thomas — sympathique.

6. Mes copains — amusants.

7. Vous — un portable.

8. Est-ce que vous — faim?

Review ...
• adjectives: pp. 164-165, 166-167

❸ The right adjectives

Complete the following descriptions with the appropriate forms of the adjectives in parentheses.

1. (français)	une amie …	des copains …
2. (américain)	des filles …	des garçons …
3. (sympathique)	une copine …	des personnes …
4. (intelligent)	une personne …	des amies …
5. (sportif)	une fille …	des copines …
6. (gentil)	des amies …	des copains …
7. (rouge)	une voiture …	un vélo …
8. (blanc)	une moto …	des bicyclettes …
9. (japonais)	une mini-chaîne …	des ordinateurs …

4 The right choice

Complete the following sentences with the appropriate option suggested in parentheses.

(Note: ⊬ means that no word is needed.)

1. Qui est — fille là-bas? **(le, la, l')**
2. — ordinateur est sur la table. **(L', Le, La)**
3. Jean-Paul aime — musique classique. **(⊬, la, une)**
4. Léa a — copines canadiennes. **(⊬, une, des)**
5. Philippe n'a pas — portable. **(⊬, un, de)**

6. Ma mère a une voiture — . **(jaune, jolie, grande)**
7. Nous avons un — professeur. **(bon, sympathique, intéressant)**

8. Voici Catherine. — une amie sympathique. **(Il est, Elle est, C'est)**
9. Voici Marc. — canadien. **(Il est, Elle est, C'est)**

Review...
- definite and indefinite articles: pp. 153-156, 158

Review ...
- position of adjectives: pp. 168, 175

Review ...
- il est or c'est: p. 177

5 Composition: Mon cousin / Ma cousine

Write a paragraph of five or six sentences describing one of your cousins, real or imaginary. Give your cousin's name, nationality and age, plus a brief description. Say why your cousin is interesting (or not interesting). Use only vocabulary and expressions that you know in French.

STRATEGY Writing

a) Make a list of the things you want to say about your cousin.

b) Organize your ideas and write your description.

c) Check that all the adjectives have the right endings.

nom: _____

nationalité: _____

âge: _____

description physique: _____

personnalité: _____

intéressant(e)? (pourquoi) _____

Vocabulaire

POUR COMMUNIQUER

Talking about people

Qui est-ce?	*Who is it?*
Comment est il/elle?	*What is he/she like?*
Quel âge a-t-il/elle?	*How old is he/she?*

Talking about things

Qu'est-ce que c'est?	*What is it? What's that?*	**Il y a …**	*There is …, There are …*
C'est …	*It's …*	**Est-ce qu'il y a …?**	*Is there …? Are there …?*
		Qu'est-ce qu'il y a …?	*What is there …?*
Est-ce que tu as …?	*Do you have …?*		
Oui, j'ai …	*Yes, I have …*	**De quelle couleur …?**	*What color …?*
Regarde ça.	*Look at that.*		
Quoi?	*What?*		
Ça, là-bas.	*That, over there.*		

Expressing opinions

C'est …   *It's …*

bien	*good*	**drôle**	*funny*	**génial**	*terrific*	**super**	*great*
chouette	*neat*	**facile**	*easy*	**mal**	*bad*	**vrai**	*true*
difficile	*hard, difficult*	**faux**	*false*	**pénible**	*a pain, annoying*		

MOTS ET EXPRESSIONS

Les personnes

un camarade	*classmate*	**une camarade**	*classmate*	**un prof**	*teacher*	**une prof**	*teacher*
un élève	*pupil, student*	**une élève**	*pupil, student*	**un professeur**	*teacher*	**une personne**	*person*
un étudiant	*student*	**une étudiante**	*student*	**un voisin**	*neighbor*	**une voisine**	*neighbor*

Quelques possessions

un appareil-photo	*camera*	**une affiche**	*poster*
un baladeur	*portable CD player*	**une auto**	*car*
un cahier	*notebook*	**une bicyclette**	*bicycle*
un CD	*CD*	**une calculatrice**	*calculator*
un crayon	*pencil*	**une cassette vidéo**	*videotape*
un DVD	*DVD*	**une chaîne hi-fi**	*stereo set*
un livre	*book*	**une chose**	*thing*
un objet	*object*	**une guitare**	*guitar*
un ordinateur	*computer*	**une mini-chaîne**	*compact stereo*
un portable	*cell phone*	**une mobylette**	*motorbike, moped*
un sac	*bag*	**une montre**	*watch*
un scooter	*motor scooter*	**une moto**	*motorcycle*
un stylo	*pen*	**une radio**	*radio*
un téléphone	*phone*	**une radiocassette**	*boom box*
un vélo	*bicycle, bike*	**une raquette**	*tennis racket*
		une télé	*TV set*
		une voiture	*car*

La chambre

un bureau	desk	**une chaise**	chair	**une porte**	door
un lit	bed	**une fenêtre**	window	**une table**	table
		une lampe	lamp		

Où?

dans	in	**devant**	in front of	**sur**	on, on top of
derrière	behind, in back of	**sous**	under		

La description

amusant(e)	amusing, fun	**jeune**	young		
beau (belle)*	beautiful, handsome	**joli(e)***	pretty		
bête	silly, dumb	**mauvais(e)***	bad		
blond(e)	blonde	**méchant(e)**	mean, nasty		
bon (bonne)*	good	**mignon (mignonne)**	cute		
brun(e)	brown, dark-haired	**petit(e)***	small, little, short	**assez**	rather
gentil (gentille)	nice, kind	**sportif (sportive)**	athletic	**très**	very
grand(e)*	big, large, tall	**sympathique**	nice, pleasant		
intelligent(e)	intelligent, smart	**timide**	timid, shy		
intéressant(e)	interesting				

* Adjectives that come before the noun

Les adjectifs de nationalité

américain(e)	American	**espagnol(e)**	Spanish	**mexicain(e)**	Mexican
anglais(e)	English	**français(e)**	French	**suisse**	Swiss
canadien (canadienne)	Canadian	**italien (italienne)**	Italian		
chinois(e)	Chinese	**japonais(e)**	Japanese		

Les couleurs

blanc (blanche)	white	**jaune**	yellow	**orange***	orange	**vert(e)**	green
bleu(e)	blue	**marron***	brown	**rose**	pink		
gris(e)	grey	**noir(e)**	black	**rouge**	red		

* Invariable adjectives

Verbes réguliers en -er

marcher	to work, to run (to function)
	to walk

Verbes irréguliers

avoir	to have
avoir faim	to be hungry
avoir soif	to be thirsty
avoir … ans	to be … (years old)

Expressions utiles

Dis!	Say! Hey!	**Je sais.**	I know.	**lundi**	on Monday
Dis donc!	Hey there!	**Je ne sais pas.**	I don't know.	**le lundi**	on Mondays
alors	so, then	**Si!**	Yes!	**le week-end**	on weekends

VOCABULAIRE SUPPLÉMENTAIRE: L'informatique

un CD-ROM (cédérom)	CD-ROM	**une imprimante**	printer	**chatter**	to chat (online)
un clavier	keyboard	**une souris**	mouse	**envoyer un mail**	to send an e-mail
un écran	screen			**surfer sur l'Internet**	to surf the Internet
un jeu d'ordinateur	computer game			**télécharger**	to download
un mail (un mél)	e-mail				
un ordinateur portable	laptop				
un PC	PC				

TEST PREP
CLASSZONE.COM

FLASHCARDS
AND MORE!

Petit catalogue des compliments ... et des insultes

LANGUAGE COMPARISONS

Over the centuries, French and English have influenced one another.

- Which of the compliments and insults did French borrow from English? Which word has English borrowed from French? Sometimes French and English express themselves in different ways.

- Which of the animal comparisons on the next page are the same in French and English? Which are different?

LES ANIMAUX et LE LANGAGE

Selon° toi, est-ce que les animaux ont une personnalité? Pour les Français, les animaux ont des qualités et des défauts,° comme° nous. Devine° comment on° complète les phrases suivantes° en français.

1 Philippe n'aime pas étudier. Il préfère dormir.° Il est paresseux° comme° …

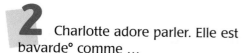
un tigre   **un chat**   **un lézard**

2 Charlotte adore parler. Elle est bavarde° comme …

une poule   **une pie**   **un lion**

3 Isabelle est une excellente élève. Elle a une mémoire extraordinaire. Elle a une mémoire de (d') …

éléphant   **hippopotame**   **kangourou**

4 Le petit frère de Christine est jeune, mais il est très intelligent. Il est malin° comme …

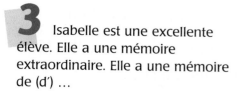  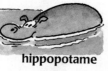 
un cheval   **un singe**   **une girafe**

5 Où est Jacques? Il n'est pas prêt!° Oh là là! Il est lent° comme …

une tortue   **un poisson**   **un rhinocéros**

6 Nicole a très, très faim. Elle a une faim de (d') …

lion   **ours**   **loup**

Selon *According to*   **défauts** *shortcomings*   **comme** *like*   **Devine** *Guess*   **on** *one*   **phrases suivantes** *following sentences*   **dormir** *to sleep* **paresseux** *lazy*   **comme** *as*   **bavarde** *talkative*   **malin** *clever*   **prêt** *ready*   **lent** *slow*

Voici les réponses:
1. un lézard 2. une pie 3. éléphant 4. un singe 5. une tortue 6. loup

Le scooter, c'est génial!

Je m'appelle Mélanie et j'ai 15 ans. J'ai un scooter. C'est un cadeau° d'anniversaire de ma grand-mère. Il est rouge et il est très confortable.

Ma copine Élodie a une mobylette. C'est une MBK. Nous allons° au collège ensemble.° Nous avons le BSR et nous sommes prudentes.° Nous portons° un casque° et nous respectons la limite de vitesse:° 45 kilomètres l'heure.

Le week-end, nous allons au centre-ville. Nous n'avons pas de problème de stationnement.° Quand il fait beau, nous allons à la campagne.° Quand nous sommes sur nos° petites machines, nous avons l'impression de liberté. Le scooter, c'est génial!

cadeau *gift* **allons** *go* **ensemble** *together* **prudentes** *careful*
portons *wear* **casque** *helmet* **vitesse** *speed* **stationnement** *parking*
campagne *country* **nos** *our*

Compréhension: vrai ou faux

1. Mélanie a un scooter.
2. Élodie a un scooter aussi.
3. Quand Mélanie est en scooter, elle porte un casque.
4. Avec un scooter, on a souvent un problème de stationnement.
5. En scooter, Mélanie a l'impression de liberté.

Et vous?

1. What are the advantages or disadvantages of owning a moped or a scooter?
2. What would you do if you had a motor scooter? How would this change your habits?

CONNEXIONS

Go to the Internet site of a French manufacturer of mopeds and scooters and make a poster showing some of the products you find.

Mobylette . . . ou scooter?

Modèle: MBK Club
Couleurs: noir, gris, bleu
Prix: 680 €

Modèle: MBK Booster Spirit
Couleurs: rouge, bleu, noir
Prix: 1 600 €

Et vous?

1. Which of the above would you choose? Use the following in your response:

modèle   *couleur*   *prix en €*   *prix en $*

2. Is it expensive? *(cher, chère)*

3. Why did you choose it?

NOTE culturelle

La mobylette et le scooter

Mopeds and motor scooters are very popular among French teenagers. To drive one, you must be at least 14 years old. If you are under 16, you cannot go over 45 kilometers (about 30 miles) per hour. You must also have a license known as the **BSR** or **Brevet de Sécurité Routière** *(Certificate of Highway Safety)* which you get after a short course of driver's education. And, of course, whenever you are riding, you must wear a helmet!

The most popular makes of mopeds and scooters include Peugeot, Renault, and MBK, all manufactured in France. The term **mobylette** was originally a brand name which French students shortened to **mob.** It now is used to refer to any type of moped.

French teens love their mopeds and their scooters, and they take great care of them. During the week, many students ride them to school. On weekends, they use them to go into town, to get to their sports clubs, or to go for a ride in the country with their friends.

Bonjour, Brigitte!

Chers° copains américains,

Je m'appelle Brigitte Lavie. J'ai quatorze ans. Voici ma photo. Je ne suis pas très grande, mais je ne suis pas petite. Je suis de taille° moyenne.° Je suis brune, mais j'ai les yeux verts. Je suis sportive. J'aime le ski, le jogging et la danse moderne.

J'habite à Toulouse avec ma famille. Mon père travaille dans l'industrie aéronautique. Il est ingénieur.° Ma mère travaille dans une banque. Elle est directrice° du personnel.

J'ai une soeur et un frère. Ma petite soeur s'appelle Élodie. Elle a cinq ans. Elle est très mignonne. Mon frère s'appelle Mathieu. Il a treize ans. Il est pénible. J'ai un chien. Il s'appelle Attila mais il est très gentil (Il est plus gentil que° mon frère!) J'ai aussi deux poissons rouges.° Ils n'ont pas de nom.°

J'ai un baladeur et des quantités de CD. Je n'ai pas de mini-chaîne. J'ai un ordinateur. C'est un cadeau° de ma marraine.° Je surfe sur l'Internet et j'envoie des mails. Je n'ai pas de scooter mais j'ai une mob.

J'ai beaucoup de copains, mais je n'ai pas de «petit copain».° Ça n'a pas d'importance!° Je suis heureuse° comme ça.°

Amitiés,
Brigitte

Chers *Dear*   **taille** *size*   **moyenne** *average*   **ingénieur** *engineer*   **directrice** *director*
plus gentil que *nicer than*   **poissons rouges** *goldfish*   **nom** *name*   **cadeau** *gift*   **marraine** *godmother*
petit copain *boyfriend*   **Ça n'a pas d'importance!** *It doesn't matter!*   **heureuse** *happy*   **comme ça** *like that*

STRATEGY Reading

Guessing from context As you read French, try to guess the meanings of unfamiliar words before you look at the English equivalents. Often the context provides good hints. For example, Brigitte writes:

> **Je ne suis pas très grande, mais je ne suis pas petite.**
> **Je suis de taille moyenne.**

She is neither tall nor short. She must be about average:

> **de taille moyenne** = *of medium height or size*

Sometimes you know what individual words in an expression mean, but the phrase does not seem to make sense. Then you have to guess at the real meaning. For example, Brigitte writes that she has:

> **deux poissons rouges** *?? red fish??*

If you guessed that these are most likely *goldfish*, you are right!

Activité écrite: Une lettre à Brigitte

Write a letter to Brigitte in which you describe yourself and your family. You may tell her:

- your name and how old you are
- if you are tall or short
- if you like sports, and which ones
- if you have brothers and sisters (and if so, their names and ages)
- if you have pets (and if so, give their names)
- a few things you own
- a few things you like to do

Writing Hint Use Brigitte's letter as a model.

Pour écrire une lettre

To write to a boy, begin with:	**Cher**	**Cher Patrick,**
To write to a girl, begin with:	**Chère**	**Chère Brigitte,**
End your letter with:	**Amicalement,** *(In friendship,)*	
	Amitiés, *(Best regards,)*	

NOTE culturelle

Toulouse

Toulouse, with a population of nearly one million people, is the center of the French aeronautic and space industry. It is in Toulouse that the Airbus planes and the Ariane rockets are being built in cooperation with other European countries.

UNITÉ 5

En ville

LEÇON 13 LE FRANÇAIS PRATIQUE:
La ville et la maison

LEÇON 14 Week-end à Paris

LEÇON 15 Au Café de l'Univers

LEÇON 16 Mes voisins

THÈME ET OBJECTIFS

Visiting a French city

There are many things to do in a city: places to visit, concerts to attend, sports to play.

In this unit, you will learn …

- to describe your city, its public buildings, and places of interest
- to ask for and give directions
- to talk about the various places you go to during the week and on weekends
- to describe your house or apartment

You will also be able …

- to discuss your future plans and say what you are going to do
- to talk about your friends and their families

WEBQUEST
CLASSZONE.COM

La ville et la maison

Accent sur ... les villes françaises

• Today 80% of the French population lives in cities and their surrounding suburbs.

• French cities have a long history. Paris, Lyon, Marseille, and Nice were founded well over two thousand years ago!

• Cities in France differ in urban design from cities in the United States.

—The downtown area **(le centre-ville)** is the historical district with buildings and monuments dating back several centuries. Usually no buildings are taller than six stories. With the many cafés, restaurants, stores, and movie houses, it is a very animated area that attracts many young people.

—The suburbs **(la banlieue)** is where the tall apartment buildings and office buildings are located. Young people who live in the Parisian suburbs often get together in the local shopping mall **(le centre commercial)** which offers shops, cafés, and cinemas.

The largest French cities:

	POPULATION (URBAN AREA)
Paris	11 000 000
Lyon	1 700 000
Lille	1 700 000
Marseille	1 500 000
Toulouse	970 000
Bordeaux	930 000
Nice	900 000
Nantes	700 000
Strasbourg	650 000
Toulon	550 000
Grenoble	500 000
Tours	200 000

Lille

Paris ☆   Strasbourg

Tours
Nantes

LA FRANCE

Lyon

Grenoble

Bordeaux

Nice

Toulouse   Marseille Toulon

Ici, à Tours

Tours est une ville de 200 000 (deux cent mille) habitants située à 200 kilomètres au sud-ouest de Paris. C'est une ville française typique.

L'Hôtel de Ville

Au centre, il y a l'hôtel de ville qui est le <u>bâtiment</u> administratif principal. C'est ici que les gens <u>viennent</u> <u>se marier</u>.

building
come
to get married

La place Plumereau

La place Plumereau est située dans un <u>quartier</u> très ancien. Il y a beaucoup de maisons historiques, et aussi beaucoup de cafés où viennent les jeunes de Tours. C'est un <u>endroit</u> très animé.

district

place

Le Château de Tours

Comme beaucoup de villes françaises, Tours a un château historique. Ce château est une <u>ancienne</u> forteresse royale. Aujourd'hui, c'est un bâtiment administratif.

former

Une maison près de Tours

Les Français qui n'habitent pas dans le centre-ville préfèrent habiter dans une maison individuelle. Cette maison de la région de Tours a deux <u>étages</u>.

floors

A VOCABULAIRE Où habites-tu?

J'habite à Tours.

▶ *How to talk about where one lives:*

Où habites-tu?

J'habite | à Tours.
| à Villeneuve
| dans **une grande ville** *(city, town)*
| dans **un petit village**
| dans **un joli quartier** *(neighborhood)*
| dans **une rue** *(street)* intéressante

Quelle est **ton adresse?**

J'habite | 32, **avenue** Victor Hugo.
| 14, **rue** La Fayette
| 50, **boulevard** Wilson

NOTE culturelle

Le nom des rues

En France, les rues ont très souvent le nom de personnes célèbres,° en particulier écrivains,° artistes et personnalités politiques.

- **Victor Hugo** (1802-1885) est un très grand poète. Il a aussi écrit° *Les Misérables* qui° a inspiré une comédie musicale moderne.

- **La Fayette** (1757-1834) est un aristocrate français. Ami de Georges Washington, il a joué un rôle important pendant la Révolution américaine.

célèbres *famous* **écrivains** *writers* **a écrit** *wrote* **qui** *which*

---

1 Expression personnelle

PARLER/ÉCRIRE Describe where you live by completing the following sentences.

1. J'habite à …
2. Ma ville est (n'est pas) …
   (grande? petite? moderne? jolie?)
   Mon village est (n'est pas) …
   (grand? petit? joli?)
3. Mon quartier est (n'est pas) …
   (intéressant? joli? moderne?)
4. Mon adresse est …
5. Ma ville favorite est …
6. Un jour, je voudrais visiter … *(name of city)*

2 Interview

PARLER/ÉCRIRE You are a French journalist writing an article about living conditions in the United States. Interview a classmate and find out the following information.

1. Where does he/she live?
2. Is his/her city large or small?
3. Is his/her city pretty?
4. What is his/her address?

B VOCABULAIRE Ma ville

▶ *How to talk about one's hometown:*

Dans ma rue, il y a …

un hôtel   un café   un restaurant   un supermarché   un magasin

Dans mon quartier, il y a …

un cinéma   une école   une église   un centre commercial

Dans ma ville, il y a …

une bibliothèque   un théâtre   un musée   un hôpital

Il y a aussi …

une piscine   un parc   un stade   une plage

3 Mon quartier

PARLER Say whether the following places are located in the area where you live. If so, you may want to give the name of the place.

▶ école   **Il y a une école. Elle s'appelle «Washington School».**
          (Il n'y a pas d'école.)

1. restaurant
2. cinéma
3. église
4. centre commercial
5. bibliothèque
6. café
7. plage
8. supermarché
9. hôpital
10. parc
11. stade
12. musée
13. hôtel
14. piscine
15. théâtre

HÔTEL CHÂTEAU BELLEVUE
16, rue de La Porte, Vieux-Québec,
Qc Canada G1R 4M9
Tél. : 418.692.2573
Téléc. : 418.692.4876
bellevue@vieuxquebec.com

4 À Montréal

PARLER You are visiting your friend Pauline in Montreal. For each of the situations below, decide where you would like to go. Ask Pauline if there is such a place in her neighborhood.

▶ You are hungry.

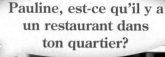

Pauline, est-ce qu'il y a un restaurant dans ton quartier?

1. You want to have a soft drink.
2. You want to see a movie.
3. You want to swim a few laps.
4. You want to run on a track.
5. You want to read a book about Canada.
6. You want to see a French play.
7. You want to buy some fruit and crackers.
8. You want to see an art exhibit.
9. You want to play frisbee on the grass.
10. You slipped and you're afraid you sprained your ankle.

COMMUNAUTÉS

Do French-speaking visitors sometimes come to your community? As a class project, prepare a map of your city on which you label key places and buildings in French. Maybe your local chamber of commerce would like to make such a map available for tourists.

C VOCABULAIRE **Pour demander un renseignement** *(information)*

▶ *How to ask for directions:*

Pardon,	monsieur.	Où est l'hôtel Normandie?
Excusez-moi,	madame	
	mademoiselle	

Il est dans la rue Jean Moulin.

Did this

Où est-ce qu'il y a un café?

Il y a un café	**rue** Saint Paul.	**une rue**
	boulevard Masséna	**un boulevard**
	avenue de Lyon	**une avenue**

Où est-ce? *(Where is it?)*
Est-ce que c'est **loin** *(far)*?

Do this

Non, ce n'est pas loin.
C'est **près** *(nearby)*.

C'est	**à gauche** *(to the left)*.	**Tournez**	à gauche.
	à droite *(to the right)*		à droite
	tout droit *(straight ahead)*	**Continuez** tout droit.

Merci beaucoup!

> Pardon, monsieur, Où est l'hôtel Normandie?

> Il est dans la rue Jean Moulin.

> Où est-ce? Est-ce que c'est loin?

> Non, ce n'est pas loin. C'est près.

---

5  **En ville**

PARLER A tourist who is visiting a French city asks a local resident how to get to the following places. Act out the dialogues.

▶ —Pardon, mademoiselle (monsieur).
  Où est le Café de la Poste?
—Le Café de la Poste? Il est dans la rue Pascal.
—Où est-ce?
—Continuez tout droit!
—Merci, mademoiselle (monsieur).

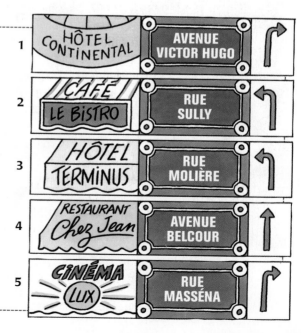

D VOCABULAIRE Ma maison

▶ *How to describe one's home:*

J'habite dans	**une maison** *(house)*.
	un appartement
	un immeuble *(apartment building)*

Ma maison/mon appartement est	**moderne.**
	confortable

Ma chambre est	**en haut** *(upstairs)*.
	en bas *(downstairs)*

J'habite dans une maison.

La maison

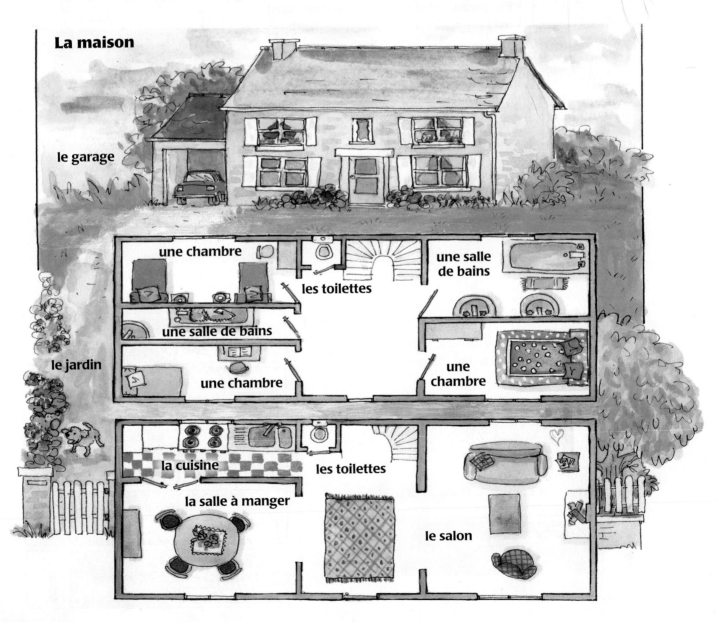

le garage

une chambre

les toilettes

une salle de bains

une salle de bains

le jardin

une chambre

une chambre

la cuisine

les toilettes

la salle à manger

le salon

6 Ma maison

PARLER/ÉCRIRE Describe your home by completing the following sentences.

1. J'habite dans … (une maison? un appartement?)
2. Mon appartement est … (grand? petit? confortable? joli?)
   Ma maison est … (grande? petite? confortable? jolie?)
3. La cuisine est … (grande? petite? moderne?)
4. La cuisine est peinte *(painted)* en … (jaune? vert? gris? blanc?   ??)
5. Ma chambre est peinte en … (bleu? rose?   ??)
6. Dans le salon, il y a … (une télé? un sofa? des plantes vertes?   ??)
7. En général, nous dînons dans … (la cuisine? la salle à manger?)
8. Ma maison/mon appartement a … (un jardin? un garage?   ??)

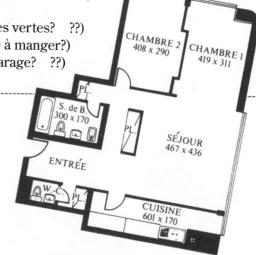

7 En haut ou en bas?

PARLER Imagine that you live in a two-story house. Indicate where the following rooms are located.

▶ ma chambre

Ma chambre est en haut.

Ma chambre est en bas.

1. la cuisine
2. la salle à manger
3. les toilettes
4. la salle de bains
5. la chambre de mes *(my)* parents
6. le salon

COMPARAISON CULTURELLE

In traditional French homes, the toilet **(WC)** is in a small room separate from the main bathroom.

8 Où sont-ils?

PARLER/ÉCRIRE From what the following people are doing, guess where they are — in or around the house.

▶ Madame Martin répare *(is repairing)* la voiture.
  Elle est dans le garage.

1. Nous dînons.
2. Tu regardes la télé.
3. Antoine et Juliette jouent au frisbee.
4. J'étudie le français.
5. Monsieur Martin prépare le dîner.
6. Henri se lave *(is washing up)*.
7. Ma sœur téléphone à son copain.

À votre tour!

OBJECTIFS

Now you can ...
- describe your town and your neighborhood
- ask and give directions

1 🎧 Écoutez bien!

ÉCOUTER Look at the map of Villeneuve. You will hear where certain people are. If they are somewhere on the left side of the map, mark A. If they are on the right side of the map, mark B.

on Quiz

	1	2	3	4	5	6	7	8
A								
B								

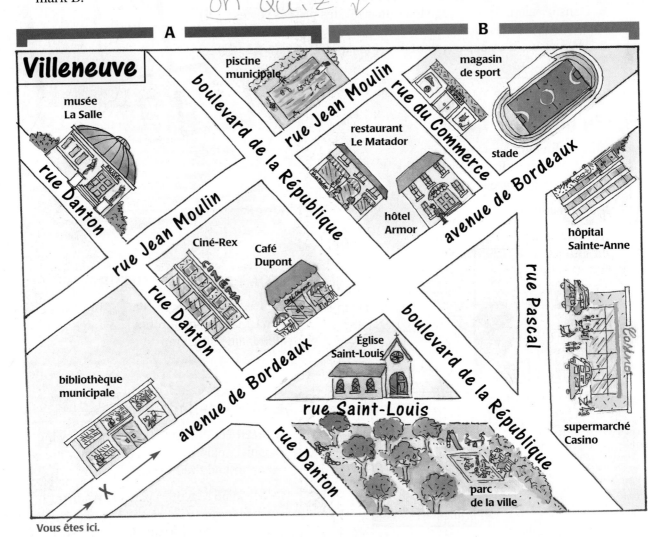

Vous êtes ici.

2 ✎ Mon quartier

ÉCRIRE Describe your neighborhood, listing five places and giving their names.

▶ Dans mon quartier, il y a un supermarché. C'est le supermarché Casino.

3  **Créa-dialogue** -

PARLER You have just arrived in Villeneuve, where you will spend the summer.
Ask a pedestrian where you can find the places represented by the symbols.
He (She) will give you the location of each place, according to the map.

▶ —Pardon, monsieur
  (madame). Où est-ce
  qu'il y a <u>un hôtel</u>?
  —Il y a <u>un hôtel avenue
  de Bordeaux.</u>
  —Est-ce que c'est loin?
  —<u>Non, c'est près.</u>
  —Merci beaucoup!

4 **Où est-ce?** -

PARLER Now you have been in
Villeneuve for several weeks
and are familiar with the city.
You meet a tourist on the **avenue
de Bordeaux** at the place indicated by an X
on the map. The tourist asks you where certain
places are and you indicate how to get there.

▶ l'hôpital Sainte-Anne

1. le musée La Salle
2. le supermarché Casino
3. l'hôtel Armor
4. le restaurant Le Matador
5. l'église Saint-Louis

Pardon, monsieur. Où est
l'hôpital Sainte-Anne?

Merci bien,
monsieur.

C'est tout droit,
mademoiselle.

5 **Composition: La maison idéale** - - - - - - - - - - - - - - -

ÉCRIRE Briefly describe your dream house. You may use the
following adjectives to describe the various rooms: **grand,
petit, moderne, confortable, joli,** as well as colors. If you
wish, sketch and label a floor plan.

▶

```
La maison
idéale est
grande et
moderne. Le
salon est ...
```

Week-end à Paris AUDIO

Aujourd'hui c'est samedi.
Les élèves <u>ne vont pas</u> en classe. *are not going*
Où est-ce qu'ils vont alors?
Ça dépend!

Thomas <u>va</u> au café. *is going*
Il a un <u>rendez-vous</u> avec une copine. *date*

Florence et Karine vont aux Champs-Élysées.
Elles vont regarder les <u>vêtements</u> dans les magasins. *clothes*
<u>Après</u>, elles vont <u>aller</u> au cinéma. *Afterward / to go*

Daniel va <u>chez</u> <u>son</u> copain Laurent. *to the house of / his*
Les garçons vont jouer aux jeux vidéo.
Après, ils vont aller au musée des sciences de la Villette.
Ils vont jouer avec les machines électroniques.

Béatrice a un grand sac et des <u>lunettes de soleil</u>. *sunglasses*
Est-ce qu'elle va à un rendez-vous secret?
Non! Elle va au Centre Pompidou.
Elle va regarder les acrobates.
Et après, elle va aller à un concert.

Et Jean-François? Qu'est-ce qu'il va faire aujourd'hui?
Est-ce qu'il va visiter le Centre Pompidou?
Est-ce qu'il va regarder les acrobates?
Est-ce qu'il va aller à un concert?
<u>Hélas</u>, non! *Alas (Unfortunately)*
Il va <u>rester</u> à la maison. *to stay*
Pourquoi? Parce qu'il est <u>malade</u>. *sick*
<u>Pauvre</u> Jean-François! *Poor*
Il fait <u>si</u> beau <u>dehors</u>! *so / outside*

Answer in French

Compréhension

1. Quel jour est-ce aujourd'hui?
2. Pourquoi est-ce que Thomas va au café?
3. Avec qui est-ce que Florence va au cinéma?
4. Où va Daniel? Qu'est-ce qu'il fait avec Laurent?
5. Où va Béatrice?
6. Pourquoi est-ce que Jean-François ne va pas en ville?
7. Quel temps fait-il aujourd'hui?

NOTE culturelle

À Paris

Paris offre beaucoup d'attractions diverses pour les jeunes.

Les Champs-Élysées

Les Champs-Élysées sont une très longue et très large° avenue avec beaucoup de cafés, de restaurants, de cinémas et de boutiques élégantes.

Le Centre Pompidou

Le Centre Pompidou est un grand musée d'art moderne. C'est aussi un centre culturel avec un grand nombre de salles° multimédia pour les jeunes. Devant le musée, il y a une place où les acrobates, les mimes, les jongleurs° et les musiciens démontrent leurs° talents. Ici, le spectacle est permanent.

Le Parc de la Villette

Le Parc de la Villette est un musée scientifique pour les jeunes. À la Géode, ils peuvent° voir° des films sur un grand écran panoramique Omni. Au Zénith, ils peuvent assister à° des concerts de rock et de musique techno.

---

large *wide*   **salles** *large rooms*   **jongleurs** *jugglers*   **leurs** *their*   **peuvent** *can*   **voir** *see*   **assister à** *attend*

A Le verbe *aller*

Aller *(to go)* is the only IRREGULAR verb that ends in **-er**. Note the forms
of **aller** in the present tense.

aller	*to go*	J'aime **aller** au cinéma.
je **vais**	*I go, I am going*	Je **vais** à un concert.
tu **vas**	*you go, you are going*	**Vas**-tu à la boum?
il/elle **va**	*he/she goes, he/she is going*	Paul **va** à l'école.
nous **allons**	*we go, we are going*	Nous **allons** au café.
vous **allez**	*you go, you are going*	Est-ce que vous **allez** là-bas?
ils/elles **vont**	*they go, they are going*	Ils ne **vont** pas en classe.

→ Remember that **aller** is used in asking people how they feel.

Ça **va?**   Oui, ça **va.**
Comment **vas**-tu?   Je **vais** bien, merci.
Comment **allez**-vous?   Très bien.

→ **Aller** is used in many common expressions.

- To encourage someone to do something:
  Vas-y!   *Come on! Go ahead! Do it!*

- To tell someone to go away:
  Va-t'en!   *Go away!*

- To tell friends to start doing something:
  Allons-y!   *Let's go!*

1 Les vacances

PARLER/ÉCRIRE The following students at a boarding school in Nice are going home for vacation. Indicate to which of the cities they are going, according to the luggage tags shown below.

Jean-Michel va à Québec.

▶ Jean-Michel est canadien.

1. Je suis suisse.
2. Charlotte est américaine.
3. Nous sommes italiens.
4. Tu es français.
5. Vous êtes espagnols.
6. Michiko est japonaise.
7. Mike et Shelley sont anglais.
8. Ana et Carlos sont mexicains.

▶

QUÉBEC ACAPULCO Lyon Madrid TOKYO Londres (London) ROME Genève CHICAGO

2 Jamais le dimanche! *(Never on Sunday!)*

PARLER/ÉCRIRE On Sundays, French students do not go to class. They all go somewhere else. Express this according to the model.

▶ nous / en ville
   Le dimanche, nous n'allons pas en classe.
   Nous allons en ville.

1. Philippe / au café
2. vous / au cinéma
3. Céline et Michèle / à un concert
4. Jérôme / au restaurant
5. je / à un match de foot
6. tu / à la piscine
7. Éric et Léa / à la plage
8. Mes copains / au stade
9. Hélène / au centre commercial
10. Vous / dans les magasins

B La préposition *à; à* + l'article défini

The preposition **à** has several meanings:

in	Patrick habite **à** Paris.	*Patrick lives **in** Paris.*
at	Nous sommes **à** la piscine.	*We are **at** the pool.*
to	Est-ce que tu vas **à** Toulouse?	*Are you going **to** Toulouse?*

CONTRACTIONS

Note the forms of **à** + DEFINITE ARTICLE in the sentences below.

Voici **le** café.	Marc est **au** café.	Corinne va **au** café.
Voici **les** Champs-Élysées.	Tu es **aux** Champs-Élysées.	Je vais **aux** Champs-Élysées.
Voici **la** piscine.	Anne est **à la** piscine.	Éric va **à la** piscine.
Voici **l'**hôtel.	Je suis **à l'**hôtel.	Vous allez **à l'**hôtel.

The preposition **à** contracts with **le** and **les,** but not with **la** and **l'.**

CONTRACTION	NO CONTRACTION		
à + le → **au**	à + la = **à la**	**au** cinéma	**à la** piscine
à + les → **aux**	à + l' = **à l'**	**aux** Champs-Élysées	**à l'**école

→ There is liaison after **aux** when the next word begins with a vowel sound.
Le professeur parle **aux élèves.**   Je téléphone **aux amis** de Claire.

3 🗣 **Dans la rue**

PARLER Two friends meet in the street and talk about where they are going.

Tu vas au café?

Non, je vais à la plage.

4 Préférences

PARLER Ask your classmates about their preferences. Be sure to use contractions when needed.

▶ aller à (le concert ou le théâtre?)

1. dîner à (la maison ou le restaurant)?
2. étudier à (la bibliothèque ou la maison)?
3. nager à (la piscine ou la plage)?
4. regarder un match de foot à (la télé ou le stade)?
5. aller à (le cinéma ou le musée)?

> Tu préfères aller au concert ou au théâtre?

> **Je préfère aller au concert.**
> (Je préfère aller au théâtre.)

5 À Paris

PARLER You are living in Paris. A friend asks you where you are going and why. Act out the dialogues with a classmate.

▶ —Où vas-tu?
  —Je vais à l'Opéra.
  —Pourquoi?
  —Parce que j'aime la danse classique.

OÙ?	POURQUOI?
▶ l'Opéra	J'aime la danse classique.
1. l'Alliance Française	J'ai une classe de français.
2. le Centre Pompidou	J'aime l'art moderne.
3. le musée d'Orsay	C'est un musée intéressant.
4. les Champs-Élysées	J'ai un rendez-vous là-bas.
5. la tour Eiffel	Il y a une belle vue *(view)* sur Paris.
6. le Zénith	Il y a un concert de rock.
7. la Villette	Il y a une exposition *(exhibit)* intéressante.
8. le stade de France	Il y a un match de foot.

6 Où vont-ils?

PARLER/ÉCRIRE Say where the following people are going, according to what they like to do.

▶ Daniel aime danser.
  Il va à la discothèque.

1. Corinne aime l'art moderne.
2. Jean-François aime manger.
3. Delphine aime les westerns.
4. Marina aime nager.
5. Éric aime regarder les magazines.
6. Denise aime faire des promenades.
7. Philippe aime la musique.
8. Alice aime le football.
9. Cécile aime le shopping.
10. Léa aime surfer sur l'Internet.

le stade
la bibliothèque
le cinéma
le centre commercial
la discothèque
le musée
le cybercafé
le parc
le restaurant
la piscine
le concert

PISCINE SERVICE
Didier Souchoy • Camaruche • Saint-Barthélemy • Tel: 0590 27 81 23

VOCABULAIRE En ville

▶ *Quelques endroits et quelques événements où aller*

un endroit	*place*	**un match**	*game*	**une boum**	*party*
un événement	*event*	**un pique-nique**	*picnic*	**une fête**	*party*
un concert	*concert*	**un rendez-vous**	*appointment,*	**une soirée**	*evening party*
un film	*movie*		*date*		

Verbes

arriver	*to arrive, come*	**J'arrive** à l'école à 9 heures.
rentrer	*to go back, come back*	À quelle heure **rentres**-tu à la maison?
rester	*to stay*	Les touristes **restent** à l'hôtel.

Expressions

à pied	*on foot*	**en voiture**	*by car*	**en métro**	*by subway*
à vélo	*by bicycle*	**en bus**	*by bus*	**en taxi**	*by taxi*
		en train	*by train*		

faire une promenade à pied	*to go for a walk*
faire une promenade à vélo	*to go for a ride (by bike)*
faire une promenade en voiture	*to go for a drive*

7 ## Questions personnelles **PARLER/ÉCRIRE**

1. En général, à quelle heure est-ce que tu arrives à l'école?
2. À quelle heure est-ce que tu rentres à la maison?
   Qu'est-ce que tu fais quand tu rentres à la maison?
3. Comment vas-tu à l'école? à pied, à vélo, en voiture ou en bus?
4. Le week-end, est-ce que tu restes à la maison? Où vas-tu?
5. Comment vas-tu à la piscine? à la plage? au cinéma?
6. Est-ce que tu aimes faire des promenades à pied? Où vas-tu? avec qui?
7. Est-ce que tu aimes faire des promenades à vélo? Où vas-tu?
8. En général, est-ce que tu aimes regarder les films à la télé? Quels films est-ce que tu préfères? (les films d'action? les films de science-fiction? les comédies?)
9. Quand tu as un rendez-vous avec un copain ou une copine, où allez-vous?
10. À quels événements aimes-tu aller? Pourquoi?

C La préposition *chez*

Note the use of **chez** in the following sentences.

Paul est **chez Céline**.	*Paul is **at Céline's (house)**.*
Je dîne **chez un copain**.	*I am having dinner **at a friend's (home)**.*
Nathalie va **chez Juliette**.	*Nathalie is going **to Juliette's (apartment)**.*
Tu vas **chez ta cousine**.	*You are going **to your cousin's (place)**.*

The French equivalent of *to* or *at someone's (house, home)* is the construction:

chez + PERSON	**chez** Béatrice	**chez** ma cousine

→ Note the interrogative expression: **chez qui?**

    Chez qui vas-tu?   ***To whose house** are you going?*

8 En vacances

PARLER/ÉCRIRE When we are on vacation, we often like to visit friends and relatives. Say where the following people are going.

▶ Claire / Marc
Claire va chez Marc.

1. Hélène / Jérôme
2. Jean-Paul / Lucie
3. tu / un copain
4. Corinne / une cousine
5. vous / des copines à Québec
6. nous / un cousin à Paris

9 Week-end

PARLER On weekends, we often like to visit friends and do things together. Say how the following people are spending Sunday afternoon.

▶ Cécile / jouer au ping-pong / Robert

1. Julie / aller / Béatrice
2. Claire / dîner / des cousins
3. Antoine / jouer au croquet / Sylvie
4. Marc / écouter des CD / un copain
5. Mathieu / regarder la télé / une copine
6. Élodie / jouer aux jeux vidéo / Thomas
7. Nous / manger une pizza / Léa
8. Vous / regarder un DVD / Éric
9. Tu / jouer au basket / Alice

Cécile joue au ping-pong chez Robert.

D La construction *aller* + l'infinitif

The following sentences describe what people are *going to do*.
Note how the verb **aller** is used to describe these FUTURE events.

Nathalie **va nager.**
Paul et Marc **vont jouer** au tennis.

Nathalie *is going to swim.*
Paul and Marc *are going to play tennis.*

Nous **allons rester** à la maison.
Je **vais aller** en ville.

We *are going to stay home.*
I *am going to go downtown.*

To express the NEAR FUTURE, the French use the construction:

> PRESENT of **aller** + INFINITIVE

➔ In negative sentences, the construction is:

> SUBJECT + **ne** + PRESENT of **aller** + **pas** + INFINITIVE ...
>
> | Sylvie | **ne** | va | **pas** | écouter le concert avec nous. |

➔ Note the interrogative forms:
Qu'est-ce que tu vas faire?
Quand est-ce que vous allez rentrer?

What are you going to do?
When are you going to come back?

LANGUAGE COMPARISON
To talk about FUTURE plans and intentions, French and English frequently use similar verbs: **aller** *(to be going to).*

10 Tourisme

PARLER/ÉCRIRE Say where the following people are going this summer and what they are going to visit.

▶ Monique (à Paris / le Louvre)
   Monique va à Paris. Elle va visiter le Louvre.

1. Alice (à New York / la statue de la Liberté)
2. nous (en Égypte / les pyramides)
3. vous (à Rome / le Colisée)
4. tu (à La Nouvelle Orléans / le Vieux Carré)
5. je (à San Francisco / Chinatown)
6. les élèves (à San Antonio / l'Alamo)
7. Madame Lambert (à Beijing / la Cité interdite
   [Forbidden City])
8. les touristes (à Kyoto / les temples)

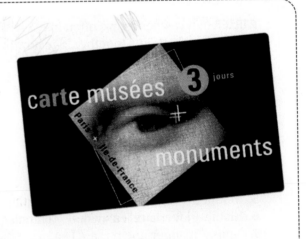

11 *Qu'est-ce que tu vas faire?*

PARLER Ask your classmates if they are going to do the following things this weekend.

 **▶ étudier**

1. travailler
2. surfer sur le Net
3. regarder la télé
4. aller au cinéma
5. inviter des amis

6. aller à une boum
7. jouer aux jeux vidéo
8. rester à la maison
9. faire une promenade à vélo

Est-ce que tu vas étudier?

Oui, je vais étudier.
(Non, je ne vais pas étudier.)

12 *Un jeu: Descriptions*

PARLER/ÉCRIRE Choose a person from Column A and say where the person is, what he or she has, and what he or she is going to do. Use the verbs **être, avoir,** and **aller** with the phrases in columns B, C, and D. How many logical descriptions can you make?

 ▶ Monique est en ville. Elle a un vélo. Elle va faire une promenade.

A	B (être)	C (avoir)	D (aller)
tu	sur le court	des livres	aller dans les magasins
Monique	à la bibliothèque	un vélo	étudier
je	au salon	20 euros	faire une promenade
les amis	en ville	une télé	regarder un film
nous	à la maison	une chaîne hi-fi	faire un match
vous	au café	une raquette	écouter des CD

PRONONCIATION /w/   /j/

Les semi-voyelles /w/ et /j/

In French, the semi-vowels /w/ and /j/ are pronounced very quickly, almost like consonants.

oui

très bien

Répétez:

/w/   **oui chouette Louise**

/wa/, /wɛ̃/   **moi toi pourquoi voiture loin**
           Chouette! La voiture de Louise n'est pas loin.

/j/   **bien chien radio piano Pierre Daniel violon pied étudiant**
           Pierre écoute la radio avec Daniel.

À votre tour!

OBJECTIFS

Now you can …
- talk about places you go to
- discuss what you are going to do in the future

1 Allô!

PARLER Anne is calling Jérôme. Match Jérôme's answers with Anne's questions. Then act out the dialogue with a friend.

1. Tu restes chez toi samedi?
2. Qu'est-ce que vous allez faire?
3. Est-ce que vous allez aller au cinéma?
4. À quelle heure est-ce que tu vas rentrer?

a. À dix heures.
b. Peut-être! Il y a un très bon film au Rex.
c. Nous allons faire une promenade en ville.
d. Non, j'ai un rendez-vous avec Christine.

2 Créa-dialogue

PARLER As you are going for a walk in town, you meet several friends. Ask them where they are going and what they are going to do there.

OÙ?	ACTIVITÉ
	dîner avec un copain

▶ —Salut, <u>Alison</u>. Ça va?
—Oui, ça va!
—Où vas-tu?
—Je vais au <u>restaurant</u>.
—Ah bon? Qu'est-ce que tu vas faire là-bas?
—Je vais <u>dîner avec un copain</u>.
—Avec qui?
—Avec <u>Chris</u>.

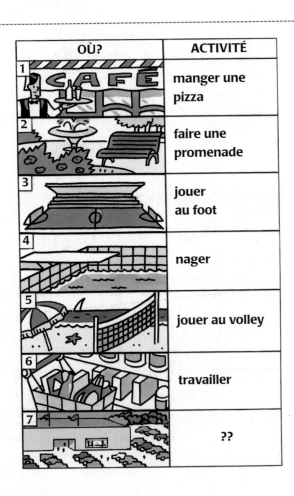

OÙ?	ACTIVITÉ
1 CAFÉ	manger une pizza
2	faire une promenade
3	jouer au foot
4	nager
5	jouer au volley
6	travailler
7	??

Conversation libre

PARLER Have a conversation with a classmate. Ask your classmate questions about what he/she plans to do on the weekend. Try to find out as much as possible, using yes/no questions.

Est-ce que tu vas rester à la maison?

Non, je ne vais pas rester à la maison.

Est-ce que tu vas aller en ville?

Oui, je vais aller en ville.

Est-ce que tu vas aller au cinéma?

Oui, je vais aller au cinéma.
(Non, je ne vais pas aller au cinéma.)

 Qu'est-ce que vous allez faire?

ÉCRIRE Leave a note for your friend Jean-Marc, telling him three things that you and your friends are going to do tonight and three things that you are going to do this weekend.

Jean-Marc
Ce soir (Tonight)
   1. Nous allons ...
   2.
   3.

Bonnes résolutions

ÉCRIRE Imagine that it is January 1 and you are making up New Year's resolutions. On a separate sheet of paper, describe six of your resolutions by saying what you are going to do and what you are not going to do in the coming year.

1er JANVIER
1. Je vais toujours parler français en classe.
2. Je ne vais pas être pénible avec mes copains...

LESSON REVIEW
CLASSZONE.COM

LEÇON 15

Au Café de l'Univers

AUDIO

Où vas-tu <u>après les cours</u>? *after school*

Est-ce que tu vas <u>directement</u> <u>chez toi?</u> *straight/home*

Valérie, elle, ne va pas directement <u>chez elle.</u> *to her house*

Elle va au Café de l'Univers avec ses copines Fatima et Zaïna.

Elle <u>vient</u> souvent ici avec elles. *comes*

À la table de Valérie, la conversation est toujours très <u>animée</u>. *lively*

<u>De quoi</u> parlent les filles aujourd'hui? *About what*

Est-ce qu'elles parlent | de l'<u>examen d'histoire?</u> *history test*
| du problème de maths?
| de la classe de sciences?

Non!

Est-ce qu'elles parlent | du week-end <u>prochain?</u> *next*
| des vacances?

<u>Non plus!</u> *Not that either!*

Est-ce qu'elles parlent | du <u>nouveau</u> copain de Marie-Claire? *new*
| de la cousine de Pauline?
| des amis de Véronique?

<u>Pas du tout!</u> *Not at all!*

Aujourd'hui, les filles parlent d'un <u>sujet</u> beaucoup <u>plus</u> important! *subject/more*
Elles parlent du nouveau prof d'anglais! (C'est un jeune professeur
américain. Il est très intéressant, très amusant, très sympathique …
et <u>surtout</u> il est très mignon!) *above all*

Compréhension

1. Où va Valérie après les cours?
2. Avec qui est-ce qu'elle va au café?
3. Qu'est-ce que les filles font au café?
4. Est-ce qu'elles parlent de l'école?
5. Est-ce qu'elles parlent des activités du week-end?
6. De quelle *(which)* personne parlent-elles aujourd'hui?
7. De quelle nationalité est le professeur d'anglais?
8. Comment est-il?

Et toi?

Describe what you do by completing the following sentences.

1. En général, après les cours,
   je vais …
   je ne vais pas …

   - à la bibliothèque
   - chez mes *(my)* copains
   - au café
   - directement chez moi

2. Avec mes copains,
   je parle …
   je ne parle pas …

   - de la classe de français
   - du prof de français
   - des examens
   - du week-end

3. Avec mes parents,
   je parle …
   je ne parle pas …

   - de l'école
   - de la classe de français
   - de mes notes *(grades)*
   - de mes copains

4. Avec mon frère ou ma soeur,
   je parle …
   je ne parle pas …

   - de mes copains
   - du week-end
   - de mes problèmes
   - des vacances

NOTE culturelle

Au café

On peut° faire beaucoup de choses différentes dans un café français. On peut manger un sandwich. On peut commander° un jus de fruits. On peut étudier. On peut jouer aux jeux électroniques. Dans les cybercafés, on peut aussi surfer sur l'Internet. Les jeunes Français vont au café principalement pour retrouver° leurs° copains et passer° un bon moment avec eux.°

Un café français est divisé en deux parties: l'intérieur et la terrasse.° Au printemps et en été, les Français préfèrent s'asseoir° à la terrasse. Là, ils peuvent° profiter du soleil° et regarder les gens qui passent dans la rue.

On peut *One can*   **commander** *order*   **retrouver** *meet*   **leurs** *their*   **passer** *spend*   **eux** *them*
la terrasse *terrace (outdoor section of a café)*   **s'asseoir** *to sit*   **peuvent** *can*   **profiter du soleil** *enjoy the sun*

A Le verbe *venir*

The verb **venir** *(to come)* is irregular. Note the forms of **venir** in the present tense.

venir	Nous allons **venir** avec des amis.
je **viens**	Je **viens** avec toi.
tu **viens**	Est-ce que tu **viens** au cinéma?
il/elle **vient**	Monique ne **vient** pas avec nous.
nous **venons**	Nous **venons** à cinq heures.
vous **venez**	À quelle heure **venez**-vous à la boum?
ils/elles **viennent**	Ils **viennent** de Paris, n'est-ce pas?

→ **Revenir** *(to come back)* is conjugated like **venir.**
—À quelle heure **revenez**-vous?
—Nous **revenons** à dix heures.

→ Note the interrogative expression: **d'où?** *(from where?)*

D'où viens-tu? **Where** do you come **from?**

1 Tu viens?

PARLER Tell a friend where you are
going and ask him or her to come along.

▶ à la pizzeria

1. au café
2. à la bibliothèque
3. à la piscine
4. au cybercafé
5. au centre commercial
6. au magasin de CD
7. au stade
8. en classe

Je vais à la pizzeria. Tu viens avec moi?

D'accord, je viens.
(Non, je ne viens pas.)

2 Le pique-nique du Club français

PARLER/ÉCRIRE The French Club has organized a picnic. Say who is coming and who is not.

▶ Philippe (non)
Philippe ne vient pas.

1. Alice (oui)
2. Jean-Pierre (non)
3. Paul et Caroline (oui)
4. vous (non)
5. je (oui)
6. nous (non)
7. tu (non)
8. le prof de français (oui)
9. le prof d'anglais (oui)

B La préposition *de; de* + l'article défini

The preposition **de** has several meanings:

from	Nous venons **de** la bibliothèque.	*We are coming **from** the library.*
of	Quelle est l'adresse **de** l'école?	*What is the address **of** the school?*
about	Je parle **de** mon copain.	*I am talking **about** my friend.*

CONTRACTIONS

Note the forms of **de** + DEFINITE ARTICLE in the sentences below.

Voici **le** café.   Marc vient **du** café.
Voici **les** Champs-Élysées.   Nous venons **des** Champs-Élysées.

Voici **la** piscine.   Tu reviens **de la** piscine.
Voici **l'**hôtel.   Les touristes arrivent **de l'**hôtel.

The preposition **de** contracts with **le** and **les,** but not with **la** and **l'.**

CONTRACTION	NO CONTRACTION			
de + le → **du**	de + la = **de la**	**du** café		**de la** plage
de + les → **des**	de + l′ = **de l'**	**des** magasins		**de l'**école

→ There is liaison after **des** when the next word begins with a vowel sound.
    Où sont les livres **des étudiants?**
    z

3 Rendez-vous

PARLER The following students live in Paris. On a Saturday afternoon they are meeting in a café. Say where each one is coming from.

▶ Jacques: le musée d'Orsay

1. Sylvie: le Louvre
2. Isabelle: le parc de la Villette
3. Jean-Paul: le Centre Pompidou
4. François: le Quartier latin
5. Cécile: l'avenue de l'Opéra
6. Nicole: la tour Eiffel
7. Marc: le jardin du Luxembourg
8. André: les Champs-Élysées
9. Pierre: les Galeries Lafayette
10. Corinne: la rue Bonaparte

Jacques vient du musée d'Orsay.

4 *D'où viens-tu?*

PARLER During vacation, Olivier goes out every day. When he gets home, his sister Sophie asks him where he is coming from.

▶ mardi

D'où viens-tu?

Je viens du cybercafé.

1. lundi
2. mercredi
3. vendredi
4. dimanche
5. samedi
6. jeudi

LUNDI	le restaurant
MARDI	le cybercafé
MERCREDI	la bibliothèque
JEUDI	l'opéra
VENDREDI	le concert de rock
SAMEDI	le pique-nique de Monique
DIMANCHE	la boum de Christine

VOCABULAIRE Les sports, les jeux et la musique

▶ **Les sports**

le foot(ball)	**le volley(ball)**
le basket(ball)	**le tennis**
le ping-pong	**le baseball**

▶ **Les jeux** (games)

les échecs (chess)	**les dames** (checkers)
les jeux vidéo	**les cartes** (cards)
les jeux d'ordinateur	

▶ **Les instruments de musique**

le piano	**le saxo(phone)**	**la flûte**	**la clarinette**
le violon	**le clavier** (keyboard)	**la guitare**	**la batterie** (drums)

jouer à + le, la, les + SPORT or GAME	*to play*	Nous **jouons au** tennis.
jouer de + le, la, les + INSTRUMENT	*to play*	Alice **joue du** piano.

5 *Activités*

PARLER Ask your classmates if they play the following instruments and games.

▶ —Est-ce que tu joues au ping-pong?
—Oui, je joue au ping-pong.
(Non, je ne joue pas au ping-pong.)
▶ —Est-ce que tu joues du piano?
—Oui, je joue du piano.
(Non, je ne joue pas du piano.)

Les pronoms accentués

In the answers to the questions below, the nouns in heavy print are replaced by pronouns. These pronouns are called STRESS PRONOUNS. Note their forms.

—François dîne avec **Florence?**	*Is François having dinner with **Florence?***
—Oui, il dîne avec **elle.**	*Yes, he is having dinner with **her.***
—Tu parles de **Jean-Paul?**	*Are you talking about **Jean-Paul?***
—Non, je ne parle pas de **lui.**	*No, I'm not talking about **him.***

FORMS

(SUBJECT PRONOUNS)	STRESS PRONOUNS	(SUBJECT PRONOUNS)	STRESS PRONOUNS
(je)	moi	(nous)	nous
(tu)	toi	(vous)	vous
(il)	lui	(ils)	eux
(elle)	elle	(elles)	elles

USES

Stress pronouns are used:

- to reinforce a subject pronoun
  Moi, je parle français.
  Vous, vous parlez anglais.

  I speak French.
  You speak English.

- after **c'est** and **ce n'est pas**
  —C'est Paul là-bas?
  —Non, ce n'est pas **lui.**

  *No, it's not **him.***

- in short sentences where there is no verb
  —Qui parle français ici?
  —**Moi!**

  I do!

- before and after **et** and **ou**
  Lui et moi, nous sommes copains.

  He and I, (we) are friends.

- After prepositions such as **de, avec, pour, chez**
  Voici Marc et Paul. Je parle souvent **d'eux.**
  Voici Isabelle. Je vais au cinéma **avec elle.**
  Voici M. Mercier. Nous travaillons **pour lui.**

  *I often talk **about them.***
  *I go to the movies **with her.***
  *We work **for him.***

  → Note the meaning of **chez** + STRESS PRONOUN:
  Je vais **chez moi.**
  Paul étudie **chez lui.**

  *I am going **home.***
  *Paul is studying **at home.***

  Tu viens **chez nous?**
  Je suis chez Alice. Je dîne **chez elle.**

  *Are you coming **to our house?***
  *I am having dinner **at her place.***

6 Samedi soir *(Saturday night)*

PARLER/ÉCRIRE On Saturday night, some people stay home and others do not. Read what the following people are doing and say whether or not they are at home.

▶ Alice étudie.
  Elle est chez elle.

▶ Paul va au cinéma.
  Il n'est pas chez lui.

1. François regarde la télé.
2. Mélanie va au cinéma.
3. Marc et Pierre dînent en ville.
4. Léa et Pauline écoutent des CD.
5. Les voisins font une promenade.
6. Je travaille avec mon père.
7. Tu vas au théâtre.
8. Nous allons à la bibliothèque.
9. Tu prépares le dîner.

7 Questions personnelles

PARLER/ÉCRIRE Use stress pronouns in your answers.

1. Tu étudies souvent avec tes *(your)* copains?
2. Tu vas souvent chez ta cousine?
3. Tu travailles pour les voisins?
4. Tu parles français avec ton père?
5. Tu vas souvent au cinéma avec tes copines?
6. Tu restes chez toi le week-end?
7. Tu restes chez toi pendant *(during)* les vacances?
8. Tu voyages avec tes parents?
9. Tu joues aux jeux vidéo avec ton copain?
10. Tu vas souvent chez tes voisins?

VOCABULAIRE Expressions pour la conversation

▶ *How to express surprise:*

Vraiment?!   *Really?!*
—Je parle chinois.
—**Vraiment?!**

▶ *How to contradict someone:*

Pas du tout!   *Not at all! Definitely not!*
—Tu es anglais?
—**Pas du tout!** Je suis français!

8 Commérage *(Gossip)*

PARLER Élodie likes to gossip. Act out the dialogues between her and her friend Thomas.

▶ Marina dîne avec Jean-Pierre.

1. Éric dîne avec Alice.
2. Thérèse va chez Paul.
3. Jérôme est au cinéma avec Delphine.
4. Monsieur Mercier travaille pour Mademoiselle Duval.
5. Philippe travaille pour le voisin.
6. Marc et Vincent dansent avec Mélanie et Juliette.

Marina dîne avec Jean-Pierre.

Vraiment?

Mais oui! Elle dîne avec lui!

D La construction: nom + *de* + nom

Compare the word order in French and English.

J'ai une raquette.   C'est une **raquette de tennis.**   *It's a **tennis racket.***

Paul a une voiture.   C'est une **voiture de sport.**   *It's a **sports car.***

When one noun is used to modify another noun, the French construction is:

MAIN NOUN + **de** + MODIFYING NOUN	**une classe de français.**
d' (+ VOWEL SOUND)	**une classe d'espagnol.**

→ There is no article after **de.**

> **LANGUAGE COMPARISON**
>
> In French, when one noun modifies another, the main noun comes FIRST.
>
> In English, the main noun comes SECOND.
>
> un **jeu** d'ordinateur   *a computer **game***

9 Précisions

PARLER/ÉCRIRE Complete the following sentences with an expression consisting of **de** + underlined noun.

▶ J'aime le <u>sport</u>. J'ai une voiture …

J'ai une voiture de sport!

1. Claire aime le <u>ping-pong</u>. Elle a une raquette …
2. Nous adorons le <u>rock</u>. Nous écoutons un concert …
3. Jacques aime le <u>jazz</u>. Il écoute un programme …
4. Vous étudiez l'<u>anglais</u>. Vous avez un livre …
5. Tu étudies le <u>piano</u>. Aujourd'hui, tu as une leçon …
6. Léa étudie l'<u>espagnol</u>. Elle a un bon prof …
7. Je regarde mes <u>photos</u>. J'ai un album …
8. Pierre joue au <u>baseball</u>. Il a une batte …
9. J'aime la <u>musique africaine</u>. J'ai des CD …
10. Paul est bon en <u>maths</u>. Il fait un problème …

PRONONCIATION 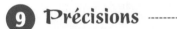   /ø/   /œ/

Les voyelles /ø/ et /œ/

The letters "**eu**" and "**oeu**" represent vowel sounds that do not exist in English but that are not very hard to pronounce.

2   **9**

d<u>eu</u>x   n<u>eu</u>f

Répétez:

/ø/   d<u>eu</u>x   <u>eu</u>x   je v<u>eu</u>x   je p<u>eu</u>x   un p<u>eu</u>   j<u>eu</u>x   il pl<u>eu</u>t   un <u>eu</u>ro
     Tu p<u>eu</u>x aller chez <u>eu</u>x.

/œ/   n<u>eu</u>f   s<u>oeu</u>r   h<u>eu</u>re   profess<u>eu</u>r   j<u>eu</u>ne
     Ma s<u>oeu</u>r arrive à n<u>eu</u>f h<u>eu</u>res.

À votre tour!

1 🎧 Conversation

PARLER Saturday afternoon, Henri meets Stéphanie downtown. Match Henri's questions with Stéphanie's answers. Then act out the conversation with a classmate.

1. Salut, Stéphanie! D'où viens-tu?

2. Et où vas-tu maintenant?

3. Tu ne veux pas venir au cinéma avec moi?

4. Ah bon? Pourquoi?

a. J'ai un examen d'anglais lundi.

b. Du supermarché.

c. Je rentre chez moi.

d. Je ne peux pas. Je dois étudier.

2 🎧 Créa-dialogue

PARLER Ask your classmates whom they are going to visit and what they are going to do. Then decide if you are going to come along.

▶ —Où vas-tu?
—Je vais chez <u>Jean-Claude</u>. Tu viens?
—Ça dépend! Qu'est-ce que tu vas faire chez <u>lui</u>?
—Nous allons <u>jouer au ping-pong</u>.
—D'accord, je viens!
  (Non, je ne viens pas.)

Jean-Claude	CHEZ QUI?	1. Françoise	2. Corinne et Claire	3. Nicolas et Patrick	4. mon cousin	5. ma cousine	6. des copains
	ACTIVITÉ						

3 Retour à la maison

PARLER This afternoon, the following people went downtown. Say which places they are coming from.

▶ Nous venons de l'école.

▶ nous

1. tu
2. vous
3. Madame Simon
4. Monsieur Dupont
5. Claire et Diane
6. Daniel et Philippe

4 ✏ Message illustré

ÉCRIRE Frédéric likes to use illustrations in his diary. Transcribe what he has written about himself and others, replacing the pictures with the corresponding missing words.

Je joue [image]
J'aime aussi aller [image]
Ma soeur Catherine joue très bien [image]
Elle est musicienne aussi. Elle joue [image] et [image]

Mon frère Marc préfère jouer [image]
Tiens, voilà ma copine Stéphanie.
Elle vient [image].
Elle joue très bien [image]

5 🖊 Un mail à Sandrine

ÉCRIRE In a recent e-mail, Sandrine, your French pen pal, mentioned various hobbies she enjoys. In a short e-mail, tell her …

- which sports you play
- which musical instruments you play
- which games you play

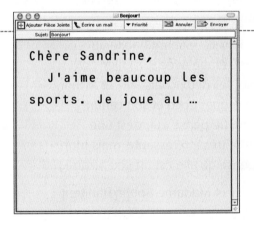

Chère Sandrine,
    J'aime beaucoup les sports. Je joue au …

parc   supermarché   stade

école   bibliothèque   piscine

LEÇON 16

Mes voisins

AUDIO

Bonjour!
Je m'appelle Frédéric Mallet.
J'habite à Paris avec ma famille.
Nous habitons dans un <u>immeuble</u> de   *building*
six <u>étages</u>.   *floors*
Voici mon immeuble et voici <u>mes</u> voisins.   *my*

Monsieur Lacroche habite au <u>sixième</u>   *sixth*
étage avec sa femme. Ils sont
musiciens. Lui, il joue du piano et elle,
elle chante. Oh là là, <u>quelle</u> musique!   *what*

Mademoiselle Jolivet habite au
<u>cinquième</u> étage avec <u>son</u> oncle et   *fifth / her*
<u>sa</u> tante.   *her*
Paul, mon <u>meilleur</u> ami, habite au   *best*
<u>quatrième</u> étage avec <u>sa</u> soeur et   *fourth / his*
<u>ses</u> parents.   *his*

Mademoiselle Ménard habite au
<u>troisième</u> étage avec son chien   *third*
Pomme, ses deux chats Fritz et Arthur,
son <u>perroquet</u> Coco et son canari   *parrot*
Froufrou. (Je <u>pense</u> <u>que</u> c'est une   *think / that*
personne très intéressante, mais mon
père pense qu'elle est un peu bizarre.)

Monsieur et Madame Boutin habitent
au <u>deuxième</u> étage avec <u>leur</u>   *second / their*
<u>fils</u> et leurs deux <u>filles</u>.   *son / daughters*

Et qui habite au premier étage?
C'est un garçon super-intelligent,
super-cool et très sympathique!
Et ce garçon … c'est moi!

Compréhension

1. Où habite Frédéric Mallet?
2. Combien *(How many)* d'étages a son immeuble?
3. Qui habite à chaque *(each)* étage?
4. Quelle est la profession des Lacroche?
5. Selon toi *(In your opinion)*, est-ce que Mademoiselle Ménard est une personne bizarre ou intéressante? Pourquoi?

COMPARAISONS CULTURELLES

The floors of buildings are numbered differently in France and in the United States. Compare:

• **rez-de-chaussée**	*ground floor or first floor*
• **premier étage (1ᵉʳ étage)**	*second floor*
• **deuxième étage (2ᵉᵐᵉ étage)**	*third floor*

NOTE: In the older downtown areas of French cities, apartment houses have a maximum of six stories. This is because until the twentieth century there were no elevators and people had to use the stairs.

NOTE culturelle

Les animaux domestiques en France

La France a une population de 60 millions d'habitants et de 42 millions d'animaux domestiques.° Les Français adorent les animaux. Une famille sur deux° a un animal domestique. Par ordre de préférence, les principaux animaux domestiques sont les chiens (39%: trente-neuf pour cent), les chats (35%), les poissons (12%), les oiseaux (5%) et les hamsters (4%). Il y a aussi un certain nombre de serpents, de tortues et de lapins.

un hamster

un lapin

une tortue

un oiseau

un poisson

un poisson rouge

animaux domestiques *pets*   **une … sur deux** *one out of two*

La possession avec *de*

Note the words in heavy print:

Voici une moto.	C'est la moto **de Frédéric.**	*It's **Frédéric's** motorcycle.*
Voici un vélo.	C'est le vélo **de Sophie.**	*It's **Sophie's** bike.*

To express POSSESSION, French speakers use the construction:

le/la/les + NOUN + **de** + OWNER	la radio **de** Thomas
↓	les livres **de** Claire
d' (+ VOWEL SOUND)	la maison **d'**Émilie

→ The same construction is used to express RELATIONSHIP:

    C'est **le copain de Daniel.**   *That's **Daniel's** friend.*

    C'est **la mère de Paul.**   *That's **Paul's** mother.*

→ Remember that **de** contracts with **le** and **les**:

    Où est le chat **du voisin?**   *Where is the **neighbor's** cat?*

    C'est la chambre **des enfants.**   *This is the **children's** room.*

→ While English often indicates possession with **'s,** French always uses **de.**

    la copine **de Monique**   ***Monique's** friend (the friend **of Monique**)*

NOUVEAU

DÉJAZET
THEATRE
CRÉATIONS D'YVES LE GUILLOCHET

NOUVEAU

ARTHÉÂTRE
L'HÉDONÉ

ARTHÉÂTRE
L'HÉDONÉ

41, boulevard du Temple · métro République · Paris 3ème

Les aventures de
PinocchiO
du 27 octobre au 25 avril

1 **Présentations** *(Introductions)*

PARLER Imagine that you are hosting a party in France. Introduce the following people.

▶ Jean-Marc (cousin/Sylvie)

Jean-Marc est le cousin de Sylvie.

1. Carole (cousine/Jacques)
2. Michel (copain/Caroline)
3. Philippe (camarade/Charles)
4. Robert (frère/Guillaume)
5. Marina (copine/Paul)
6. Pauline (amie/Éric)
7. Alice (soeur/Karine)

2 **Échanges**

PARLER/ÉCRIRE The following friends have decided to trade a few of their possessions. On a separate sheet of paper, write out what each person has, once the exchange has been completed.

Marc   Alice   Éric   Laure

VOCABULAIRE La famille

la famille (family)

les grands-parents
  le grand-père   **la grand-mère**

les parents (parents)   **les parents** (relatives)
  le père   **la mère**   **l'oncle**   **la tante** (aunt)
  le mari (husband)   **la femme** (wife)

les enfants (children)
  un enfant   **une enfant**
  le frère   **la soeur**   **le cousin**   **la cousine**
  le fils (son)   **la fille** (daughter)

3 La famille de Frédéric

PARLER/ÉCRIRE Frédéric has drawn his family tree. Study it and explain the relationships between the people below.

▶ Éric/Alice Vidal
  Éric est le fils d'Alice Vidal.

1. Léa/Frédéric
2. Martine Mallet/Léa
3. Albert et Julie Mallet/Éric
4. Alice Vidal/Frédéric
5. Jean Mallet/Martine Mallet
6. Alice Vidal/Maurice Vidal
7. Julie Mallet/Éric
8. Élodie/Maurice Vidal
9. Léa/Éric
10. Frédéric/Élodie

▶ Marc a la guitare d'Alice et …

Marc   Alice   Éric   Laure

B Les adjectifs possessifs: *mon, ton, son*

Note the forms of the possessive adjectives in the chart below:

(POSSESSOR)		SINGULAR		PLURAL			
		MASCULINE	FEMININE				
(je)	*my*	mon	ma	mes	mon frère	ma soeur	mes copains
(tu)	*your*	ton	ta	tes	ton oncle	ta tante	tes cousins
(il)	*his*	son	sa	ses	son père	sa mère	ses parents
(elle)	*her*	son	sa	ses	son père	sa mère	ses parents

→ The feminine singular forms **ma, ta, sa** become **mon, ton, son** before a vowel sound.

| **une** amie | **mon** amie | **ton** amie | **son** amie |
| **une** auto | **mon** auto | **ton** auto | **son** auto |

→ There is liaison after **mon, ton, son, mes, tes, ses** before a vowel sound.

mon oncle   **mes** amis

→ The choice between **son, sa,** and **ses** depends on the gender (masculine or feminine) and the number (singular or plural) of the noun that *follows*.

It does NOT depend on the gender of the possessor (that is, whether the owner is male or female). Compare:

4 **Marc et Hélène**

PARLER Marc never knows where his things are, but Hélène does. Play both roles.

▶ le vélo/dans le garage
—Où est mon vélo?
—Ton vélo? Il est dans le garage.

1. les CD/ici
2. la raquette/là-bas
3. la montre/sur toi
4. les livres/dans le sac
5. le portable/sur le bureau
6. le chat/derrière la porte
7. l'appareil-photo/dans la chambre
8. le baladeur/sur la table

5 **Invitations**

PARLER/ÉCRIRE Say whom each person is inviting to the school party, using the appropriate possessive adjectives.

▶ Michel/la copine
Michel invite sa copine.

1. André/la cousine
2. Jean-Claude/la soeur
3. Marie-Noëlle/les frères
4. Pascal/l'amie Sophie
5. Monique/les cousins
6. Nathalie/l'ami Marc
7. Georges/l'amie Cécile
8. Paul/l'amie Thérèse

6 **Chez Marie et Christophe Boutin**

PARLER/ÉCRIRE Items 1 to 8 belong to Marie. Items 9 to 16 belong to Christophe. Point these things out.

Marie	
▶ le vélo	**C'est son vélo.**
1. le baladeur	5. l'ordinateur
2. le sac	6. la guitare
3. le chien	7. les CD
4. l'album	8. les cassettes

Christophe	
▶ les CD	**Ce sont ses CD.**
9. la guitare	13. les livres
10. la chaîne hi-fi	14. la montre
11. le chat	15. les photos
12. le scooter	16. les skis

VOCABULAIRE **Expression pour la conversation**

▶ *How to question a statement or express a doubt:*

Tu es sûr(e)? *Are you sure?* —C'est mon pantalon (*pants*)!
—**Tu es sûr?**

7 **Après la soirée**

PARLER Last night Frédéric and Paul gave a party. They realize that their friends left certain things behind. Frédéric thinks he knows what belongs to whom.

▶ le sac/Claire
FRÉDÉRIC: **Voici le sac de Claire.**
PAUL: **Tu es sûr?**
FRÉDÉRIC: **Mais oui, c'est son sac!**

1. le sac/Jean-Pierre
2. la guitare/Antoine
3. l'appareil-photo/Cécile
4. le baladeur/Stéphanie
5. les CD/Léa
6. le portable/Thomas

Les adjectifs possessifs: *notre, votre, leur*

Note the forms of the possessive adjectives in the chart below:

(POSSESSOR)		SINGULAR	PLURAL		
(nous)	*our*	**notre**	**nos**	**notre** prof	**nos** livres
(vous)	*your*	**votre**	**vos**	**votre** ami	**vos** copains
(ils/elles)	*their*	**leur**	**leurs**	**leur** radio	**leurs** amies

→ There is liaison after **nos, vos, leurs** when the next word begins with a vowel sound.

nos amis   **vos** amies   **leurs** ordinateurs

C'est son vélo.   C'est leur vélo.

8 Aux Galeries Lafayette

PARLER At the Galeries Lafayette department store, a customer is looking for various things. The person at the information desk indicates where they can be found. Play both roles.

▶ les CD/là-bas

S'il vous plaît, où sont vos CD?

Nos CD sont là-bas.

1. les livres/à gauche
2. les affiches/à droite
3. le restaurant/en haut
4. le garage/en bas
5. les ordinateurs/ici
6. la cafétéria/tout droit

9 Les millionnaires

PARLER/ÉCRIRE Imagine you are showing a millionaire's estate to French visitors.

▶ la maison
   Voici leur maison.

1. la piscine
2. la Rolls Royce
3. les chiens
4. le parc
5. l'hélicoptère
6. les courts de tennis

10 En famille

PARLER/ÉCRIRE We often do things with our family. Complete each sentence with a possessive adjective: **son, sa, ses, leur,** or **leurs.**

▶ Pascal joue au tennis avec <u>sa</u> cousine.
▶ Éric et Paul jouent aux cartes avec <u>leurs</u> cousins.

1. Frédéric dîne chez … oncle.
2. André dîne chez … grands-parents.
3. Caroline et Paul vont chez … grand-mère.
4. Mlle Vénard fait une promenade avec … chien.
5. Antoine va à la piscine avec … soeur.
6. Stéphanie et Céline vont au cinéma avec … parents.
7. M. et Mme Boutin voyagent avec … fille.
8. Mme Denis visite Paris avec … fils, Marc et Frédéric.

D Les nombres ordinaux

Compare the following regular numbers and the ordinal numbers in French:

(2)   deux   **deuxième**   Février est le **deuxième** mois de l'année.
(3)   trois   **troisième**   Mercredi est le **troisième** jour de la semaine.
(4)   quatre   **quatrième**   J'habite au **quatrième** étage *(floor)*.

To form ordinal numbers, French speakers use the following pattern:

NUMBER (minus final **-e**, if any) + **-ième**
(6) six : **six** + **-ième** → **sixième**
(11) onze : **onz-** + **-ième** → **onzième**

→ EXCEPTIONS: (1)   un (une) → **premier (première)**
                (5)   cinq   → **cinquième**
                (9)   neuf   → **neuvième**

→ Ordinal numbers are adjectives and come BEFORE the noun.

> ### LEARNING ABOUT LANGUAGE
>
> Numbers like *first, second, third, fourth, fifth* are used to rank persons or things—to put them in a given order.
>
> They are called ORDINAL NUMBERS.
>
> In English, most ordinal numbers end in *-th*.

11 La course *(The race)*

PARLER/ÉCRIRE Frédéric and his friends are participating in a five-kilometer race. Announce the order of arrival of the following runners.

▶ Paul (6)

1. Frédéric (4)
2. Jérôme (7)
3. Christophe (8)
4. Sophie (2)
5. Christine (1)
6. Claire (10)
7. Karine (11)
8. Olivier (12)

Paul est sixième.

PRONONCIATION   /o/   /ɔ/

Les voyelles /o/ et /ɔ/

The French vowel /o/ is pronounced with more tension than in English. It is usually the last sound in a word.

vél<u>o</u>   **téléph<u>o</u>ne**

Répétez: /o/   **vél<u>o</u> radi<u>o</u> n<u>o</u>s v<u>o</u>s <u>eau</u> chât<u>eau</u> ch<u>au</u>d**
                    N<u>o</u>s vél<u>o</u>s sont <u>au</u> chât<u>eau</u>.

The French vowel /ɔ/ occurs in the middle of a word. Imitate the model carefully.

Répétez: /ɔ/   **téléph<u>o</u>ne éc<u>o</u>le Nic<u>o</u>le n<u>o</u>tre v<u>o</u>tre c<u>o</u>pain pr<u>o</u>f d<u>o</u>mmage**
                    C<u>o</u>mment s'appelle v<u>o</u>tre pr<u>o</u>f?

À votre tour!

OBJECTIFS

Now you can …
• talk about your family and your relatives
• identify things as belonging to you or to someone else
• talk about your pets

1  **Allô!**

PARLER Émilie is on the phone with Bernard. Match Émilie's questions with Bernard's answers. Then act out the dialogue with a classmate.

1. Avec qui est-ce que tu vas au cinéma?

2. C'est le cousin de Monique?

3. Tu connais leurs parents?

4. Ils sont canadiens, n'est-ce pas?

a. Non, c'est son frère.

b. Bien sûr, ils sont très sympathiques.

c. Avec mon copain Marc.

d. Non, mais leurs voisins sont de Québec.

2  **Créa-dialogue**

PARLER We often identify objects by their color. Create conversations with your classmates according to the model.

le vélo / Paul?

▶ —C'est le vélo de Paul?
—Non, ce n'est pas son vélo.
—Tu es sûr?
—Mais oui. Son vélo est bleu.

1. la guitare / Alice?

2. le scooter / Paul et Anne?

3. le chien / tes cousins?

4. la mobylette / Isabelle?

5. la maison / M. et Mme Lavoie?

6. la voiture / ton oncle?

Composition: un animal domestique -----------------------------------

ÉCRIRE Write a short composition about a pet: either your own pet, a pet belonging to a friend, or an imaginary pet. You may mention …

- the type of animal
- its name
- its age
- its colors
- its size
- its eating habits
- some physical and personality traits

 Composition: Ma famille -----------------------------------

ÉCRIRE Select five people in your family and write one to three sentences about each person.

Mon cousin s'appelle John. Il habite à San Francisco. Il a seize ans.

 Arbre généalogique *(Family tree)* -----------------------------------

ÉCRIRE On a separate sheet of paper, draw your own (real or imaginary) family tree. Label the people and indicate their relationships to you.

LESSON REVIEW
CLASSZONE.COM

Tests de contrôle

By taking the following tests, you can check your progress in French and also prepare for the unit test. Write your answers on a separate sheet of paper.

1 The right place

Review...
• places and rooms of the house: pp. 197 and 200

Complete each of the following sentences by filling in the blank with one of the places in the box. Be logical and do not use the same word more than once.

> bibliothèque chambre cuisine école église immeuble
> jardin magasin piscine plage salle de bains salle à manger

1. Le réfrigérateur est dans la —.
2. Quand il y a des invités *(guests)*, nous dînons dans la —.
3. Dans le —, il y a un lilas *(lilac tree)*.
4. Dans le complexe sportif où nous allons, il y a une — olympique.
5. Il y a beaucoup de livres à la — de la ville.
6. Dans ma —, il y a une table et un grand lit.
7. En été, nous allons en vacances sur une — de l'Atlantique.
8. Il y a une — catholique dans notre quartier.
9. Le samedi, les élèves américains ne vont pas à l'—.
10. Le shampooing *(shampoo)* est dans la —.
11. Mes cousins habitent dans un grand — moderne.
12. Je vais acheter un ordinateur dans un — d'équipement électronique.

2 The right choice

Review...
• use of à, de, and chez pp. 208, 210, 211, 219, 220, and 223

Choose the word or expression in parentheses which logically completes each of the following sentences.

1. Marc dîne — restaurant. **(à, au)**
2. Thomas nage — piscine. **(la, à la)**
3. Le professeur parle — élèves. **(aux, les)**
4. Les élèves vont — école en bus. **(à la, à l')**
5. Nous faisons une promenade — pied. **(à, au)**
6. Pauline va — sa copine Isabelle. **(à, chez)**
7. Nous revenons — école à trois heures. **(à l', de l')**
8. Les touristes arrivent — musée. **(du, de l')**
9. J'aime jouer — football. **(au, du)**
10. Est-ce que tu joues — clarinette? **(à la, de la)**
11. Comment s'appelle la copine — Monique? **(de, à)**
12. Voici la maison — voisins. **(des, de)**

3 The right owner

Complete each of the following sentences with the possessive adjective that corresponds to the underlined subject.

▶ Jean-Paul regarde **ses** photos.

1. Tu téléphones à — copine.

2. Je vais souvent au cinéma avec — amis.

3. Marc dîne chez — tante.

4. Alice invite — voisins à la boum.

5. Isabelle n'a pas — appareil-photo avec elle.

6. Thomas et Charlotte sont en vacances chez — oncle.

7. Les élèves respectent — professeurs.

8. Vous parlez avec — amie Mélanie.

9. Nous allons visiter Paris avec — professeur de français.

10. Est-ce que vous écoutez toujours — parents?

Review...
• possessive adjectives: pp. 230 and 232

4 Aller and venir

Complete the following sentences with the appropriate forms of **aller** or **venir.**

1. Attendez-moi *(Wait for me)*! Je —.

2. Thomas et Céline — très souvent au cinéma.

3. Qu'est-ce que tu — faire samedi?

4. Nous — aller à une boum.

5. Le professeur est canadien. Il — de Montréal.

6. Je — souvent à la piscine parce que j'aime nager.

7. Nicolas n'a pas faim. Il — du restaurant.

8. D'où est-ce que vous —?

Review...
• aller and venir: pp. 206, 212, and 218

5 Composition: La maison idéale

Write a short paragraph of five or six sentences describing your ideal house and its rooms. Does it have a garden? Where is it located? What do you especially like about it?

STRATEGY Writing		
a	**b**	**c**
Sketch out a floor plan of your ideal house, labelling the rooms.	Organize your paragraph, concluding with why you like this house.	Reread your composition to be sure you have spelled all the names of the rooms correctly.

Vocabulaire

POUR COMMUNIQUER

Asking where people are going

Où vas-tu?
    Je vais à + PLACE, EVENT   **Je vais au concert.**
    Je vais chez + PERSON   **Je vais chez Pierre.**
    Je vais chez + STRESS PRONOUN   **Je vais chez moi.**

Where are you going?
I am going to the concert.
I am going to Pierre's house.
I am going to my house.

Asking where people are coming from

D'où est-ce que tu viens?
    Je viens de + PLACE   **Je viens de la piscine.**

Where are you coming from?
I am coming from the pool.

Asking for directions

Excusez-moi, où est [le théâtre]?
Excuse me, where is [the theater]?

Est-ce que c'est | **loin?**
                      | **près?**

Is it | *far?*
     | *nearby, close?*

Tournez | **à gauche.**
        | **à droite.**
Continuez tout droit.

Turn | *to the left.*
     | *to the right.*
Continue straight ahead.

Pardon, où sont [les toilettes]?
Excuse me, where are [the toilets]?

Elles sont | **en haut.**
          | **en bas**

They are | *upstairs.*
      | *downstairs.*

Talking about future plans

Qu'est-ce que tu vas faire?
    Je vais [travailler].

What are you going to do?
I am going [to work].

Expressing possession

C'est mon (ton, son ...) livre.   *That's my (your, his/her, ...) book.*

MOTS ET EXPRESSIONS

Moyens de transport *(means of transportation)*

à pied	*on foot*	**en bus**	*by bus*	**en train**	*by train*
à vélo	*by bicycle*	**en métro**	*by subway*	**en voiture**	*by car*
		en taxi	*by taxi*		

La ville

un boulevard	*boulevard*	**une adresse**	*address*
un café	*café*	**une avenue**	*avenue*
un centre commercial	*mall, shopping center*	**une bibliothèque**	*library*
un cinéma	*movie theater*	**une école**	*school*
un hôpital	*hospital*	**une église**	*church*
un hôtel	*hotel*	**une piscine**	*(swimming) pool*
un magasin	*store*	**une plage**	*beach*
un musée	*museum*	**une rue**	*street*
un parc	*park*	**une ville**	*city, town*
un quartier	*neighborhood*		
un restaurant	*restaurant*		
un stade	*stadium*		
un supermarché	*supermarket*		
un théâtre	*theater*		
un village	*town, village*		

La maison

un appartement	apartment	une chambre	bedroom
un garage	garage	une cuisine	kitchen
un immeuble	apartment building	une maison	house
un jardin	garden, yard	une salle à manger	dining room
un salon	living room	une salle de bains	bathroom
		les toilettes	bathroom, toilet

Quelques endroits où aller

un concert	concert	un film	movie	une boum	party (casual)
un endroit	place	un pique-nique	picnic	une fête	party
un événement	event	un rendez-vous	date, appointment	une soirée	party (evening)

La famille

les parents	parents; relatives	la famille	family
les grands-parents	grandparents		
le grand-père	grandfather	la grand-mère	grandmother
le père	father	la mère	mother
le mari	husband	la femme	wife
un enfant	child	une enfant	child
le fils	son	la fille	daughter
le frère	brother	la soeur	sister
l'oncle	uncle	la tante	aunt
le cousin	cousin	la cousine	cousin

Verbes en -er

arriver	to arrive, to come
rentrer	to go back, come back
rester	to stay
jouer à + SPORT, GAME	to play (a sport, game)
jouer de + INSTRUMENT	to play (an instrument)

Verbes irréguliers

aller	to go
faire une promenade à pied	to go for a walk
faire une promenade à vélo	to go for a bike ride
faire une promenade en voiture	to go for a drive
venir	to come
revenir	to come back

Les sports

le baseball	baseball
le basket(ball)	basketball
le foot(ball)	soccer
le ping-pong	ping-pong
le tennis	tennis
le volley(ball)	volleyball

Les jeux

les échecs	chess	les cartes	cards
les jeux d'ordinateur	computer games	les dames	checkers
les jeux vidéo	video games		

Les instruments de musique

le clavier	keyboard	la batterie	drums
le piano	piano	la clarinette	clarinet
le saxo(phone)	saxophone	la flûte	flute
le violon	violin	la guitare	guitar

Les nombres ordinaux

premier (première)	first	septième	seventh
deuxième	second	huitième	eighth
troisième	third	neuvième	ninth
quatrième	fourth	dixième	tenth
cinquième	fifth	onzième	eleventh
sixième	sixth	douzième	twelfth

Expressions utiles

Pas du tout!	Not at all! Definitely not!
Vraiment?!	Really?!
Tu es sûr(e)?	Are you sure?
Vas-y!	Go on!
Va-t'en!	Go away!

TEST PREP CLASSZONE.COM FLASHCARDS AND MORE!

LES JEUNES FRANÇAIS ET

le cinéma

Le samedi, les jeunes Français adorent aller au cinéma. C'est pour eux l'occasion de voir° un bon film et aussi d'être avec leurs copains. Quand ils sont en ville, ils peuvent° aller dans les cinémas de quartier. Mais en général, ils préfèrent les «multiplexes». Là, ils ont le choix entre 6 et 12 films différents. Dans les grands multiplexes, il y a aussi des restaurants, des boutiques et des salles de jeux vidéo où ils peuvent aller avant° et après le film. Les jeunes qui vont souvent au cinéma peuvent acheter° une carte de multiplexe.° Avec cette° carte qui coûte dix-huit euros par mois, ils peuvent voir un nombre illimité de films dans leur multiplexe favori.

Les jeunes Français vont au cinéma pour voir les films français récents. Ils aiment aussi les films américains, en particulier les films d'action, les films de science-fiction et les comédies. Les jeunes qui parlent bien anglais peuvent voir ces films en «version originale» — avec, bien sûr, des sous-titres° en français.

voir *to see* **peuvent** *can* **avant** *before* **acheter** *buy* **carte de multiplexe** *movie pass*
cette *that* **ces** *these* **sous-titres** *subtitles*

COMPARAISONS CULTURELLES

Compare the movie-going preferences of French and American teenagers by filling in the following chart:

Les préférences	Les jeunes Français	Moi	Différence ou similarité?
• Quel jour?	_____	_____	_____
• Dans quelle sorte de cinéma?	_____	_____	_____
• Quels films?	_____	_____	_____

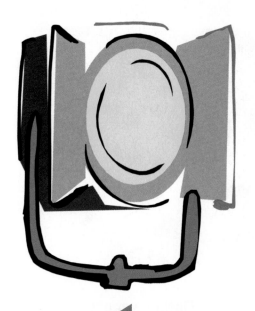

Films américains, public français

Voici une liste de films américains qui ont eu° beaucoup de succès en France. Est-ce que vous pouvez° identifier ces films? Lisez° le titre° français de chaque° film. Faites correspondre° le titre de ce film avec le titre américain.

---

ont eu *have had* **pouvez** *can* **Lisez** *Read* **titre** *title* **chaque** *each*
Faites correspondre *Match*

TITRES FRANÇAIS

1. Blanche-Neige et les sept nains (1937)
2. Le Magicien d'Oz (1939)
3. La mélodie du bonheur (1965)
4. Devine qui vient dîner? (1967)
5. Le Parrain (1972)
6. Les aventuriers de l'arche perdue (1981)
7. E.T. l'extra-terrestre (1982)
8. Le roi Lion (1994)
9. Il faut sauver le soldat Ryan (1998)
10. En pleine tempête (2000)

TITRES AMÉRICAINS

A. E.T. the Extra-Terrestrial
B. The Lion King
C. The Godfather
D. Snow White and the Seven Dwarves
E. Guess Who's Coming to Dinner?
F. The Perfect Storm
G. Raiders of the Lost Ark
H. Saving Private Ryan
I. The Sound of Music
J. The Wizard of Oz

CONNEXIONS

Use the Internet to find out which American films are currently playing in Paris. As you read the French titles, can you guess the original English titles?

Tintin et ses amis

Tintin et Milou

Tous° les jeunes Français connaissent° Tintin. Tintin n'est pas une personne réelle. C'est le héros d'une bande dessinée° très populaire en France et dans le monde° entier. «Les Aventures de Tintin» ont été publiées en français, mais aussi en anglais, en espagnol, en italien, en chinois, en japonais ... au total dans 40 langues° différentes.

Tintin a dix-sept ans et il est belge.° C'est un journaliste-détective. Il est intelligent et courageux et il adore voyager. Il va en Égypte, au Congo, en Chine, au Tibet, au Mexique et en Amérique. Il va même° sur° la lune, bien avant° les astronautes américains. Dans ses voyages, il connaît° des aventures extraordinaires. Tintin est l'ami de la justice et l'ennemi du mal.° Il protège ses amis et il s'attaque aux dictateurs, aux trafiquants de drogue° et aux marchands d'armes.° Il est souvent en danger, mais il triomphe toujours.

Dans ses aventures, Tintin est toujours accompagné de son chien, Milou. Milou est un petit fox terrier blanc intuitif et courageux qui protège son maître quand il est attaqué. Il accompagne Tintin dans toutes ses aventures. Quand il va avec lui sur la lune, il est équipé d'une combinaison spatiale° pour chiens.

Voilà qui est fait.°

EN BREF: LA BELGIQUE

Capitale: Bruxelles
Population: 10 250 000
Langues officielles: français, flamand° et allemand°

La Belgique est une monarchie constitutionnelle avec un roi,° le roi Albert II. Sa capitale, Bruxelles, est le siège° de la Commission Européenne.

---

flamand *Flemish* **allemand** *German*
roi *king* **siège** *seat*

Tous *All* **connaissent** *know* **bande dessinée** *comic strip* **monde** *world* **langues** *languages* **belge** *Belgian*
même *even* **sur** *on* **avant** *before* **connaît** *experiences* **mal** *evil* **trafiquants de drogue** *drug dealers*
armes *weapons* **combinaison spatiale** *space suit* **Voila qui est fait.** *There, you're all set.*

Tintin a d'autres compagnons d'aventures, très sympathiques, mais un peu bizarres.

le capitaine Haddock

Le capitaine Haddock habite au château° de Moulinsart en Belgique. C'est un ancien° officier de la marine marchande. Il est brave et courageux ... mais il est aussi très irritable.

Garnements! *Rascals!* **Iconoclastes!** *Iconoclasts! (people who attack and seek to overthrow traditional ideas)* **château** *castle* **ancien** *former*

Dupont et Dupond

Dupont et Dupond sont presque° identiques, mais ils ne sont pas frères. Ce sont des policiers méthodiques ... mais incompétents.

presque *almost*

le professeur Tournesol

Le professeur Tournesol est un génie scientifique. Il est modeste et réservé et comme° beaucoup de professeurs, il est très distrait.°

comme *like* **distrait** *absent-minded*

STRATEGY Reading

Recognizing Cognate Patterns Recognizing French-English cognate patterns will help you increase your reading vocabulary and improve your reading comprehension. Here are some common patterns:

FRENCH	ENGLISH	FRENCH	ENGLISH
-aire	*-ar, -ary*	extraordinaire	*extraordinary*
-eux, -euse	*-ous*	courageux	*courageous*
-ique	*-ic, -ical*	identique	*identical*
-iste	*-ist, istic*	journaliste	*journalist*
-é	*-ed*	réservé	*reserved*

COMMUNAUTÉ

Organize a **fête Tintin** for the language classes in your school. You may display Tintin books in French and other languages and show a video or DVD of some of Tintin's adventures. Encourage your classmates to come dressed as Tintin characters.

Et vous?

Quelle est ta bande dessinée favorite? Qui sont les héros? Pourquoi est-ce que tu aimes cette bande dessinée?

Bonjour, Ousmane!

Bonjour! Je m'appelle Ousmane. J'adore la musique. J'aime surtout le rap et le rock. Mon chanteur° préféré est MC Solaar. Il chante très bien. J'ai beaucoup de CD de lui. Ma soeur, elle, préfère le blues et le jazz.

Je suis un peu musicien. Je joue de la guitare. Et je ne joue pas trop mal. J'ai organisé° un petit orchestre° de rock avec des copains. Nous répétons° le mercredi après-midi. Nous ne répétons pas chez moi, parce que ma mère déteste ça.° Parfois,° le week-end, nous jouons à des boums pour nos amis.

---

chanteur *singer* **ai organisé** *organized* **orchestre** *band*
répétons *rehearse* **ça** *that* **Parfois** *Sometimes*

Compréhension

1. Quelle est la musique préférée d'Ousmane?
2. De quel instrument est-ce qu'il joue?
3. Quand est-ce qu'il répète avec ses copains?
4. Pourquoi est-ce qu'il ne répète pas à la maison?

Activité écrite

Write a short note to Ousmane in which you describe your musical preferences. Use the following suggestions:

- J'aime … (quelles musiques?)
- Je déteste … (quelles musiques?)
- Mon groupe préféré est … (qui?)
- Ils/Elles chantent … (comment?)

MC Solaar

le «Monsieur Rap» français

MC Solaar est né° à Dakar au Sénégal. Il s'appelle en réalité Claude M'Barali. Ses parents émigrent en France quand il a six mois. Il fait ses études dans la région parisienne. Après° le bac, il s'intéresse à° la musique. Il compose des chansons° françaises sur des rythmes de rap américain. Ses chansons ont beaucoup de succès. MC Solaar donne° des concerts en France, mais aussi en Angleterre,° en Allemagne,° en Russie et dans les pays° d'Afrique.

Aujourd'hui, MC Solaar est le «Monsieur Rap» français! Dans ses chansons, il exprime° des messages positifs contre° la violence et pour la paix.° Voilà pourquoi il est très populaire en France et dans le monde° francophone.

---

est né *was born* **Après** *After* **s'intéresse à** *becomes interested in* **chansons** *songs* **donne** *gives* **Angleterre** *England* **Allemagne** *Germany* **pays** *countries* **exprime** *expresses* **contre** *against* **la paix** *peace* **monde** *world*

CONNEXIONS

With 2 or 3 classmates, select a French singer, such as MC Solaar. Go on the Internet and obtain as much information as you can about the person you have chosen. If possible, get samples of his or her music. Share your findings with the rest of the class.

COMMUNAUTÉ

Prepare a short program about music from the French-speaking world. You may want to include pictures of the performers, selections of their recordings, and perhaps a world map showing their countries of origin. Present your program to another class at school or at a local senior center.

À Paris

Bonjour, Paris!

Quelques faits

- Paris est la capitale de la France.

- Paris est une très grande ville. La ville de Paris a deux millions d'habitants. La région parisienne a onze millions d'habitants. Vingt pour cent (20%) des Français habitent dans la région parisienne.

- Paris est situé° sur la Seine. Ce fleuve° divise° la ville en deux parties: la rive° droite (au nord) et la rive gauche (au sud).

- Administrativement, Paris est divisé en vingt arrondissements.°

- Paris est une ville très ancienne.° Elle a plus de° deux mille° ans.

- Paris est aussi une ville moderne et dynamique. C'est le centre économique, industriel et commercial de la France.

- Avec ses musées, ses théâtres, ses bibliothèques et ses écoles d'art, Paris est un centre culturel et artistique très important.

- Avec ses nombreux° monuments et ses larges avenues, Paris est une très belle ville. Pour beaucoup de gens, c'est la plus° belle ville du monde.° Chaque année,° des millions de touristes visitent Paris.

---

situé *located* **fleuve** *river* **divise** *divides*
rive *(river)bank* **arrondissements** *districts*
ancienne *old* **plus de** *more than* **mille** *thousand*
nombreux *many* **la plus** *the most* **monde** *world*
Chaque année *Each year*

GARE DE LYON

BASTILLE

RÉPUBLIQUE

Mairie du XIème

Le Paris
TRADITIONNEL

PORTE DE LA VILLETTE

LA VILLE CITÉ DES SC ET DE L'IND

SACRÉ-COEUR

BUTTE MONTMARTRE

ARC DE TRIOMPHE

OPÉRA

MADELEINE

PLACE DE LA CONCORDE

GRAND PALAIS

LOUVRE

CENTRE POMPIDOU

RIVE DROITE

INVALIDES

TOUR EIFFEL

MUSÉE D'ORSAY

NOTRE-DAME

OPÉRA DE LA BASTILLE

RIVE GAUCHE

Seine

TOUR MONTPARNASSE

SORBONNE

QUARTIER LATIN

Seine

PALAIS OMNISPORTS

PORTE BERCY

LA TOUR EIFFEL

Pour beaucoup de gens, **la tour Eiffel** est le symbole de Paris. Cette° immense tour de fer° a trois cent mètres de haut.° Elle a été inaugurée en 1889 (dix-huit cent quatre-vingt-neuf) par l'ingénieur Gustave Eiffel. Du sommet de la tour Eiffel, on° a une très belle vue sur Paris.

NOTRE-DAME

Notre-Dame est la cathédrale de Paris. Elle est située au centre de Paris sur une île,° l'île de la Cité. Notre-Dame a été construite° aux douzième et treizième siècles.°

Cette *This* **fer** *iron* **a trois cent mètres de haut** *is 300 meters high* **on** *one* **île** *island* **a été construite** *was built* **siècles** *centuries*

LE SACRÉ-COEUR

Le Sacré-Coeur est une église de pierre° blanche qui domine Paris. Cette église est située sur la butte° Montmartre. Montmartre est un quartier pittoresque. Les artistes viennent ici pour peindre° et les touristes viennent pour regarder les artistes. Si vous voulez° avoir un souvenir personnel de Paris, allez à Montmartre et demandez à° un artiste de faire votre portrait.

LE QUARTIER LATIN

Le Quartier latin est le quartier des étudiants. C'est un quartier très animé avec des cafés, des cinémas, des librairies° et des restaurants exotiques et bon marché.° Pourquoi est-ce que ce quartier s'appelle «Quartier latin»? Parce qu'autrefois° les étudiants parlaient° latin ici.

L'ARC DE TRIOMPHE ET LES CHAMPS-ÉLYSÉES

L'Arc de Triomphe est un monument qui° commémore les victoires de Napoléon (1769–1821). Ce monument est situé en haut° des Champs-Élysées.

Les Champs-Élysées sont une très grande et très belle avenue. Pour les Parisiens, c'est la plus° belle avenue du monde.

Activité Culturelle

Imaginez que vous passez une journée° à Paris. Où allez-vous aller le matin? Où allez-vous aller l'après-midi? Choisissez deux endroits à visiter et expliquez° votre choix.°

---

pierre *stone* **butte** *hill* **peindre** *to paint* **voulez** *want* **demandez à** *ask* **librairies** *bookstores*
bon marché *inexpensive* **autrefois** *in the past* **parlaient** *used to speak* **qui** *which* **en haut** *at the top*
la plus *the most* **passez une journée** *are spending a day* **expliquez** *explain* **choix** *choice*

deux cent quarante-neuf
Lecture et Culture 249

Le nouveau Paris

● Le Louvre et la pyramide du Louvre

Le Louvre est une ancienne° résidence royale transformée en musée. C'est dans ce° musée que se trouve° la fameuse «Mona Lisa». On entre dans le Louvre par° une pyramide de verre.° Cette pyramide moderne a été construite° par l'architecte américain I.M. Pei. Avec sa pyramide, le Louvre est le symbole du nouveau° Paris, à la fois° moderne et traditionnel.

● Le Centre Pompidou

Le Centre Pompidou est le monument le plus° visité de Paris. C'est un musée d'art moderne. C'est aussi une bibliothèque, une cinémathèque et un centre audio-visuel. À l'extérieur,° sur l'esplanade, il y a des musiciens, des mimes, des acrobates, des jongleurs° … Un peu plus loin,° il y a une place° avec des fontaines, un bassin° et des sculptures mobiles.

● Le musée d'Orsay

Autrefois,° c'était° une gare.° Aujourd'hui, c'est un musée. On vient ici admirer les chefs-d'oeuvre° des grands peintres° et sculpteurs français du dix-neuvième siècle.° On peut,° par exemple, admirer les oeuvres° de Monet, de Claudel, de Renoir, de Morisot et de Toulouse-Lautrec. À l'extérieur, il y a des sculptures qui représentent les cinq continents.

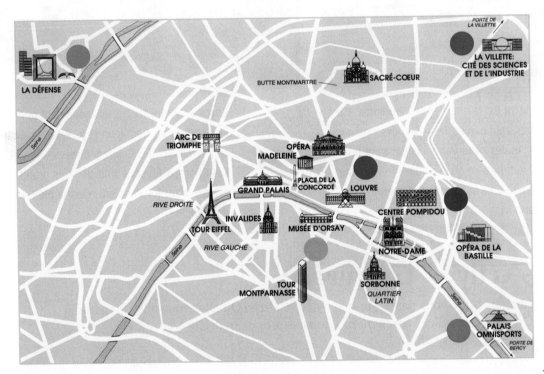

---

ancienne *former* **ce** *this* **se trouve** *is located* **par** *by* **verre** *glass* **a été construite** *was built* **nouveau** *new*
à la fois *at the same time* **le plus** *the most* **À l'extérieur** *Outside* **jongleurs** *jugglers* **plus loin** *farther away* **place** *square*
bassin *ornamental pool* **Autrefois** *Formerly* **c'était** *it used to be* **gare** *train station* **chefs-d'oeuvre** *masterpieces*
peintres *painters* **siècle** *century* **peut** *can* **oeuvres** *works*

LE PALAIS OMNISPORTS DE BERCY

Sport ou musique? **Bercy** est un stade couvert° pour tous les sports. C'est aussi une immense salle° de concert. On vient ici écouter et applaudir les vedettes° de la chanson° française … et de la chanson américaine.

LE PARC DE LA VILLETTE

Le parc de la Villette est un lieu° de récréation pour les jeunes de tout âge.° On trouve ici des parcs pour enfants,° des terrains de jeu° et différentes° constructions ultra-modernes.

- Le Zénith est une salle de concert où viennent les vedettes du monde° entier.
- La Géode est un cinéma omnimax avec un écran° circulaire géant.
- La Cité des sciences et de l'industrie est un grand musée scientifique où les jeunes peuvent° faire leurs propres° expériences° et jouer avec toutes sortes de gadgets électroniques.

LA DÉFENSE ET SON ARCHE

La Défense est le nouveau centre d'affaires° situé à l'ouest de Paris. Chaque° jour, des milliers° de Parisiens viennent travailler dans ses gratte-ciel° de verre. Il y a aussi des magasins, des cinémas, des restaurants et une patinoire.° La Grande Arche a été construite pour commémorer le deux centième anniversaire de la Révolution française.

Activité Culturelle

Vous êtes à Paris pour une semaine. Pendant votre séjour, vous voulez faire les choses suivantes. Dites où vous allez pour cela.

▶ Lundi, je veux voir une exposition d'art moderne. Je vais au Centre Pompidou.

Quand?	Pourquoi?	Où?
▶ lundi	voir *(to see)* une exposition d'art moderne	??
mardi	voir une exposition sur les lasers	??
mercredi	voir la «Mona Lisa»	??
jeudi	voir un match de basket	??
vendredi	voir une exposition sur Toulouse-Lautrec	??
samedi	aller dans les magasins et faire du shopping	??

---

couvert *covered* **salle** *hall* **vedettes** *stars* **chanson** *song* **lieu** *place* **de tout âge** *of all ages* **parcs pour enfants** *playgrounds*
terrains de jeu *playing fields* **différentes** *several* **monde** *world* **écran** *screen* **peuvent** *can* **propres** *own*
expériences *experiments* **affaires** *business* **Chaque** *Each* **des milliers** *thousands* **gratte-ciel** *skyscrapers*
patinoire *skating rink*

| Précédente | Suivante | Recharger | Accueil | Rechercher | Images | Imprimer | Sécurité | Arrêter |

Salut, les amis!

Je m'appelle Jean-Marc Lacoste. Je suis parisien. J'habite rue Racine. C'est une petite rue du Quartier latin. Notre appartement est situé au quatrième étage° d'un vieil° immeuble. L'immeuble est très ancien (il n'y a pas d'ascenseur°), mais notre appartement est moderne et confortable.

Je vais à l'École Alsacienne où je suis élève de seconde. En général, je vais là-bas en bus. Quand il fait beau, je prends° mon scooter, ou bien° je vais à pied. C'est assez loin, mais j'adore marcher.

En semaine, j'ai beaucoup de travail et je n'ai pas le temps° de sortir.° Le week-end, c'est différent. Qu'est-ce que je fais? Ça dépend! Quand j'ai de l'argent,° je vais au concert. Le week-end prochain,° j'espère aller à Bercy écouter le groupe U2. Quand je n'ai pas d'argent, je vais au Centre Pompidou. Là, au moins,° le spectacle° est gratuit.°

J'aime aussi me promener° dans mon quartier avec mes copains. Il y a toujours quelque chose° à faire au Quartier latin. On° va au cinéma. On va dans les magasins de musique pour écouter les nouveaux albums. On va dans les librairies° pour regarder les vieux livres et les bandes dessinées.° On va au café. Là, on regarde les gens qui passent dans la rue. Parfois,° on rencontre° des filles …

Et vous, quand est-ce que vous allez venir à Paris? Bientôt,° j'espère. Je vous attends!°

Amitiés,°
Jean-Marc

étage *floor* **vieil** *old* **ascenseur** *elevator* **prends** *take* **ou bien** *or else* **temps** *time* **sortir** *go out* **argent** *money*
prochain *next* **au moins** *at least* **spectacle** *show* **gratuit** *free* **me promener** *to go for walks* **quelque chose** *something*
On *We* **librairies** *bookstores* **bandes dessinées** *comics* **Parfois** *Sometimes* **rencontre** *meet* **Bientôt** *Soon*
Je vous attends! *I'm expecting you!* **Amitiés** *In friendship*

PARIS en BATEAU-MOUCHE

Comment visiter Paris? On peut° visiter Paris en taxi, mais c'est cher.° On peut prendre° le bus. C'est amusant, mais la circulation° à Paris est souvent difficile. On peut prendre le métro. C'est pratique, rapide et bon marché,° mais on ne voit rien.°

Pourquoi ne pas faire une promenade° en bateau-mouche?° Les bateaux-mouches sont des bateaux modernes et confortables qui circulent sur la Seine. Pendant° la promenade, on peut prendre des photos et admirer les monuments le long de° la Seine. Le soir, on peut voir les monuments illuminés!

Activité Culturelle

Vous faites une promenade en bateau-mouche.
- Combien coûte le billet?
- Quels° monuments est-ce que vous pouvez° voir?

On peut *One can* **cher** *expensive* **prendre** *take* **circulation** *traffic* **bon marché** *inexpensive* **ne voit rien** *sees nothing*
Pourquoi ne pas faire une promenade *Why not take a ride* **bateau-mouche** *sight-seeing boat* **Pendant** *During* **le long de** *along*
Quels *Which* **pouvez** *can*

UNITÉ 6

Le shopping

LEÇON 17 LE FRANÇAIS PRATIQUE: L'achat des vêtements

LEÇON 18 Rien n'est parfait!

LEÇON 19 Un choix difficile

LEÇON 20 Alice a un job

THÈME ET OBJECTIFS

Buying clothes

Are you interested in clothes? When you visit France, you will enjoy going window shopping. In fact, you will probably want to try on a few items and buy something special to bring home.

In this unit, you will learn …

- to name and describe the clothes you wear
- to discuss style
- to shop for clothes and other items
- to talk about money

You will also be able …

- to make comparisons
- to point out certain people or objects to your friends

WEBQUEST
CLASSZONE.COM

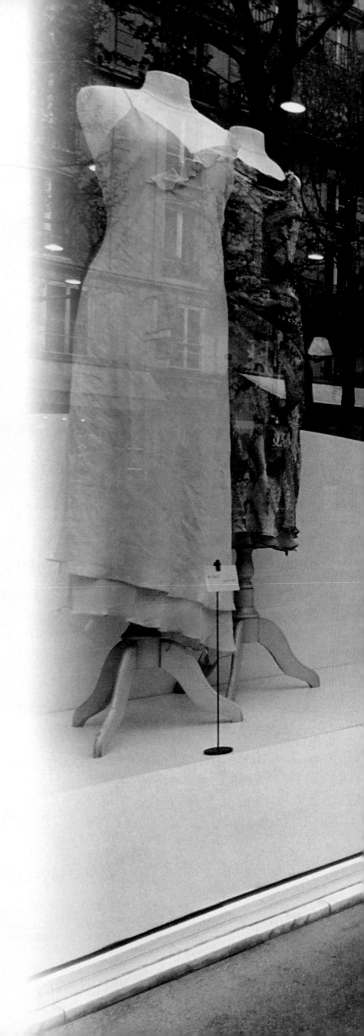

LEÇON
17

LE FRANÇAIS
PRATIQUE
VIDÉO   DVD   AUDIO

L'achat des vêtements

Accent sur ... l'élégance française

France is a leader in high fashion. French fashion design houses, such as Dior, Chanel, Yves Saint Laurent and Pierre Cardin, are known all over the world for the style and quality of their creations.

French young people like to be in style, even if their clothes are casual and not too expensive. Depending on their budgets, they buy their clothes at ...

- **une grande surface** (*low-cost chain store*)
- **un grand magasin** (*department store*)
- **une boutique de vêtements** (*clothing store*)
- **une boutique de soldes** (*discount clothing shop*)
- **le marché aux puces** (*flea market*)

Mélanie cherche une robe pour aller au mariage de sa cousine. Quelle robe est-ce qu'elle va acheter?

Fatima est dans une boutique de vêtements. Ici les vêtements sont très élégants …
et très chers aussi.

Patrick et Béatrice achètent leurs vêtements dans
une grande surface. Ici les vêtements sont de
bonne qualité et ils ne sont pas trop chers.

Michel est dans un magasin de chaussures. Quelles chaussures
est-ce qu'il va acheter? Des baskets ou des chaussures de sport?

A VOCABULAIRE Les vêtements

Je vais dans un magasin.

▶ **How to talk about shopping for clothes:**

Où vas-tu?

Je vais | dans **une boutique** *(shop).*
| dans **un magasin** *(store)*
| dans **un grand magasin** *(department store)*

Qu'est-ce que tu vas **acheter** *(to buy)*?

Je vais acheter **des vêtements** *(clothes).*

Les vêtements

Pour hommes et femmes

une casquette

un chapeau

100€

50€

60€

80€

un blouson

une veste

un pull

un manteau

un pantalon

un imper
(un imperméable)

30€

20€

un jean

25€

une chemise

un polo

des chaussettes
(une chaussette)

➔ Nouns that end in **-eau** in the singular end in **-eaux** in the plural.

un chap**eau**   des chap**eaux**   un mant**eau**   des mant**eaux**

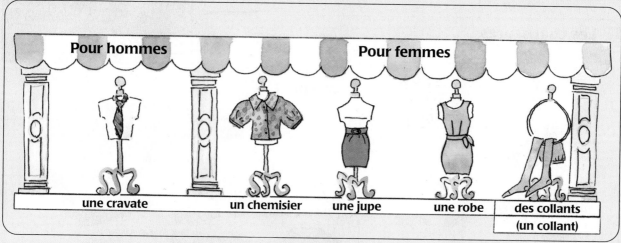

Pour hommes   **Pour femmes**

| une cravate | un chemisier | une jupe | une robe | des collants (un collant) |

acheter	*to buy*	Je vais **acheter** une cravate.
porter	*to wear*	Qu'est-ce que tu vas **porter** demain?
mettre	*to put on, wear*	Oh là là, il fait froid. Je vais **mettre** un pull.

→ **Mettre** is irregular. (Its forms are presented in Leçon 18.)

---

1 🖊 Shopping

PARLER Below are the names of several Paris stores. Using the illustrations as a guide, talk to a classmate about where you are going shopping and what you plan to buy.

▶ —Où vas-tu?
—Je vais au Monoprix.
—Qu'est-ce que tu vas acheter?
—Je vais acheter une chemise.

▼

(au) MONOPRIX
1. (au) PRINTEMPS
2. (au) BON MARCHÉ
3. (chez) KOOKAÏ
4. (chez) CÉLINE
5. (aux) GALERIES LAFAYETTE
6. (chez) LECLERC
7. (chez) DIOR
8. (à) LA SAMARITAINE

2 Quels vêtements?

PARLER/ÉCRIRE What we wear often depends on the circumstances: where we are, what we will be doing, what the weather is like. Complete the following sentences with the appropriate items of clothing.

1. Aujourd'hui, je porte …
2. Le professeur porte …
3. L'élève à ma gauche porte …
4. L'élève à ma droite porte …
5. Quand je vais à une boum, je porte …
6. Quand je vais dans un restaurant élégant, je porte …
7. S'il pleut (*If it rains*) demain, je vais mettre …
8. S'il fait chaud demain, je vais mettre …
9. Si (*If*) je vais en ville samedi, je vais mettre …
10. Si je vais à un concert dimanche, je vais mettre …

B VOCABULAIRE D'autres vêtements et accessoires

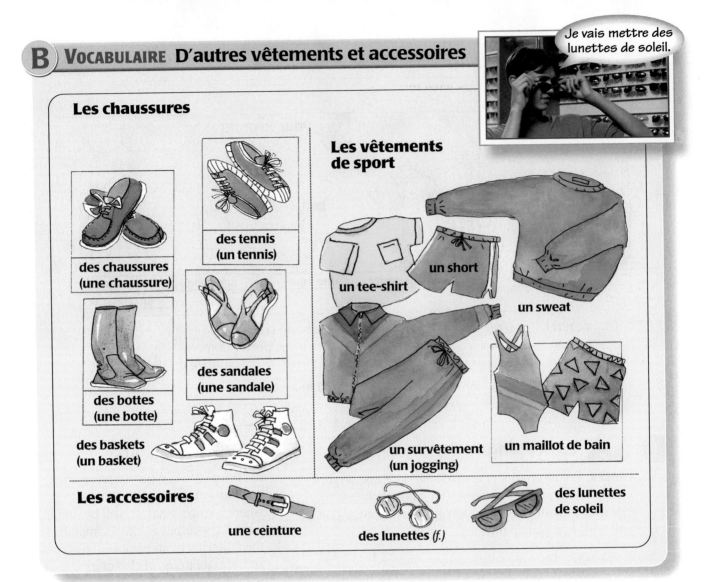

Je vais mettre des lunettes de soleil.

Les chaussures

des chaussures
(une chaussure)

des tennis
(un tennis)

des bottes
(une botte)

des sandales
(une sandale)

des baskets
(un basket)

Les vêtements de sport

un tee-shirt

un short

un sweat

un survêtement
(un jogging)

un maillot de bain

Les accessoires

une ceinture

des lunettes *(f.)*

des lunettes
de soleil

3 À la plage de Deauville

PARLER/ÉCRIRE You are spending the summer vacation in Deauville, a popular seaside resort in Normandy. Describe what you and your friends are wearing.

▶ Paul porte un maillot de bain ...

▶ **Paul**   1. **Anne**   2. **Sophie**   3. **Michel**   4. **Catherine**   5. **moi**

Qu'est-ce que tu portes?

PARLER Ask your classmates what they wear in the following circumstances. Let them use their imagination.

▶ jouer au tennis

1. aller à la piscine
2. aller à la plage
3. jouer au basket
4. travailler dans le jardin
5. aller au gymnase *(gym)*
6. faire une promenade dans la forêt *(forest)*
7. faire une promenade dans la neige *(snow)*

Qu'est-ce que tu portes quand tu joues au tennis?

Je porte un tee-shirt, un short et des tennis.

5 **Un jeu**

PARLER/ÉCRIRE When you see what people are wearing, you can often tell what they are going to do. How many different logical sentences can you make in five minutes using the elements of A, B, and C? Follow the model below.

A	B	C
André	un maillot de bain	nager
Sylvie	des lunettes de soleil	aller à la plage
Paul et Éric	un short	aller à un concert
Michèle et Anne	des chaussettes blanches	jouer au tennis
	un sweat	jouer au volley
	un pantalon très chic	jouer au foot
	des chaussures noires	aller à la campagne *(country)*
	des bottes	faire du jogging *(to jog)*
	un costume *(suit)*	dîner en ville
	une robe	
	une casquette	

Sylvie porte un short. Elle va jouer au foot.

6 **Joyeux anniversaire!**

PARLER/ÉCRIRE The following people are celebrating their birthdays. Find a present for each person by choosing an item of clothing from pages 258, 259, or 260.

1. Pour mon père (ma mère), je vais acheter …
2. Pour ma grand-mère (mon grand-père), …
3. Pour ma petite cousine Élodie (10 ans), …
4. Pour mon grand frère Guillaume (18 ans), …
5. Pour le professeur, …
6. Pour mon meilleur *(best)* ami, …
7. Pour ma meilleure amie, …

C VOCABULAIRE Dans un magasin

Pardon,
madame.

Vous désirez,
mademoiselle?

Je cherche
un pantalon.

▶ **How to get help from a salesperson:**

Pardon, monsieur (madame).

Vous désirez *(May I help you)*, | **monsieur?**
| **madame**
| **mademoiselle**

Je cherche *(I'm looking for)* …
  un pantalon.
Quel est le prix *(What is the price)* du pantalon?
Combien *(How much)* **coûte** le pantalon?
Combien est-ce qu'il coûte?
  Il coûte 40 euros.

Je cherche …
  une veste.
Quel est le prix de la veste?
Combien coûte la veste?
Combien est-ce qu'elle coûte?
  Elle coûte 65 euros.

▶ **How to discuss clothes with a friend:**

Qu'est-ce que tu penses du pantalon vert?
  (What do you think of …?)
Comment trouves-tu le pantalon vert?
  (What do you think of …?)

Qu'est-ce que tu penses de
  la veste verte?
Comment trouves-tu
  la veste verte?

Comment trouves-tu
le pantalon vert?

Il est
trop petit.

Il est	**joli.**		Elle est	**jolie.**
	élégant			**élégante**
	génial *(terrific)*			**géniale**
	chouette *(neat)*			**chouette**
	à la mode *(in style)*			**à la mode**
Il est	**moche** *(plain, ugly)*.		Elle est	**moche.**
	démodé *(out of style)*			**démodée**
Il est **trop** *(too)*	**petit.**		Elle est **trop**	**petite.**
	grand *(big)*			**grande**
	court *(short)*			**courte**
	long *(long)*			**longue**
Il est	**cher** *(expensive)*.		Elle est	**chère.**
	bon marché *(cheap)*			**bon marché**

→ The expression **bon marché** is INVARIABLE. It does not take adjective endings.
  Les chaussures blanches sont **bon marché.**

VERBES

chercher	*to look for*	Je **cherche** un jean.
coûter	*to cost*	Les chaussures **coûtent** 60 euros.
penser	*to think*	Qu'est-ce que tu **penses** de cette *(this)* robe?
penser que	*to think (that)*	Je **pense qu'**elle est géniale!
trouver	*to find*	Je ne **trouve** pas ma veste.
	to think of	Comment **trouves**-tu mes lunettes de soleil?

→ The verb **penser** is often used alone.
  Tu **penses?** *Do you think so?*   Je **ne pense pas.** *I don't think so.*

Les nombres de 100 à 1000

100	cent	200	deux cents	500	cinq cents	800	huit cents
101	cent un	300	trois cents	600	six cents	900	neuf cents
102	cent deux	400	quatre cents	700	sept cents	1000	mille

7 *Au marché aux puces*

PARLER You are at the Paris flea market looking for clothes with a French friend. Explain why you are not buying the following items. Use your imagination … and expressions from the **Vocabulaire.**

▶ —Tu vas acheter le blouson?
   —Non, je ne pense pas.
   —Pourquoi pas?
   —Il est trop grand.

▶

8 *C'est combien?*

PARLER Ask your friends how much the following items cost.

▶ —Combien coûte la veste?
   —Elle coûte cent vingt euros.

▶ 120€ 1 150€ 2 200€ 3 250€ 4 180€

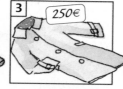

5 350€ 6 1400€ 7 275€ 8 725€ 9 890€

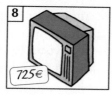

À votre tour!

OBJECTIFS

Now you can ...
• name and describe the clothes you wear
• discuss their style and their fit
• count to 1000

1 🎧 Écoutez bien!

ÉCOUTER Thomas and Frédéric are both getting ready to leave on vacation. Listen to the following sentences which mention items that they are packing. If the item belongs to Thomas, mark A. If the item belongs to Frédéric, mark B.

	1	2	3	4	5	6
A: Thomas						
B: Frédéric						

A. Thomas

B. Frédéric

2 🎧 Créa-dialogue

PARLER You are at Place Bonaventure in Montreal looking at clothes in various shops. You like what the salesperson shows you and ask how much each item costs. React to the price.

▶ joli / $60

1. élégant / $30

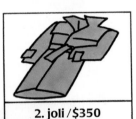

2. joli / $350

3. à la mode / $250

4. génial / $15

▶ —Vous désirez, monsieur (mademoiselle)?
—Je cherche <u>un pantalon</u>.
—Comment trouvez-vous <u>le pantalon gris</u>?
—Il est <u>joli</u>. Combien est-ce qu'<u>il</u> coûte?
—<u>Soixante</u> dollars.
—Oh là là, <u>il</u> est cher! (<u>Il</u> est bon marché.)

 **3**  **Conversation dirigée** ----------------------------------

PARLER Sophie and Christophe are shopping in a department store. Act out their conversation in French.

Sophie					Christophe
	asks Christophe what he is looking for	→ ↙	answers that he is looking for a baseball cap		
	asks him what he thinks of the yellow cap	→ ↙	says that it is terrific but adds that he is going to buy the blue cap		
	asks how much it costs	⇄	answers 5 euros		
	says that it is inexpensive but adds that it is too small				

4 **Qu'est-ce qui ne va pas?** *(What's wrong?)* ------------------------------

PARLER Explain what is wrong with the clothes that these people just bought at a sale.

▶ **Le chapeau de Monsieur Dupont est trop grand.**

Monsieur Dupont   **Édouard**

5 **Les valises** --

ÉCRIRE You are an exchange student in Paris. Your host family has invited you to spend:

• one weekend in Nice to go sailing
• one weekend in Chamonix to go skiing

Make a list of the different clothes you will take on each trip.

6 **À l'aéroport** ---

ÉCRIRE You are flying to Paris tomorrow on an exchange program. Your hosts plan to meet you at the airport, but don't have your picture. Write them an e-mail explaining what you look like and what you will be wearing.

Je suis …
Je vais porter …

LESSON REVIEW
CLASSZONE.COM

LEÇON 18

Rien n'est parfait!

VIDÉO   DVD   AUDIO

<u>Cet</u> après-midi, Frédéric et Jean-Claude vont acheter des vêtements.
Ils vont acheter <u>ces</u> vêtements dans un grand magasin. <u>Ce</u> magasin
s'appelle le Bon Marché.

This

these/This

Scène 1.

Frédéric et Jean-Claude regardent les pulls.

Frédéric:	Regarde! Comment trouves-tu ce pull?
Jean-Claude:	<u>Quel</u> pull?
Frédéric:	Ce pull bleu.
Jean-Claude:	Il est chouette.
Frédéric:	C'est vrai, il est très chouette.
Jean-Claude:	*(qui regarde le prix)* Il est aussi très cher.
Frédéric:	Combien est-ce qu'il coûte?
Jean-Claude:	Deux cents euros.
Frédéric:	Deux cents euros! <u>Quelle horreur!</u>

Which

What a scandal!

NOTE culturelle

Le grand magasin

Le grand magasin est un magasin de 4 ou 5 étages où on peut° acheter toutes° sortes de produits différents: vêtements, parfums, meubles,° alimentation° générale, etc. … Le grand magasin est une idée française. Le premier grand magasin a été créé° en 1852 par Aristide Boucicaut (1810-1877). Ce magasin existe toujours° et s'appelle «le Bon Marché». L'idée de Monsieur Boucicaut était° d'offrir à sa clientèle une marchandise de bonne qualité à des prix bon marché … d'où° le nom «Bon Marché». Son idée a été vite° copiée dans toutes les villes.

on peut *one can*   **toutes** *all*   **meubles** *furniture*   **alimentation** *food*
a été créé *was created*   **toujours** *still*   **était** *was*   **d'où** *hence*   **vite** *quickly*

COMPARAISONS CULTURELLES

French department stores, such as **le Bon Marché, la Samaritaine,
le Printemps,** and **les Galeries Lafayette** have Internet sites. Check out one
of these stores. How do its products compare to what you find in your local
department stores?

Scène 2.

Maintenant Frédéric et Jean-Claude regardent les vestes.

Frédéric: Quelle veste est-ce que tu préfères?

Jean-Claude: Je préfère cette veste jaune. Elle est très élégante et elle n'est pas très chère.

Frédéric: Oui, mais elle est trop grande pour toi!

Jean-Claude: Dommage!

Scène 3.

Frédéric est au <u>rayon</u> des chaussures.   *department*
Quelles chaussures est-ce qu'il va acheter?

Jean-Claude: Alors, quelles chaussures est-ce que tu achètes?

Frédéric: J'achète ces chaussures noires. Elles sont très confortables … et elles ne sont pas chères. Regarde, elles sont <u>en solde</u>.   *on sale*

Jean-Claude: C'est vrai, elles sont en solde … mais elles <u>ne sont plus</u> à la mode.   *are no longer*

Frédéric: <u>Hélas, rien n'est parfait</u>!   *Too bad/nothing is perfect*

Compréhension

1. Où vont Frédéric et Jean-Claude cet après-midi?
2. Qu'est-ce qu'ils vont faire?
3. Qu'est-ce qu'ils regardent d'abord *(first)*?
4. Combien coûte le pull bleu?
5. Quelle est la réaction de Frédéric?
6. Qu'est-ce que Jean-Claude pense de la veste jaune?
7. Pourquoi est-ce qu'il n'achète pas la veste?
8. Qu'est-ce que Frédéric pense des chaussures noires?
9. Pourquoi est-ce qu'il n'achète pas les chaussures?

A Les verbes *acheter* et *préférer*

Verbs like **acheter** *(to buy)* end in: **e** + CONSONANT + **-er.**
Verbs like **préférer** *(to prefer)* end in: **é** + CONSONANT + **-er.**

Note the forms of these two verbs in the chart, paying attention to:
- the **e** of the stem of **ach<u>e</u>ter**
- the **é** of the stem of **préf<u>é</u>rer**

INFINITIVE	acheter	préférer
PRESENT	J' ach**è**te une veste. Tu ach**è**tes une cravate. Il/Elle ach**è**te un imper.	Je préf**è**re la veste bleue. Tu préf**è**res la cravate jaune. Il/Elle préf**è**re l'imper gris.
	Nous achetons un jean. Vous achetez un short. Ils/Elles ach**è**tent un pull.	Nous préférons le jean noir. Vous préférez le short blanc. Ils/Elles préf**è**rent le pull rouge.

→ Verbs like **acheter** and **préférer** take regular endings and have the following changes in the stem:

> **ach<u>e</u>ter** e → è ⎫ in the **je, tu, il,** and **ils**
> **préf<u>é</u>rer** é → è ⎭ forms of the present

1 Achats *(Purchases)*

PARLER/ÉCRIRE What we buy depends on how much money we have. Complete the sentences below with **acheter** and one or more of the items from the list.

1. Avec dix dollars, tu …
2. Avec quinze dollars, j' …
3. Avec trente dollars, nous …
4. Avec cinquante dollars, Jean-Claude …
5. Avec cent dollars, vous …
6. Avec quinze mille dollars, mes parents …
7. Avec ?? dollars, mon cousin …
8. Avec ?? dollars, j' …

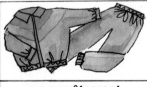

une voiture

des chaussures

un survêtement

une cravate

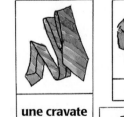

des lunettes de soleil

un polo

une veste

un CD

un jean

??

VOCABULAIRE Verbes comme (like) *acheter* et *préférer*

acheter	*to buy*	Qu'est-ce que tu **achètes?**
amener	*to bring (a person)*	François **amène** sa copine à la boum.
préférer	*to prefer*	**Préfères**-tu le manteau ou l'imper?
espérer	*to hope*	J'**espère** visiter Paris en été.

→ In French, there are two verbs that correspond to the English *to bring*:

amener + PEOPLE   J'**amène** une copine au pique-nique.

apporter + THINGS   J'**apporte** des sandwichs au pique-nique.

2 Pique-nique

PARLER/ÉCRIRE Everyone is bringing someone or something to the picnic. Complete the sentences below with the appropriate forms of **amener** or **apporter.**

▶ Nous **amenons** un copain.   Marc **apporte** des sandwichs.

1. Tu … ta guitare.
2. Philippe … sa soeur.
3. Nous … nos voisins.
4. Vous … un dessert.
5. Michèle … des sodas.

6. Antoine et Vincent … leur cousine.
7. Raphaël … ses CD.
8. Mon cousin … sa copine.
9. J' … ma radiocassette.
10. Léa et Émilie … leurs portables.

3 Expression personnelle

PARLER/ÉCRIRE Complete the sentences below with one of the suggested options or an expression of your choice. Note: You may wish to make some of the sentences negative.

1. Quand je vais à une fête, j'amène … (des copains, une copine, ma grand-mère, ??)
J'apporte … (des sandwichs, ma guitare, mes CD, mon portable, ??)
2. Quand je vais à un pique-nique, j'amène … (ma soeur, une copine, mon chien, ??)
J'apporte … (mon baladeur, mon livre de français, des sandwichs, ??)
3. Le week-end, je préfère … (étudier, aller au cinéma, rester à la maison, ??)
Ce *(This)* week-end, j'espère … (avoir un rendez-vous avec un copain ou une copine, travailler, jouer au volley, ??)

Quand je vais à une fête, j'apporte mon portable.

Et moi, j'apporte ma guitare.

4. Pendant *(During)* les vacances, j'espère … (rester à la maison, trouver un job, voyager, ??)
5. Un jour, j'espère … (visiter la France, parler français, aller à l'université, être millionnaire, ??)

B L'adjectif démonstratif *ce*

Note the forms of the demonstrative adjective **ce** in the chart below.

	SINGULAR *(this, that)*	PLURAL *(these, those)*		
MASCULINE	ce ↓ cet (+ VOWEL SOUND)	ces	ce blouson / cet homme	ces blousons / ces hommes
FEMININE	cette	ces	cette veste / cette amie	ces vestes / ces amies

→ There is liaison after **cet** and **ces** when the next word begins with a vowel sound.

→ To distinguish between a person or an object that is close by and one that is further away, the French sometimes use **-ci** or **-là** after the noun.

Philippe achète **cette chemise-ci.**   *Philippe is buying **this shirt** (over here).*

François achète **cette chemise-là.**   *François is buying **that shirt** (over there).*

4 À la Samaritaine

PARLER Marc and Nathalie are at the Samaritaine department store. Marc likes everything that Nathalie shows him. Play both roles.

▶ une robe (jolie)   NATHALIE: **Regarde cette robe!**
                         MARC: **Elle est jolie!**

1. un imper (élégant)
2. des bottes (à la mode)
3. une casquette (géniale)
4. un survêtement (chouette)
5. des livres (amusants)
6. un ordinateur (génial)
7. une télé (moderne)
8. une ceinture (jolie)
9. des sandales (jolies)

5  Différences d'opinion

PARLER Whenever they go shopping together, Éric and Brigitte cannot agree on what they like. Play both roles.

▶ un short

1. une chemise
2. un blouson
3. des chaussures
4. des lunettes
5. une casquette
6. une affiche
7. un stylo
8. un ordinateur

J'aime ce short-ci.

Eh bien, moi, je préfère ce short-là.

C L'adjectif interrogatif *quel?*

The interrogative adjective **quel** *(what? which?)* is used in questions. It agrees with the noun it introduces and has the following forms:

	SINGULAR	PLURAL		
MASCULINE	quel	quels	**Quel** garçon?	**Quels** cousins?
FEMININE	quelle	quelles	**Quelle** fille?	**Quelles** copines?

→ Note the liaison after **quels** and **quelles** when the next word begins with a vowel sound.
  Quelles affiches est-ce que tu préfères?

6 *Vêtements d'été*

PARLER You are shopping for the following items before going on a summer trip to France. A friend is asking you which ones you are buying. Identify each item by color.

J'achète un pantalon.

Quel pantalon est-ce que tu achètes?

Ce pantalon noir.

▶ un pantalon/noir

1. un maillot de bain/bleu

2. des chaussettes/ vertes

3. une jupe/jaune

4. une veste/bleue

5. des chaussures/ blanches

6. des sandales/ marron

7. un sweat/gris

8. une chemise /orange

9. un pull/rouge

7 *Questions personnelles* **PARLER/ÉCRIRE**

1. À quelle école vas-tu?
2. Dans quel magasin achètes-tu tes vêtements?
3. Dans quel magasin achètes-tu tes chaussures?
4. Quels CD aimes-tu écouter?
5. Quels programmes aimes-tu regarder à la télé?
6. Quel est ton restaurant préféré?
7. Quelle est ta classe préférée?

D Le verbe *mettre*

The verb **mettre** *(to put, place)* is irregular. Note its forms in the chart below.

INFINITIVE	mettre	
PRESENT	je **mets**	nous **mettons**
	tu **mets**	vous **mettez**
	il/elle **met**	ils/elles **mettent**

→ In the singular forms, the "**t**" of the stem is silent. The "**t**" is pronounced in the plural forms.

→ The verb **mettre** has several English equivalents:

to put, place	Je **mets** mes livres sur la table.
to put on, wear	Caroline **met** une robe rouge.
to turn on	Nous **mettons** la télé.

8 Où?

PARLER/ÉCRIRE Say where the people of Column A put the objects of Column B, by choosing a place from Column C. Be logical!

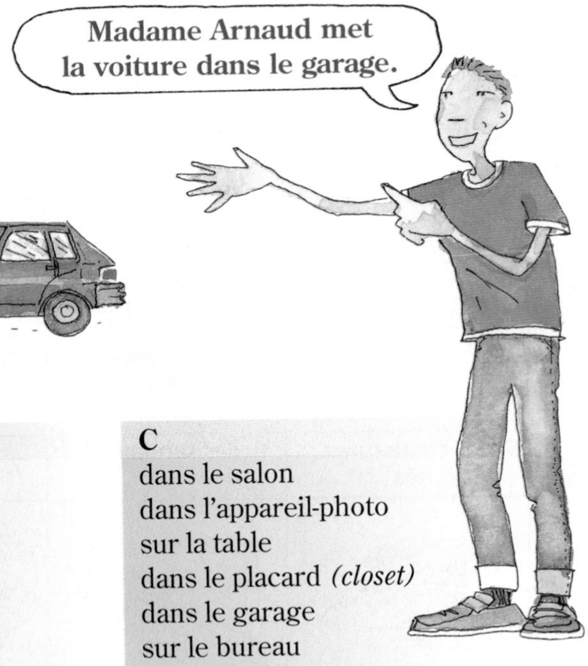

> Madame Arnaud met la voiture dans le garage.

A	B	C
moi	la glace	dans le salon
nous	la voiture	dans l'appareil-photo
toi	les livres	sur la table
vous	le téléphone	dans le placard *(closet)*
Christine	les vêtements	dans le garage
le professeur	des plantes vertes	sur le bureau
Madame Arnaud	une pellicule *(film)*	dans le réfrigérateur
Marc et Philippe	les cartes	sous le lit

9 *Questions personnelles* **PARLER/ÉCRIRE**

1. Est-ce que tu mets la radio quand tu étudies?
2. Chez vous, est-ce que vous mettez la télé quand vous dînez?
3. Est-ce que tu mets des lunettes de soleil quand tu vas à la plage?
4. Où est-ce que tes parents mettent leur voiture? (dans le garage? dans la rue?)
5. Quels programmes de télé est-ce que tu mets le dimanche? le samedi?
6. Quels CD est-ce que tu mets quand tu vas à une boum?
7. Quels vêtements est-ce que tu mets quand il fait froid?
8. Quels vêtements est-ce que tu mets quand tu joues au basket?

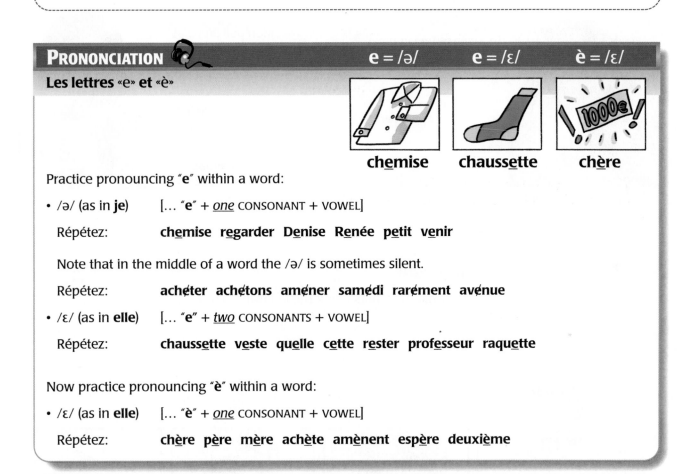

PRONONCIATION

Les lettres «e» et «è»

e = /ə/	e = /ɛ/	è = /ɛ/
chemise	chaussette	chère

Practice pronouncing "**e**" within a word:

• /ə/ (as in **je**)   [... "**e**" + *one* CONSONANT + VOWEL]

Répétez: ch**e**mise r**e**garder D**e**nise R**e**née p**e**tit v**e**nir

Note that in the middle of a word the /ə/ is sometimes silent.

Répétez: ach**e̸**ter ach**e̸**tons am**e̸**ner sam**e̸**di rar**e̸**ment av**e̸**nue

• /ɛ/ (as in **elle**)   [... "**e**" + *two* CONSONANTS + VOWEL]

Répétez: chauss**e**tte v**e**ste qu**e**lle c**e**tte r**e**ster prof**e**sseur raqu**e**tte

Now practice pronouncing "**è**" within a word:

• /ɛ/ (as in **elle**)   [... "**è**" + *one* CONSONANT + VOWEL]

Répétez: ch**è**re p**è**re m**è**re ach**è**te am**è**nent esp**è**re deuxi**è**me

NOS CHEMISES

À votre tour!

OBJECTIFS

Now you can ...
• talk about what you plan to buy
• discuss your preferences
• point out certain people or objects

1 La bonne réponse

PARLER Alice is talking to her cousin Jérôme. Match Alice's questions with Jérôme's answers. Act out the dialogue with a classmate.

Alice

1. Je vais à la soirée de Delphine. Et toi?

2. Tu amènes une copine?

3. Qu'est-ce que vous allez apporter?

4. Qu'est-ce que tu vas mettre?

Jérôme

a. Oui, Christine.

b. Mon pull jaune et mon blouson marron.

c. Nous allons acheter des pizzas.

d. Moi aussi.

2 Créa-dialogue

PARLER Ask your classmates what they think about the following. They will answer affirmatively or negatively.

▶ —Comment trouves-tu <u>cette fille</u>?
—<u>Quelle fille</u>?
—<u>Cette fille-là</u>!
—Eh bien, je pense qu'<u>elle</u> est <u>jolie</u>.
(<u>Elle</u> n'est pas <u>jolie</u>.)

▶ jolie?

1. intéressants?

2. sympathique?

3. courte?

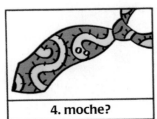
4. moche?

5. bon marché?

6. ??

7. ??

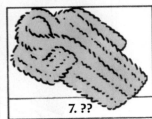

3 Shopping

PARLER You and a friend are shopping by catalog. Choose an object and tell your friend what you are buying. Identify it by color and explain why you like it.

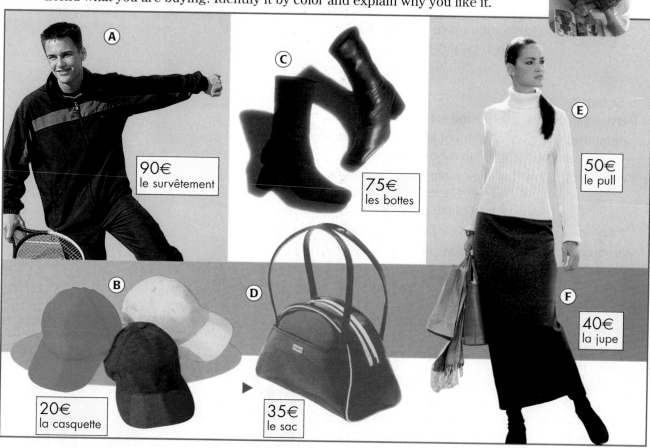

90€
le survêtement

75€
les bottes

50€
le pull

20€
la casquette

35€
le sac

40€
la jupe

▶ —Je vais acheter un sac.
—Quel sac?
—Ce sac rouge.
—Pourquoi?
—Parce qu'il est joli.

4 Composition: La soirée

ÉCRIRE You have been invited to a party by a French friend. In a short paragraph, describe …

• what clothes you are going to wear
• whom you are going to bring along
• what things you are going to bring (food? CDs? boombox? camera?)

LESSON REVIEW
CLASSZONE.COM

Un choix difficile

VIDÉO   DVD   AUDIO

Dans un mois, Delphine va aller au mariage de sa cousine. Elle va acheter une <u>nouvelle</u> robe pour cette occasion. Pour cela, elle va dans un magasin de vêtements avec sa copine Véronique. Il y a beaucoup de jolies robes dans ce magasin.

new

Delphine <u>hésite</u> <u>entre</u> une robe jaune et une robe rouge. Quelle robe est-ce que Delphine va <u>choisir</u>? Ah là là, le <u>choix</u> n'est pas facile.

is hesitating/between
to choose
choice

SCÈNE 1.

Véronique: Alors, quelle robe est-ce que tu choisis?

Delphine: Eh bien, <u>finalement</u> je choisis la robe rouge. Elle est <u>plus jolie que</u> la robe jaune.

finally
prettier than

Véronique: C'est vrai, elle est plus jolie … mais la robe jaune est <u>moins</u> chère et elle est <u>plus grande</u>. Regarde. La robe rouge est trop petite pour toi.

less/larger

Delphine: Mais non, elle n'est pas trop petite.

Véronique: Bon, écoute, <u>essaie-la</u>!

try it!

NOTE culturelle

Les jeunes et la mode

Les jeunes Français aiment être à la mode. Ils dépensent° trente pour cent (30%) de leur budget pour les vêtements. Parce que ce budget est limité, ils font très attention quand ils choisissent leurs vêtements. Heureusement,° il y a des boutiques spécialisées dans la mode des jeunes, comme Zara, Mango et Etam, où les vêtements ne sont pas trop° chers.

Certains jeunes préfèrent la «mode rétro». Ils achètent leurs vêtements au marché aux puces.°

dépensent *spend*   **Heureusement** *Fortunately*   **trop** *too*
marché aux puces *flea market*

SCÈNE 2.

Delphine <u>sort</u> de la <u>cabine d'essayage</u>.

| | | | |

Delphine: C'est vrai, la robe rouge est <u>plus petite</u> mais ce n'est pas un problème.

Véronique: Pourquoi?

Delphine: Parce que j'ai un mois pour <u>maigrir</u>.

Véronique: Et <u>si</u> tu <u>grossis</u>?

Delphine: Toi, <u>tais-toi</u>!

comes out/fitting room

smaller

to lose weight

if/gain weight

be quiet

Compréhension

1. Où vont Delphine et Véronique?

2. Qu'est-ce que Delphine va acheter?

3. Pourquoi?

4. Delphine hésite entre deux robes. De quelle couleur sont-elles?

5. Quelle robe est-ce qu'elle choisit?

6. Pourquoi est-ce qu'elle préfère la robe rouge?

7. Selon *(According to)* Véronique, quel est le problème avec la robe rouge?

8. Qu'est-ce que Delphine doit *(must)* faire pour porter la robe?

A Les verbes réguliers en -ir

Many French verbs end in **-ir**. Most of these verbs are conjugated like **finir** *(to finish)*.
Note the forms of this verb in the present tense, paying special attention to the endings.

INFINITIVE	finir	STEM (infinitive minus -ir)	ENDINGS
PRESENT	Je **finis** à deux heures. Tu **finis** à une heure. Il/Elle **finit** à cinq heures. Nous **finissons** à midi. Vous **finissez** à une heure. Ils/Elles **finissent** à minuit.	fin-	-is -is -it -issons -issez -issent

1 Le marathon de Paris

PARLER/ÉCRIRE Not all runners finish the Paris marathon. Say who does and who does not.

▶ Philippe (non)   **Philippe ne finit pas.**

1. moi (oui)   **3.** nous (oui)   **5.** Éric (oui)   **7.** Frédéric et Marc (non)
2. toi (non)   **4.** vous (non)   **6.** Stéphanie (non)   **8.** Anne et Cécile (oui)

VOCABULAIRE Verbes réguliers en -ir

choisir	*to choose*	Quelle veste **choisis**-tu?
finir	*to finish*	Les classes **finissent** à midi.
grossir	*to gain weight, get fat*	Marc **grossit** parce qu'il mange beaucoup.
maigrir	*to lose weight, get thin*	Je **maigris** parce que je mange peu.
réussir	*to succeed*	Tu vas **réussir** parce que tu travailles!
réussir	*to pass an exam*	Nous **réussissons à nos examens.**
à un examen		

2 Le régime (Diet)

PARLER/ÉCRIRE Read about the following people. Say if they are gaining or losing weight.

▶ Philippe mange beaucoup de pizzas.
  Il grossit. Il ne maigrit pas.

1. Vous faites des exercices.
2. Nous allons souvent au gymnase.
3. Vous êtes inactifs.
4. Je mange des carottes.

5. Monsieur Moreau adore la bonne cuisine.
6. Vous n'êtes pas très sportifs.
7. Ces personnes mangent trop *(too much)*.
8. Je nage, je joue au volley et je fais des promenades.

3 **Questions personnelles** PARLER/ÉCRIRE

1. À quelle heure finissent les classes?
2. À quelle heure finit la classe de français?
3. Quand finit l'école cette année *(year)*?
4. Tu es invité(e) au restaurant ou au cinéma. Où choisis-tu d'aller?

5. Quand tu vas au cinéma avec ta famille, qui choisit le film?
6. En général, est-ce que tu réussis à tes examens? Est-ce que tu vas réussir à l'examen de français? Et tes copains?

B Les adjectifs *beau, nouveau* et *vieux*

The adjectives **beau** *(beautiful, good-looking)*, **nouveau** *(new)*, and **vieux** *(old)* are irregular.

		beau	nouveau	vieux
SINGULAR	**MASC.**	le **beau** manteau (le **bel** imper)	le **nouveau** manteau (le **nouvel** imper)	le **vieux** manteau (le **vieil** imper)
	FEM.	la **belle** veste	la **nouvelle** veste	la **vieille** veste
PLURAL	**MASC.**	les **beaux** manteaux	les **nouveaux** manteaux	les **vieux** manteaux
	FEM.	les **belles** vestes	les **nouvelles** vestes	les **vieilles** vestes

→ The adjectives **beau, nouveau,** and **vieux** usually come BEFORE the noun. If the noun begins with a vowel sound, there is liaison between the adjective and the noun.

 les **nouveaux** ordinateurs   les **belles** affiches   les **vieux** impers

→ In the masculine singular, the liaison forms **bel, nouvel,** and **vieil** are used before a vowel sound. Note that **vieil** is pronounced like **vieille:**

 un **vieil** imper   une **vieille** robe

4 **La collection de printemps**

PARLER Mod Boutique is presenting its spring collection. Point out all the items you like to a French friend, using the appropriate forms of **beau.**

▶ une chemise
 Regarde la belle chemise!

1. une robe
2. un pantalon
3. des jeans
4. des blousons
5. une veste

6. un imper
7. des sandales
8. un manteau
9. un chapeau
10. des tee-shirts

5 **Différences d'opinion**

PARLER François is showing the new things he bought to his sister Valérie. She prefers his old things.

▶ des chaussures

1. un polo
2. des lunettes de soleil
3. un imper
4. des affiches
5. une casquette
6. une montre
7. un ordinateur
8. des baskets
9. un survêtement

Tu aimes mes nouvelles chaussures?

En bien, non, je préfère tes vieilles chaussures.

C La comparaison avec les adjectifs

Note how COMPARISONS are expressed in French.

Cet imper est **plus cher que** ce manteau.	*… more expensive than …*
Cette jupe est **plus jolie que** cette robe.	*… prettier than …*
Paul est **moins sportif que** Patrick.	*… less athletic than …*
Il est **moins amusant que** lui.	*… less amusing than …*
Je suis **aussi grand que** toi.	*… as tall as …*
Tu **n'**es **pas aussi timide que** moi.	*… not as timid as …*

To make comparisons with adjectives, French speakers use the following constructions:

+ **plus**		**plus cher (que)**	*more expensive (than)*
− **moins**	+ ADJECTIVE (+ **que** …)	**moins cher (que)**	*less expensive (than)*
= **aussi**		**aussi cher (que)**	*as expensive (as)*

→ Note the irregular **plus**-form of **bon** *(good):*

plus + bon(ne) → meilleur(e) *(better)*

Ta pizza est **bonne**, mais mon sandwich est **meilleur**.

→ There is liaison after **plus** and **moins** when the next word begins with a vowel sound.

Cette robe-ci est **plus élégante**.   Ce livre-là est **moins intéressant**.

→ In comparisons, the adjective always agrees with the noun (or pronoun) it describes.

La jupe est plus **chère** que le chemisier.

Les vestes sont moins **chères** que les manteaux.

→ In comparisons with people, STRESS PRONOUNS are used after **que**.

Paul est plus petit **que moi**.   Je suis plus grand **que lui**.

6 Comparaisons

PARLER/ÉCRIRE How much do you think the following pairs of items cost? Give your opinion, saying whether the first one is more expensive, less expensive, or as expensive as the second one.

▶ une guitare/une raquette   **Une guitare est plus (moins, aussi) chère qu'une raquette.**

1. un vélo/un scooter
2. une mobylette/une moto
3. une pizza/un sandwich
4. une télé/un ordinateur
5. des chaussures/des sandales

6. une casquette/des lunettes de soleil
7. des bottes/des tennis
8. un short/un maillot de bain
9. un baladeur/une montre
10. un portable/une mini-chaîne

VOCABULAIRE Expression pour la conversation

▶ *How to introduce a personal opinion:*

à mon avis …   *in my opinion …*   **À mon avis**, le français est facile.

7 *Expression personnelle*

PARLER/ÉCRIRE Compare the following by using the adjectives suggested. Give your personal opinion.

▶ le tennis/intéressant/le ping-pong

À mon avis, le tennis est plus (moins, aussi) intéressant que le ping-pong.

1. le basket/intéressant/le foot
2. l'anglais/facile/le français
3. la classe de français/amusant/la classe d'anglais
4. la Floride/beau/la Californie
5. les Yankees/bon/les Red Sox
6. la cuisine américaine/bon/la cuisine française
7. les filles/intelligent/les garçons
8. l'argent *(money)*/important/l'amitié *(friendship)*

8 *Et toi?*

PARLER Use the appropriate stress pronouns in answering the questions below.

▶ —Es-tu plus grand(e) que ton copain?   (Non, je suis moins grand(e) que lui.)
   —Oui, je suis plus grand(e) que lui.   (Je suis aussi grand(e) que lui.)

1. Es-tu plus grand(e) que ta mère?
2. Es-tu aussi riche que Bill Gates?
3. Es-tu plus sportif (sportive) que tes copains?
4. Es-tu plus intelligent(e) qu'Einstein?

PRONONCIATION   **ill** /j/

Les lettres «ill»

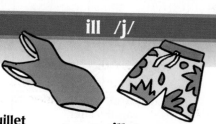

In the middle of a word, the letters "**ill**" usually represent the sound /j/ like the "**y**" of *yes*.

Répétez: ma**ill**ot trava**ill**ez ore**ill**e vie**ill**e f**ill**e fam**ill**e ju**ill**et
En ju**ill**et, Mire**ill**e va trava**ill**er pour sa vie**ill**e tante.

maill**ot**

At the end of a word, the sound /j/ is sometimes spelled **il**.

Répétez: appare**il**-photo vie**il** trava**il** *(job)*
Mon oncle a un vie**il** appare**il**-photo.

EXCEPTION: The letters **ill** are pronounced /il/ in the following words:

Répétez: v**ill**e v**ill**age m**ill**e L**ill**e

À votre tour!

OBJECTIFS

Now you can ...
• make comparisons
• discuss your choices

1  La bonne réponse

PARLER François and Stéphanie are shopping. Match François's questions with Stéphanie's answers. You may act out the dialogue with a friend.

François

1. Tu aimes cette veste verte?

2. Combien est-ce qu'elle coûte?

3. Et qu'est-ce que tu penses de cette veste rouge?

4. Alors, qu'est-ce que tu vas choisir?

a. 300 euros.

b. À mon avis, elle est moins jolie.

c. La veste bleue. Elle est meilleur marché et elle est aussi élégante.

d. Oui, mais elle est très chère.

Stéphanie

2 Créa-dialogue

PARLER With a classmate, prepare a dialogue comparing the items in one of the following pictures. Use the suggested verb and some of the suggested adjectives.

▶ —Tu <u>choisis</u> <u>la voiture rouge</u> ou <u>la voiture noire</u>?
—Je <u>choisis</u> <u>la voiture rouge</u>.
—Pourquoi?
—Parce qu'<u>elle</u> est <u>plus petite</u> et <u>moins chère</u>.

▶ **choisir**

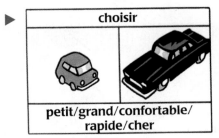

petit/grand/confortable/
rapide/cher

1. acheter

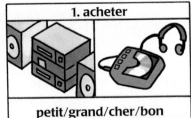

petit/grand/cher/bon

2. préférer

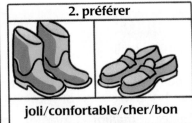

joli/confortable/cher/bon

3. choisir

petit/grand/mignon/joli

4. amener

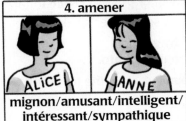

ALICE   ANNE

mignon/amusant/intelligent/
intéressant/sympathique

5. inviter

PAUL   PHILIPPE

??

❸ Choix personnels

PARLER Select two people or two items in each of the following categories and ask a classmate to indicate which one he/she prefers. You may ask your classmate to explain why.

▶ 2 actors

Tu préfères Tom Hanks ou Brad Pitt?

Je préfère Brad Pitt.

Pourquoi?

Parce que Brad Pitt est plus mignon que Tom Hanks.
(plus beau, plus jeune ...)

CATEGORIES:

- ▶ 2 actors
- • 2 actresses
- • 2 singers (male)
- • 2 singers (female)
- • 2 baseball teams
- • 2 cities
- • 2 restaurants in your town
- • 2 stores in your town

❹ Composition: Portrait comparatif

ÉCRIRE Write a description of yourself, comparing yourself to six other people (your friends, your family, well-known personalities, etc.) You may use some of the following adjectives:

> grand petit jeune vieux amusant intelligent bête
> sportif sympathique timide gentil génial optimiste

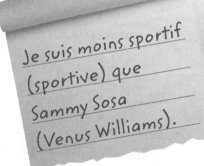

Je suis moins sportif (sportive) que Sammy Sosa (Venus Williams).

❺ Composition: Comparaisons personnelles

Mon cousin s'appelle Patrick. Il a quinze ans. Je suis plus jeune que lui, mais il est moins grand que moi ...

ÉCRIRE Choose a friend or relative about your age. Give this person's name and age. Then, in a short paragraph, compare yourself to that person in terms of physical appearance and personality traits.

LESSON REVIEW
CLASSZONE.COM

LEÇON 20

Alice a un job

VIDÉO   DVD   AUDIO

Alice a un nouveau job. Elle travaille dans un magasin de matériel audio-visuel. Dans ce magasin, <u>on</u> <u>vend</u> <u>toutes</u> sortes de choses: des baladeurs, des chaînes hi-fi, des radiocassettes/CD, des lecteurs de DVD …

one, they / sell(s) / all

Un jour, son cousin Jérôme <u>lui rend visite</u>.

comes to visit her

Jérôme:	Salut, ça va?
Alice:	Oui, ça va.
Jérôme:	Et ce nouveau job?
Alice:	C'est super.
Jérôme:	Qu'est-ce qu'on vend dans ton magasin?
Alice:	Eh bien, tu <u>vois</u>, on vend toutes sortes de matériel audio-visuel … Moi, je vends des mini-chaînes.
Jérôme:	Tu es bien <u>payée</u>?
Alice:	Non, on n'est pas très bien payé, mais on a des réductions sur l'équipement stéréo et sur les CD et les DVD.
Jérôme:	Qu'est-ce que tu vas faire avec ton <u>argent</u>?
Alice:	Je ne sais pas … J'<u>ai envie de</u> voyager cet été.
Jérôme:	Tu <u>as de la chance</u>. Moi aussi, j'ai envie de voyager, mais je n'ai pas d'argent.
Alice:	Écoute, Jérôme, si tu as <u>besoin</u> d'argent, <u>fais comme moi</u>.
Jérôme:	<u>Comment</u>?
Alice:	<u>Cherche</u> un job!

see

paid

money

feel like

are lucky

need / do as I do

What?

Find

Compréhension

1. Où travaille Alice?
2. Qu'est-ce qu'elle vend?
3. Qu'est-ce qu'elle espère faire cet été?

4. Pourquoi est-ce que Jérôme ne va pas voyager?
5. Qu'est-ce que Jérôme doit *(must)* faire pour avoir de l'argent?

NOTE culturelle

L'argent° des jeunes

Contrairement à beaucoup de jeunes Américains, les jeunes Français n'ont pas de travail° régulier. Par exemple, ils ne travaillent pas dans les supermarchés, les boutiques ou les stations-service. Occasionnellement, ils font des petits jobs pour leurs voisins: baby-sitting, promenade de chiens,° lavage° de voitures, etc.

En général, ils dépendent de la générosité de leurs parents pour leur argent. Le montant° qu'ils reçoivent varie avec l'âge, les résultats scolaires,° et la situation économique de la famille. Ils reçoivent aussi de l'argent de leur famille et de leurs parrains° et marraines° pour des occasions spéciales: Noël, jour de l'An° et anniversaire.

Voici combien d'argent les jeunes Français ont en moyenne: °

ÂGE	MONTANT PAR MOIS
2-7 ans	5 euros
8-14 ans	15 euros
15-17 ans	100 euros

argent *money* **travail** *work*
promenade de chiens *dog walking* **lavage** *washing*
montant *amount* **résultats scolaires** *report cards*
parrains *godfathers* **marraines** *godmothers*
jour de l'An *New Year's Day* **en moyenne** *on the average*

COMPARAISONS CULTURELLES

• Compare how teenagers in France and in the United States get their spending money.

• Why do you think French teenagers do not have regular jobs?

VOCABULAIRE L'argent

NOMS

l'argent *(m.)*	money	une pièce *coin*	
un billet	bill, paper money		

ADJECTIFS

riche ≠ pauvre   *rich ≠ poor*

VERBES

dépenser	to spend	Je n'aime pas **dépenser** mon argent.
gagner	to earn,	Je **gagne** 10 dollars par *(per)* jour.
	to win	Tu joues bien. Tu vas **gagner** le match.
payer	to pay, pay for	Qui va **payer** aujourd'hui?

EXPRESSIONS

combien + VERB	*how much*	**Combien** coûte cette chaîne hi-fi?
combien de + NOUN	*how much*	**Combien d'**argent as-tu?
	how many	**Combien de** CD as-tu?
avoir besoin de + NOUN	*to need*	J'**ai besoin de** 5 dollars.
+ INFINITIVE	*to need to, have to*	J'**ai besoin de** travailler.
avoir envie de + NOUN	*to want*	J'**ai envie d'**une pizza.
+ INFINITIVE	*to feel like, want to*	J'**ai envie de** manger.

→ Verbs like **payer** that end in **-yer,** have the following stem change:

y → i in the **je, tu, il, ils** forms of the verb

je **paie**   tu **paies**   il/elle **paie**   ils/elles **paient**

but: nous **payons**   vous **payez**

L'ARGENT NE FAIT PAS LE BONHEUR

Money does not buy happiness.

1 *Combien?*

PARLER Ask your classmates how many of the following they have.

▶ des CD   —**Combien de CD as-tu?**
              —**J'ai vingt CD.**
                  (Je n'ai pas de CD.)

1. des frères   **3.** des casquettes   **5.** des tee-shirts   **7.** des billets d'un dollar
2. des soeurs   **4.** des affiches   **6.** des jeans   **8.** des pièces de dix cents

2 Qu'est-ce que tu as envie de faire?

PARLER Ask your classmates if they feel like doing the following things.

▶ aller au cinéma

1. aller au restaurant
2. manger une pizza
3. aller à la piscine
4. parler français
5. écouter un CD
6. visiter Paris
7. jouer au Frisbee
8. acheter une moto
9. faire une promenade
10. surfer sur l'Internet

Est-ce que tu as envie d'aller au cinéma?

Oui, j'ai envie d'aller au cinéma.

Et toi?

Non, je n'ai pas envie d'aller au cinéma.

3 Au restaurant

PARLER/ÉCRIRE The following students are in a restaurant in Quebec. Say what they feel like buying and estimate how much money they need.

▶ Hélène/une pizza
Hélène a envie d'une pizza. Elle a besoin de cinq dollars.

1. Marc/un sandwich
2. nous/une glace
3. moi/un soda
4. toi/un jus d'orange
5. vous/une salade
6. mes copains/un steak

4 Questions personnelles **PARLER/ÉCRIRE**

1. Est-ce que tu as un job? Où est-ce que tu travailles? Combien est-ce que tu gagnes par *(per)* heure? par semaine?
2. Quand tu vas au cinéma, qui paie? toi ou ton copain (ta copine)?
3. Combien est-ce que tu paies quand tu achètes un hamburger? une pizza? une glace?
4. Est-ce que tu as des pièces dans ta poche *(pocket)*? quelles pièces?
5. Qui est représenté sur le billet d'un dollar? sur le billet de cinq dollars? sur le billet de dix dollars?
6. Est-ce que tu préfères dépenser ou économiser *(to save)* ton argent? Pourquoi?
7. Est-ce que tu espères être riche un jour? Pourquoi?

Le Vendôme
36, Côte de la Montagne
Québec
tél 692.0557

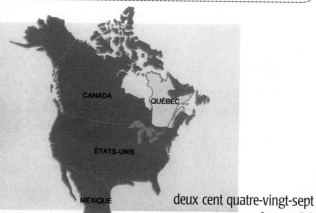

CANADA

QUÉBEC

ÉTATS-UNIS

MEXIQUE

A Le pronom *on*

Note the use of the subject pronoun **on** in the sentences below.

Qu'est-ce qu'**on** vend ici?	*What do **they** (do you) sell here?*
Où est-ce qu'**on** achète ce CD?	*Where does **one** (do people) buy that CD?*
En France, **on** parle français.	*In France, **people** (you, they) speak French.*

The pronoun **on** is used in GENERAL statements, according to the construction:

on + il/elle - form of verb	**On** travaille beaucoup.	**One** works a lot. **They** work a lot. **You** work a lot. **People** work a lot.

▶ There is liaison after **on** when the next word begins with a vowel sound.
   Est-ce qu'**on** invite Stéphanie à la boum?

▶ In conversation, **on** is often used instead of **nous:**
   —Est-ce qu'**on** dîne à la maison? *Are **we** having dinner at home?*
   —Non, **on** va au restaurant. *No, **we** are going to the restaurant.*

5 Ici on parle ...

PARLER/ÉCRIRE Imagine that you have won a grand prize of a world tour.
Say which of the following languages is spoken in each of the cities
that you will be visiting.

▶ Acapulco

À Acapulco, on parle espagnol.

1. Québec
2. Boston
3. Madrid
4. Bruxelles
5. Genève

6. Tokyo
7. Buenos Aires
8. Londres *(London)*
9. Rome
10. Beijing

anglais	espagnol	français
japonais	italien	chinois

COMMUNAUTÉS

In a multi-cultural society, people speak different languages and have different customs.
How many different languages are spoken at home by classmates in your school? What are
some of their different customs and different celebrations? As a class project, put up a wall
map showing their countries of origin. Do some come from French-speaking areas?

VOCABULAIRE Expression pour la conversation

▶ *How to indicate approval:*

C'est une bonne idée!   *That's a good idea!*

6  *Projets de week-end*

PARLER Suggest possible weekend activities to your classmates. They will let you know whether they think each idea is a good one or not.

▶ aller au café

1. jouer aux jeux vidéo?
2. aller à la bibliothèque?
3. aller à la plage?
4. téléphoner au professeur?
5. faire une promenade à vélo?
6. aller dans les magasins?
7. acheter des vêtements?
8. écouter des CD?

On va au café?

Oui, c'est une bonne idée!

Non, ce n'est pas une bonne idée.

7 *En Amérique et en France*

PARLER An American student and a French student are comparing certain aspects of life in their own countries. Play both roles.

▶ jouer au baseball (au foot)

En Amérique, on joue au baseball.

En France, on joue au foot.

1. parler anglais (français)
2. étudier le français (l'anglais)
3. dîner à six heures (à huit heures)
4. manger des hamburgers (des omelettes)
5. voyager souvent en avion *(by plane)* (en train)
6. skier dans le Colorado (dans les Alpes)
7. aller à l'école le mercredi après-midi (le samedi matin)
8. chanter «la Bannière étoilée» *("The Star-Spangled Banner")* («la Marseillaise»)

8 *Expression personnelle*

PARLER/ÉCRIRE Describe what you, your friends, and your relatives generally do. Complete the following sentences according to your personal routine.

1. À la maison, on dîne … (à quelle heure?)
2. À la télé, on regarde … (quel programme?)
3. À la cafétéria de l'école, on mange … (quoi?)
4. En été, on va … (où?)
5. Le week-end, avec mes copains, on va … (où?)
6. Avec mes copains, on joue … (à quel sport? à quel jeu?)
7. On a une classe de français … (quels jours?)
8. On a un examen de français … (quel jour?)

B Les verbes réguliers en -re

Many French verbs end in **-re**. Most of these are conjugated like **vendre** *(to sell)*. Note the forms of this verb in the present tense, paying special attention to the endings.

INFINITIVE	vendre	STEM (infinitive minus **-re**)	ENDINGS
PRESENT	Je **vends** ma raquette. Tu **vends** ton scooter. Il/Elle/On **vend** son ordinateur. Nous **vendons** nos livres. Vous **vendez** vos CD. Ils/Elles **vendent** leur voiture.	vend-	-s -s — -ons -ez -ent

→ The "**d**" of the stem is silent in the singular forms, but it is pronounced in the plural forms.

VOCABULAIRE Verbes réguliers en -re

attendre	*to wait, wait for*	Pierre **attend** Michèle au café.
entendre	*to hear*	Est-ce que tu **entends** la radio?
perdre	*to lose, waste*	Jean-Claude **perd** le match.
rendre visite à	*to visit (a person)*	Je **rends visite à** mon oncle.
répondre à	*to answer*	Nous **répondons à** la question du prof.
vendre	*to sell*	À qui **vends**-tu ton vélo?

→ There are two French verbs that correspond to the English verb *to visit*.

visiter (+ PLACES) Nous **visitons** Québec.

rendre visite à (+ PEOPLE) Nous **rendons visite à** nos cousins canadiens.

---

9 Rendez-vous

PARLER/ÉCRIRE The following people have been shopping and are now waiting for their friends at a café. Express this, using the appropriate forms of the verb **attendre**.

▶ Jérôme (Michèle) **Jérôme attend Michèle.**

1. nous (nos copains)
2. vous (vos cousines)
3. moi (Antoine)
4. toi (Julie)
5. Olivier et Éric (Élodie et Sophie)
6. les étudiants (les étudiantes)
7. Julien et moi, nous (Pauline et Mélanie)
8. Annette et toi, vous (Jean-Marc)
9. on (notre copine)
10. Stéphanie (Léa)

⑩ Qui?

PARLER/ÉCRIRE Who is doing what? Answer the following questions, using the suggested subjects.

1. Qui perd le match?
   (toi, vous, Alice)
2. Qui rend visite à Pierre?
   (Paul, Léa et Hélène, toi)
3. Qui entend l'avion *(plane)*?
   (moi, vous, les voisins)
4. Qui vend des CD?
   (on, ce magasin, ces boutiques)
5. Qui attend le bus?
   (les élèves, le professeur, on, vous)
6. Qui répond au professeur?
   (toi, nous, les élèves)

⑪ Qu'est-ce qu'ils font?

PARLER/ÉCRIRE Say what the following people do by completing each sentence with the appropriate form of one of the verbs from the list. Be logical!

1. Guillaume est patient. Il … ses amis.
2. Vous êtes à Paris. Vous … à vos cousins français.
3. Tu joues mal. Tu … le match.
4. Je suis chez moi. J' … un bruit *(noise)* curieux.
5. Nous sommes en classe. Nous … aux questions du professeur.
6. Julie travaille dans une boutique. Elle … des robes.
7. On est au café. On … nos copains.

attendre	entendre	rendre visite
vendre	perdre	répondre

Ⓒ L'impératif

LEARNING ABOUT LANGUAGE
The IMPERATIVE is used to make suggestions and to give orders and advice. The commands or suggestions may be affirmative or negative.

Compare the French and English forms of the imperative.

Écoute ce CD! — *Listen to this CD!*
Ne vendez pas votre voiture! — *Don't sell your car!*
Allons au cinéma! — *Let's go to the movies!*

Note the forms of the imperative in the chart below.

INFINITIVE	parler	finir	vendre	aller
IMPERATIVE				
(tu)	parle	finis	vends	va
(vous)	parlez	finissez	vendez	allez
(nous)	parlons	finissons	vendons	allons

For regular verbs and most irregular verbs, the forms of the imperative are the same as the corresponding forms of the present tense.

→ NOTE: For all **-er** verbs, including **aller,** the **-s** of the **tu** form is dropped. Compare:

   Tu **parles** anglais.   **Parle** français, s'il te plaît!
   Tu **vas** au café.   **Va** à la bibliothèque!

→ The negative imperative is formed as follows:

| ne + VERB + pas … | **Ne choisis pas** ce blouson. |

12 **Mais oui!**

J'apporte
une pizza?

PARLER You have organized
a party at your home. Valérie
offers to do the following. You accept.

▶ apporter une pizza?

Mais oui, apporte une pizza!

1. faire une salade?
2. inviter nos copains?
3. acheter des sodas?
4. apporter des CD?
5. choisir la musique de danse?
6. venir à huit heures?
7. téléphoner aux voisins?
8. apporter une mini-chaîne?
9. faire des sandwichs?

 13 **L'ange et le démon** *(The angel and the devil)*

PARLER Véronique is wondering whether she should do certain things. The
angel gives her good advice. The devil gives her bad advice. Play both roles.

▶ étudier les verbes
  Étudie les verbes.
  N'étudie pas les verbes.

1. téléphoner à ta tante
2. attendre tes copains
3. faire attention en classe
4. aller à l'école
5. finir la leçon

6. écouter tes professeurs
7. mettre *(set)* la table
8. aider tes amis
9. rendre visite à ta grand-mère

10. choisir des copains
    sympathiques
11. faire tes devoirs
    (homework)
12. réussir à l'examen

14 **Oui ou non?**

PARLER For each of the following situations, give your classmates advice
as to what to do and what not to do. Be logical.

▶ Nous sommes en vacances. (étudier? voyager?)
  N'étudiez pas! Voyagez!

1. Nous sommes à Paris. (parler anglais? parler français?)
2. C'est dimanche. (aller à la bibliothèque? aller au cinéma?)
3. Il fait beau. (rester à la maison? faire une promenade?)
4. Il fait froid. (mettre un pull? mettre un tee-shirt?)
5. Il est onze heures du soir. (rester au café? rentrer à la maison?)
6. Il fait très chaud. (aller à la piscine? regarder la télé?)

15 *L'esprit de contradiction* (Disagreement)

PARLER Make suggestions to your friends about things to do. Your friends will not agree and will suggest something else.

▶ aller au cinéma (à la plage)

Allons au cinéma!

Non, n'allons pas au cinéma! Allons à la plage!

1. jouer au tennis (aux jeux vidéo)
2. écouter la radio (des CD)
3. regarder la télé (un film vidéo)
4. dîner au restaurant (à la maison)
5. inviter Michèle (Sophie)

6. organiser un barbecue (une boum)
7. faire des sandwichs (une pizza)
8. aller au musée (à la bibliothèque)
9. faire une promenade à pied (en voiture)
10. rendre visite à nos voisins (à nos copains)

PRONONCIATION

an, en /ɑ̃/

Les lettres «an» et «en»

The letters "**an**" and "**en**" represent the nasal vowel /ɑ̃/.
Be sure not to pronounce the sound "**n**" after the vowel.

enfant

Répétez:

/ɑ̃/ enf<u>an</u>t <u>an</u> m<u>an</u>teau coll<u>an</u>ts gr<u>an</u>d élég<u>an</u>t
    <u>An</u>dré m<u>an</u>ge un gr<u>an</u>d s<u>an</u>dwich.

/ɑ̃/ <u>en</u>fant <u>en</u> arg<u>en</u>t dép<u>en</u>ser att<u>en</u>ds <u>en</u>t<u>en</u>d v<u>en</u>d <u>en</u>vie
    Vinc<u>en</u>t dép<u>en</u>se rarem<u>en</u>t son arg<u>en</u>t.

À votre tour!

OBJECTIFS

Now you can …
• make suggestions
• tell others what to do

1 🎧 La bonne réponse

PARLER Anne is talking to Jean-François. Match Anne's questions with Jean-François's answers. You may act out the conversation with a classmate.

Anne

1 Est-ce que tu rends visite à tes cousins ce week-end?

2 Tu veux aller dans les boutiques avec moi?

3 Est-ce que tu as envie d'aller au cinéma?

4 Et après (afterwards) qu'est-ce qu'on fait?

a Eh bien, allons au restaurant!

b Bonne idée! Il y a un nouveau film au «Majestic».

c Écoute! Je n'ai pas besoin de vêtements.

d Non, je reste ici.

Jean-François

2 🎧 Créa-dialogue

PARLER When we are with our friends, it is not always easy to agree on what to do. With your classmates, discuss the following possibilities.

Qu'est-ce qu'on fait samedi?

Allons au cinéma.

Je n'ai pas envie d'aller au cinéma.

Eh bien, rendons visite à nos amis. D'accord?

Oui, c'est une bonne idée.

Quand?	Première suggestion	Deuxième suggestion
▶ samedi	aller au cinéma	rendre visite à nos amis
1. ce soir (tonight)	étudier	regarder la télé
2. dimanche	aller en ville	dîner au restaurant
3. après (after) les classes	jouer au basket	faire une promenade
4. cet été	chercher un job	voyager
5. ce week-end	faire un pique-nique	??
6. demain	aller à la bibliothèque	??

Conseils ---

PARLER Your friends tell you what they would like to do. Give them appropriate
advice, either positive or negative. Use your imagination.

▶ Je voudrais maigrir.   **Alors, mange moins.**
                        (Alors, ne mange pas de pizza.)

1. Je voudrais avoir un «A» en français.   **3.** Je voudrais organiser une boum.
2. Je voudrais gagner beaucoup d'argent.   **4.** Je voudrais préparer un barbecue.

 Que faire? ---

PARLER Give a classmate advice about what to do or not to do in the following
circumstances.

Pendant *(During)* la classe	Ce soir	Ce week-end	Pendant les vacances
écouter le prof	étudier	rester à la maison	voyager
parler à tes copains	aller au cinéma	aller en ville	travailler
regarder les bandes dessinées *(comics)*	préparer tes leçons	dépenser ton argent	grossir
manger un sandwich	aider *(help)* ta mère	organiser une boum	oublier *(forget)* ton français
répondre en français	surfer sur l'Internet	faire une promenade à pied	??
??	??	??	

▶ 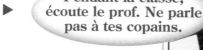 **Pendant la classe, écoute le prof. Ne parle pas à tes copains.**

 Bon voyage! ---

ÉCRIRE Your French friend Ariane is going to visit the United States
next summer with her cousin. They are traveling on a low budget and
are asking you for advice as to how to save money. Make a list of
suggestions, including five things they could do and five things they
should not do. You may want to use some of the following ideas:

▶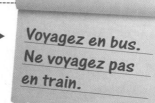
  Voyagez en bus.
  Ne voyagez pas
  en train.

▶ • voyager (comment?)
    • rester (dans quels hôtels?)
    • dîner (dans quels restaurants?)
    • visiter (quelles villes?)

    • aller (où?)
    • acheter (quelles choses?)
    • apporter (quelles choses?)

 **LESSON REVIEW** CLASSZONE.COM

Tests de contrôle

By taking the following tests, you can check your progress in French and also prepare for the unit test. Write your answers on a separate sheet of paper.

Review...
• items of clothing: pp. 258, 259, and 260

1 The right item

Give the names of the following items of clothing, using the appropriate article: **un, une,** or **des.**

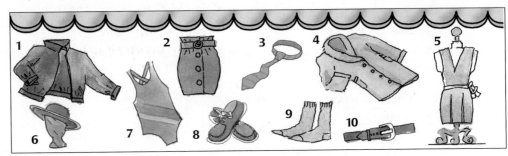

Dans ce magasin, il y a ...

1. —   3. —   5. —   7. —   9. —
2. —   4. —   6. —   8. —   10. —

Review...
• new verbs: pp. 259, 262, 269, 278, and 290

2 The right activity

Complete each of the following sentences with the appropriate forms of the verbs in the box. Be logical in your choice of verbs and do not use the same word more than once.

1. Philippe — ses CD à la boum.
2. Caroline — sa nouvelle robe.
3. Thomas — parce qu'il mange trop *(too much)*.
4. Léa — un copain au pique-nique.
5. Céline — aux examens parce qu'elle étudie beaucoup.
6. Mélanie ne — pas son stylo. Où est-il?
7. Charlotte est en vacances. Elle — à son oncle.
8. Pierre — à un mail.
9. Je n' — pas bien. Répète, s'il te plaît.
10. Cécile regarde sa montre. Elle — un copain.

amener
apporter
attendre
entendre
grossir
porter
rendre visite
répondre
réussir
trouver

Review...
• beau, nouveau, and vieux: p. 279

3 The right form

Complete the following sentences with the appropriate forms of **beau, nouveau,** and **vieux.** Be logical in your choices.

1. Dans ce quartier moderne, il y a beaucoup de — immeubles.
2. Ma grand-mère a 82 ans. Elle est —.
3. Catherine est très jolie. C'est une — fille, n'est-ce pas?
4. Mon ordinateur ne marche pas. J'ai besoin d'un — ordinateur.
5. Nicolas va nettoyer *(to clean)* le garage. Il met ses — vêtements.

4 The right comparison

Make logical comparisons using the adjectives in parentheses.

(grand)   **1.** La France est — les États-Unis *(United States)*.
(élégant) **2.** Une belle chemise est — un vieux tee-shirt.
(rapide)   **3.** Les voitures de sport sont — les limousines.
(bon)   **4.** À l'examen, un «A» est — un «C».

Review...
• comparisons:
  p. 280

5 Ce or quel?

Complete the following sentences with the appropriate forms of **ce** or **quel**.

1. — blouson préfères-tu?
2. J'aime — lunettes!
3. — veste est chère!
4. — casquette achetez-vous?
5. — copains invites-tu?
6. — chaussures mets-tu?
7. Comment s'appelle — garçon?
8. Qui est — homme?

Review...
• ce and **quel**
  pp. 270 and 271

6 The right verb

Complete the following sentences with the appropriate forms of the verbs in parentheses.

1. (acheter)
J'— une chemise.   Nous — des CD.   Qu'est-ce que tu —?
2. (mettre)
Marc — un tee-shirt.   Je — un short.   Qu'est-ce que vous —?
3. (choisir)
Vous — des vêtements.   Ils — des CD.   Éric — un polo.
4. (finir)
Nous — les devoirs.   Je — un livre.   Pauline — la pizza.
5. (vendre)
Ils — leur maison.   Je — mon vélo.   Claire — sa voiture.
6. (attendre)
Les touristes — le train.   J'— le bus.   Nous — un copain.

Review...
• verb forms:
  pp. 268, 272, 278
  and 290

7 Composition: Un mariage

Imagine that you are a reporter for the society column of your local newspaper. You are attending an elegant wedding. Describe what the following people are wearing: **la mariée** *(the bride)*, **le marié** *(the groom)*, and **les demoiselles d'honneur** *(the bridesmaids)*. Be imaginative but use only vocabulary and expressions that you know in French.

STRATEGY Writing

a For each of the following, list the clothes and their colors.

la mariée	le marié	les demoiselles d'honneur
_____	_____	_____
_____	_____	_____

b Write three short paragraphs describing what each person is wearing.

c Reread your composition and be sure you have spelled all the items of clothing correctly and have used the correct forms of the color adjectives.

Vocabulaire

POUR COMMUNIQUER

Shopping for clothes

Pardon...	*Excuse me …*	**Quel est le prix de …?**	*What is the price of …?*
Vous désirez, (monsieur)?	*May I help you, (Sir)?*	**Combien coûte …**	*How much does … cost?*
Je cherche …	*I'm looking for …*		

Expressing opinions and making comparisons

Qu'est-ce que tu penses de [la robe rose]?		*What do you think of [the pink dress]?*
Comment tu trouves [la robe noire]?		*What do you think of [the black dress]?*

La robe rose est	**plus belle que** **moins belle que** **aussi belle que**	**la robe noire.**	*The pink dress is*	*more beautiful than* *less beautiful than* *as beautiful as*	*the black dress.*

MOTS ET EXPRESSIONS

Les magasins

un magasin	*store*	**une boutique**	*shop*
un grand magasin	*department store*		

L'argent

l'argent	*money*	**une pièce**	*coin*
un billet	*bill, paper money*		

Les vêtements et les accessoires

des baskets	*(hightop) sneakers*	**des bottes**	*boots*
un blouson	*jacket*	**une casquette**	*baseball cap*
un chapeau	*hat*	**une ceinture**	*belt*
un chemisier	*blouse*	**des chaussettes**	*socks*
des collants	*tights*	**des chaussures**	*shoes*
un imper(méable)	*raincoat*	**une chemise**	*shirt*
un jean	*jeans*	**une cravate**	*tie*
un jogging	*jogging suit*	**une jupe**	*skirt*
un maillot de bain	*bathing suit*	**des lunettes**	*glasses*
un manteau	*overcoat*	**des lunettes de soleil**	*sunglasses*
un pantalon	*pants*	**une robe**	*dress*
un polo	*polo shirt*	**des sandales**	*sandals*
un pull	*sweater*	**une veste**	*jacket*
un short	*shorts*		
un survêtement	*track suit*		
un sweat	*sweatshirt*		
un tee-shirt	*t-shirt*		
des tennis	*sneakers*		

La description

à la mode	in style	joli(e)	pretty
beau (belle)	beautiful	long(ue)	long
bon marché	cheap	meilleur(e)	better
cher (chère)	expensive	moche	ugly
chouette	neat	nouveau (nouvelle)	new
court(e)	short	pauvre	poor
démodé(e)	out of style	petit(e)	small
élégant(e)	elegant	riche	rich
génial(e)	terrific	vieux (vieille)	old
grand(e)	big		

Verbes réguliers en -er

chercher	to look for
coûter	to cost
dépenser	to spend
gagner	to earn; to win
penser (que)	to think (that)
porter	to wear
trouver	to find; to think of

Verbes avec changements orthographiques

acheter	to buy
amener	to bring (a person)
espérer	to hope
préférer	to prefer
payer	to pay, to pay for

Verbes réguliers en -ir

choisir	to choose
finir	to finish
grossir	to gain weight
maigrir	to lose weight
réussir	to succeed
réussir à un examen	to pass an exam

Verbes réguliers en -re

attendre	to wait, to wait for
entendre	to hear
perdre	to lose, to waste
rendre visite à	to visit (a person)
répondre à	to answer
vendre	to sell

Verbes irréguliers

avoir besoin de + *noun*	to need	avoir envie de + *noun*	to want
avoir besoin de + *infinitive*	to need to, to have to	avoir envie de + *infinitive*	to feel like, to want to
		mettre	to put, to put on

Les nombres de 100 à 1000

100	cent	200	deux cents	500	cinq cents	800	huit cents
101	cent un	300	trois cents	600	six cents	900	neuf cents
102	cent deux	400	quatre cents	700	sept cents	1000	mille

Expressions utiles

à mon avis	in my opinion	combien + *verb*	how much
Eh bien!	Well!	combien de + *noun*	how much, how many
C'est une bonne idée!	That's a good idea!	trop + *adjective*	too
ce, cet, cette, ces	this, that, these, those		
quel, quelle, quels, quelles	what, which		

TEST PREP CLASSZONE.COM FLASHCARDS AND MORE!

Achats° par INTERNET

En France, comme° aux États-Unis,° on peut
faire beaucoup d'achats par Internet. Ces
vêtements figurent° sur le catalogue-en-ligne
de «la Redoute», une compagnie française
spécialisée dans la vente° de vêtements par
correspondance.°

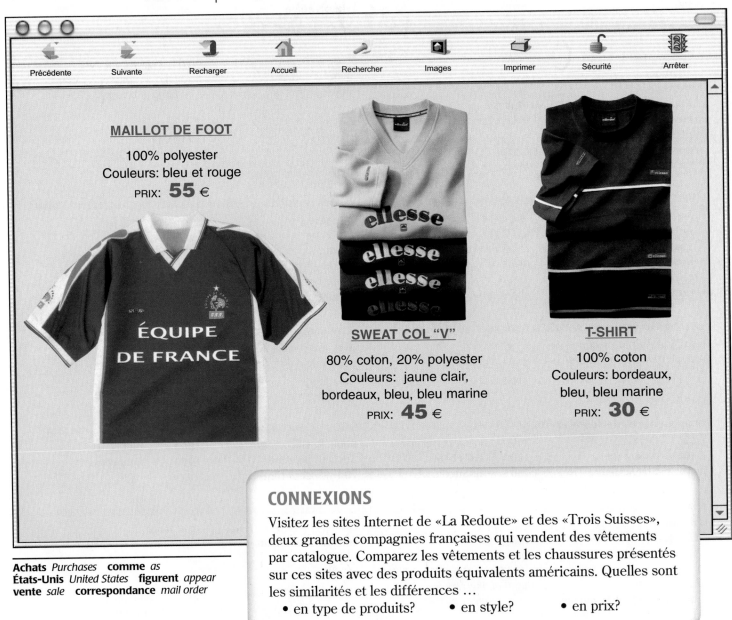

Précédente Suivante Recharger Accueil Rechercher Images Imprimer Sécurité Arrêter

MAILLOT DE FOOT

100% polyester
Couleurs: bleu et rouge
PRIX: **55** €

ÉQUIPE DE FRANCE

SWEAT COL "V"

80% coton, 20% polyester
Couleurs: jaune clair,
bordeaux, bleu, bleu marine
PRIX: **45** €

T-SHIRT

100% coton
Couleurs: bordeaux,
bleu, bleu marine
PRIX: **30** €

Achats *Purchases* **comme** *as*
États-Unis *United States* **figurent** *appear*
vente *sale* **correspondance** *mail order*

CONNEXIONS

Visitez les sites Internet de «La Redoute» et des «Trois Suisses»,
deux grandes compagnies françaises qui vendent des vêtements
par catalogue. Comparez les vêtements et les chaussures présentés
sur ces sites avec des produits équivalents américains. Quelles sont
les similarités et les différences …

- en type de produits?
- en style?
- en prix?

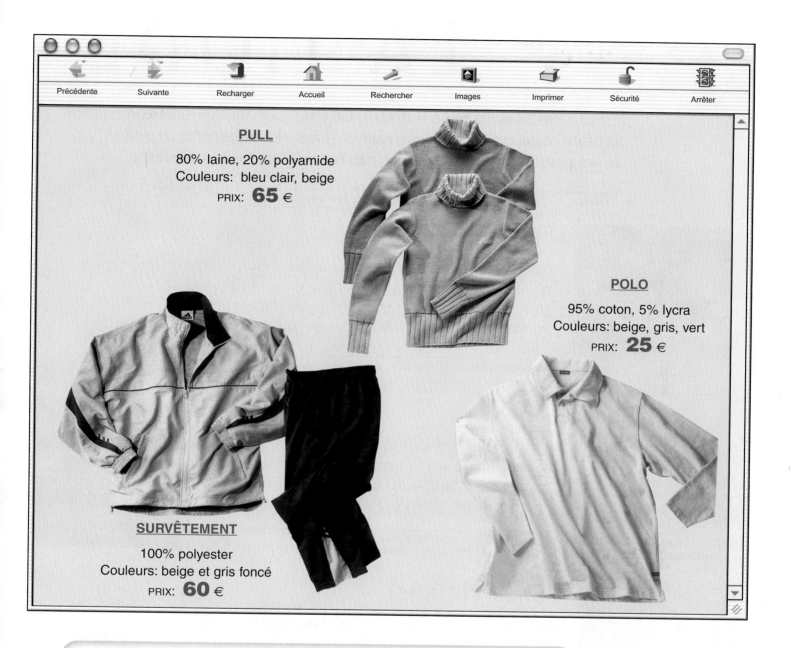

PULL

80% laine, 20% polyamide
Couleurs: bleu clair, beige
PRIX: **65** €

POLO

95% coton, 5% lycra
Couleurs: beige, gris, vert
PRIX: **25** €

SURVÊTEMENT

100% polyester
Couleurs: beige et gris foncé
PRIX: **60** €

Précédente Suivante Recharger Accueil Rechercher Images Imprimer Sécurité Arrêter

Et vous?

Vous êtes en France et vous voulez acheter deux vêtements différents comme cadeaux *(presents)* pour des amis aux États-Unis. Votre budget est limité à un total de 100 euros. Faites votre sélection.

	Pour qui?	Vêtement	Textile	Couleur	Prix
1.					
2.					
				Prix total:	

Les jeunes Français et LA MODE

Est-ce que vous aimez être à la mode?° Où est-ce que vous achetez vos vêtements? Et qu'est-ce qui compte° le plus° pour vous? le style? la qualité? le prix? Nous avons posé° ces questions à cinq jeunes Français. Voilà leurs réponses.

à la mode *in style* **compte** *counts* **le plus** *the most* **avons posé** *asked*

Florence (16 ans)

J'aime être à la mode. Malheureusement,° mon budget est limité. La solution? Le samedi après-midi je travaille dans une boutique de mode. Là, je peux acheter mes jupes et mes pulls à des prix très avantageux.° Pour le reste, je compte sur la générosité de mes parents.

Malheureusement *Unfortunately* **avantageux** *reasonable*

Chloé (15 ans)

Pour moi, le style, c'est tout.° Hélas, la mode n'est pas bon marché. Heureusement,° j'ai une cousine qui a une machine à coudre° et qui est très adroite.° Alors, nous cousons° des rubans° et des patchs sur nos vêtements. De cette façon,° nous créons notre propre° style. C'est génial, non?

tout *everything* **Heureusement** *Fortunately* **machine à coudre** *sewing machine*
adroite *skillful* **cousons** *sew* **rubans** *ribbons* **façon** *manner, way* **propre** *own*

Julien (14 ans)

Vous connaissez° le proverbe: «L'habit ne fait pas le moine*.» Eh bien, pour moi, les vêtements n'ont pas d'importance. Avec mon argent, je préfère° acheter des CD. Quand j'ai besoin de jeans ou de tee-shirts, je vais aux puces.° C'est pas cher et c'est marrant!°

connaissez *know* **[marché] aux puces** *flea market* **marrant** *fun*
Clothes don't make the man. (The habit doesn't make the monk.)

Robert (15 ans)

Aujourd'hui la présentation extérieure est très importante. Mais il n'est pas nécessaire d'être à la mode pour être bien habillé.° Pour moi, la qualité des vêtements est aussi importante que leur style. En général, j'attends les soldes. J'achète peu de vêtements mais je fais attention à la qualité.

habillé *dressed*

Éric (12 ans)

Moi, je n'ai pas le choix!° C'est ma mère qui choisit mes vêtements. En ce qui concerne° la mode, elle n'est pas dans le coup.° Elle achète tout sur catalogue et elle choisit ce qui est le moins cher.° C'est pas drôle.

---

choix *choice* **En ce qui concerne** *As for* **dans le coup** *with it*
le moins cher *the cheapest (the least expensive)*

STRATEGY Reading

Understanding casual French speech
The interviews you read were conducted orally. Notice how casual French speech is different from standard written language.

- Spoken language often contains slang expressions.
  Elle n'est pas dans le coup! C'est marrant! C'est génial!

- Spoken French sometimes drops the **ne** in **ne … pas.**
  C'est pas cher. = Ce n'est pas cher.

NOTE culturelle

Les soldes

En France, les boutiques de vêtements ont des soldes deux fois par an.° Les dates de ces soldes sont déterminées par le gouvernement et sont les mêmes° dans tout le pays.° Au moment des soldes, on peut acheter des vêtements de bonne qualité à des prix avantageux.

---

deux fois par an *twice a year* **mêmes** *same*
tout le pays *the entire country*

Et vous?

Voici ce que disent les jeunes Français. Est-ce que c'est vrai pour vous aussi?

Oui, c'est vrai pour moi!

Non, ce n'est pas vrai pour moi!

OUI OU NON?

1. J'aime être à la mode.
2. Mon budget est limité.
3. J'attends les soldes.
4. Je fais attention à la qualité.

OUI OU NON?

5. Je couds des patchs sur mes jeans.
6. Ma mère choisit mes vêtements.
7. Je préfère acheter des CD.
8. J'achète mes vêtements aux puces.

Bonjour, Fatima!

Je m'appelle Fatima et j'ai quinze ans. J'habite dans la banlieue° de Paris. Mes parents sont généreux mais ils ne sont pas très riches. Alors, je n'ai pas beaucoup d'argent de poche: cinquante euros par mois. Ce n'est pas une fortune! Heureusement,° je fais du baby-sitting pour les voisins quand ils vont au cinéma le week-end. Je gagne cinq euros par heure.

J'adore les vêtements. Avec ma copine Djemila, on achète des magazines de mode et on va dans les magasins. Quand on entre dans une boutique, c'est généralement plus pour regarder que pour acheter. J'achète mes nouveaux pulls pendant la période des soldes. Par contre,° j'achète assez souvent des bracelets et des boucles d'oreille.° On trouve des choses géniales dans les petites boutiques de mon quartier. Quand je veux changer de «look», je change de boucles d'oreille et je change de vernis à ongles° et de rouge à lèvres.° C'est facile et ça ne coûte pas cher!

banlieue *suburbs*   **Heureusement** *Fortunately*   **Par contre** *On the other hand*   **boucles d'oreille** *earrings*
vernis à ongles *nail polish*   **rouge à lèvres** *lipstick*

NOTE culturelle

Prénoms arabes

Fatima et **Djemila** sont des jeunes filles d'origine «maghrébine». Elles portent° des noms typiquement arabes.

Le Maghreb est une région géographique constituée par **le Maroc,**° **l'Algérie** et **la Tunisie**. Quatre millions de Français (sur une population totale de soixante millions) sont d'origine maghrébine. Beaucoup parlent arabe et pratiquent la religion musulmane.°

portent = ont   **Maroc** *Morocco*
musulmane *Moslem*

Compréhension

1. Comment est-ce que Fatima gagne son argent?
2. Qu'est-ce qu'elle fait avec sa copine?
3. Qu'est-ce qu'elle achète avec son argent?
4. Qu'est-ce qu'elle fait pour changer de look?

Et vous?

Quelles ressemblances *(similarities)* et quelles différences est-ce que vous
trouvez entre Fatima et vous? Faites une liste de ces ressemblances et de
ces différences.

- âge
- parents
- argent de poche
- achats de vêtements
- achats d'accessoires
- comment changer de look

EN BREF: L'ALGÉRIE

Population: 32 millions
Capitale: Alger
Langues: arabe, berbère, français

L'Algérie est un pays° d'Afrique
du Nord. Colonie française pendant
plus de 100 ans, l'Algérie est
devenue indépendante en 1962.
La majorité des Algériens sont
arabes et pratiquent la religion
musulmane. Des millions
d'Algériens ont immigré en
France et sont devenus Français.
Pour cette raison,° la France est
maintenant le pays avec la plus
grande population musulmane
d'Europe.

La présence algérienne
influence la vie° ordinaire des
Français. Par exemple, les Français mangent du couscous*
qui est une spécialité d'Afrique du Nord, et beaucoup de
jeunes écoutent le raï qui est une musique d'origine algérienne.

---

pays *country* **raison** *reason* **vie** *life*

* **Couscous** *is a type of semolina (white gritty wheat) which is usually cooked with meat and vegetables as a main
dish, but which can also be steamed and served cold in salads.*

COMMUNAUTÉS

Explore Internet sources to find out more about the Muslim religion.
Or perhaps there is a Muslim person in your school or in your community
whom you could invite to talk to your class. Use the information you gather to
make a bulletin board display explaining the basic tenets of the Muslim faith.

UNITÉ 7

Le temps libre

LEÇON 21 LE FRANÇAIS PRATIQUE:
Le week-end et les vacances

LEÇON 22 Vive le week-end!

LEÇON 23 L'alibi

LEÇON 24 Qui a de la chance?

THÈME ET OBJECTIFS

Leisure-time activities

We work hard during the week, but we also need
time to relax.

In this unit, you will learn ...

• to discuss your weekend activities

• to talk about individual summer and winter
sports

• to describe your vacation and travel plans

You will also be able ...

• to describe what you did and where you went
yesterday, last week, or last summer

• more generally, to narrate what happened
at any time in the past

WEBQUEST
CLASSZONE.COM

LEÇON

21

LE FRANÇAIS
P R A T I Q U E
VIDÉO · DVD · AUDIO

Le week-end et les vacances

Accent sur … les loisirs

When given the choice, French people would rather have more free time than more money. For them, leisure time is an essential component of what they call **la qualité de la vie** (*quality of life*). By law, they work only thirty-five hours per week and they have a minimum of five weeks of vacation per year.

Like their parents, French teenagers value their leisure time and try to make the most of it. What are their favorite activities? Here is what they do when they have a free evening.

Qu'est-ce que tu aimes faire le soir?	GARÇONS	FILLES
Je regarde la télé.	24%	18%
Je sors° avec mes copains.	20%	18%
Je vais au cinéma.	16%	14%
Je lis.°	14%	20%
Je vais au concert ou au théâtre.	10%	12%
Je vais danser.	8%	12%
Je fais du sport.	6%	4%
Je bricole.°	2%	2%

sors *go out*   **lis** *read*   **bricole** *do things around the house*

Michèle est très sportive. Elle fait souvent du jogging dans le parc de la ville.

Thomas adore faire du skate. Le samedi, il va au skatepark avec ses copains.

À la Martinique il fait beau tout le temps.
À la plage, on fait du surfing ou de la planche
à voile.

En hiver, beaucoup de jeunes Français vont à la montagne
avec leur famille ou leur école. Le snowboard — ou
le surf — est un sport très populaire.

A VOCABULAIRE Le week-end

▶ *How to plan your weekend activities:*

> *Qu'est-ce que tu vas faire samedi?*

> *Je vais rester chez moi pour réparer mon vélo.*

Qu'est-ce que tu vas faire | samedi?
| samedi **matin**
| dimanche **après-midi**
| demain **soir**
| ce **week-end**
| le week-end **prochain** *(next)*

le matin *morning*
l'après-midi *(m.) afternoon*
le soir *evening*

Je vais rester chez moi **pour** *(in order to)* | faire mes **devoirs** *(homework)*.
| **réparer** *(to fix)* mon vélo
| **préparer** le dîner
| **aider** *(to help)* mes parents
| **laver** *(to wash)* la voiture
| **nettoyer** *(to clean)* le garage
| **ranger** *(to pick up)* ma chambre

Je vais aller … | pour …
en ville | **faire des achats**
dans les magasins | *(to go shopping)*.
au centre commercial | **louer** *(to rent)* un film

au cinéma | **voir** *(to see)* un film
au café | **rencontrer** *(to meet)* des copains
au stade | **assister à** *(to go to, attend)*
| un match de foot
à la campagne *(countryside)* | **faire un pique-nique**
| *(to have a picnic)*

> *Moi, je vais aller en ville pour faire des achats.*

Je vais aller à une boum.
Avant *(Before)* la boum, je vais faire des achats.
Pendant *(During)* la boum, je vais écouter des CD.
Après *(After)* la boum, je vais faire mes devoirs.

→ The verb **nettoyer** is conjugated like **payer**:

je **nettoie**   tu **nettoies**   il/elle/on **nettoie**   ils/elles **nettoient**
but: nous **nettoyons**   vous **nettoyez**

1 Et toi?

PARLER/ÉCRIRE Décris tes activités.
Pour cela, complète les phrases suivantes.

1. En général,
   je vais au cinéma …
   - le vendredi soir
   - le samedi soir
   - le dimanche après-midi
   - … ?

2. En général,
   je fais mes devoirs …
   - avant le dîner
   - après le dîner
   - pendant la classe
   - … ?

3. Je préfère assister à …
   - un match de foot
   - un match de baseball
   - un concert de rock
   - … ?

4. En général, quand je rentre
   chez moi après les classes, …
   - je fais mes devoirs
   - je regarde la télé
   - j'aide ma mère ou mon père
   - … ?

5. J'aime aller en ville pour …
   - voir un film
   - rencontrer mes copains
   - faire des achats
   - … ?

6. En général, je préfère faire
   mes achats …
   - seul(e) *(by myself)*
   - avec mes copains
   - avec mes frères et mes soeurs
   - … ?

7. En été, je préfère faire
   un pique-nique …
   - dans mon jardin
   - à la campagne
   - à la plage
   - … ?

8. Pour aider mes parents à
   la maison, je préfère …
   - ranger le salon
   - laver la voiture
   - nettoyer le garage
   - … ?

2 Qu'est-ce qu'ils font?

PARLER/ÉCRIRE Informez-vous sur les personnes
suivantes. Décrivez ce qu'elles font ou ce qu'elles
vont faire. Pour cela, complétez les phrases avec
une expression du **Vocabulaire** à la page 310.

▶ Sandrine est au garage.
  Elle <u>répare son vélo</u> (<u>sa mobylette</u>).

1. Mme Jolivet est dans la cuisine. Elle …
2. Vincent Jolivet est aussi dans la cuisine. Il …
3. Anne et Sylvie sont au Bon Marché. Elles …
4. Je suis dans ma chambre et je regarde mon
   livre de français. Je …
5. Olivier et ses copains achètent des billets
   (tickets) de cinéma. Ils vont …
6. Mes amis vont à Yankee Stadium. Ils vont …
7. Tu vas au café. Tu vas …
8. Vous faites des sandwichs. Vous allez … à
   la campagne.

3 Mon calendrier personnel

PARLER/ÉCRIRE Décrivez ce que
vous allez faire.

MERCREDI

1. Après la classe, je vais …
2. Avant le dîner, …
3. Après le dîner, …
4. Demain soir, …
5. Vendredi soir, …
6. Samedi après-midi, …
7. Samedi soir, …
8. Dimanche après-midi, …
9. Pendant les vacances, …

B VOCABULAIRE Les vacances

Qu'est-ce que tu vas faire cet été?

Je vais aller à la mer.

▶ *How to plan your vacation activities:*

Qu'est-ce que tu vas faire	à **Noël?**	**Noël** *Christmas*
	à **Pâques**	**Pâques** *Easter*
	pendant *(during)* **les vacances** de printemps	**les vacances** *vacation*
	pendant **les grandes vacances**	**les grandes vacances**
	cet été	*summer vacation*

| Je vais aller | à **la mer** *(ocean, shore).* |
| | à **la montagne** *(mountains)* |

Je vais voyager	en avion.	**un avion** *plane*
	en train	**un train** *train*
	en autocar	**un autocar, un car** *touring bus*
	en bateau	**un bateau** *boat, ship*
	en voiture	

Je vais voyager en avion.

| Je vais voyager | **seul(e)** *(alone).* |
| | avec ma famille |

Je vais **passer** *(to spend)*	dix jours	là-bas.	**un jour** *day*
	six semaines		**une semaine** *week*
	deux mois		**un mois** *month*

| J'aime | **le ski** *(skiing).* | En hiver, je vais à la montagne pour **faire du ski** *(to ski).* |
| | **le ski nautique** *(water-skiing)* | En été, je vais à la mer pour **faire du ski nautique** *(to water-ski).* |

J'aime le ski!

VOCABULAIRE **Activités sportives**

le sport	*sport(s)*	Je **fais du sport.**	*I practice sports.*
le jogging	*jogging*	Nous **faisons du jogging.**	*We jog.*
la natation	*swimming*	Tu **fais de la natation?**	*Do you go swimming?*
l'escalade *(f.)*	*rock climbing*	J'aime **faire de l'escalade.**	*I like to go rock climbing.*
le ski	*skiing*	Tu **fais du ski?**	*Do you ski?*
le ski nautique	*water-skiing*	Anne **fait du ski nautique.**	*Anne water-skis.*
la voile	*sailing*	Paul **fait de la voile.**	*Paul sails.*
la planche à voile	*windsurfing*	Vous **faites de la planche à voile?**	*Do you windsurf?*

le roller	*in-line skating*	**des rollers**	*in-line skates*
le skate	*skateboarding*	**un skate**	*skateboard*
le snowboard	*snowboarding*	**un snowboard**	*snowboard*
le VTT	*mountain biking*	**un VTT**	*mountain bike*

➜ To describe participation in individual sports or other activities, the French use the construction:

faire	$\begin{cases} \textbf{du} \\ \textbf{de la} \\ \textbf{de l'} \end{cases}$ +	*SPORT* or *ACTIVITY*	**le roller** → **faire du roller** **la voile** → **faire de la voile** **l'escalade** → **faire de l'escalade**

NOTE *culturelle*

Les sports d'hiver

À Noël et pendant les vacances de février, beaucoup de jeunes Français vont à la montagne avec leur famille pour faire des sports d'hiver. Certaines écoles organisent des «classes de neige». Les élèves étudient le matin et font du sport l'après-midi.

Le ski est un sport très populaire. Mais beaucoup de jeunes préfèrent faire du snowboard, une spécialité dans laquelle° plusieurs° Françaises ont été° championnes olympiques.

laquelle *which* **plusieurs** *several* **ont été** *have been*

4 Et toi?

PARLER/ÉCRIRE Indique tes préférences personnelles en complétant les phrases suivantes.

1. Mes vacances préférées sont ...
   - les vacances de Noël
   - les vacances de printemps
   - les grandes vacances
   - ... ?

2. Pendant les grandes vacances, je préfère ...
   - aller à la mer
   - aller à la montagne
   - aller à la campagne
   - ... ?

3. En été, je vais à la plage spécialement *(especially)* pour ...
   - nager
   - faire du ski nautique
   - bronzer *(to get a tan)*
   - ... ?

4. Je voudrais aller dans le Colorado pour ...
   - faire du ski
   - faire de l'escalade
   - faire du VTT
   - ... ?

5. Je voudrais aller à la Martinique principalement *(mainly)* pour ...
   - parler français
   - faire de la planche à voile
   - faire de la plongée *(scuba diving)*
   - ... ?

5 Leurs activités favorites

PARLER/ÉCRIRE Les personnes suivantes ont certaines activités favorites. Lisez où elles sont et dites ce qu'elles font. Pour cela choisissez une activité appropriée de la liste à droite.

▶ Anne est dans un studio de danse.
  Elle fait de la danse moderne.

1. Jean-Pierre est au stade.
2. Je suis à la plage.
3. En juillet, nous allons dans le Colorado.
4. Tu passes les vacances de Noël en Suisse.
5. Mes copains passent les vacances à la campagne.
6. Pauline et Marie sont à la salle *(room)* de gymnastique.
7. Vous êtes à la mer.
8. Nous sommes à Tahiti.
9. Avant le dîner, nous allons au parc municipal.
10. Je suis à la Martinique.

la gymnastique

la danse moderne

le sport

le jogging

le camping

la voile

la planche à voile

le ski

le ski nautique

l'escalade

6. Mon sport préféré est …

- la natation
- le snowboard
- le roller
- … ?

7. Pour mon anniversaire, je préfère avoir …

- un skate
- des rollers
- un VTT
- … ?

8. Avec mes copains, je préfère …

- faire du roller
- faire du skate
- faire du jogging
- … ?

9. Quand je voyage pendant les vacances, je préfère voyager …

- seul(e)
- avec mes copains
- avec ma famille
- … ?

10. Je voudrais aller à Paris et rester là-bas pendant *(for)* …

- dix jours
- trois semaines
- six mois
- … ?

6 *Questions personnelles* PARLER/ÉCRIRE

1. En général, qu'est-ce que tu fais pendant les vacances de Noël?
2. Est-ce que tu vas voyager pendant les grandes vacances? Où vas-tu aller? Combien de temps *(How long)* est-ce que tu vas rester là-bas?
3. Qu'est-ce que tu aimes faire quand tu es à la plage?
4. Est-ce que tu voyages souvent? Comment voyages-tu?

COMMUNAUTÉS

During summer vacation, some American teenagers spend a month in a French-speaking region doing community service. At the same time they have the opportunity to meet other young people and to use their French skills.

You can go on the Internet to research some of the non-profit organizations that sponsor such exchanges. It is not too early to begin planning ahead.

À votre tour!

OBJECTIFS

Now you can ...
- discuss your weekend and vacation plans
- talk about individual sports

① 🎧 Écoutez bien!

ÉCOUTER On weekends, you can stay in and take care of things at home, or you can go out and have fun. Listen carefully to what the people are saying. If they refer to an indoor activity, mark A. If they refer to an outdoor activity, mark B.

	1	2	3	4	5	6
A: À l'intérieur						
B: À l'extérieur						

A. À l'intérieur

B. À l'extérieur

② ✍️ Composition: Le week-end prochain

ÉCRIRE Make plans for next weekend. Prepare a list of activities describing ...

- four things that you are going to do at home
- four things that you are going to do outside

Samedi, je vais ranger ma chambre. Après, je ...

③ ✍️ Composition: Mes sports préférés

ÉCRIRE Describe two sports that you engage in during each of the following times of year.

- Pendant les vacances d'été
- En hiver
- En toute (any) saison

4 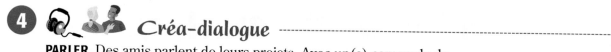 *Créa-dialogue* ---

PARLER Des amis parlent de leurs projets. Avec un(e) camarade de classe, choisissez une scène et composez le dialogue correspondant.

▶ —Où vas-tu <u>vendredi</u>?
—Je vais <u>en ville</u>.
—Qu'est-ce que tu vas faire là-bas?
—Je vais <u>faire des achats</u>.

▶	vendredi	en ville	

1. samedi matin			2. samedi après-midi			3. à Noël	à Aspen	

4. pendant les vacances de printemps	en Floride		5. en juillet			6. en août		

7. demain matin	?		8. dimanche après-midi	?	?	9. cet été	?	?

5 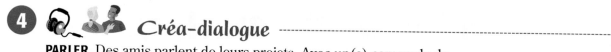 *Conversation dirigée* --

PARLER Avec un(e) camarade, composez un dialogue basé sur les instructions suivantes. Thomas demande à Hélène si elle a des projets de vacances.

Thomas			Hélène
asks Hélène where she is going this summer	→ ↙	says that she is going to the ocean with friends	
asks her if they are going to travel by car	→ ↙	answers that they are going to travel by train because they do not have a car	
asks her if she is going to go sailing	→ ↙	answers yes and says that she is also going to windsurf	
says good-bye to Hélène and wishes her a good vacation **(Bonnes vacances!)**	→	answers good-bye	

LESSON REVIEW
CLASSZONE.COM

trois cent dix-sept
Leçon 21 317

LEÇON 22

Vive le week-end!

AUDIO

Le week-end, nous avons nos occupations préférées.
Certaines personnes aiment aller en ville et rencontrer leurs amis.

<u>D'autres</u> préfèrent rester à la maison et <u>bricoler</u>.
Qu'est-ce que les personnes suivantes <u>ont fait</u>
le week-end <u>dernier</u>?

Others / do things around the house
did … do
last

Le week-end	**Le week-end dernier**

J'aime acheter des vêtements.

J'<u>ai acheté</u> des vêtements. *bought*

Tu aimes réparer ton vélo.

Tu <u>as réparé</u> ton vélo. *fixed*

M. Lambert aime travailler dans le jardin.

Il <u>a travaillé</u> dans le jardin. *worked*

Nous aimons organiser des boums.

Nous <u>avons organisé</u> une boum. *organized*

Le week-end

Vous aimez jouer au foot.

Pluton et Philibert aiment rencontrer leurs amis.

Le week-end dernier

Vous <u>avez joué</u> au foot. *played*

Ils <u>ont rencontré</u> leurs amis. *met*

Et toi?

Indique si oui ou non tu as fait les choses suivantes le week-end dernier.
Pour cela complète les phrases suivantes.

1. (J'ai/Je n'ai pas) … acheté des vêtements.
2. (J'ai/Je n'ai pas) … réparé mon vélo.
3. (J'ai/Je n'ai pas) … travaillé dans le jardin.

4. (J'ai/Je n'ai pas) … organisé une boum.
5. (J'ai/Je n'ai pas) … joué au foot.
6. (J'ai/Je n'ai pas) … rencontré mes amis.

NOTE culturelle

Le week-end

Le week-end ne commence pas° le vendredi soir pour tout le monde.° Dans beaucoup d'écoles françaises, les élèves ont classe le samedi matin. Pour eux, le week-end commence seulement° le samedi à midi.

Que font les jeunes Français le samedi? Ça dépend. Beaucoup° vont en ville. Ils vont dans des magasins pour écouter les nouveaux CD ou pour regarder, essayer° et parfois° acheter des vêtements. Ils vont au café ou au cinéma avec leurs copains. Certains° préfèrent louer un film et rester chez eux ou aller chez des copains. Parfois

ils vont à une soirée. Là on écoute de la musique, on mange des sandwichs et on danse …

En général, le dimanche est réservé aux activités familiales.° Un week-end, on invite des cousins. Un autre° week-end, on rend visite aux grands-parents … Le dimanche, on déjeune° et on dîne en famille.° Le soir, on regarde la télé et souvent on fait ses devoirs pour les classes du lundi matin.

ne commence pas *does not begin* **tout le monde** *everyone* **seulement** *only* **Beaucoup** *Many* **essayer** *try on*
parfois *sometimes* **Certains** *Some of them* **activités familiales** *family activities* **Un autre** *Another* **déjeune** *has lunch*
en famille *at home (with the family)*

A Les expressions avec *avoir*

Note the use of **avoir** in the following sentences:

J'**ai faim**. *I **am hungry**.*
Brigitte **a soif**. *Brigitte **is thirsty**.*

French speakers use **avoir** in many expressions where English speakers use the verb *to be*.

VOCABULAIRE Expressions avec *avoir*

avoir chaud	to be (feel) warm	Quand j'**ai chaud** en été, je vais à la plage.
avoir froid	to be (feel) cold	Est-ce que tu **as froid?** Voici ton pull.
avoir faim	to be hungry	Tu **as faim?** Est-ce que tu veux une pizza?
avoir soif	to be thirsty	J'**ai soif.** Je voudrais une limonade.
avoir raison	to be right	Est-ce que les profs **ont** toujours **raison?**
avoir tort	to be wrong	Marc ne fait pas ses devoirs. Il **a tort!**
avoir de la chance	to be lucky	J'**ai de la chance.** J'ai des amis sympathiques.

1 Tort ou raison?

PARLER/ÉCRIRE Informez-vous sur les personnes suivantes et dites si, à votre avis, elles ont tort ou raison.

▶ Les élèves ne font pas leurs devoirs.
 Ils ont tort!

▶ Tu écoutes le prof.
 Tu as raison!

1. Catherine est généreuse avec ses copines.
2. Nous aidons nos parents.
3. Tu fais tes devoirs.
4. Vous êtes très impatients avec vos amis.
5. Mes copains étudient le français.
6. Jean-François dépense son argent inutilement *(uselessly)*.
7. M. Legros mange trop *(too much)*.
8. Alain et Nicolas sont impolis *(impolite)*.
9. Vous rangez votre chambre.
10. Léa est polie *(polite)* avec les voisins.

2 De bonnes questions

PARLER/ÉCRIRE Étudiez ce que font les personnes suivantes. Ensuite, posez une question logique sur chaque personne. Pour cela, utilisez l'une des expressions suivantes:

avoir faim	avoir soif	avoir chaud
	avoir froid	avoir de la chance

▶ Philippe va au restaurant.
 Est-ce que Philippe a faim?

1. Tu veux un soda.
2. Jean-Pierre mange une pizza.
3. Cécile porte un manteau.
4. Vous gagnez à la loterie.
5. Vous faites des sandwichs.
6. Tu mets ton blouson.
7. Mes copains vont aller à la piscine.
8. Ces élèves n'étudient pas beaucoup, mais ils réussissent toujours à leurs examens.
9. Tu as des grands-parents très généreux.

B Le passé composé des verbes en *-er*

The sentences below describe past events. In the French sentences, the verbs are in the PASSÉ COMPOSÉ. Note the forms of the passé composé and its English equivalents.

Hier j'**ai réparé** mon vélo.

Le week-end dernier, Marc **a organisé** une boum.

Pendant les vacances, nous **avons visité** Paris.

*Yesterday I **fixed** my bicycle.*

*Last weekend, Marc **organized** a party.*

*During vacation, we **visited** Paris.*

FORMS

The PASSÉ COMPOSÉ is composed of two words. For most verbs, it is formed as follows:

PRESENT of **avoir** + PAST PARTICIPLE

Note the forms of the passé composé for **visiter.**

PASSÉ COMPOSÉ	PRESENT OF avoir + PAST PARTICIPLE	
J'**ai visité** Québec.	j' **ai**	
Tu **as visité** Paris.	tu **as**	
Il/Elle/On **a visité** Montréal.	il/elle/on **a**	**visité**
Nous **avons visité** Genève.	nous **avons**	
Vous **avez visité** Strasbourg.	vous **avez**	
Ils/Elles **ont visité** Fort-de-France.	ils/elles **ont**	

→ For all **-er** verbs, the past participle is formed by replacing the **-er** of the infinitive by **-é**.

jou er	→	jou é	Nous **avons joué** au tennis.
parl er	→	parl é	Éric **a parlé** à Nathalie.
téléphon er	→	téléphon é	Vous **avez téléphoné** à Cécile.

LEARNING ABOUT LANGUAGE

The PASSÉ COMPOSÉ, as its name indicates, is a "past" tense "composed" of two parts. It is formed like the present perfect tense in English.

AUXILIARY VERB + PAST PARTICIPLE of the main verb

Nous **avons** **travaillé**.

We have *worked.*

USES

The passé composé is used to describe past actions and events. It has several English equivalents.

J'ai visité Montréal.
*I **visited** Montreal.*
*I **have visited** Montreal.*
*I **did visit** Montreal.*

Profitez de cette offre imbattable et venez visiter les grandes attractions de Montréal!

Découvrez Montréal

La Ronde

3 Achats

PARLER/ÉCRIRE Samedi dernier *(Last Saturday)*, les personnes suivantes ont fait des achats. Dites ce que chaque personne a acheté.

▶ Philippe (des CD)
   Philippe a acheté des CD.

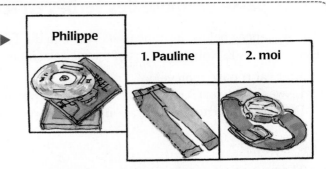

| | Philippe | 1. Pauline | 2. moi |

| 3. toi | 4. vous | 5. nous | 6. Stéphanie et Isabelle | 7. Patrick et Jean-Paul | 8. M. et Mme Dupont |

4 Vive la différence!

PARLER Caroline et Jean-Pierre sont des copains, mais ils aiment faire des choses différentes. Ils parlent de ce qu'ils ont fait ce week-end.

▶ jouer au volley (au tennis)

J'ai joué au volley.

Eh bien, moi, j'ai joué au tennis.

1. acheter des CD (des magazines)
2. dîner au restaurant (chez moi)
3. inviter mon cousin (un ami)
4. téléphoner à ma tante (à mon grand-père)
5. aider ma mère (mon père)
6. nettoyer la cuisine (le garage)
7. réparer ma mobylette (mon vélo)
8. assister à un match de foot (à un concert)
9. laver mes tee-shirts (mes jeans)
10. regarder un film (une comédie)
11. ranger ma chambre (le salon)
12. louer un DVD (une cassette vidéo)

5 La boum

PARLER Anne et Éric organisent une boum ce week-end. Anne demande à Éric s'il a fait les choses suivantes. Il répond oui.

▶ acheter des sodas?   —**Tu as acheté des sodas?**
                        —**Mais oui, j'ai acheté des sodas.**

1. préparer les sandwichs?
2. ranger le salon?
3. réparer la chaîne hi-fi?
4. apporter un DVD?
5. inviter nos copains?
6. téléphoner aux voisins?

6 Un jeu

PARLER/ÉCRIRE Décrivez ce que certaines personnes ont fait samedi dernier. Pour cela, faites des phrases logiques en utilisant les éléments des Colonnes A, B et C.

▶Vous avez assisté à un concert de jazz.

NICE, L'ARÈNE DU JAZZ

A	B	C
nous	acheter	une boum
vous	assister	un musée
Marc	dîner	des vêtements
Hélène et Juliette	jouer	un film
Éric et Stéphanie	organiser	aux jeux vidéo
mes copains	louer	dans le jardin
les voisins	travailler	dans un restaurant vietnamien
	visiter	à un concert de jazz

VOCABULAIRE   Expressions pour la conversation

▶ *How to indicate the order in which actions take place:*

d'abord	*first*	**D'abord,** nous avons invité nos copains à la boum.
après	*after, afterwards*	**Après,** tu as préparé des sandwichs.
ensuite	*then, after that*	**Ensuite,** Jacques a acheté des jus de fruit.
enfin	*at last*	**Enfin,** vous avez décoré le salon.
finalement	*finally*	**Finalement,** j'ai apporté ma radiocassette.

---

7 Dans quel ordre?

PARLER/ÉCRIRE Décrivez ce que les personnes suivantes ont fait dans l'ordre logique.

▶nous (manger / préparer la salade / acheter des pizzas)
D'abord, nous avons acheté des pizzas.
Après, nous avons préparé la salade.
Ensuite, nous avons mangé.

1. Alice (travailler / trouver un job / acheter une moto)
2. les touristes canadiens (voyager en avion / visiter Paris / réserver les billets [*tickets*])
3. tu (assister au concert / acheter un billet / acheter le programme)
4. vous (danser / apporter des CD / inviter des copains)
5. nous (payer l'addition [*check*]/dîner / trouver un restaurant)

C Le passé composé: forme négative

Compare the affirmative and negative forms of the passé composé in the sentences below.

AFFIRMATIVE	NEGATIVE	
Alice **a travaillé.**	Éric **n'a pas travaillé.**	*Éric **has not worked.*** *Éric **did not work.***
Nous **avons visité** Paris.	Nous **n'avons pas visité** Lyon.	*We **have not visited** Lyon.* *We **did not visit** Lyon.*

In the negative, the passé composé follows the pattern:

> negative form of **avoir** + PAST PARTICIPLE

Note the negative forms of the passé composé of **travailler.**

PASSÉ COMPOSÉ (NEGATIVE)	PRESENT of **avoir** (NEGATIVE) + PAST PARTICIPLE	
Je **n'ai pas travaillé.**	je **n'ai pas**	
Tu **n'as pas travaillé.**	tu **n'as pas**	
Il/Elle/On **n'a pas travaillé.**	il/elle/on **n'a pas**	
		travaillé
Nous **n'avons pas travaillé.**	nous **n'avons pas**	
Vous **n'avez pas travaillé.**	vous **n'avez pas**	
Ils/Elles **n'ont pas travaillé.**	ils/elles **n'ont pas**	

8   *Oublis* *(Things forgotten)*

PARLER Nicole demande à Jean-Marc s'il a fait *(did)* les choses suivantes. Jean-Marc a oublié *(forgot)*.

▶ acheter *Paris-Match*?

1. réparer ta chaîne hi-fi?
2. apporter tes livres?
3. étudier?
4. téléphoner à ta tante?
5. inviter tes copains?
6. ranger ta chambre?
7. laver tes chemises?
8. louer un film?
9. aider ta mère?
10. nettoyer le garage?
11. chercher le programme de télé?
12. trouver ton livre?

— Tu as acheté *Paris Match*?

— Euh, non ... Je n'ai pas acheté *Paris Match.*

9 Quel mauvais temps!

PARLER/ÉCRIRE Ce week-end, il a fait mauvais et les personnes suivantes sont restées *(stayed)* chez elles. Dites qu'elles n'ont pas fait les choses suivantes.

▶ nous/nager
   Nous n'avons pas nagé.

1. vous/jouer au tennis
2. Philippe/rencontrer ses copains à la plage
3. Nathalie/dîner en ville
4. les voisins/travailler dans le jardin
5. Mlle Lacaze/laver sa voiture
6. mes copains/organiser un pique-nique
7. nous/assister au match de foot
8. toi/visiter le musée

10 Une question d'argent

PARLER/ÉCRIRE Les personnes suivantes n'ont pas beaucoup d'argent. Décrivez leur choix. Pour cela, dites ce qu'elles ont fait et ce qu'elles n'ont pas fait.

▶ nous/dîner au restaurant ou chez nous?
   Nous avons dîné chez nous.
   Nous n'avons pas dîné au restaurant.

1. Philippe/acheter un tee-shirt ou une chemise?
2. vous/manger un steak ou un sandwich?
3. nous/assister au concert ou au match de foot?
4. les touristes/voyager en car ou en avion?
5. mes voisins/louer une petite maison ou un grand appartement?
6. Marc/passer dix jours ou trois semaines à Paris?

11 Impossibilités

PARLER/ÉCRIRE Sans *(Without)* certaines choses il n'est pas possible de faire certaines activités. Expliquez cela logiquement en choisissant une personne de la Colonne A, un objet de la Colonne B et une activité de la Colonne C.

▶ **Je n'ai pas d'aspirateur. Je n'ai pas nettoyé le salon.**

A	B	C
je	une raquette	surfer sur l'Internet
vous	un billet *(ticket)*	voyager en Europe
nous	un passeport	nettoyer le salon
Frédéric	un ordinateur	regarder la comédie
Éric et Olivier	une télé	assister au concert
Claire et Caroline	un aspirateur *(vacuum cleaner)*	jouer au tennis

D Les questions au passé composé

Compare the statements and questions in the passé composé.

STATEMENT	QUESTION	
Tu as travaillé.	Tu as travaillé? **Est-ce que** tu as travaillé?	*Did you work?*
Philippe a voyagé cet été.	**Quand est-ce que** Philippe a voyagé? **Où est-ce qu'**il a voyagé?	*When did Philippe travel?* *Where did he travel?*

For most verbs, questions in the passé composé are formed as follows:

> interrogative form of **avoir** + PAST PARTICIPLE

	YES/NO QUESTIONS	INFORMATION QUESTIONS
WITH INTONATION	Tu as voyagé? Paul a téléphoné?	— —
WITH est-ce que	**Est-ce que** tu as voyagé? **Est-ce qu'**Alice a téléphoné?	**Avec qui est-ce que** tu as voyagé? **À qui est-ce qu'**Alice a téléphoné?

→ When the subject is a pronoun, questions in the passé composé can also be formed by inversion.

As-tu assisté au match de foot?   *Did you go to the soccer game?*
Avec qui **avez-vous joué** au foot?   *With whom did you play soccer?*
                            Who(m) did you play soccer with?

12 Expériences personnelles

PARLER Demandez à vos camarades s'ils ont déjà *(already)* fait les choses suivantes.

▶ visiter Paris?

Est-ce que tu as visité Paris?

Oui, j'ai visité Paris.
(Non, je n'ai pas visité Paris.)

1. visiter le Tibet?
2. voyager en Alaska?
3. piloter un avion?
4. dîner dans un restaurant vietnamien?
5. manger des escargots *(snails)*?
6. gagner à la loterie?
7. assister à un match de catch *(wrestling)*?
8. rencontrer un fantôme *(ghost)*?

13 Curiosité

PARLER Lisez ce que les personnes suivantes ont fait et posez des questions sur leurs activités.

▶ Paul a joué au tennis. (avec qui?)
Avec qui est-ce qu'il a joué au tennis?

1. Thomas a visité Québec. (quand?)
2. Corinne a téléphoné. (à quelle heure?)
3. Nathalie a voyagé en Italie. (comment?)
4. Marthe a acheté une robe. (où?)
5. Léa a rencontré sa copine. (où?)
6. Michèle a visité Genève. (avec qui?)
7. Philippe a trouvé un job. (où?)
8. Éric et Véronique ont dîné en ville. (dans quel restaurant?)
9. Les voisins ont téléphoné. (quand?)

14 *Jérôme et Valérie*

PARLER Jérôme est très curieux. Il veut toujours savoir ce que Valérie a fait. Valérie répond à ses questions.

▶ où/dîner? (dans un restaurant italien)
JÉRÔME: **Où est-ce que tu as dîné?**
VALÉRIE: **J'ai dîné dans un restaurant italien.**

1. avec qui / jouer au tennis? (avec Marc)
2. quand / assister au concert? (samedi après-midi)
3. qui / inviter au café? (ma copine Nathalie)
4. où / rencontrer Pierre? (dans la rue)

5. où / acheter ta veste? (au Bon Marché)
6. combien / payer ce CD? (10 euros)
7. à qui / téléphoner? (à ma grand-mère)
8. chez qui / passer le week-end? (chez une amie)

15 *Conversation*

PARLER Demandez à vos camarades ce qu'ils ont fait hier.

▶ à quelle heure / dîner?

1. avec qui / dîner?
2. à qui / téléphoner?
3. quel programme / regarder à la télé?
4. quel programme / écouter à la radio?
5. qui / rencontrer après les classes?
6. quand / étudier?

Dis, Hélène, à quelle heure est-ce que tu as dîné?
J'ai dîné à six heures.

PRONONCIATION ain = /ɛ̃/   aine = /ɛn/   in = /ɛ̃/   ine = /in/

Les lettres «ain» et «in»

sa main   **semaine**   **magasin**   **magazine**

When the letters "**ain**," "**aim**," "**in**," "**im**" are at the end of a word or are followed by a *consonant,* they represent the nasal vowel /ɛ̃/.

REMEMBER: Do not pronounce an /n/ after the nasal vowel /ɛ̃/.

Répétez: /ɛ̃/ **dem**ai**n** **f**ai**m** **tr**ai**n** **m**ai**n** **vois**in **cous**in **jard**in **magas**in
mai**ntenant** **i**n**telligent** **i**n**téressant** **i**m**portant**

When the letters "**ain**," "**aim**," "**in(n)**," "**im**" are followed by a *vowel,* they do NOT represent a nasal sound.

Répétez: /ɛn/ **sem**aine **améric**aine
/ɛm/ **j'**aime

/in/ **vois**ine **cous**ine **cuis**ine **magaz**ine **c**in**éma** **Cor**inne **f**in**ir**
/im/ **t**im**ide** **d**im**anche** **M**im**i** **cent**ime

Alain **M**in**ime a un rendez-vous** **i**m**portant** **dem**ain **mat**in, **avenue du M**aine.

À votre tour!

OBJECTIFS

Now you can ...
- talk with friends about what you did and did not do last weekend
- talk about past events in general

1 Allô!

PARLER Reconstituez la conversation entre Alain et Christine. Pour cela, faites correspondre les réponses de Christine avec les questions d'Alain.

1 À quelle heure est-ce que tu as dîné hier soir?

2 Et après, tu as regardé la télé?

3 Qu'est-ce que tu as regardé après?

4 Qui a gagné?

5 Dis, tu as préparé la leçon pour demain?

a Le match Marseille-Nice.

b Nice. Par un score de trois à un.

c Mais oui! J'ai étudié avant le dîner.

d Oui, mais d'abord j'ai aidé ma mère.

e À sept heures et demie.

2 Dis-moi ...

PARLER *I will tell you a few things that I did yesterday after school and a few things that I did not do, then you will tell me what you did and did not do.*

- J'ai étudié.
- J'ai dîné avec mes parents.
- J'ai téléphoné à une copine.

- Je n'ai pas rangé ma chambre.
- Je n'ai pas rencontré mes copains.
- Je n'ai pas regardé la télé.

Et maintenant, dis-moi ...

3 Créa-dialogue

PARLER Demandez à vos camarades s'ils ont fait les choses suivantes le week-end dernier. En cas de réponse affirmative, continuez la conversation.

▶ —Est-ce que tu as <u>dîné au restaurant</u>?
—Oui, j'ai <u>dîné au restaurant</u>.
—<u>Avec qui?</u>
—<u>Avec mes cousins.</u>
—<u>Où</u> est-ce que <u>vous avez dîné?</u>
—<u>Nous avons dîné Chez Tante Lucie</u> (à l'Hippopotamus, etc.).

▶ avec qui?
où?

1 avec qui?
quand?

2 quand?
où?

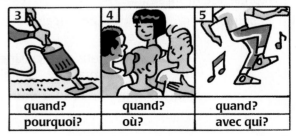

3 quand?
pourquoi?

4 quand?
où?

5 quand?
avec qui?

4 **Composition: Hier soir** (Last night) ----------------------------------

ÉCRIRE In one or two paragraphs describe what you did yesterday evening. You may wish to use the following suggestions:

- étudier (quoi?)
- dîner (à quelle heure?)
- manger (quoi?)
- téléphoner (à qui?)
- parler (de quoi?)
- écouter (quel type de musique?)
- regarder (quel programme à la télé?)
- aider (qui? comment?)
- ranger (quoi?)

STRATEGY Writing

Narrating the past When you write about past events, it is helpful to indicate the order in which these events occurred. In your composition, you can indicate the sequence in which you did certain things last night by using expressions such as **d'abord, après, ensuite, enfin,** and **finalement**.

COMMENT DIT-ON ...?

How to wish somebody a nice time:

Bon week-end! (Have a nice weekend!)

Bonnes vacances! (Have a good vacation!)

Bonne journée! (Have a nice day!)

Bon voyage! (Have a good trip!)

LESSON REVIEW
CLASSZONE.COM

LEÇON 23

L'alibi AUDIO

l'inspecteur Leflic

Êtes-vous bon (bonne) détective? <u>Pouvez</u>-vous trouver la solution
du mystère <u>suivant</u>?

Can
following

Samedi dernier à deux heures de l'après-midi, <u>il y a eu</u> une <u>panne</u>
<u>d'électricité</u> dans la petite ville de Marcillac-le-Château. La panne <u>a duré</u>
une heure. Pendant la panne, un <u>cambrioleur a pénétré</u> dans
la Banque Populaire de Marcillac-le-Château. Bien sûr, l'alarme
n'a pas fonctionné et c'est <u>seulement</u> lundi matin que le
directeur de la banque <u>a remarqué</u> le <u>cambriolage</u>: un million d'euros.

there was / power
failure / lasted
burglar / entered

only
noticed / burglary

Lundi après-midi, l'<u>inspecteur</u> Leflic a interrogé quatre suspects,
mais <u>chacun</u> a un alibi.

police detective
each one

Sophie Filou

Euh, … excusez-moi, Monsieur l'Inspecteur.
Ma mémoire n'est pas très bonne.
<u>Voyons</u>, qu'est-ce que <u>j'ai fait</u> samedi après-midi?
Ah oui, <u>j'ai fini</u> un livre.
Le <u>titre</u> du livre? *Le crime ne paie pas!*

Let's see / did I do
finished
title

Marc Laroulette

Qu'est-ce que j'ai fait samedi?
<u>J'ai rendu visite à</u> mes copains.
Nous avons joué aux cartes.
C'est moi qui ai gagné!

visited

Patrick Lescrot

Voyons, samedi dernier …
Ah oui … cet après-midi-là, j'ai invité des amis chez moi.
Nous avons regardé la télé.
Nous <u>avons vu</u> le match de foot France-<u>Allemagne</u>.
Quel match! <u>Malheureusement</u>, c'est la France qui <u>a perdu</u>!
Dommage!

saw / Germany
Unfortunately / lost

Pauline Malin

Ce n'est pas moi, Monsieur l'Inspecteur!
Samedi j'ai fait un pique-nique à la campagne avec une copine.
Nous <u>avons choisi</u> un <u>coin</u> près d'une rivière.
Ensuite, nous avons fait une promenade à vélo.
Nous <u>avons eu de la chance</u>!
<u>Il a fait un temps extraordinaire</u>!

chose / spot

were lucky
The weather was great!

Lisez <u>attentivement</u> les quatre déclarations. À votre avis, qui est
le cambrioleur ou la cambrioleuse? Pourquoi? (Vous pouvez comparer
votre réponse avec la réponse de l'inspecteur à la page 337.)

carefully

Compréhension

Certains événements ont eu lieu *(took place)* samedi dernier. Indiquez si oui ou non les événements suivants ont eu lieu.

1. Le directeur de la banque a vu *(saw)* le cambrioleur.

2. Un cambriolage a eu lieu *(took place)* à Marcillac-le-Château.

3. L'inspecteur Leflic a arrêté *(arrested)* quatre personnes.

4. Sophie Filou a vu le film *Le crime ne paie pas* à la télé.

5. Marc Laroulette a perdu un million d'euros.

6. L'Allemagne a gagné un match de foot.

7. Pauline Malin a fait une promenade à vélo à la campagne.

8. Il a fait beau.

Et toi?

Dis si oui ou non tu as fait les choses suivantes le week-end dernier.

1. (J'ai/Je n'ai pas) … rendu visite à mes copains.

2. (J'ai/Je n'ai pas) … vu un match de foot à la télé.

3. (J'ai/Je n'ai pas) … fini un livre.

4. (J'ai/Je n'ai pas) … fait une promenade à vélo.

5. (J'ai/Je n'ai pas) … fait un pique-nique.

NOTE *culturelle*

Les jeunes Français et la télé

Combien d'heures par° jour est-ce que tu regardes la télé? Une heure? deux heures? trois heures? plus? moins? En général, les jeunes Français regardent la télé moins souvent et moins longtemps° que les jeunes Américains: en moyenne° 1 heure 15 les jours d'école et 2 heures 15 les autres° jours (mercredi, samedi et dimanche). Dans beaucoup de familles, les parents contrôlent l'usage° de la télé. Souvent ils exigent° que leurs enfants finissent leurs devoirs avant de regarder la télé. Ainsi,° beaucoup de jeunes regardent la télé seulement° après le dîner.

Quels sont leurs programmes favoris? Les jeunes Français aiment surtout° les films, les programmes de sport, les variétés et les jeux télévisés,° comme «Qui veut gagner° des millions?». Les séries américaines sont aussi très populaires.

par *per* **moins longtemps** *for a shorter time* **en moyenne** *on an average of* **autres** *other* **usage** *use* **exigent** *insist* **Ainsi** *Thus* **seulement** *only* **surtout** *especially* **jeux télévisés** *game shows* **gagner** *to win*

A Le verbe *voir*

The verb **voir** *(to see)* is irregular. Note the forms of **voir** in the present tense.

INFINITIVE	voir	
PRESENT	Je **vois** Marc. Tu **vois** ton copain. Il/Elle/On **voit** un accident.	Nous **voyons** un film. Vous **voyez** un match de baseball. Ils/Elles **voient** le professeur.

1 Week-end à Paris

PARLER/ÉCRIRE Les personnes suivantes passent le week-end à Paris. Décrivez ce que chacun voit.

▶ Olivier   **Olivier voit Notre-Dame.** ▶

Notre-Dame

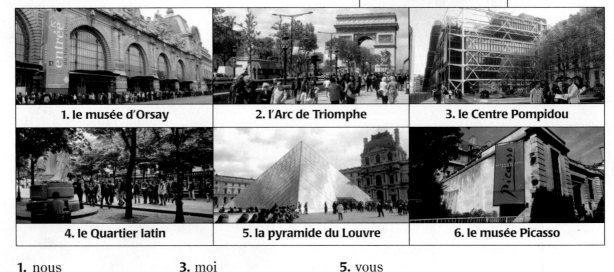

| 1. le musée d'Orsay | 2. l'Arc de Triomphe | 3. le Centre Pompidou |
| 4. le Quartier latin | 5. la pyramide du Louvre | 6. le musée Picasso |

1. nous   3. moi   5. vous
2. toi   4. Sophie   6. les touristes japonais

2 Questions personnelles   PARLER/ÉCRIRE

1. Est-ce que tu vois bien? Est-ce que tu portes des lunettes?
2. Est-ce que tu vois tes amis pendant les vacances? Est-ce que tu vois tes professeurs?
3. Est-ce que tu vois souvent tes cousins? Est-ce que tu vois tes cousins pendant les vacances? à Noël?
4. Qu'est-ce que tu préfères voir à la télé? un match de football ou un match de baseball?
5. Quand tu vas au cinéma, quels films aimes-tu voir? les comédies? les films d'aventures? les films policiers *(detective movies)*?

B Le passé composé des verbes réguliers en *-ir* et *-re*

Note the passé composé of the verbs below, paying special attention to the ending of the past participle.

choisir	J'**ai choisi** cette casquette.	Je **n'ai pas choisi** cette chemise.
finir	Nous **avons fini** le magazine.	Nous **n'avons pas fini** le livre.
vendre	Tu **as vendu** ton vélo.	Tu **n'as pas vendu** ta moto.
attendre	Jacques **a attendu** Paul.	Il **n'a pas attendu** François.
répondre	J'**ai répondu** au professeur.	Tu **n'as pas répondu** à la question.

The past participle of regular **-ir** and **-re** verbs is formed as follows:

-ir	→	-i		-re	→	-u
chois ir	→	chois i		vend re	→	vend u
fin ir	→	fin i		attend re	→	attend u

3 Besoins d'argent *(Money needs)*

PARLER/ÉCRIRE Parce qu'elles ont besoin d'argent, les personnes suivantes ont vendu certains objets. Dites ce que chaque personne a vendu.

▶ Philippe/sa guitare   **Philippe a vendu sa guitare.**

1. M. Roche/sa voiture
2. mes copains/leur chaîne hi-fi
3. moi/mon appareil-photo
4. toi/ton skate
5. les voisins/leur piano
6. nous/nos livres
7. vous/votre ordinateur
8. François et Vincent/ leurs CD

À vendre
INSTRUMENTS DE MUSIQUE

4 Bravo!

PARLER/ÉCRIRE Les personnes suivantes méritent *(deserve)* des félicitations *(congratulations)*. Expliquez pourquoi.

▶ les élèves/réussir à l'examen   **Les élèves ont réussi à l'examen.**

1. M. Bedon/maigrir
2. Mlle Legros/perdre dix kilos
3. Florence/gagner le match de tennis
4. les élèves/finir la leçon
5. moi/ranger ma chambre
6. nous/choisir une classe difficile
7. toi/finir les exercices
8. Marc/rendre visite à un copain à l'hôpital
9. vous/attendre vos copains
10. les élèves/répondre en français

5 **Non!**

PARLER Jean-Louis répond négativement aux questions de Béatrice. Jouez les deux rôles.

Tu as gagné le match?

Non! J'ai perdu!

▶ gagner le match/perdre

1. étudier ce week-end/rendre visite à un copain
2. acheter un DVD/choisir un CD
3. finir ce livre/regarder la télé
4. vendre ta guitare/vendre mon appareil-photo
5. téléphoner à Marc/rendre visite à son cousin
6. maigrir/grossir
7. répondre à la lettre/téléphoner

6 **Aujourd'hui et hier**

PARLER/ÉCRIRE Dites ce que les personnes suivantes font aujourd'hui et ce qu'elles ont fait hier.

▶ Paul/acheter un blouson/un pantalon
Aujourd'hui, Paul achète un blouson.
Hier, il a acheté un pantalon.

1. moi/téléphoner à mon cousin/à mes copains
2. toi/finir ce livre/ce magazine
3. nous/manger des sandwichs/une pizza
4. Mélanie/choisir une jupe/un chemisier
5. les élèves/réussir à l'examen de français/ à l'examen d'anglais
6. Philippe/vendre sa chaîne hi-fi/ses vieilles cassettes
7. Philippe et Jean-Pierre/rendre visite à leurs cousins/à leur grand-mère
8. les touristes/attendre le train/le car

7 **Excuses**

PARLER Quand Michel ne fait pas une chose, il a toujours une excuse. Jouez le dialogue entre Michel et sa soeur Laure.

Tu as étudié?

Non, je n'ai pas étudié.

Pourquoi est-ce que tu n'as pas étudié?

Parce que j'ai perdu mon livre.

▶ étudier/perdre mon livre

1. travailler/jouer au foot
2. répondre/entendre la question
3. jouer au tennis/perdre ma raquette
4. acheter une veste/choisir un blouson
5. finir le livre/regarder la télé
6. rendre visite à Marc/étudier
7. réussir à l'examen/perdre mes notes
8. écouter tes CD/vendre mon baladeur

C Le passé composé des verbes *être, avoir, faire, mettre* et *voir*

The verbs **être, avoir, faire, mettre,** and **voir** have irregular past participles.

être	→	été	Nous **avons été** à Paris.
avoir	→	eu	M. Lambert **a eu** un accident.
faire	→	fait	Qu'est-ce que tu **as fait** hier?
mettre	→	mis	Nous **avons mis** des jeans.
voir	→	vu	J'ai **vu** un bon film.

→ In the passé composé, the verb **être** has two different meanings:

Mme Lebrun **a été** malade.   *Mme Lebrun* **has been** *sick.*
Elle **a été** à l'hôpital.   *She* **was** *in the hospital.*

8 Dialogue

PARLER Demandez à vos camarades s'ils ont fait les choses suivantes récemment *(recently)*.

▶ faire une promenade?
—Est-ce que tu as fait une promenade récemment?
—Oui, j'ai fait une promenade. (Non, je n'ai pas fait de promenade.)

1. faire un pique-nique?
2. faire une promenade en voiture?
3. être malade *(sick)*?
4. avoir la grippe *(flu)*?
5. avoir une dispute *(fight)* avec ton copain?

6. avoir une bonne surprise?
7. avoir un «A» en français?
8. voir un film?
9. voir tes cousins?
10. mettre des affiches dans ta chambre?

9 Pourquoi?

PARLER Avec vos camarades de classe, parlez des personnes suivantes.

▶ Fabrice est content.
(avoir un «A» à l'examen)

1. Mes copains sont furieux. (avoir un «F» à l'examen)
2. Pauline est très contente. (voir son copain)
3. Mon père n'est pas content. (avoir une dispute avec son chef [*boss*])
4. Philippe est pâle. (voir un accident)
5. Juliette est fatiguée *(tired)*. (faire du jogging)
6. Alice et Laure sont bronzées *(tanned)*. (être à la mer)
7. Mon frère est fatigué. (faire de la gymnastique [*to work out*])
8. Patrick et Marc sont contents. (voir un bon film)
9. Isabelle est très élégante. (mettre une jolie robe)

Fabrice est content.

Il a eu un «A» à l'examen.

Ah bon? Pourquoi?

10 **Vive les vacances!**

PARLER/ÉCRIRE Dites où les personnes suivantes ont été pendant les vacances. Dites aussi si oui ou non elles ont fait les choses entre parenthèses. Soyez logique *(Be logical)*.

▶ Christophe: à la piscine (étudier/nager)
Christophe a été à la piscine. Il n'a pas étudié. Il a nagé.

1. Élodie: à la montagne (nager/faire du VTT)
2. nous: à la campagne (visiter des monuments/faire du camping)
3. vous: à Paris (parler italien/voir la tour Eiffel)
4. moi: à la mer (faire de la planche à voile/travailler)
5. mes parents: en Égypte (voir les pyramides/visiter Paris)
6. vous: dans un club de sport (faire de la gymnastique/grossir)
7. Christine: à la plage (mettre des lunettes de soleil/jouer au tennis)

VOCABULAIRE *Quand?*

	maintenant	avant	après
le jour	**aujourd'hui**	**hier**	**demain**
le matin	**ce matin**	**hier matin**	**demain matin**
l'après-midi	**cet après-midi**	**hier après-midi**	**demain après-midi**
le soir	**ce soir**	**hier soir**	**demain soir**
le jour	**samedi**	**samedi dernier** *(last)*	**samedi prochain** *(next)*
le week-end	**ce week-end**	**le week-end dernier**	**le week-end prochain**
la semaine	**cette semaine**	**la semaine dernière**	**la semaine prochaine**
le mois	**ce mois-ci**	**le mois dernier**	**le mois prochain**

11 **Quand?**

PARLER Demandez à vos camarades quand ils ont fait les choses suivantes. Ils vont répondre en utilisant une expression du **Vocabulaire.**

▶ faire tes devoirs?

1. faire des achats?
2. ranger ta chambre?
3. rencontrer tes voisins?
4. voir ton copain?
5. voir un film?
6. avoir un examen?
7. faire une promenade à pied?
8. être en ville?
9. mettre *(set)* la table?

Quand est-ce que tu as fait tes devoirs?

J'ai fait mes devoirs hier après-midi.
(vendredi soir, le week-end dernier, ...)

⑫ Le passé et le futur

PARLER/ÉCRIRE Décrivez ce que vous avez fait (phrases 1 à 5) et ce que vous allez faire (phrases 6 à 10). Dites la vérité … ou utilisez votre imagination!

1. Ce matin, j'ai … ____
2. Hier matin, j'ai … ____
3. Samedi après-midi, j'ai … ____
4. La semaine dernière, j'ai … ____
5. Le mois dernier, j'ai … ____

6. Ce soir, je vais … ____
7. Demain soir, je vais … ____
8. Vendredi soir, je vais … ____
9. Le week-end prochain, je vais … ____
10. La semaine prochaine, je vais … ____

⑬ Questions personnelles PARLER/ÉCRIRE

1. En général, est-ce que tu étudies avant ou après le dîner?
2. En général, est-ce que tu regardes la télé avant ou après le dîner?
3. À quelle heure est-ce que tu as dîné hier soir?
4. Quel programme de télé est-ce que tu as regardé hier après-midi?
5. Qu'est-ce que tu vas faire le week-end prochain?
6. Où vas-tu aller le week-end prochain?

PRONONCIATION   gn = /ɲ/

Les lettres «gn»

The letters "**gn**" represent a sound similar to the "**ny**" in *canyon*. First, practice with words you know.

Répétez: **espagnol   gagner   mignon**
          la montagne   la campagne

espagnol

Now try saying some new words. Make them sound French!

Répétez: **Champagne   Espagne** *(Spain)*   **un signe**
          la vigne *(vineyard)*   **la ligne** *(line)*   **un signal**
          la dignité   ignorer   magnétique   magnifique   Agnès

          Agnès Mignard a gagné son match. C'est magnifique!

(L'alibi, p. 330)

LA RÉPONSE DE L'INSPECTEUR:

C'est Patrick Lescrot le cambrioleur. Samedi après-midi, il y a eu une panne d'électricité. Patrick Lescrot n'a pas pu *(was not able to)* regarder la télé. Son alibi n'est pas valable *(valid)*.

À votre tour!

OBJECTIFS

Now you can …
• talk about what you did last week
• find out what others did recently

1  Allô!

PARLER Reconstituez la conversation entre Robert et Julien. Pour cela, faites correspondre les réponses de Julien avec les questions de Robert.

1. Tu as fini tes devoirs de français?
2. Qu'est-ce que tu as fait alors?
3. Tu as gagné?
4. Mais d'habitude (usually) tu joues bien?
5. Peut-être que Caroline a joué mieux (better) que toi?

a. Non, j'ai perdu!
b. Non, je n'ai pas étudié cet après-midi.
c. C'est vrai, mais aujourd'hui, je n'ai pas eu de chance …
d. J'ai joué au tennis avec Caroline.
e. Tu as raison. Elle a joué comme une championne.

2 Dis-moi …

PARLER *I will tell you about some nice things that happened to me recently; then you will tell me about three nice things that happened to you.*

• J'ai réussi à mon examen d'anglais. (J'ai eu un «A».)
• J'ai eu un rendez-vous avec une personne très intéressante.
• J'ai vu un très bon film.

Et maintenant, dis-moi …

3  Créa-dialogue

PARLER Avec vos camarades, discutez de ce que vous avez fait récemment (recently). Vous pouvez utiliser les expressions et les activités suggérées. Continuez la conversation avec des questions supplémentaires.

Quand?	
dimanche après-midi	lundi dernier
hier soir	la semaine dernière
samedi soir	le mois dernier
le week-end dernier	

Quoi?	
jouer aux jeux vidéo	dîner au restaurant
faire des achats	voir un film
faire du skate	avoir un rendez-vous
voir mes cousins	rendre visite à un copain
	faire du roller

▶ —Qu'est-ce que tu as fait <u>dimanche après-midi</u>?
—J'<u>ai joué au tennis avec ma soeur</u>.
—<u>Est-ce que tu as gagné</u>?
—<u>Non, j'ai perdu</u>.
—<u>Dommage!</u>

4 Le week-end dernier

ÉCRIRE Write a short composition in which you describe what you did last weekend. You may adopt some of the following suggestions. Do not use **aller.**

- voir (qui? où? quand?)
- voir (quel film? où?)
- faire (de quel sport? de quelle activité? avec qui?)
- jouer (à quel jeu? à quel sport?)
- jouer (de quel instrument? où?)
- avoir un rendez-vous (avec qui?)
- faire une promenade (où? avec qui?)
- dîner (où? avec qui?)
- être (à quel endroit? avec qui? quand?)
- faire des achats (où? quand?)
- acheter (quoi? pourquoi?)
- regarder (quel programme de télé? quel DVD?)
- assister (à quel match? à quel concert?)

Vendredi soir, j'ai vu le film *Casablanca* au Palace avec mon copain ...

COMMENT DIT-ON ...?

How to wish someone good luck or give encouragement:

Bonne chance!

Bon courage!

LESSON REVIEW
CLASSZONE.COM

LEÇON 24

Qui a de la chance?

AUDIO

VENDREDI APRÈS-MIDI

Anne et Valérie parlent de leurs projets pour le week-end.

Anne: Qu'est-ce que tu vas faire samedi soir?

Valérie: Je vais aller au cinéma avec Jean-Pierre.

Anne: Tu as de la chance! Moi, je dois rester à la maison.

Valérie: Mais pourquoi?

Anne: Les amis de mes parents viennent chez nous ce week-end. Mon père insiste <u>pour que</u> je reste pour le dîner. <u>Quelle barbe!</u>

that / What a pain!

Valérie: C'est vrai! Tu n'as pas de chance!

LUNDI MATIN

Anne et Valérie parlent de leur week-end.

Anne: Alors, tu as passé un bon week-end?

Valérie: Euh non, pas très bon.

Anne: Mais tu <u>es sortie</u> avec Jean-Pierre!

went out

Valérie: C'est vrai. Je <u>suis allée</u> au cinéma avec lui …

went

Nous avons vu un très, très mauvais film! Après le film, j'ai eu une <u>dispute</u> avec Jean-Pierre. Et, <u>en plus</u>, j'ai perdu mon <u>porte-monnaie</u> … et je <u>suis rentrée</u> chez moi à pied! Et toi, tu <u>es restée</u> chez toi?

quarrel

in addition

wallet / went back

stayed

Anne: Non.

Valérie: Comment? Les amis de tes parents <u>ne sont pas venus</u>?

didn't come

Anne: Si, si, ils sont venus … avec leur fils!

Valérie: Et alors?

Anne: Eh bien, c'est un garçon très <u>sympa</u> et très amusant …

sympa = sympathique

Après le dîner, nous <u>sommes allés</u> au Zénith.[*] Nous avons assisté à un concert de rock absolument extraordinaire. Après, nous sommes allés dans un café et nous avons fait des projets pour le week-end prochain.

went

Valérie: Qu'est-ce que vous allez faire?

Anne: Nous allons faire une promenade à la campagne dans la nouvelle voiture de sport de Thomas. (C'est le nom de mon nouveau copain!)

Valérie: Toi, vraiment, tu as de la chance!

[*] Une salle *(hall)* de concert à Paris, parc de la Villette.

Compréhension

1. Qu'est-ce que Valérie va faire samedi soir?
2. Pourquoi est-ce qu'Anne doit *(must)* rester à la maison?
3. Est-ce que Valérie a aimé le film?
4. Qu'est-ce qu'elle a perdu?
5. Comment est-ce qu'elle est rentrée chez elle?
6. Où et avec qui est-ce qu'Anne a dîné?
7. Où est-ce qu'elle est allée après le dîner?
8. Qu'est-ce qu'elle va faire le week-end prochain?
9. Comment s'appelle son nouveau copain?

Et toi?

Dis si oui ou non tu as fait les choses suivantes samedi dernier.

1. (Je suis/Je ne suis pas) … allé(e) en ville.
2. (Je suis/Je ne suis pas) … allé(e) au cinéma.
3. (Je suis/Je ne suis pas) … allé(e) à un concert.
4. (Je suis/Je ne suis pas) … rentré(e) chez moi pour le dîner.
5. (Je suis/Je ne suis pas) … resté(e) chez moi le soir.

NOTE **culturelle**

Les jeunes Français et la musique

«Pour moi, la musique c'est tout!»° déclare Anne, une jeune Française de quinze ans. Sa copine Hélène est d'accord: «Aujourd'hui, on ne peut pas° vivre° sans° musique.»

Comme les jeunes Américains, les jeunes Français sont des «fanas»° de la musique. Ils aiment particulièrement le rock, le rap français ou américain, la techno, le pop, le reggae et le ska, mais certains préfèrent la musique classique. En semaine, ils écoutent leur musique préférée sur leurs baladeurs et leurs chaînes hi-fi. Le week-end, ils vont au concert écouter les stars de la chanson° française, anglaise ou américaine.

Le 21 juin de chaque année, les jeunes célèbrent la «Fête de la Musique» avec tous° les Français. C'est une grande fête nationale avec des concerts publics gratuits° dans toutes les villes et tous les villages de France. Ce jour-là, 800 000 musiciens jouent pour 60 millions de spectateurs. Pour la «Fête de la Musique» tout le monde° fait de la musique.

COMPARAISONS CULTURELLES

- Do you think American teenagers would agree with Anne: **"On ne peut pas vivre sans musique?"** Explain.
- Do French and American teenagers listen to the same types of music?
- Do you think that the United States should declare a national music day like the French **"Fête de la Musique"**? Why or why not?

tout *everything*   **ne peut pas** *cannot*   **vivre** *live*   **sans** *without*   **fanas = fanatiques**   **chanson** *song*   **tous** *all*
gratuits *free*   **tout le monde** *everyone*

Le passé composé avec *être*

Note the forms of the passé composé of **aller** in the sentences below, paying attention to the endings of the past participle (**allé**).

Jean-Paul **est allé** au cinéma.   *Jean-Paul **went** to the movies.*
Mélanie **est allée** à la plage.   *Mélanie **went** to the beach.*

Éric et Patrick **sont allés** en ville.   *Éric and Patrick **went** downtown.*
Mes copines **sont allées** à la campagne. *My friends **went** to the country.*

The passé composé of **aller** and certain verbs of motion is formed with **être** according to the pattern:

> PRESENT of **être** + PAST PARTICIPLE

→ When the passé composé of a verb is conjugated with **être** (and not with **avoir**), the PAST PARTICIPLE *agrees* with the SUBJECT in gender and number.

INFINITIVE	aller	
PASSÉ COMPOSÉ	je **suis** allé tu **es** allé il **est** allé nous **sommes** allé[s] vous **êtes** allé[s] ils **sont** allé[s]	je **suis** allé[e] tu **es** allé[e] elle **est** allé[e] nous **sommes** allé[es] vous **êtes** allé[es] elles **sont** allé[es]
NEGATIVE	je **ne suis pas** allé	je **ne suis pas** allé[e]
INTERROGATIVE	est-ce que tu **es** allé? tu **es** allé? (**es**-tu allé?)	est-ce que tu **es** allé[e]? tu **es** allé[e]? (**es**-tu allé[e]?)

→ When **vous** refers to a single person, the past participle is in the singular:

Mme Mercier, est-ce que vous êtes **allée** au concert hier soir?

1 À Paris

PARLER/ÉCRIRE Des amis sont allés à Paris samedi dernier. Chacun est allé à un endroit différent. Dites qui est allé aux endroits suivants. Complétez chaque phrase avec le sujet approprié et la forme correspondante du verbe **être**.

Olivier

Éric et Jacques

Claire

Anne et Monique

▶ **Anne et Monique** sont allées au Louvre.

1. … allée à la tour Eiffel.
2. … allé au Centre Pompidou.
3. … allés au Stade de France.
4. … allées aux Galeries Lafayette.
5. … allé à la Villette.
6. … allés au Zénith.
7. … allé au musée d'Orsay.
8. … allées au Quartier latin.

2 Conversation

PARLER Demandez à vos camarades s'ils sont allés aux endroits suivants.

▶ ce matin/à la bibliothèque?

1. hier matin/à l'école?
2. hier soir/au cinéma?
3. dimanche dernier/au restaurant?
4. samedi dernier/dans les magasins?
5. l'été dernier/chez tes cousins?
6. le week-end dernier/à la campagne?
7. le mois dernier/à un concert?
8. la semaine dernière/chez le coiffeur *(barber, hairdresser)*?
9. les vacances dernières/à la mer?

Ce matin, est-ce que tu es allé à la bibliothèque?

Oui, je suis allé à la bibliothèque.
(Non, je ne suis pas allé à la bibliothèque.)

3 Le week-end dernier

PARLER/ÉCRIRE Dites ce que les personnes de la Colonne A ont fait en choisissant une activité de la Colonne B. Puis dites où ces personnes sont allées en choisissant un endroit de la Colonne C. Soyez logiques!

A	B	C
je	voir des clowns	à la campagne
tu	nager	au zoo
nous	dîner en ville	dans un magasin de chaussures
Catherine	regarder les éléphants	à la bibliothèque
vous	choisir des livres	à la plage
mon petit frère	faire un pique-nique	au restaurant
André et Thomas	acheter des sandales	au cirque *(circus)*
les filles	faire du roller	dans la rue

▶ J'ai nagé. Je suis allé(e) à la plage.

4 **Week-end**

PARLER Des amis parlent de leur week-end. Jouez ces dialogues.

▶ en ville / acheter des vêtements

1. au stade / regarder un match de foot
2. à la plage / jouer au volley
3. à une boum / danser
4. à la campagne / faire une promenade à pied
5. au Bon Marché / acheter un blouson
6. dans un restaurant italien / manger des spaghetti

Où est-ce que tu es allée?

Je suis allée en ville.

Ah bon! Qu'est-ce que tu as fait?

J'ai acheté des vêtements.

VOCABULAIRE Quelques verbes conjugués avec *être* au passé composé

INFINITIVE	PAST PARTICIPLE		
aller	allé	*to go*	Nous **sommes allés** en ville.
arriver	arrivé	*to arrive*	Vous **êtes arrivés** à midi.
rentrer	rentré	*to return, go back, come back*	Nous **sommes rentrés** à la maison à onze heures.
rester	resté	*to stay*	Les touristes **sont restés** à l'hôtel Ibis.
venir	venu	*to come*	Qui **est venu** hier?

---

5 **Qui est resté à la maison?**

PARLER/ÉCRIRE Samedi après-midi, les personnes suivantes ont fait certaines choses. Dites si oui ou non elles sont restées à la maison.

▶ Paul a regardé la télé. **Il est resté à la maison.**
▶ Mélanie a fait des achats. **Elle n'est pas restée à la maison.**

1. Mlle Joly a lavé sa voiture.
2. Nous avons fait une promenade à vélo.
3. Tu as nettoyé le garage.
4. Éric et Olivier ont joué aux jeux vidéo.
5. Christine et Isabelle ont travaillé dans le jardin.
6. Vous avez fait du roller.
7. Mes cousins ont fait de la voile.
8. J'ai fait du jogging.

JOGGING

INFOS *Sport* magazine

6 **La journée de Sandrine**

PARLER/ÉCRIRE Pendant les vacances, Sandrine travaille dans une agence de tourisme. Le soir, elle raconte *(tells about)* sa journée à son père.

▶ aller au bureau *(office)*

1. arriver à neuf heures
2. téléphoner à un client anglais
3. parler avec des touristes japonais
4. aller au restaurant à midi et demi
5. rentrer au bureau à deux heures
6. copier des documents
7. préparer des billets *(tickets)* d'avion
8. rester jusqu'à *(until)* six heures
9. dîner en ville
10. rentrer à la maison à neuf heures

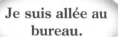

Je suis allée au bureau.

7 **Une question de circonstances** *(A matter of circumstances)*

PARLER/ÉCRIRE Nos activités dépendent souvent des circonstances.
Dites si oui ou non les personnes suivantes ont fait les choses indiquées.

▶ On est mardi aujourd'hui.
 • les élèves/rester à la maison?
  Les élèves ne sont pas restés à la maison.

1. On est dimanche.
 • M. Boulot/travailler?
 • nous/aller à l'école?
 • vous/dîner à la cantine *(school cafeteria)*?

2. Il fait très beau aujourd'hui.
 • moi/aller à la campagne?
 • mes copines/regarder la télé?
 • toi/venir à la piscine avec nous?

3. Il fait très mauvais!
 • Marc/faire un pique-nique?
 • Hélène et Juliette/rester à la maison?
 • ma mère/rentrer à la maison à pied?

4. Mes copains et moi, nous n'avons pas beaucoup d'argent.
 • toi/aller dans un restaurant cher?
 • mes copains/venir chez moi en taxi?
 • moi/acheter des vêtements?

B La construction négative *ne ... jamais*

Compare the following negative constructions.

Éric **ne** parle **pas** à Paul.	*Éric does **not** speak to Paul.*
Éric **ne** parle **jamais** à Paul.	*Éric **never** speaks to Paul.*
Nous **n'**étudions **pas** le dimanche.	*We do **not** study on Sundays.*
Nous **n'**étudions **jamais** le dimanche.	*We **never** study on Sundays.*

To say that one NEVER does something, French speakers use the construction **ne ... jamais,** as follows:

SUBJECT	+	**ne**	+	VERB	+	**jamais ...**
Nous		**ne**		regardons		**jamais** la télé.

→ **Ne** becomes **n'** before a vowel sound.

Nous **n'**allons **jamais** à l'opéra.

→ Note the use of **ne ... jamais** in the passé composé:

Nous **n'**avons **jamais** visité Québec.	*We **never** visited Quebec.*
Je **ne** suis **jamais** allé à Genève.	*I **never** went to Geneva.*

8 Jamais le dimanche

PARLER/ÉCRIRE Le dimanche les personnes suivantes ne font jamais ce qu'elles font pendant la semaine. Exprimez cette situation.

▶ François va à l'école.
Le dimanche, il ne va jamais à l'école.

1. Anne étudie.
2. Marc travaille.
3. Nous parlons français.
4. Vous allez à la bibliothèque.
5. M. Bernard va en ville.
6. Les élèves mangent à la cantine.
7. Tu rends visite à tes copains.
8. Vous dînez chez vous.
9. Je range ma chambre.
10. Je lave la voiture.

9 Et toi?

PARLER/ÉCRIRE Dites si vous avez jamais *(ever)* fait les choses suivantes.

▶ aller en France
Oui, je suis allé(e) en France.
Non, je ne suis jamais allé(e) en France.

1. aller en Chine?
2. visiter Paris?
3. voyager en limousine?
4. voir un opéra?
5. voir un fantôme *(ghost)*?
6. téléphoner au Président?
7. surfer sur l'Internet en français?
8. dîner dans un restaurant vietnamien?
9. jouer aux échecs?
10. faire une promenade en scooter?

C Les expressions *quelqu'un, quelque chose* et leurs contraires

Compare the affirmative and negative constructions in heavy print.

—Tu attends **quelqu'un?** *Are you waiting for **someone (anyone)?***
—Non, je **n'**attends **personne.** *No, I'm **not** waiting for **anyone.***

—Vous faites **quelque chose** ce soir? *Are you doing **something (anything)** tonight?*
—Non, nous **ne** faisons **rien.** *No, we're **not** doing **anything.***
  *No, we're doing **nothing.***

To refer to unspecified people or things, French speakers use the following expressions:

quelqu'un	someone, anyone somebody, anybody	ne ... personne	no one, not anyone nobody, not anybody
quelque chose	something, anything	ne ... rien	nothing, not anything

→ Like all negative expressions, **personne** and **rien** require **ne** before the verb.

→ In short answers, **personne** and **rien** may be used alone.

Qui est là? **Personne.**
Qu'est-ce que tu fais? **Rien.**

10 **Florence est malade**

 Tu dînes avec quelqu'un?

 Non, je ne dîne avec personne.

PARLER Florence est malade *(sick)* aujourd'hui. Elle répond négativement aux questions de Paul.

▶ dîner avec quelqu'un?

1. inviter quelqu'un?
2. faire quelque chose ce soir?
3. manger quelque chose à midi?
4. regarder quelque chose à la télé?
5. attendre quelqu'un ce matin?

6. voir quelqu'un cet après-midi?
7. préparer quelque chose pour le dîner?
8. rencontrer quelqu'un après le dîner?

PRONONCIATION qu = /k/

Les lettres «qu»

The letters "**qu**" represent the sound /k/.

Répétez: **qui quand quelque chose quelqu'un quatre
quatorze Québec Monique Véronique sympathique
un pique-nique le ski nautique**

Véronique pense que Monique aime la musique classique.

un bouquet

À votre tour!

OBJECTIFS

Now you can …
• say where you went and when you came back
• talk about things you have never done

1  Allô!

PARLER Reconstituez la conversation entre Sophie et Charlotte. Pour cela, faites correspondre les réponses de Charlotte avec les questions de Sophie.

1 Tu es restée chez toi samedi soir?

2 Qu'est-ce que vous avez vu?

3 Qu'est-ce que vous avez fait ensuite?

4 Vous avez mangé quelque chose?

5 À quelle heure es-tu rentrée chez toi?

a Oui, des sandwichs.

b À onze heures et demie.

c Un vieux western avec Gary Cooper.

d Nous sommes allées dans un café sur le boulevard Saint Michel.

e Non! J'ai téléphoné à une copine et nous sommes allées au cinéma.

2 Dis-moi …

PARLER *I will tell you about some places I have never visited. Then you will tell me about a few places where you have been.*

• Je ne suis jamais allée à la Martinique.
• Je n'ai jamais vu la Statue de la Liberté.
• Je n'ai jamais été à New York.
• Je n'ai jamais visité San Francisco.

Et maintenant, dis-moi …

3 Créa-dialogue

PARLER Avec vos copains, discutez de ce que vous avez fait récemment *(recently)*. Utilisez les suggestions suivantes.

▶ —**Tu es resté(e) chez toi hier matin?**
  —**Oui, je suis resté(e) chez moi.**
  —Qu'est-ce que tu as fait?
  —**J'ai rangé ma chambre.**

▶ —**Tu es resté(e) chez toi hier matin?**
  —**Non, je ne suis pas resté(e) chez moi.**
  —Qu'est-ce que tu as fait?
  —**Je suis allé(e) à l'école.**

▶
rester chez toi
hier matin
??

1. aller en ville
samedi après-midi
??

2. rentrer chez toi
vendredi soir
??

3. rester à la maison
samedi matin
??

4 ✎ Composition: *Samedi dernier*

ÉCRIRE Read what Céline did last Saturday. Then write a short composition in the **passé composé** telling how a friend of yours (real or imaginary) spent the day. Use only familiar vocabulary.

Le matin, Céline est restée à la maison. Elle a rangé sa chambre et après elle a fini ses devoirs.

L'après-midi, elle est allée au cinéma avec son copain Trinh. Ils ont vu une comédie. Ensuite ils sont allés dans un magasin de vêtements. Céline a acheté un tee-shirt et Trinh a acheté une nouvelle casquette. Finalement, Céline est rentrée chez elle.

Le soir, elle a dîné avec ses parents. Après, elle est restée dans sa chambre. Elle a surfé sur l'Internet et elle a téléchargé de la musique reggae. Elle adore la musique reggae!

▶
```
Samedi dernier
Le matin, mon ami
Kevin n'est pas
resté à la maison.
Il a fait du jogging
et après …
```

STRATEGY Writing

Narration in the *passé composé* Read the description of Céline's activities again. Note that the author wrote **Céline est restée, elle est allée,** and **Céline est rentrée,** adding a final "e" to the past participles because the subject, **Céline/elle** is feminine. In referring to Céline and Trinh, the author wrote **ils sont allés** and added a final "s" to **allé** because the subject, **ils,** is plural.

When you are writing in the passé composé, it is important to go back over your composition and check all the verb forms. If you have used the verbs **aller, venir, arriver, rester,** or **rentrer,** look to be sure that you formed the passé composé with **être,** rather than **avoir,** and that in each case the past participle agrees with the subject.

COMMENT DIT-ON ...?

How to celebrate a happy occasion:

Bon anniversaire!

Bonne année!

4. aller à la plage	5. aller à la campagne	6. aller à une boum	7. faire un voyage	8. travailler
dimanche dernier	le week-end dernier	la semaine dernière	le mois dernier	l'été dernier
??	??	??	??	??

Tests de contrôle

By taking the following tests, you can check your progress in French and also prepare for the unit test. Write your answers on a separate sheet of paper.

Review...
new words and
expressions
• verbs: p. 310
• sports: pp. 312, 313
• expressions with
  avoir: p. 320
• expressions of time:
  p. 336
• **quelqu'un** and
  quelque chose: p. 347

1 The right choice

Choose the expressions (a), (b), or (c) which best complete the following sentences.

1. Céline va au cinéma. Elle va — une comédie.
   a. aider   **b.** rencontrer   **c.** voir
2. Thomas va au stade. Il va — un match de foot.
   a. assister à   **b.** attendre   **c.** nettoyer
3. Mathieu va rester à la maison. Il va — la voiture de sa mère.
   a. aider   **b.** laver   **c.** rencontrer
4. Charlotte va au café. Elle va — ses copines.
   a. rencontrer   **b.** assister à   **c.** louer

5. Julien est à la mer. Il fait —.
   a. du ski   **b.** du roller   **c.** de la planche à voile
6. Léa est à la montagne. Elle fait —.
   a. de la voile   **b.** de l'escalade   **c.** ses devoirs

7. Clément met un pull parce qu'il a —.
   a. faim   **b.** chaud   **c.** froid
8. Mélanie commande (*orders*) un soda parce qu'elle a —.
   a. soif   **b.** tort   **c.** de la chance

9. Je suis allé au cinéma—.
   a. demain   **b.** hier soir   **c.** samedi prochain
10. Je vais aller à une boum —.
    a. hier matin   **b.** demain après-midi   **c.** la semaine dernière

11. Catherine est au café. Elle attend —.
    a. un   **b.** quelqu'un   **c.** personne
12. Pierre n'a pas faim. Il ne mange —.
    a. rien   **b.** quelque chose   **c.** une pizza

Review...
the **passé composé**
• **-er** verbs: p. 321
• **-ir** and **-re** verbs:
  p. 333
• irregular verbs: p. 335

2 The right verb

Complete the following sentences with the appropriate forms of the **passé composé** of the verbs in parentheses.

1. **(louer)**   La semaine dernière, nous — un DVD.
2. **(jouer)**   Hier après-midi, Céline et Thomas — au tennis.
3. **(ranger)**   Samedi matin, Pauline — sa chambre.

4. (finir) Est-ce que vous — les exercices?

5. (vendre) À qui est-ce que tu — ton vélo?

6. (avoir) Monsieur Lescure — un accident avec sa nouvelle voiture.

7. (faire) Pendant les vacances, les élèves — un voyage au Canada.

8. (être) Moi, j'— à Paris l'année dernière.

9. (voir) Quel film est-ce que tu — mardi soir?

10. (mettre) Mathieu — un CD de rock.

3 Être or avoir?

Complete the following sentences with the **passé composé** forms of the verbs in parentheses. Be sure to use the appropriate forms of **être** or **avoir**.

1. (acheter) Nous — un livre sur Paris.

2. (aller) Marie — à la tour Eiffel.

3. (rester) Mes copains — à l'hôtel.

4. (téléphoner) Ils — à des amis.

5. (arriver) Pierre — à l'aéroport.

6. (rentrer) Nous — le 15 août.

7. (visiter) Tu — le musée d'Orsay.

8. (venir) Mes amis — avec nous.

> **Review...**
> • passé composé with être: pp. 342 and 344

4 Non!

Transform the statements below into **negative** sentences. Replace the underlined words with the expressions in parentheses.

1. Léa a voyagé en bus. **(en train)**

2. J'ai joué au foot hier. **(au basket)**

3. Tu es resté à l'hôtel. **(chez tes cousins)**

4. Éric a invité sa cousine. **(son copain)**

> **Review...**
> • the negative passé composé: p. 324

5 Composition: Thanksgiving

Write a short paragraph of five or six sentences about what you and your family did last Thanksgiving. Did you travel somewhere or did people come to your house? What did you do together? Use the **passé composé**, limiting yourself to words and expressions that you know in French.

STRATEGY Writing

a Make a list of the verbs you will use to describe your activities. Review which ones use **avoir** in the **passé composé** and which use **être**.

	avoir	être
dîner chez mes cousins	x	

b Organize your ideas and write your paragraph.

c Check the **passé composé** forms of all the verbs in your composition.

Vocabulaire

POUR COMMUNIQUER

Talking about past activities

Qu'est-ce que tu as fait hier?	What did you do yesterday?
J'ai vu un film.	I saw a film.
Je suis allé au cinéma.	I went to the movies.
Je n'ai pas travaillé.	I didn't work.
Je ne suis pas allé à l'école.	I didn't go to school.

Explaining why

Pourquoi est-ce que tu es allé en ville?	Why did you go downtown?
Je suis allé en ville pour louer un DVD.	I went downtown to rent a DVD.

Talking about one's activities

Est-ce que tu fais	du roller?	Do you do in-line skating?
	de la voile?	sailing?
	de l'escalade?	rock climbing?
Marc ne fait pas de sport.		Marc doesn't do sports.

MOTS ET EXPRESSIONS

Activités sportives

le jogging	jogging	l'escalade	rock climbing
le roller	in-line skating	la natation	swimming
le skate	skateboarding	la planche à voile	windsurfing
le ski	skiing	la voile	sailing
le ski nautique	water-skiing		
le snowboard	snowboarding		
le sport	sport(s)		
le VTT	mountain biking		

Équipement sportif

des rollers	in-line skates
un skate	skateboard
un snowboard	snowboard
un VTT	mountain bike

Vacation travel

un autocar, un car	touring bus
un avion	plane
un bateau	boat, ship
un train	train

Vacation destinations

la campagne	countryside
la mer	ocean, shore
la montagne	mountains

Les contraires

souvent	often	ne ... jamais	never
quelque chose	something, anything	ne ... rien	nothing, not anything
quelqu'un	someone, anyone, somebody	ne ... personne	no one, not anyone, nobody

Verbes en -er

aider	to help
assister à	to go to, to attend
laver	to wash
louer	to rent
nettoyer	to clean
passer	to spend
préparer	to prepare
ranger	to clean, to pick up
rencontrer	to meet
réparer	to fix

Verbes irréguliers

avoir chaud/froid	to be (feel) hot/cold
avoir faim/soif	to be hungry/thirsty
avoir raison/tort	to be right/wrong
avoir de la chance	to be lucky
faire des achats	to go shopping
faire les devoirs	to do homework
faire un pique-nique	to have a picnic
voir	to see

Le passé composé avec *avoir*

parler	j'ai parlé	I spoke
finir	j'ai fini	I finished
vendre	j'ai vendu	I sold
avoir	j'ai eu	I had
être	j'ai été	I was, I have been
faire	j'ai fait	I did
mettre	j'ai mis	I put
voir	j'ai vu	I saw

Le passé composé avec *être*

aller	je suis allé(e)	I went
arriver	je suis arrivé(e)	I arrived
rentrer	je suis rentré(e)	I came back
rester	je suis resté(e)	I stayed
venir	je suis venu(e)	I came

Le calendrier

Noël	Christmas
un jour	day
un mois	month
l'après-midi	afternoon
le matin	morning
le soir	evening
le week-end	weekend

Pâques	Easter
une semaine	week
les vacances	vacation
les grandes vacances	summer vacation

Expressions pour indiquer quand

aujourd'hui	today
hier	yesterday
demain	tomorrow
prochain(e)	next
dernier (dernière)	last

d'abord	first
avant	before
pendant	during
après	after, afterwards
ensuite	then, after that
enfin	at last
finalement	finally

Expressions utiles

pour	in order to
seul(e)	alone

TEST PREP
CLASSZONE.COM

FLASHCARDS
AND MORE!

Le roller: un sport qui roule!°

Beaucoup de jeunes Français participent aux sports d'équipe° comme° le foot, le basket et le volley, mais certains préfèrent les sports individuels comme le jogging ou la natation. Aujourd'hui, beaucoup de jeunes pratiquent aussi les «sports de glisse»° comme le roller, le skate, la planche à voile (en été) et le ski et le snowboard (en hiver).

Le roller est particulièrement populaire parce qu'il peut être pratiqué en toute° saison et par les gens de tout âge. Deux millions de Français font régulièrement du roller, principalement dans les grandes villes et surtout° dans la région parisienne. «Pour moi,» dit Clément, 15 ans, «le roller est l'occasion° de me faire des nouveaux copains.» Mélanie, 17 ans, dit qu'elle fait du roller «parce que j'ai l'impression de vitesse,° d'indépendance et de liberté. Je suis libre° comme un oiseau.» Pour Charlotte, 21 ans, «le roller est un excellent moyen° de faire de l'exercice et de rester en bonne forme° physique.»

Pour certaines personnes qui habitent dans les grandes villes, le roller est un nouveau moyen de transport urbain. Philippe Tardieu, un jeune avocat° de la région parisienne, va à son bureau° en roller. «Le roller est plus économique, moins polluant° et souvent plus rapide que l'auto. Le roller, ça roule...!»

Le roller a beaucoup d'avantages, mais c'est aussi un sport qui peut être dangereux si on ne fait pas attention. Pour faire du roller, on doit être en bonne forme physique et avoir l'équipement nécessaire. On doit toujours porter un casque pour se protéger° la tête. On doit aussi porter des genouillières pour se protéger les genoux° et des protège-poignets pour se protéger les poignets.°

On peut faire du roller dans la rue ou sur toute surface plane, mais il est préférable de pratiquer ce sport dans les endroits réservés pour cette activité. Dans les grandes villes, il y a des «rollerparks» où les jeunes peuvent aussi faire du roller acrobatique et jouer au hockey sur roller.

À Paris, une association sportive nommée Pari-Roller organise tous les vendredis soirs° une grande randonnée° en roller dans les rues de la ville. Cette randonnée commence à dix heures du soir et finit à une heure du matin. Il y a souvent 12 000 (douze mille) participants de tout âge accompagnés de policiers en roller. Pendant cet événement, les rues du circuit sont interdites° aux voitures. Pour beaucoup de Parisiens, cet événement est l'occasion de redécouvrir° leur ville dans une ambiance° d'amitié, de bonne humeur et de fête populaire.

---

roule *rolls* **équipe** *team* **comme** *like* **glisse** *gliding* **toute** *any* **surtout** *above all* **occasion** *opportunity* **vitesse** *speed* **libre** *free* **moyen** *means* **forme** *shape* **avocat** *lawyer* **bureau** *office* **polluant** *polluting* **protéger** *to protect* **genoux** *knees* **poignets** *wrists* **tous les vendredis soirs** *every Friday evening* **randonnée** *long ride* **interdites** *closed* **redécouvrir** *to rediscover* **ambiance** *atmosphere*

L'équipement du roller

le casque
(pour protéger la tête)

le protège-coude
(pour protéger les coudes)

le protège-poignet
(pour protéger les poignets)

les genouillières
(pour protéger les genoux)

les rollers

Compréhension

Faites correspondre *(Match)* les personnes et leurs opinions.

> **a.** Clément
> **b.** Mélanie
> **c.** Charlotte
> **d.** Philippe

1. «Le roller, ça roule!»

2. «Le roller est moins polluant que l'auto.»

3. «Quand je fais du roller, je suis libre comme un oiseau.»

4. «Le roller est l'occasion de me faire des nouveaux copains.»

5. «Le roller est un excellent moyen de faire de l'exercice.»

6. «Quand je fais du roller, j'ai l'impression de vitesse.»

7. «En ville, le roller est un bon moyen de transport.»

Et vous?

Classez *(Rank)* les avantages du roller par ordre d'importance personnelle — de 6 (plus important) à 1 (moins important). Comparez votre classement avec vos camarades.

Le roller, c'est ...

- un moyen de faire de l'exercice
- un moyen de rester en forme
- un moyen de rencontrer des copains
- un moyen de transport urbain
- l'impression d'indépendance
- l'impression de vitesse

Les activités du week-end

Qu'est-ce que vous faites le week-end? Qu'est-ce que vous avez fait le week-end dernier? Voici les réponses de quatre jeunes du monde° francophone.

Pierre
(16 ans)
Basse Terre, Guadeloupe

Le samedi, je joue généralement au foot. Je fais partie° de l'équipe° junior de mon village. Le week-end dernier, nous avons fait un match. Nous avons bien joué, mais nous avons perdu! Après le match, je suis allé à la plage. Le soir, je suis allé chez des copains. Nous avons mis de la musique et nous avons dansé.

Aïcha
(14 ans)
Casablanca, Maroc

Samedi dernier, nous avons eu une grande réunion de famille chez mon oncle Karim. Une centaine° de personnes sont venues. Nous avons fait un «méchoui».
(C'est un repas° où on rôtit° un mouton° entier à la broche.°) J'ai eu l'occasion° de voir tous° mes cousins et cousines. On s'est bien amusé.°

Élisabeth
(15 ans)
Bruxelles, Belgique

Samedi matin, j'ai fait des achats. J'ai choisi un cadeau pour l'anniversaire de mon père. (J'ai acheté une cravate en soie.°) L'après-midi, je suis allée au ciné-club avec un copain. Nous avons vu *Les Temps modernes*, un vieux film de Charlie Chaplin. Après, nous sommes allés dans un café et nous avons rencontré d'autres° copains. J'ai passé la soirée° en famille.

monde *world* **fais partie** *am a member* **équipe** *team*
soie *silk* **d'autres** *other* **soirée** *evening*

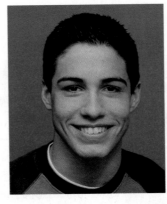

Yvan
(14 ans)
Montréal, Québec

Le matin, je suis allé à un rollerpark avec des copains et nous avons joué au hockey. À midi, je suis rentré chez moi. L'après-midi, j'ai aidé mes parents à repeindre° la cuisine. Pour le dîner, nous sommes allés au restaurant.

une centaine *about 100* **repas** *meal* **rôtit** *roasts* **mouton** *sheep*
à la broche *on the spit* **occasion** *opportunity* **tous** *all*
On s'est bien amusé. *We had a good time.* **repeindre** *repaint*

CONNEXIONS

Pick one of the above French-speaking cities, and find out more about it on the Internet. Imagine that you will be spending a week in that city.

• What kinds of things would you like to do?
• What places would you like to visit?
• What would be the best season to go?

STRATEGY Reading

More cognate patterns
Here are two important cognate patterns that will help you read French more easily.

- French verbs in **-er** sometimes correspond to English verbs in *-ate.*

FRENCH	ENGLISH		FRENCH	ENGLISH
situer	*situate*		**situé**	*situated*
indiquer	*indicate*		**indiqué**	*indicated*

- The ending **-ment** usually corresponds to the English ending *-ly.*
  généralement *generally*

Activité écrite: Une carte postale

Imaginez que vous avez passé le week-end avec l'une des quatre personnes: Pierre, Yvan, Élisabeth ou Aïcha. Dans une carte postale, décrivez ce week-end de votre point de vue personnel.

Chers amis,

   J'ai passé le week-end avec Yvan. Nous avons ....

Writing Hint Be sure to use the **passé composé.**

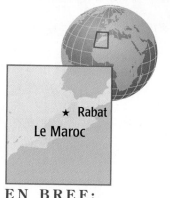

★ Rabat
Le Maroc

EN BREF: LE MAROC

Population: 30 millions
Capitale: Rabat
Langues: arabe, français,
             espagnol

Le Maroc est un pays° d'Afrique du Nord° situé entre la Méditerranée au nord, l'Atlantique à l'est° et le Sahara au sud.° Autrefois° administré par la France, ce pays est maintenant gouverné par un roi,° le roi Mohammed VI. Le sud du pays est habité par les Touareg, un peuple nomade qui traverse le Sahara en caravanes de chameaux.°

De culture islamique, le Maroc est un pays moderne avec une longue tradition intellectuelle et artistique. Les artisans marocains créent° des produits d'excellente qualité: textiles, céramiques et objets de cuir° et de cuivre.°

Il y a aujourd'hui un million de Marocains qui habitent en France où ils ont introduit le couscous, le thé à la menthe° et d'autres° spécialités de leur pays.

---

pays *country* **nord** *north* **est** *east* **sud** *south* **Autrefois** *In the past* **roi** *king*
chameaux *camels* **créent** *create* **cuir** *leather* **cuivre** *copper* **menthe** *mint*
d'autres *other*

Les quatre erreurs de Sophie

Pendant les vacances, Sophie Lambert, une jeune Française, a fait un grand voyage dans les pays° francophones. Dans chaque° pays où elle est allée, elle a écrit° des cartes postales à ses copains. Dans chaque carte postale, Sophie a fait une erreur.° Quelle est cette erreur? (Les erreurs de Sophie concernent la géographie ou les gens.) Lisez attentivement chaque carte et cherchez l'erreur que Sophie a faite.

pays *countries* **chaque** *each* **a écrit** *wrote* **erreur** *error, mistake*

Marrakech, le 10 juillet

Ma chère Pauline,

Je suis au Maroc. C'est un pays d'Afrique du Sud° où on parle arabe et où beaucoup de gens parlent aussi français. Samedi, je suis allée à la «médina» qui est le vieux quartier° de Marrakech. Là, j'ai acheté un beau sac de cuir° à un artisan local.

Amitiés,
Sophie

Sud *south* **quartier** *district* **cuir** *leather*

Québec, le 25 juillet

Mon cher Guillaume,

Je passe une semaine à Québec, la capitale du Canada. Hier j'ai téléphoné à une copine et nous sommes allées dans la vieille ville. Ensuite, nous sommes allées à la Citadelle et nous avons vu le changement de la garde.° Ici, les gens parlent un français un peu ancien.° Par exemple, pour dire «au revoir», on dit° «bonjour». C'est amusant, non?

Amicalement,
Sophie

changement de la garde *changing of the guard* **ancien** *old* **dit** *says*

Fort-de-France, le 3 août

Ma chère Élodie,

Un grand bonjour de la Martinique qui est une petite île° de l'Océan Pacifique. Je suis arrivée ici la semaine dernière. Ici, il fait toujours chaud et les gens vont à la plage toute l'année!° Hier j'ai acheté un maillot de bain et des lunettes de soleil dans une boutique de l'hôtel. Ensuite, j'ai nagé et j'ai fait de la planche à voile et de la plongée sous-marine.° J'ai vu des poissons de toutes les couleurs!

Affectueusement,
Sophie

île *island* **toute l'année** *all year long*
plongée sous-marine *scuba diving*

Port-au-Prince, le 14 août

Mon cher Mathieu,

Je suis arrivée à Haïti dimanche dernier. J'ai trouvé une chambre dans une pension° à Port-au-Prince, la capitale du pays. Les gens d'ici parlent créole et espagnol. Hier soir, je suis allée écouter un orchestre de musique «compas». Génial! J'aime aussi la cuisine créole. C'est épicé,° mais c'est très bon!

Amitiés,
Sophie

---

pension *boarding house* **épicé** *spicy, hot*

Les 4 erreurs:

1. Le Maroc est en Afrique du Nord (et non pas en Afrique du Sud).
2. La capitale du Canada est Ottawa (et non pas Québec).
3. La Martinique est dans l'Océan Atlantique (et non pas dans l'Océan Pacifique).
4. À Haïti, on parle créole et français (et non pas espagnol).

UNITÉ 8

Les repas

LEÇON 25 LE FRANÇAIS PRATIQUE:
Les repas et la nourriture

LEÇON 26 À la cantine

LEÇON 27 Un client difficile

LEÇON 28 Pique-nique

THÈME ET OBJECTIFS

Food and meals

Eating well is not only essential for our health, it should be an enjoyable experience as well.

In this unit, you will learn ...

- to talk about your favorite foods
- to describe the different meals of the day
- to prepare a shopping list and do the grocery shopping
- to order a meal in a restaurant
- to set the table

You will also be able ...

- to ask people to do things for you

WEBQUEST
CLASSZONE.COM

LEÇON 25

Les repas et la nourriture

Accent sur … Les repas français

For the French, a meal is more than just food served on a plate. It is a happy social occasion where people gather around a table to enjoy one another's company. Dinner is the most important family time of the day. Parents and children sit down together and talk about the day's events and topics of common interest. Special events are celebrated by more elaborate meals.

In traditional homes, children do not go to the refrigerator to fix their own sandwiches nor do they help themselves to snacks. They are expected to sit down at the table with everyone else at mealtime, eat what is served, join in the conversation, and not ask to be excused until the adults are finished.

Le petit déjeuner (breakfast)

Le petit déjeuner français traditionnel est un repas simple: tartines° de pain avec du beurre° et de la confiture° et un grand bol de café au lait ou de chocolat chaud. Dans les familles modernes, les enfants mangent «à l'américaine»: ils prennent° des céréales et du jus d'orange.

tartines *slices* **beurre** *butter* **confiture** *jam* **prennent** *have*

Le déjeuner (lunch)

Le déjeuner est généralement servi entre° midi et demi et une heure et demie. Il se compose de hors-d'oeuvre divers (saucisson,° radis,° salade de concombres, etc.), d'un plat principal (viande° ou poisson° avec des légumes°), d'une salade verte, d'un fromage° et d'un dessert (gâteau,° fruits ou glace). Le café est toujours servi à la fin du repas.

entre *between* **saucisson** *salami* **radis** *radishes* **viande** *meat* **poisson** *fish* **légumes** *vegetables* **fromage** *cheese* **gâteau** *cake*

Le goûter *(afternoon snack)*

Après les cours, beaucoup de jeunes vont à la pâtisserie. Là, ils achètent un pain au chocolat,° un croissant ou un éclair.

pain au chocolat *chocolate croissant*

Le dîner *(dinner)*

Le dîner est le repas familial principal. Il est servi entre huit heures et neuf heures avec tout le monde° présent. C'est un repas simple qui se compose d'une soupe, d'un plat principal (viande ou poisson, omelette ou pâtes°), d'une salade et d'un dessert léger° (yaourt ou fruit).

tout le monde *everybody*
pâtes *pasta* **léger** *light*

A VOCABULAIRE Les repas et la table

▶ *How to talk about meals:*

—En général, à quelle heure est-ce que tu **prends le petit déjeuner** *(have breakfast)?*

—Je prends le petit déjeuner à sept heures et demie.

—Où est-ce que tu vas **déjeuner** *(to have lunch)* aujourd'hui?

—Je vais déjeuner à **la cantine de l'école** *(school cafeteria).*

> À quelle heure est-ce que tu prends le petit déjeuner?
>
> Je prends le petit déjeuner à sept heures et demie.

Les repas et la nourriture

NOMS		VERBES	
un repas	*meal*		
le petit déjeuner	*breakfast*	**prendre le petit déjeuner**	*to have breakfast*
le déjeuner	*lunch*	**déjeuner**	*to have lunch*
le dîner	*dinner*	**dîner**	*to have dinner*
la nourriture	*food*		
la cuisine	*cooking, cuisine*		

—Tu peux **mettre** *(set)* la table?

—D'accord. Je vais mettre la table.

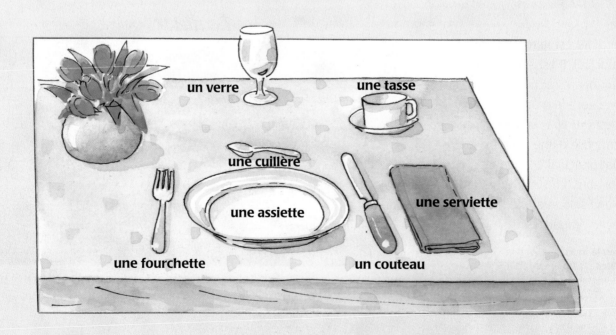

un verre   une tasse

une cuillère

une serviette

une assiette

une fourchette   un couteau

1 *Et toi?*

PARLER/ÉCRIRE Exprime tes préférences. Pour cela complète les phrases suivantes.

1. Mon repas préféré est …
   - le petit déjeuner
   - le dîner
   - le déjeuner

2. Je préfère déjeuner …
   - chez moi
   - à la cantine de l'école
   - dans un fast-food
   - …?

3. En général, la nourriture de la cantine de l'école est …
   - excellente
   - bonne
   - mauvaise
   - …?

4. Je préfère dîner …
   - chez moi
   - chez mes copains
   - au restaurant
   - …?

5. Je préfère la nourriture …
   - mexicaine
   - italienne
   - chinoise
   - …?

6. Quand je dois aider pour le dîner, je préfère …
   - préparer la salade
   - mettre la table
   - laver les assiettes
   - …?

2 *Questions personnelles* **PARLER/ÉCRIRE**

1. À quelle heure est-ce que tu prends ton petit déjeuner le lundi? Et le dimanche?
2. En général, à quelle heure est-ce que tu dînes?
3. Où est-ce que tu déjeunes pendant la semaine? le samedi? le dimanche?
4. Où est-ce que tu as déjeuné hier? Avec qui?
5. Où est-ce que tu vas dîner ce soir? Avec qui?
6. Est-ce que tu vas souvent au restaurant? Quand? Avec qui? Quel est ton restaurant préféré?
7. Est-ce que tu as jamais *(ever)* déjeuné dans un restaurant français? (dans un restaurant mexicain? dans un restaurant italien? dans un restaurant chinois? dans un restaurant vietnamien?) Quand et avec qui?
8. Est-ce que tu mets la table chez toi? Qui a mis la table pour le petit déjeuner? Et pour le dîner?

3 *Au restaurant*

PARLER Vous êtes dans un restaurant français. Vous avez commandé *(ordered)* les choses suivantes. Le serveur a oublié *(forgot)* d'apporter le nécessaire (les ustensiles, etc.).

▶ pour le jus d'orange

Monsieur, je voudrais un verre pour le jus d'orange.

Pardon. Voici un verre.

1. pour l'eau minérale *(mineral water)*
2. pour le thé
3. pour la soupe
4. pour les frites
5. pour le steak
6. pour le gâteau *(cake)*

B VOCABULAIRE La nourriture et les boissons

▶ *How to express food preferences:*

—Est-ce que tu aimes **le poisson** *(fish)*?
—Oui, j'aime le poisson mais je préfère **la viande** *(meat)*.
—Quelle viande est-ce que tu aimes?
—J'aime **le rosbif** *(roast beef)* et **le poulet** *(chicken)*.

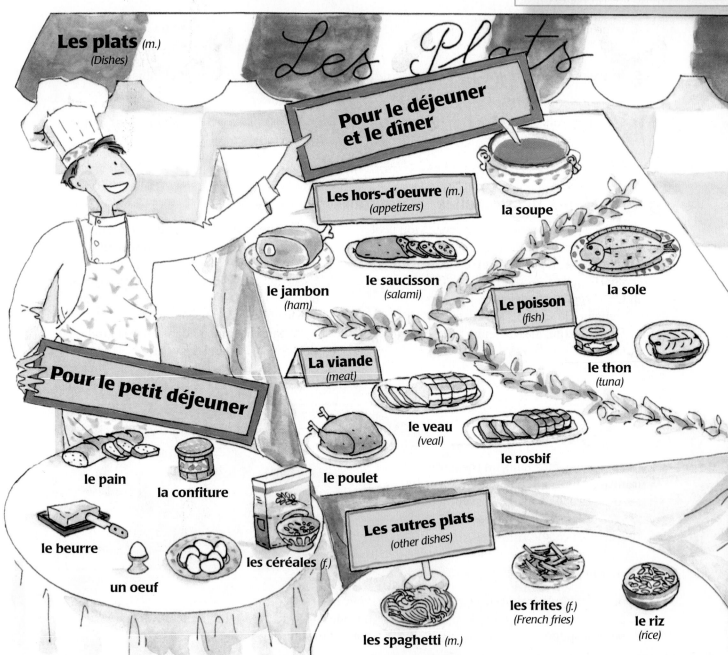

Les plats *(m.)*
(Dishes)

Les Plats

Pour le déjeuner et le dîner

Les hors-d'oeuvre *(m.)*
(appetizers)

la soupe

le saucisson
(salami)

le jambon
(ham)

Le poisson
(fish)

la sole

La viande
(meat)

le thon
(tuna)

le veau
(veal)

le rosbif

Pour le petit déjeuner

le poulet

le pain

la confiture

Les autres plats
(other dishes)

le beurre

un oeuf

les céréales *(f.)*

les frites *(f.)*
(French fries)

le riz
(rice)

les spaghetti *(m.)*

Quelle viande est-ce que tu aimes?

J'aime le rosbif et le poulet.

aimer	*to like*	Alice **aime** le poulet.
préférer	*to prefer*	Philippe **préfère** le rosbif.
détester	*to hate*	Paul **déteste** le poisson.

Les Plats

Les ingrédients (m.)

la mayonnaise

le ketchup

le sucre
(sugar)

le sel
(salt)

La salade et le fromage

le fromage
(cheese)

la salade
(lettuce)

le yaourt

Le dessert

le gâteau
(cake)

la glace
(ice cream)

la tarte
(pie)

**Les boissons
(une boisson)**
(drink, beverage)

le jus
d'orange

le thé
glacé
(iced tea)

l'eau (f.)
(water)

le jus
de pomme
(apple juice)

le lait
(milk)

l'eau
minérale

4 Vous aimez ça?

PARLER/ÉCRIRE Dites si oui ou non vous aimez les choses suivantes.

- J'aime …
- J'aime beaucoup …
- Je n'aime pas …
- Je déteste …

▶ J'aime le fromage.
   (Je n'aime pas
   le fromage.)

5 **Dîner avec André**

PARLER Vous dînez avec André, un ami canadien. Demandez à André de vous passer les choses suivantes.

▶ —S'il te plaît, André, passe-moi le pain.
   —Tiens. Voilà le pain.
   —Merci.

6 **La Petite Marmite**

PARLER Vous dînez au restaurant français La Petite Marmite. Le garçon demande ce que vous préférez. Répondez-lui.

La Petite Marmite
m e n u

- soupe / saucisson
- viande / poisson
- poulet / veau
- sole / thon
- frites / spaghetti
- fromage / salade
- yaourt / glace
- tarte / gâteau
- thé / café

Vous avez choisi?

Oui, j'ai choisi la soupe.

7 **Dans le réfrigérateur ou sur la table?**

PARLER Choisissez un produit et demandez à vos camarades où est le produit.
Ils vont dire si le produit est dans le réfrigérateur ou sur la table.

▶ Où est la confiture?

Elle est sur la table.

8 **Les préférences**

PARLER/ÉCRIRE Indiquez les préférences culinaires des personnes
suivantes en complétant les phrases.

1. J'aime …
2. Je déteste …
3. Ma mère aime …
4. Mon petit frère (ma petite soeur)
    déteste …

5. Mon copain aime …
6. Ma copine déteste …
7. Les enfants aiment …
8. En général, les Italiens aiment …
9. En général, les Japonais aiment …

9 **Les courses** (Food shopping)

ÉCRIRE Vous passez les vacances en France avec votre famille.
Faites la liste des courses pour les repas suivants.

▶ un repas végétarien

1. un pique-nique à la campagne
2. un bon petit déjeuner
3. un repas d'anniversaire
4. le dîner de ce soir
5. le déjeuner de demain
6. un repas de régime (diet)

LISTE

▶ Un repas végétarien:
— oeufs
— salade
— fromage
— pain
— yaourt
— eau minérale

C VOCABULAIRE Les fruits et les légumes *(Fruits and vegetables)*

▶ **How to shop for food:**

À la maison

—Où vas-tu?
—Je vais au **marché**.
 Je vais **faire les courses** *(to do the food shopping)*.
—Qu'est-ce que tu vas acheter?
—Je vais acheter des **tomates** et des **oranges**.

Au marché

—Pardon, madame. Combien coûtent les **pommes**?
—Elles coûtent un euro cinquante le kilo.
—Donnez-moi deux **kilos de** pommes, s'il vous plaît.
—Voilà. Ça fait trois euros.

Où vas-tu?

Je vais au marché.

Pardon, madame. Combien coûtent les pommes?

Elles coûtent un euro 50 le kilo.

🔟 Qu'est-ce que vous préférez?

PARLER/ÉCRIRE Indiquez vos préférences.

▶ pour le petit déjeuner: (un oeuf ou des céréales?)   **Je préfère des céréales.**

1. pour le petit déjeuner: (un pamplemousse ou une banane?)
2. après le déjeuner: (une pomme ou une poire?)
3. avec le poulet: (des haricots verts ou des petits pois?)
4. avec le steak: (des pommes de terre ou des carottes?)
5. comme *(as)* salade: (une salade de tomates ou une salade de concombres *(cucumbers)*?)
6. pour le dessert: (une tarte aux cerises ou une tarte aux poires?)
7. comme glace: (une glace à la vanille ou une glace à la fraise?)

🔟🔟  Les achats

PARLER Vos copains reviennent du marché. Demandez ce qu'ils ont acheté.

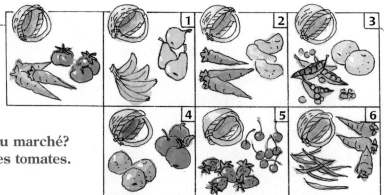

▶ —Qu'est-ce que tu as acheté au marché?
   —J'ai acheté des carottes et des tomates.

Les fruits (un fruit)

une orange
une banane
une pomme
une poire
une fraise
une cerise
un pamplemousse

Les légumes (un légume)

une tomate
une pomme de terre
une carotte
une salade
des petits pois *(m.)*
des haricots verts *(m.)*

LES QUANTITÉS

une livre (de)	*pound*	
un kilo (de)	*kilo (2.2 pounds)*	
une douzaine (de)	*dozen*	

Donnez-moi
- **une livre** de tomates.
- **un kilo de** pommes.
- **une douzaine d'**oeufs.

---

12   *Au marché*

PARLER Vous êtes au marché. Demandez au vendeur combien coûtent certaines choses. Dites aussi quelle quantité vous voulez acheter.

> Pardon, monsieur. Combien coûtent les pommes de terre?

> Elles coûtent un euro vingt-cinq le kilo.

> Alors, donnez-moi deux kilos de pommes de terre, s'il vous plaît.

> Voici. Ça fait deux euros cinquante.

1 euro 25 le kilo — 2 kilos
3 euros la douzaine — 1 douzaine
3 euros la livre — 1 livre
2 euros le kilo — 3 kilos
2 euros 50 le kilo — 2 kilos
2 euros 25 la livre — 1 livre
1 euro 50 le kilo — 3 kilos
1 euro 50 le kilo — 1 kilo
3 euros la livre — 1 livre

À votre tour!

OBJECTIFS

Now you can …
- talk about what you like to eat and drink
- prepare a shopping list

1 🎧 Écoutez bien!

ÉCOUTER Pauline et Thomas ont fait les courses dans deux supermarchés différents. Écoutez bien les phrases. Si vous entendez le nom d'un produit acheté par Pauline, marquez A. Si vous entendez le nom d'un produit acheté par Thomas, marquez B.

	1	2	3	4	5	6
A: Pauline						
B: Thomas						

A. Pauline

B. Thomas

2 🎧 Conversation dirigée

PARLER Avec un(e) camarade, composez un dialogue basé sur les instructions suivantes. C'est samedi aujourd'hui. Ce matin Marc et Juliette ont fait des achats en ville. Il est midi et demi maintenant.

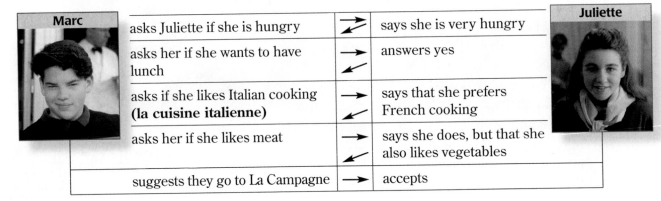

Marc		Juliette
asks Juliette if she is hungry	↗	says she is very hungry
asks her if she wants to have lunch	→ ↙	answers yes
asks if she likes Italian cooking **(la cuisine italienne)**	→ ↙	says that she prefers French cooking
asks her if she likes meat	→ ↙	says she does, but that she also likes vegetables
suggests they go to La Campagne	→	accepts

3 Créa-dialogue

PARLER Vous êtes à Deauville avec un(e) ami(e).
Essayez de découvrir *(try to discover)* ce que votre ami(e)
aime manger. Proposez à votre ami(e) de déjeuner dans
le restaurant correspondant à ses préférences.

▶ —Tu aimes <u>la viande</u>?
　—Non, je n'aime pas <u>la viande</u>.
　—Tu aimes <u>les légumes</u>?
　—Non, je n'aime pas <u>les légumes</u>.
　—Tu aimes <u>le poisson</u>?
　—Oui, j'aime beaucoup <u>le poisson</u>.
　—On déjeune <u>à La Marine</u>?
　—D'accord.

La marine
spécialités
de la mer

CHEZ RIGOLETTO
spécialités italiennes
1

AU PALAIS DES GLACES
spécialités de glaces
2

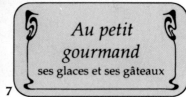

À la Normandie
spécialités de fromages
3

À LA CAMPAGNE
Restaurant végétarien
4

L'Auvergnat
spécialités de jambon
5

CHEZ OBÉLIX
spécialités de bonnes viandes
6

Au petit gourmand
ses glaces et ses gâteaux
7

4 Comparaisons

ÉCRIRE Avec un(e) camarade de classe, préparez
le menu de trois repas américains et trois repas
français typiques. Comparez ces menus.

Repas américains	Repas français
• petit déjeuner	• petit déjeuner
_____	_____
• déjeuner	• déjeuner
_____	_____
• dîner	• dîner
_____	_____

CONNEXIONS

La France exporte beaucoup de produits
alimentaires *(food products)*, en particulier des
fromages et des eaux minérales.

Allez dans votre supermarché local et visitez
le rayon *(department)* de ces produits.

• Est-ce qu'il y a des fromages français?
　Quelles sortes de fromage?

• Est-ce qu'il y a des eaux minérales françaises?
　Quelles marques *(brands)*?

LESSON REVIEW
CLASSZONE.COM

LEÇON 26

À la cantine ^{AUDIO}

Il est midi et demi. Suzanne va à la cantine. Elle rencontre Jean-Marc.

Suzanne:	Est-ce que tu veux déjeuner avec moi?
Jean-Marc:	Ça dépend. Qu'est-ce qu'il y a aujourd'hui?
Suzanne:	Il y a du poisson!
Jean-Marc:	Du poisson?
Suzanne:	Oui, du poisson.
Jean-Marc:	<u>Quelle horreur</u>! Bon, aujourd'hui, je ne veux pas déjeuner.
Suzanne:	Il y a aussi du gâteau.
Jean-Marc:	Du gâteau! Hm …
Suzanne:	Et de la glace!
Jean-Marc:	Une minute … je vais <u>prendre</u> un <u>plateau</u>.

How disgusting!

to take / tray

Compréhension

1. À quelle heure est-ce que Suzanne va déjeuner?
2. Qui est-ce qu'elle rencontre?
3. Est-ce que Jean-Marc aime le poisson?
4. Qu'est-ce qu'il aime?
5. Est-ce qu'il va déjeuner avec Suzanne? Pourquoi?

Et toi?

1. En général, où est-ce que tu déjeunes?
2. À quelle heure est-ce que tu déjeunes?
3. En général, est-ce que tu aimes la nourriture de la cantine?
4. Qu'est-ce que tu fais quand tu n'aimes pas la nourriture de la cantine?

NOTE culturelle

À la cantine

Où est-ce que tu déjeunes pendant la semaine? Quand on habite près de l'école, on peut° rentrer à la maison. Quand on habite loin, on déjeune à la cantine. À midi, beaucoup de jeunes Français déjeunent à la cantine de leur école.

À la cantine, chacun° prend° un plateau et va chercher° sa nourriture. Cette nourriture est généralement bonne, abondante° et variée. Le menu change chaque° jour de la semaine. Un repas typique inclut° les plats suivants:

- **un hors-d'oeuvre**
  salade de concombres,
  salade de pommes de terre,
  carottes râpées,° jambon …

- **un plat principal° chaud**
  poulet, steak, côtelette de porc°

- **une garniture°**
  spaghetti, frites, petits pois,
  purée de pommes de terre°

- **une salade verte**

- **du fromage**

- **un dessert**
  glace ou fruit

- **une boisson**
  eau minérale, limonade, jus de fruit

Où est-ce que tu préférerais° déjeuner?
À ton école ou dans une école française?

peut *can* **chacun** *each one* **prend** *takes* **chercher** *to get*
abondante *plentiful* **chaque** *each* **inclut** *includes*
râpées *grated* **principal** *main* **côtelette de porc** *pork chop*
garniture *side dish* **purée de pommes de terre** *mashed potatoes*
est-ce que tu préférerais *would you prefer*

A Le verbe *vouloir*

Note the forms of the irregular verb **vouloir** *(to want)*.

INFINITIVE	**vouloir**	
PRESENT	Je **veux** aller au café.	Nous **voulons** une glace.
	Tu **veux** déjeuner.	Vous **voulez** des spaghetti.
	Il/Elle/On **veut** dîner.	Ils/Elles **veulent** des frites.
PASSÉ COMPOSÉ	J'**ai voulu** dîner chez Maxim's.	

→ When making a request, French speakers often use **je voudrais** *(I would like)*, which is more polite than **je veux** *(I want)*.

Où vous voulez.
Quand vous voulez.
EXPRESS
AIR CANADA ⊛ CARGO

Je voudrais un café.   *I would like a cup of coffee.*
Je voudrais dîner.   *I would like to have dinner.*

→ When accepting an offer, French speakers often use the expression **je veux bien.**

— Est-ce que tu veux déjeuner avec moi?   *Do you want to have lunch with me?*
— Oui, **je veux bien.**   *Yes, **I do.** (Yes, **I want to.**)*

1 Vive la différence!

PARLER/ÉCRIRE Nous sommes samedi. Des amis vont en ville. Pour le déjeuner, chacun veut faire des choses différentes.

▶ Cécile/aller dans un café
Cécile veut aller dans un café.

1. nous/manger des frites
2. toi/manger une pizza
3. vous/aller dans un restaurant italien
4. moi/aller dans un restaurant chinois
5. Patrick et Alain/déjeuner à midi
6. Isabelle/déjeuner à une heure

2 Oui ou non?

PARLER/ÉCRIRE Dites si oui ou non les personnes entre parenthèses veulent faire les choses indiquées.

▶ Il est midi. (nous/déjeuner?)
Oui, nous voulons déjeuner.

▶ C'est samedi. (les élèves/étudier?)
Non, les élèves ne veulent pas étudier.

1. Il fait froid. (Éric/jouer au foot?)
2. Il fait beau. (mes copains/aller à la plage?)
3. La nourriture est mauvaise. (vous/déjeuner à la cantine?)
4. Il y a des spaghetti. (moi/dîner?)
5. Il y a une excellente comédie. (toi/regarder la télé?)
6. C'est dimanche. (nous/travailler)

3 Expression personnelle

PARLER/ÉCRIRE Complétez les phrases suivantes avec une expression personnelle.

1. Ce week-end, je voudrais …
   Je ne veux pas …
2. Cet été, je voudrais …
   Je ne veux pas …
3. Après l'école, je voudrais …
   Je ne veux pas …
4. Dans la vie *(life)*, je voudrais …
   Je ne veux pas …

B Le verbe *prendre*

Note the forms of the irregular verb **prendre** *(to take)*.

INFINITIVE	prendre	
PRESENT	Je **prends** une pizza.	Nous **prenons** le train.
	Tu **prends** un sandwich.	Vous **prenez** l'avion.
	Il/Elle/On **prend** une salade.	Ils/Elles **prennent** des photos.
PASSÉ COMPOSÉ	J'**ai pris** un steak.	

→ The singular forms follow the pattern of regular **-re** verbs. The plural forms are irregular.

VOCABULAIRE Verbes comme *prendre*

prendre	to take	Nous **prenons** le métro.
	to have (food)	Est-ce que tu **prends** un café?
apprendre	to learn	Nous **apprenons** le français.
apprendre à + *infinitive*	to learn how to	Sophie **apprend à** jouer de la guitare.
comprendre	to understand	Est-ce que vous **comprenez** l'espagnol?

4 Qu'est-ce qu'ils prennent?

PARLER/ÉCRIRE Dites ce que les personnes suivantes prennent.
Pour cela, choisissez une expression logique de la liste.

un bateau	une salade
un taxi	une limonade
le bus	un steak-frites
des photos	

▶ Philippe a faim.   **Il prend un steak-frites.**

1. J'ai très soif.
2. Vous n'avez pas très faim.
3. Hélène a un nouvel appareil-photo.
4. Tu vas à l'aéroport.
5. Nous allons à l'école.
6. Les touristes vont à la Statue de la Liberté.

5 Questions personnelles PARLER/ÉCRIRE

1. À quelle heure est-ce que tu prends le petit déjeuner le lundi? Et le dimanche?
2. Est-ce que tu prends le bus pour aller à l'école? Et tes copains?
3. Est-ce que tu prends des photos? Avec quel appareil?
4. Quand tu fais un grand voyage, est-ce que tu prends l'autocar? le train? l'avion?
5. Est-ce que tu apprends le français? l'italien? l'espagnol? Et ton copain?
6. Est-ce que tu apprends à jouer du piano? à jouer de la guitare? à faire
   du snowboard? à faire de la planche à voile?
7. Où as-tu appris à nager? À quel âge?
8. Est-ce que tu comprends quand le prof parle français? Et les autres *(other)* élèves?
9. À ton avis, est-ce que les adultes comprennent les jeunes? Est-ce que les jeunes
   comprennent les adultes?

C L'article partitif: *du, de la*

LEARNING ABOUT LANGUAGE

The pictures on the left represent *whole* items: a whole chicken, a whole cake, a whole head of lettuce, a whole fish. The nouns are introduced by INDEFINITE ARTICLES: **un, une.**

The pictures on the right represent a *part* or *some quantity* of these items: a serving of chicken, a slice of cake, some leaves of lettuce, a piece of fish. The nouns are introduced by PARTITIVE ARTICLES: **du, de la.**

Voici …

Voilà …

un poulet

du poulet

un gâteau

du gâteau

une salade

de la salade

une sole

de la sole

FORMS

The PARTITIVE ARTICLE is used to refer to A CERTAIN QUANTITY or A CERTAIN AMOUNT OF SOMETHING and corresponds to the English *some* or *any*. It has the following forms:

| MASCULINE | **du** | *some* | **du** fromage, **du** pain |
| FEMININE | **de la** | *some* | **de la** salade, **de la** limonade |

→ Note that **du** and **de la** become **de l'** before a vowel sound.

  de l'eau minérale

Mangez chaque jour …
du fromage, de la viande,
des fruits et du pain.
Santé et Bien-être social   Health and Welfare
Canada   Canada

USES

Note how the partitive article is used in the sentences below.

Philippe mange **du** fromage.	*Philippe is eating (some) cheese.*
Nous prenons **de la** salade.	*We are having (some) salad.*
—Est-ce que tu veux **du** lait?	*Do you want (any, some) milk?*
—Non, mais je voudrais **de l'**eau.	*No, but I would like some water.*

➜ While the words *some* or *any* are often omitted in English, the articles **du** and **de la** must be used in French.

➜ Partitive articles may also be used with nouns designating things other than foods and beverages. For example:

Tu as **de l'argent?**	*Do you have (any) money?*

Partitive articles are often, but not always, used after the following expressions and verbs.

voici	**Voici du** pain.	*Here is (some) bread.*
voilà	**Voilà de la** mayonnaise.	*Here is (some) mayonnaise.*
il y a	Est-ce qu'**il y a de la** salade?	*Is there (any) salad?*
acheter	Nous **achetons du** fromage.	*We are buying (some) cheese.*
avoir	Est-ce que tu **as de la** limonade?	*Do you have (any) lemon soda?*
manger	Marc **mange du** rosbif.	*Marc is eating (some) roast beef.*
prendre	Est-ce que vous **prenez du** café?	*Are you having (any) coffee?*
vouloir	Est-ce que tu **veux de la** glace?	*Do you want (any) ice cream?*

Voici un gâteau.

Voici du gâteau.

6 Le menu

PARLER/ÉCRIRE Vous avez préparé un dîner pour le Club Français.
Dites à un(e) camarade ce qu'il y a au menu.

▶ la viande   **Il y a de la viande.**

1. le rosbif	3. la salade	5. la glace	7. l'eau minérale
2. le poulet	4. le fromage	6. la tarte	8. le jus d'orange

7 Au choix

Tu veux du jus ou de l'eau minérale?

Je voudrais de l'eau minérale.

PARLER Vous déjeunez avec votre famille. Offrez aux membres de votre famille le choix entre les choses suivantes. Ils vont indiquer leurs préférences.

▶ le jus ou l'eau minérale?

1. la soupe ou la salade?
2. le poisson ou la viande?
3. le rosbif ou le poulet?
4. le ketchup ou la mayonnaise?
5. le fromage ou le yaourt?
6. le beurre ou la margarine?
7. le gâteau ou la tarte?
8. le jus d'orange ou le jus de pomme?

8 Qu'est-ce qu'on met?

PARLER/ÉCRIRE Dites quels produits de la liste on met dans ou sur les choses suivantes.

▶ On met <u>du beurre</u> (<u>de la confiture</u>) sur le pain.

1. On met … dans le café.
2. On met … dans le thé.
3. On met … dans la soupe.
4. On met … dans un sandwich.
5. On met … sur un hamburger.
6. On met … sur un hot dog.
7. On met … dans les céréales.
8. On met … sur un toast.

le fromage
le jambon
le beurre
la confiture
le ketchup
la mayonnaise
le sel
la crème
le sucre
la moutarde (mustard)
le lait

9 Les courses

PARLER/ÉCRIRE M. Simon a fait les courses. Dites ce qu'il a acheté.

▶ Il a acheté de la viande.

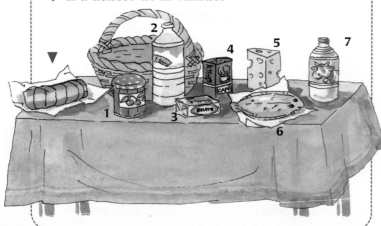

10 Le Cochon d'Or

LIRE/PARLER Émilie est allée au restaurant. Voici l'addition. Dites ce qu'elle a pris.

▶ Émilie a pris de la salade de tomates.

RESTAURANT
Le Cochon d'Or

salade de tomates	3€
poulet	4€
salade	3€
fromage	3€
glace	3€50
eau minérale	2€50
	19 €

11 *Au café*

PARLER Au café, une cliente commande *(orders)* les choses suivantes. Le serveur apporte ces choses.

> S'il vous plaît, monsieur, je voudrais de la limonade.

> Voici de la limonade, mademoiselle.

12 *Menus*

PARLER/ÉCRIRE Préparez des menus pour les personnes suivantes. Dites ce que vous allez acheter pour chaque personne.

▶ une personne qui aime manger
Je vais acheter du rosbif, du fromage, de la glace ...

1. une personne malade *(sick)*
2. un(e) athlète
3. un petit enfant
4. un végétarien (une végétarienne)

5. une personne qui veut maigrir
6. un invité *(guest)* japonais
7. une invitée française
8. un invité américain

D ## L'article partitif dans les phrases négatives

Note the forms of the partitive articles in the negative sentences below.

AFFIRMATIVE	NEGATIVE	
Tu manges **du jambon?**	Non, je **ne** mange **pas de jambon.**	*No, I don't eat ham.*
Tu veux **de la salade?**	Non, merci, je **ne** veux **pas de salade.**	*Thanks, I don't want any salad.*
Il y a **de l'eau minérale?**	Non, il **n'**y a **pas d'eau minérale.**	*No, there is no mineral water.*

In negative sentences, the PARTITIVE ARTICLE follows the pattern:

du, de la (de l')	→	ne ... pas de (d')
Marc prend **du** café.		Éric **ne** prend **pas de** café.
Sophie prend **de la** limonade.		Alain **ne** prend **pas de** limonade.
Anne prend **de l'**eau.		Nicole **ne** prend **pas d'**eau.

13 Un mauvais restaurant

PARLER Une cliente demande au serveur s'il y a certaines choses au menu. Le serveur répond négativement.

▶ le rosbif

Est-ce que vous avez du rosbif?

Je regrette mademoiselle, mais nous n'avons pas de rosbif.

1. le jambon
2. le melon
3. le thon
4. la sole
5. le veau
6. le yaourt
7. le jus de pamplemousse
8. l'eau minérale
9. la tarte aux pommes
10. le gâteau au chocolat

14 Au régime *(On a diet)*

PARLER Les personnes suivantes sont au régime parce qu'elles veulent maigrir. Répondez négativement aux questions suivantes.

▶ —Est-ce qu'Anne mange du pain?
—**Non, elle ne mange pas de pain.**

1. Est-ce que Marc prend de la mayonnaise?
2. Est-ce que Pauline veut du gâteau?
3. Est-ce que Jean-Pierre mange de la glace?
4. Est-ce qu'Alice prend du beurre?
5. Est-ce que Monsieur Ledodu veut de la tarte?
6. Est-ce que Mademoiselle Poix met de la crème dans son café?

15 Conversation

PARLER Demandez à vos camarades s'ils mangent souvent les choses suivantes.

▶ du poisson

1. de la confiture
2. du veau
3. du pain français
4. du fromage français
5. de la tarte aux fraises
6. de la soupe
7. du rosbif
8. du poulet
9. du thon
10. de la glace

Est-ce que vous mangez souvent du poisson?

Oui, je mange souvent du poisson.

Non, je ne mange pas souvent de poisson.

16 Dans le réfrigérateur

PARLER Vous préparez le dîner. Demandez à un(e) camarade s'il y a les choses suivantes dans le réfrigérateur.

▶ le lait —**Est-ce qu'il y a du lait?**
—**Non, il n'y a pas de lait.**

1. le jus d'orange?
2. le pain?
3. la glace?
4. le beurre?
5. le jambon?
6. l'eau minérale?
7. le jus de pomme?
8. le fromage?
9. la mayonnaise?
10. le ketchup?

E   Le verbe *boire*

Note the forms of the irregular verb **boire** *(to drink)*.

INFINITIVE	boire	
PRESENT	Je **bois** du lait.	Nous **buvons** du café.
	Tu **bois** de l'eau.	Vous **buvez** du thé glacé.
	Il/Elle/On **boit** du soda.	Ils/Elles **boivent** du jus d'orange.
PASSÉ COMPOSÉ	J'**ai bu** du jus de tomate.	

17 Les boissons

PARLER/ÉCRIRE Philippe et ses amis ont soif. Chacun *(Each person)* boit quelque chose de différent.

▶ **Philippe boit de l'eau.**

| Philippe | 1. nous | 2. toi | 3. vous | 4. Cécile | 5. mes copains | 6. moi |

18 Expression personnelle

PARLER/ÉCRIRE Complétez les phrases suivantes avec la forme appropriée du verbe **boire** et une expression de votre choix. Attention: utilisez le passé composé dans les phrases 6 à 8.

1. Au petit déjeuner, je …
2. Au petit déjeuner, mes parents …
3. À la cantine de l'école, nous …
4. Quand il fait chaud, on …

5. Quand il fait froid, on …
6. Hier soir au dîner, j' …
7. Hier matin, au petit déjeuner, ma mère …
8. À la dernière boum, nous …

PRONONCIATION   **ou** = /u/   **u** = /y/

Les lettres «ou» et «u»

The letters "**ou**" always represent the sound /u/.
Répétez: /u/   v**ou**s   n**ou**s   p**ou**let   s**ou**pe
f**ou**rchette   c**ou**teau   d**ou**zaine

la p**ou**le   le p**u**ll

The letter "**u**" always represents the sound /y/.
Répétez: /y/   t**u**   d**u**   **u**ne   lég**u**me   j**u**s   s**u**cre   bien s**û**r   aven**u**e   m**u**sée

Now distinguish between the two vowel sounds:
Répétez: /u/ – /y/   **poule** *(hen)* – **pull**   **roue** *(wheel)* – **rue**   **vous** – **vue** *(view)*   **je joue** – **le jus**

Vou**s b**u**vez d**u** j**u**s de pamplem**ou**sse. Je v**ou**drais de la s**ou**pe, d**u** p**ou**let et d**u** j**u**s de raisin.**

À votre tour!

OBJECTIFS

Now you can …
- describe what you eat and drink at meals
- talk about food shopping

1  Allô!

PARLER Reconstituez la conversation entre Frédéric et Sandrine. Pour cela, faites correspondre les réponses de Sandrine avec les questions de Frédéric.

1 Tu dînes au restaurant ce soir?

2 Tu as fait les courses?

3 Qu'est-ce que tu as acheté?

4 Tu n'as pas acheté de viande?

5 C'est vrai. Et pour le dessert, tu as acheté de la glace?

a. Oui, je suis allée au supermarché ce matin.
b. Du riz, des oeufs, de la salade et du fromage.
c. Non, j'ai pris un gâteau au chocolat.
d. Non, j'ai invité mon copain Fabien à dîner chez moi.
e. Mais non, tu sais *(know)* bien que Fabien est végétarien.

2 Dis-moi …

I will tell you about my breakfast this morning.

- J'ai pris le petit déjeuner à sept heures.
- J'ai mangé du pain avec du beurre et de la confiture.
- J'ai bu du jus d'orange.

PARLER *Now choose one of the meals you had yesterday and tell me …*

- *at what time you had that meal*
- *what you ate*
- *what you drank*

3  Créa-dialogue

PARLER Avec vos camarades, décrivez où vous êtes allé(e)s et ce que vous avez fait aux endroits suivants.

▶ au supermarché
acheter

Où es-tu allée?

Je suis allée au supermarché.

Qu'est-ce que tu as acheté?

J'ai acheté du pain, du lait et de la confiture.

④ Composition: *Un bon repas*

Imaginez que vous êtes allé(e) *(went)* dans un bon restaurant pour une occasion spéciale. Décrivez le repas. Voici quelques suggestions:

- Dans quel restaurant êtes-vous allé(e)?
- Avec qui et pour quelle occasion?
- Qu'est-ce que vous avez mangé comme *(as)* hors d'oeuvre?
- Comme plat principal?
- Comme dessert?
- Qu'est-ce que vous avez bu?
- Qu'est-ce que les autres *(other)* personnes ont mangé et bu?
- Est-ce que tout le monde *(everyone)* a aimé le repas?

STRATEGY Writing

Writing about food When you are writing in French about what you ate and drank at a recent meal, you have to decide whether you had a whole item (for example, **une pizza**) or whether you had a portion of that item (for example, **de la pizza**).

Before you begin your composition, make a list of the foods and beverages that you and your friends had. Then, next to each item, write the appropriate article (**un/une** or **du/de la/de l'**). Use this list as you write your composition.

un steak
du poulet

COMMENT DIT-ON ...?

How to show your appreciation for good food:

Hm ... C'est délicieux!

C'est exquis!

C'est fameux!

1. à la cantine manger	2. au restaurant manger	3. au marché acheter	4. à la boum boire

5. à la cuisine prendre	6. au café boire	7. dans un restaurant chinois ??

LESSON REVIEW
CLASSZONE.COM

trois cent quatre-vingt-cinq
Leçon 26   385

LEÇON 27

Un client difficile

VIDÉO   DVD   AUDIO

M. Ronchon a beaucoup d'appétit … mais pas beaucoup de
patience. <u>En fait</u>, M. Ronchon est rarement <u>de bonne humeur</u>.
Et quand il est de mauvaise humeur, c'est un client difficile.
Aujourd'hui, <u>par exemple</u>, au restaurant …

As a matter of fact / in
a good mood
for instance

—<u>Garçon</u>!

Waiter!

—<u>J'arrive</u>!

I'm coming!

—Qu'est-ce que vous avez <u>comme</u>
hors-d'oeuvre?

as, for

—Nous avons du jambon et du saucisson.

—Apportez-moi <u>tout ça</u> … avec du pain
et du beurre!

all of that

—Bien, monsieur.

—Et comme boisson, qu'est-ce que
je vous apporte?

—Donnez-moi de l'eau minérale …
<u>Dépêchez-vous</u>! J'ai soif!

Hurry up!

—Apportez-moi du poulet et des frites …
<u>Vite</u>! J'ai très faim!

Fast!

—Je vous apporte ça <u>tout de suite</u>.

right away

—Et apportez-moi aussi du fromage,
de la glace, de la tarte aux pommes et
de la tarte aux <u>abricots</u> … Mais, qu'est-ce
que vous attendez?

apricots

—Tout de suite, monsieur, tout de suite.

—Mais qu'est-ce que vous m'apportez?

—Je vous apporte l'<u>addition</u>!

check

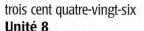

Compréhension

1. En général, est-ce que M. Ronchon est de bonne humeur ou de mauvaise humeur?
2. Qu'est-ce qu'il va prendre comme hors-d'oeuvre?
3. Qu'est-ce qu'il va prendre comme plat principal *(main course)*?
4. Qu'est-ce qu'il va boire?
5. Qu'est-ce qu'il va manger comme dessert?
6. Qu'est-ce que le garçon apporte après le dessert?
7. Quelle est la réaction de M. Ronchon? Est-ce qu'il est de bonne humeur ou de mauvaise humeur?

Et toi?

1. En général, est-ce que tu es de bonne humeur?
2. Et aujourd'hui, est-ce que tu es de bonne ou de mauvaise humeur?
3. En général, est-ce que tu as beaucoup d'appétit?
4. Est-ce que tu es une personne patiente?
5. Quand tu vas au restaurant avec un copain (une copine), qui paie l'addition?

NOTE culturelle

Les restaurants français et la cuisine française

Les Français aiment manger chez eux, mais ils aiment aussi aller au restaurant. Pour les gens pressés,° il y a la restauration rapide° et les pizzerias.

Pour les gens qui veulent faire un bon repas, il y a toutes° sortes de restaurants spécialisés: auberges,° restaurants régionaux, restaurants de poisson, … Il y a aussi les «grands restaurants» où la cuisine est extraordinaire … et très chère!

La cuisine française a une réputation internationale. Pour beaucoup de personnes, c'est la meilleure° cuisine du monde.°

Les Américains ont emprunté° un grand nombre de mots° au vocabulaire de la cuisine française. Est-ce que tu connais les mots suivants: **soupe, sauce, mayonnaise, omelette, filet mignon, tarte, purée, soufflé?** Est-ce que tu aimes **les croissants? les crêpes? la mousse au chocolat?**

INTERNET ACTIVITY

Go to the sites of restaurants in France and read their menus. Which menu/restaurant do you find tempting?

pressés *in a hurry* **restauration rapide** *fast food* **toutes** *all* **auberges** *country inns* **meilleure** *best* **du monde** *in the world* **ont emprunté** *have borrowed* **mots** *words*

A Les pronoms compléments *me, te, nous, vous*

In the sentences below, the pronouns in heavy print are called OBJECT PRONOUNS.
Note the form and the position of these pronouns in the sentences below.

Anne **me** parle.	Elle **m'**invite.	*Anne talks **to me**.*	*She invites **me**.*
Mes amis **te** parlent.	Ils **t'**invitent.	*My friends talk **to you**.*	*They invite **you**.*
Tu **nous** parles.	Tu **nous** invites.	*You talk **to us**.*	*You invite **us**.*
Je **vous** parle.	Je **vous** invite.	*I am talking **to you**.*	*I invite **you**.*

FORMS

The OBJECT PRONOUNS that correspond to the subject pronouns **je, tu, nous, vous** are:

me ↓ m´ (+ VOWEL SOUND)	me, to me	**nous**	us, to us
te ↓ t´ (+ VOWEL SOUND)	you, to you	**vous**	you, to you

Cette carte **vous** donne
l'accès à 60 musées.

C A R T E
MUSÉES ET MONUMENTS

POSITION

In French, object pronouns usually come before the verb, according to the following patterns:

AFFIRMATIVE			NEGATIVE				
SUBJECT + OBJECT PRONOUN + VERB ...			SUBJECT + **ne** + OBJECT PRONOUN + VERB + **pas** ...				
Paul	**nous**	invite.	Éric	**ne**	**nous**	invite	**pas**.

1 D'accord!

PARLER Demandez à vos camarades
de faire les choses suivantes pour vous.
Ils sont d'accord pour faire ces choses.

▶ téléphoner ce soir?

1. téléphoner demain?
2. attendre après la classe?
3. inviter à ta fête/soirée?
4. inviter à dîner?
5. rendre visite ce week-end?
6. rendre visite cet été?
7. acheter une glace?
8. apporter un sandwich?
9. vendre ton baladeur?
10. écouter?

Tu me
téléphones ce
soir?

D'accord,
je te téléphone
ce soir.

2 *Pauvre Chloé!*

PARLER Charlotte a de la chance.
Sa copine Chloé n'a pas de chance.
Jouez les deux rôles.

▶ mon copain/inviter

1. ma tante/inviter au restaurant
2. mes cousins/téléphoner souvent
3. mon frère/écouter
4. mes parents/comprendre
5. mes voisins/inviter à dîner
6. ma copine/aider avec mes devoirs
7. mon grand-père/acheter
   des cadeaux *(gifts)*
8. mes amis/attendre après la classe

> Mon copain
> m'invite.

> Tu as de la chance.
> Mon copain
> ne m'invite pas.

VOCABULAIRE Les services personnels

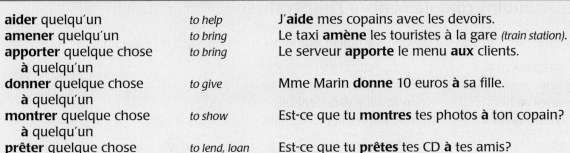

aider quelqu'un	*to help*	J'**aide** mes copains avec les devoirs.
amener quelqu'un	*to bring*	Le taxi **amène** les touristes à la gare *(train station)*.
apporter quelque chose à quelqu'un	*to bring*	Le serveur **apporte** le menu **aux** clients.
donner quelque chose à quelqu'un	*to give*	Mme Marin **donne** 10 euros **à** sa fille.
montrer quelque chose à quelqu'un	*to show*	Est-ce que tu **montres** tes photos **à** ton copain?
prêter quelque chose à quelqu'un	*to lend, loan*	Est-ce que tu **prêtes** tes CD **à** tes amis?

---

3 *Questions personnelles*

PARLER/ÉCRIRE Réponds affirmativement ou
négativement aux questions suivantes.

1. Est-ce que tes copains t'aident avec tes devoirs?
2. Est-ce que ta mère ou ton père t'aide avec les devoirs
   de français?
3. Est-ce que ton père ou ta mère te prête sa voiture?
4. Est-ce que ton frère ou ta sœur te prête ses CD?
5. Est-ce que tes profs te donnent des conseils *(advice)*?
6. Est-ce que ton copain te montre ses photos?
7. Est-ce que tes cousins t'apportent des cadeaux
   (gifts) quand ils viennent chez toi?
8. Est-ce que tes parents t'amènent au restaurant
   pour ton anniversaire?

SAMEDI devoirs

MATIÈRES	pour le	TEXTES
Histoire	lundi	questions 1-15 page 475
français	mardi	examen chapitre 8

4 Bons services

PARLER/ÉCRIRE Informez-vous sur les personnes suivantes. Dites ce que leurs amis ou leurs parents font pour eux. Pour cela, complétez les phrases avec les pronoms **me (m'), te (t'), nous** ou **vous.**

▶ J'organise une boum.   **Ma soeur <u>me</u> prête ses CD.**

▶ Nous avons faim.   **Cécile <u>nous</u> apporte des sandwichs.**

1. Nous organisons un pique-nique. Nos copains … aident.
2. Tu as soif. Je … apporte un soda.
3. Vous préparez l'examen. Le prof … donne des conseils *(advice)*.
4. J'ai besoin d'argent. Mon cousin … prête vingt euros.
5. Tu es chez les voisins. Ils … montrent leur appartement.
6. Nous sommes à l'hôpital. Nos amis … rendent visite.
7. Vous êtes sympathiques. Je … invite chez moi.
8. Nous allons prendre l'avion. Le taxi … amène à l'aéroport.
9. Je nettoie le garage. Mon frère … aide.

B Les pronoms compléments à l'impératif

Compare the position and the form of the object pronouns when the verb is in the imperative.

AFFIRMATIVE	NEGATIVE
Téléphone-**moi** ce soir!	Ne **me** téléphone pas demain!
Invite-**moi** samedi!	Ne **m'**invite pas dimanche!
Apporte-**nous** du thé!	Ne **nous** apporte pas de café!

When the IMPERATIVE verb is AFFIRMATIVE, the object pronouns come *after* the verb.

→ **me** becomes **moi**

When the imperative verb is negative, the object pronouns come *before* the verb.

5 Prêts *(Loans)*

PARLER Demandez à vos copains de vous prêter les choses suivantes. Ils vont accepter.

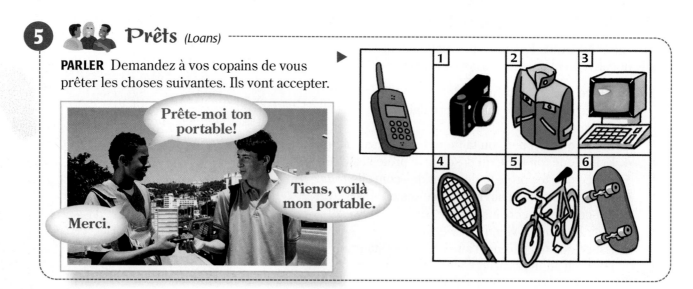

6 À Paris

PARLER/ÉCRIRE Vous visitez Paris. Demandez certains services aux personnes suivantes.

▶ au garçon de café *(waiter)*
  • apporter un sandwich
  S'il vous plaît, apportez-moi un sandwich.

1. au garçon de café
   • apporter de l'eau
   • apporter une limonade
   • donner un croissant

2. à la serveuse *(waitress)* du restaurant
   • montrer le menu
   • donner du pain
   • apporter l'addition *(check)*
3. au chauffeur de taxi *(cab driver)*
   • amener au musée d'Orsay
   • montrer Notre-Dame
   • aider avec les bagages
4. à un copain parisien
   • téléphoner ce soir
   • donner ton adresse
   • prêter ton plan *(map)* de Paris

7 Quel service?

PARLER Demandez à vos camarades certains services. Pour cela complétez les phrases en utilisant ces verbes.

aider	amener	apporter
donner	montrer	prêter

▶ J'ai soif. … de la limonade.
  S'il te plaît, apporte-moi (donne-moi) de la limonade.

1. Je ne comprends pas les devoirs de maths.
2. Je voudrais téléphoner à ta cousine.
3. Je n'ai pas d'argent pour aller au cinéma.
4. Je voudrais voir tes photos.
5. J'ai soif.
6. J'organise une boum.
7. Je vais peindre *(to paint)* ma chambre.
8. Je vais à l'aéroport.
9. Je ne sais pas où tu habites.

▶ J'ai faim. … un sandwich
  S'il te plaît, apporte-moi (donne-moi) un sandwich.

… avec le problème.
… son numéro de téléphone.
… dix dollars.
… tes photos.
… de l'eau minérale.
… tes CD.
… avec ce projet.
… là-bas avec ta voiture.
… ton adresse.

8 Non!

PARLER Proposez à vos camarades de faire les choses suivantes pour eux. Ils vont refuser et donner une explication.

▶ téléphoner ce soir (Je ne suis pas chez moi.)

1. téléphoner demain soir (Je dois faire mes devoirs.)
2. inviter ce week-end (Je vais à la campagne.)
3. inviter dimanche (Je dîne chez mes cousins.)
4. attendre après la classe (Je dois rentrer chez moi.)
5. prêter mes CD (Je n'ai pas de chaîne hi-fi.)
6. acheter un sandwich (Je n'ai pas faim.)
7. rendre visite ce soir (Je vais au cinéma.)

Je te téléphone ce soir?

Non, ne me téléphone pas. Je ne suis pas chez moi.

C Les verbes *pouvoir* et *devoir*

FORMS

Note the forms of the irregular verbs **pouvoir** *(can, may, be able)* and **devoir** *(must, have to)*.

INFINITIVE	pouvoir	devoir
PRESENT	Je **peux** venir. Tu **peux** travailler. Il/Elle/On **peut** voyager. Nous **pouvons** dîner ici. Vous **pouvez** rester. Ils/Elles **peuvent** aider.	Je **dois** rentrer avant midi. Tu **dois** gagner de l'argent. Il/Elle/On **doit** visiter Paris. Nous **devons** regarder le menu. Vous **devez** finir vos devoirs. Ils/Elles **doivent** mettre la table.
PASSÉ COMPOSÉ	J'**ai pu** étudier.	J'**ai dû** faire mes devoirs.

USES

- **Pouvoir** has several English equivalents.

can	Est-ce que tu **peux** venir au pique-nique?	*Can you come to the picnic?*
may	Est-ce que je **peux** prendre la voiture?	*May I take the car?*
to be able	Jacques ne **peut** pas réparer sa mobylette.	*Jacques is not able to fix his moped.*

- **Devoir** is used to express an OBLIGATION.

must	Vous **devez** faire vos devoirs.	*You must do your homework.*
to have to	Est-ce que je **dois** ranger ma chambre?	*Do I have to pick up my room?*

→ **Devoir** is usually followed by an infinitive. It cannot stand alone.

Est-ce que tu **dois étudier** ce soir? *Do you have to study tonight?*
Oui, je **dois étudier**. *Yes, I have to (study).*
Non, je **ne dois pas étudier**. *No, I don't have to (study).*

9 Le coût de la vie *(The cost of living)*

PARLER/ÉCRIRE Décrivez ce que les personnes suivantes peuvent acheter avec leur argent.

▶ Philippe a quinze euros.
  Il peut acheter des lunettes de soleil.

1. Alice et Françoise ont vingt euros.
2. J'ai cent euros.
3. Tu as soixante euros.
4. Vous avez quatre-vingts euros.
5. Ma copine a soixante-cinq euros.
6. Nous avons cinquante euros.
7. Mon frère a vingt-cinq euros.

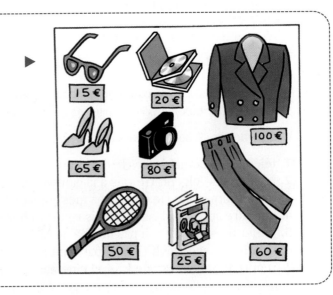

10 *Obligations?*

PARLER Demandez à vos camarades s'ils doivent faire les choses suivantes.

▶ étudier?

1. étudier ce soir?
2. ranger ta chambre?
3. mettre la table?
4. réussir à l'examen?
5. aller chez le dentiste cette semaine?
6. parler au professeur après la classe?
7. être poli(e) *(polite)* avec tes voisins?
8. rentrer chez toi après la classe?

Est-ce que tu dois étudier?

Oui, je dois étudier. (Non, je ne dois pas étudier.)

11 *Excuses*

PARLER/ÉCRIRE Thomas demande à ses amis de repeindre *(to repaint)* sa chambre avec lui, mais chacun a une excuse. Dites que les personnes suivantes ne peuvent pas aider Thomas. Dites aussi ce qu'elles doivent faire.

▶ Hélène (étudier)
Hélène ne peut pas aider Thomas.
Elle doit étudier.

1. nous (faire les courses)
2. Lise et Rose (acheter des vêtements)
3. moi (aider ma mère)
4. toi (nettoyer le garage)
5. Alice (rendre visite à sa grand-mère)
6. vous (déjeuner avec vos cousins)
7. mon frère et moi (laver la voiture)
8. Nathalie et toi (préparer l'examen)

12 *Expression personnelle*

PARLER/ÉCRIRE Complétez les phrases suivantes avec vos idées personnelles.

1. Chez moi, je peux …
   Je ne peux pas …
2. À l'école, nous devons …
   Nous ne devons pas …
3. À la maison, je dois …
   Mes frères (Mes soeurs) doivent …
4. Quand on est riche, on peut …
   On doit …
5. Quand on est malade *(sick)*, on doit …
   On ne doit pas …
6. Quand on veut maigrir, on doit …
   On ne peut pas …

PRONONCIATION s = /z/ ss = /s/

Les lettres «s» et «ss»

Be sure to distinguish between "s" and "ss" in the middle of a word.

poison   poisson

Répétez: /z/ **mauvaise cuisine fraise mayonnaise**
quelque chose   magasin

/s/ **poisson saucisson dessert boisson assiette pamplemousse**

/z/–/s/ **poison – poisson   désert** *(desert)* **– dessert**

Comme dessert nous choisissons une tarte aux fraises.

 À votre tour!

OBJECTIFS

Now you can …
• ask people for favors
• say what your friends do for you

1  Allô!

PARLER Reconstituez la conversation entre Corinne et Philippe. Pour cela, faites correspondre les réponses de Philippe avec ce que dit Corinne.

Corinne

1 Dis, Philippe, j'ai besoin d'un petit service.

2 Prête-moi ta mobylette, s'il te plaît.

3 Dans ce cas, apporte-moi Paris-Match.

4 Alors, achète-moi aussi le nouvel album d'Astérix.

5 Je t'ai prêté vingt euros hier!

Philippe

a C'est vrai … Bon, je t'achète tout ça (all that).

b D'accord! Je vais aller à la librairie (bookstore) Duchemin.

c Écoute, je n'ai pas assez d'argent.

d Ah, je ne peux pas. Je dois aller en ville cet après-midi.

e Qu'est-ce que je peux faire pour toi?

2 Créa-dialogue

PARLER Demandez certains services à vos camarades. Ils vont vous demander pourquoi. Répondez à leurs questions. Ils vont accepter le service.

▶ —S'il te plaît, prête-moi ton vélo!
—Pourquoi?
—Parce que je voudrais faire une promenade à la campagne.
—D'accord, je te prête mon vélo.

	▶ prêter 	1. prêter	2. prêter	3. apporter	4. prêter	5. donner	6. donner
QUEL SERVICE?					$1.00	$5.00	??
POURQUOI?	faire une promenade à la campagne	jouer au tennis	organiser une boum	prendre des photos	acheter une glace	??	??

3 **Au restaurant** --------------

PARLER Avec un(e) camarade, préparez un dialogue original correspondant à la situation suivante.

> You are having dinner at a French restaurant called Sans-Souci. You have a friendly but inexperienced waiter/waitress (played by your classmate) who forgets to bring you what you need. However, whenever you mention something, he/she agrees to bring it right away **(tout de suite)**.
>
> Tell your waiter/waitress …
>
> - to please show you the menu **(le menu)**
> - to please give you some water
> - to bring you a napkin
> - to give you a beverage (of your choice)
> - to bring you a dessert (of your choice)
> - to bring you the silverware that you need for eating the dessert

COMMENT DIT-ON …?

How to show your reaction to bad food:

Pouah! … C'est infect! … C'est dégoûtant! C'est infâme!

4  **Composition: Bonnes relations**

ÉCRIRE Select a person you like (a friend, a neighbor, a relative, a teacher) and write a short paragraph mentioning at least four things this person does for you. You may want to use some of the following verbs:

> acheter amener aider
> donner inviter montrer
> prêter rendre visite téléphoner

> J'ai une bonne copine.
> Elle s'appelle Stéphanie.
> Elle est très sympathique.
> Elle me téléphone souvent
> et le week-end, elle m'invite
> chez elle. Elle est très
> intelligente et quand je ne
> comprends pas, elle m'aide
> avec mes devoirs de français.
> Elle me donne toujours
> des conseils (advice) excellents.

Now tell me about a friend of yours and let me know some of the things this friend does for you.

LEÇON 28

Pique-nique  AUDIO

Mélanie et Jean-Marc organisent un pique-nique ce week-end.
Ils préparent la liste des <u>invités</u>. Qui vont-ils inviter?

guests

Pique-nique:
Stéphanie
Frédéric
Fatima
Olivier
Ousmane
Sophie

Mélanie:	Tu connais Stéphanie?
Jean-Marc:	Oui, je la connais. C'est une copine.
Mélanie:	Je l'invite au pique-nique?
Jean-Marc:	Bien sûr. Invite-la.
Mélanie:	Et son cousin Frédéric, tu le connais?
Jean-Marc:	Oui, je le connais un peu.
Mélanie:	Je l'invite aussi?
Jean-Marc:	Non, ne l'invite pas. Il est trop snob.
Mélanie:	<u>Comment</u>? Tu le trouves snob? Moi, je le trouve intelligent et sympathique. Et <u>puis</u>, il a une voiture et nous avons besoin d'une voiture pour transporter <u>tout le monde</u> …
Jean-Marc:	Mélanie, tu es <u>géniale</u> … C'est vrai, Frédéric n'est pas <u>aussi snob que ça</u> … Téléphonons-lui <u>tout de suite</u> et invitons-le au pique-nique!

What?
also

everyone
brilliant
that snobbish
right away

NOTE culturelle

Un pique-nique français

Quand ils vont à la campagne, les Français adorent faire des pique-niques. Un pique-nique est un repas froid assez simple. Il y a généralement du poulet froid et des oeufs durs° et aussi du jambon, du saucisson ou du pâté* pour les sandwichs. Quand on a l'équipement nécessaire, on peut aussi faire des grillades° sur un barbecue. Comme dessert, il y a des fruits (bananes, oranges, pommes, poires, raisin°). Comme boisson, il y a de l'eau minérale, des sodas et des jus de fruit.

*The French have created dozens of varieties of **pâté**, ranging from the expensive and refined **foie gras** (made from the livers of fattened geese) to the everyday **pâté de campagne** (a type of cold meat loaf served in thin slices with bread).

durs *hard-boiled* **grillades** *grilled meat* **raisin** *grapes* (*Note that* **raisin** *is always in the singular.*)

Compréhension

1. Qui est Stéphanie?
2. Qui est Frédéric?
3. Est-ce que Jean-Marc a une bonne ou une mauvaise opinion de Frédéric? Pourquoi?
4. Et Mélanie, comment est-ce qu'elle trouve Frédéric?
5. Finalement, est-ce que Jean-Marc va inviter Frédéric au pique-nique? Pourquoi?

Et toi?

1. Est-ce que tu aimes faire des pique-niques?
2. Quand tu fais un pique-nique avec des copains, où allez-vous?
3. Qui invites-tu?
4. En général, qu'est-ce qu'on mange à un pique-nique américain?
5. Qu'est-ce qu'on boit?
6. Dans ta famille, est-ce qu'on fait des barbecues? Où? Qui est le «chef»? Qu'est-ce qu'on mange et qu'est-ce qu'on boit?

A Le verbe *connaître*

Note the forms of the irregular verb **connaître** *(to know)*.

INFINITIVE	connaître	
PRESENT	Je **connais** Stéphanie.	Nous **connaissons** Paris.
	Tu **connais** son cousin?	Vous **connaissez** Montréal?
	Il/Elle/On **connaît** ces garçons.	Ils/Elles **connaissent** ce café.
PASSÉ COMPOSÉ	J'**ai connu** ton frère pendant les vacances.	

➔ In the passé composé, **connaître** means *to meet for the first time.*

➔ The French use **connaître** to say that they *know* or *are acquainted with people or places.* To say that they *know information,* they use **je sais, tu sais.** Compare:

PEOPLE/PLACES

Je **connais** Éric.
Tu **connais** Frédéric.
Je **connais** un bon restaurant.

INFORMATION

Je **sais** où il habite.
Tu **sais** à quelle heure il vient?
Je **sais** qu'il est près du théâtre.

Je connais Éric.

Je sais où il habite.

1 On ne peut pas tout connaître

PARLER/ÉCRIRE Les personnes suivantes connaissent la première personne ou la première chose entre parenthèses. Elles ne connaissent pas la deuxième.

▶ Philippe (Isabelle/sa soeur)
  Philippe connaît Isabelle.
  Il ne connaît pas sa soeur.

1. nous (Paul/ses copains)
2. vous (le prof d'anglais/le prof de maths)
3. moi (les voisins/leurs amis)
4. toi (Paris/Bordeaux)
5. les touristes (le Louvre/le musée d'Orsay)
6. mon copain (ce café/ce restaurant)

2 Questions personnelles   PARLER/ÉCRIRE

1. Est-ce que tu connais New York? Chicago? San Francisco? Montréal? Quelles villes est-ce que tu connais bien?
2. Dans ta ville est-ce que tu connais un bon restaurant? Comment est-ce qu'il s'appelle? Est-ce que tu connais un supermarché? un centre commercial? un magasin de CD? Comment est-ce qu'ils s'appellent?
3. Est-ce que tu connais des monuments à Paris? Quels monuments?

4. Est-ce que tu connais bien tes voisins? Est-ce qu'ils sont sympathiques? Est-ce que tu connais personnellement le directeur (la directrice) de ton école? Est-ce qu'il (elle) est strict(e)?
5. Quels acteurs de cinéma est-ce que tu connais? Quelles actrices? Quels musiciens? Quels athlètes professionnels?

B Les pronoms compléments: *le, la, les*

In the questions below, the nouns in heavy type follow the verb directly. They are the DIRECT OBJECTS of the verb. Note the forms and position of the DIRECT OBJECT PRONOUNS which are used to replace those nouns in the answers.

Tu connais **Éric?**	Oui, je **le** connais. Je **l'**invite souvent.	*Yes, I know **him**.* *I invite **him** often.*
Tu connais **Stéphanie?**	Oui, je **la** connais. Je **l'**invite aussi.	*Yes, I know **her**.* *I invite **her** also.*
Tu connais **mes copains?**	Je **les** connais bien. Je **les** invite.	*I know **them** well.* *I invite **them**.*
Tu connais **mes amies?**	Je **les** connais aussi. Je **les** invite souvent.	*I know **them** too.* *I invite **them** often.*

FORMS AND USES

Direct object pronouns have the following forms:

Qui le vend?
Qui le répare?

On le trouve dans les pages jaunes!

LA POSTE

	SINGULAR		PLURAL
MASCULINE	**le** ↓ **l'** (+ VOWEL SOUND)	*him, it*	**les** *them*
FEMININE	**la** ↓ **l'** (+ VOWEL SOUND)	*her, it*	

→ The direct object pronouns **le, la, l', les** can refer to either people or things.

Tu vois **Nicole?**	Oui, je **la** vois.	*Yes, I see **her**.*
Tu vois **ma voiture?**	Oui, je **la** vois.	*Yes, I see **it**.*
Tu comprends **le professeur?**	Oui, je **le** comprends.	*Yes, I understand **him**.*
Tu comprends **ce mot** *(word)*?	Oui, je **le** comprends.	*Yes, I understand **it**.*

POSITION

Direct object pronouns generally come *before* the verb according to the following patterns:

	AFFIRMATIVE			NEGATIVE				
	SUBJECT + **le/la/les** + VERB ...			SUBJECT + **ne** + **le/la/les** + VERB + **pas** ...				
Éric?	Je	**le**	connais bien.	Tu	**ne**	**le**	connais	**pas**.
Ces filles?	Nous	**les**	invitons.	Vous	**ne**	**les**	invitez	**pas**.

3 À la boum de Delphine

PARLER Pierre connaît tous les invités *(all the guests)* à la boum de Delphine, mais Lise ne les connaît pas. Jouez les trois rôles.

▶ ces garçons?

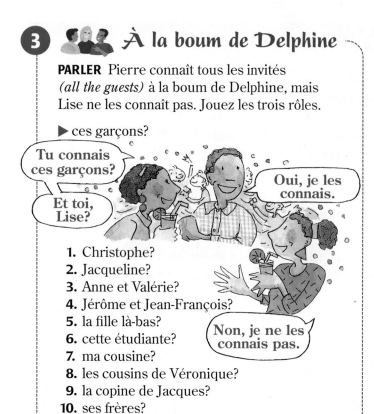

Tu connais ces garçons?

Oui, je les connais.

Et toi, Lise?

Non, je ne les connais pas.

1. Christophe?
2. Jacqueline?
3. Anne et Valérie?
4. Jérôme et Jean-François?
5. la fille là-bas?
6. cette étudiante?
7. ma cousine?
8. les cousins de Véronique?
9. la copine de Jacques?
10. ses frères?

4 Un choix difficile

PARLER Vous allez passer le mois de juillet en France. Vous êtes limité(e) à 20 kilos de bagages. Un(e) camarade demande si vous allez prendre les choses suivantes. Répondez affirmativement ou négativement.

▶ ta raquette?
  —**Tu prends ta raquette?**
  —**Oui, je la prends.**
    (Non, je ne la prends pas.)
1. tes CD?
2. ton livre de français?
3. ta guitare?
4. ton baladeur?
5. ta chaîne hi-fi?
6. ton maillot de bain?
7. ton skate?
8. tes tee-shirts?
9. tes sandales?

5 Questions et réponses

PARLER Julien pose des questions à Luc en utilisant les éléments des colonnes A et B. Jérôme répond logiquement en utilisant les éléments des colonnes B et C et un pronom complément. Avec un(e) camarade, jouez les deux rôles.

A	B	C
où	rencontrer tes copains	le samedi matin
quand	voir ta cousine	à 8 heures du matin
à quelle heure	regarder la télé	à 9 heures du soir
	ranger ta chambre	à la Boîte à Musique
	faire les courses	à Mod' Shop
	acheter tes CD	au café Le Pont Neuf
	acheter tes vêtements	dans un supermarché
	prendre le petit déjeuner	le week-end
		pendant les vacances
		dans la cuisine
		dans le salon

Où est-ce que tu rencontres tes copains?

Je les rencontre au café Le Pont Neuf.

C La place des pronoms à l'impératif

Note the position of the object pronoun when the verb is in the imperative.

	AFFIRMATIVE COMMAND	NEGATIVE COMMAND
J'invite **Frédéric?**	Oui, invite-**le!**	Non, ne **l'**invite pas!
Je prends **la guitare?**	Oui, prends-**la!**	Non, ne **la** prends pas!
J'achète **les sandales?**	Oui, achète-**les!**	Non, ne **les** achète pas!

In AFFIRMATIVE COMMANDS, the object pronoun comes *after* the verb and is joined to it by a hyphen.

In NEGATIVE COMMANDS, the object pronoun comes *before* the verb.

---

6 Invitations

PARLER/ÉCRIRE Vous préparez une liste de personnes à inviter à une boum. Vous êtes limité(e)s à quatre *(4)* des personnes suivantes. Faites vos suggestions d'après les modèles.

▶ Caroline est sympathique.
  Invitons-la!
▶ Jean-Louis est pénible.
  Ne l'invitons pas!

1. Sylvie est très sympathique.
2. Cécile et Anne aiment danser.
3. Jacques est stupide.
4. Robert joue bien de la guitare.
5. Ces filles sont intelligentes.
6. Martin et Thomas sont snobs.
7. Nicolas n'est pas mon ami.
8. Ces garçons sont pénibles.
9. Cette fille est gentille.
10. Tes copains sont méchants.

---

7   Le pique-nique

PARLER Élodie demande à Mathieu si elle doit prendre certaines choses pour le pique-nique.

▶ ma guitare (oui)

Est-ce que je prends ma guitare?

Oui, prends-la!

1. la limonade (oui)
2. les sandwichs (non)
3. la salade (oui)
4. le lait (non)
5. le gâteau (non)
6. mon appareil-photo (oui)
7. mes lunettes de soleil (oui)
8. les impers (non)

---

8   Oui ou non?

PARLER Votre petit cousin de Québec passe deux semaines chez vous. Il vous demande s'il doit ou peut faire les choses suivantes. Répondez affirmativement ou négativement.

1. Je fais les courses?
2. Je regarde tes photos?
3. Je range ma chambre?
4. J'achète le journal *(newspaper)*?
5. J'invite les voisins à déjeuner?
6. Je prépare le dîner?
7. Je prends ton vélo?
8. Je loue les DVD?
9. J'aide ta mère?
10. Je mets la télé?

Je fais les devoirs?

Oui, fais-les.
(Non, ne les fais pas.)

D Les pronoms compléments *lui, leur*

In the questions below, the nouns in heavy type are INDIRECT OBJECTS. These nouns represent PEOPLE and are introduced by **à**.

Note the forms and position of the corresponding INDIRECT OBJECT PRONOUNS in the answers on the right.

Tu téléphones **à Philippe?**   Oui, je **lui** téléphone.
Tu parles **à Juliette?**   Non, je ne **lui** parle pas.

Tu téléphones **à tes amis?**   Oui, je **leur** téléphone.
Tu prêtes ton vélo **à tes cousines?** Non, je ne **leur** prête pas mon vélo.

FORMS

INDIRECT OBJECT PRONOUNS replace **à** + <u>noun representing people</u>. They have the following forms:

	SINGULAR		PLURAL	
MASCULINE/FEMININE	**lui**	*to him, to her*	**leur**	*to them*

POSITION

Like other object pronouns, **lui** and **leur** come before the verb, except in affirmative commands.

Voici Henri.   Parle-**lui!**   Prête-**lui** ton vélo!

→ In negative sentences, **lui** and **leur,** like other object pronouns, come between **ne** and the verb.

Voici Éric.   Je ne **lui** téléphone pas.
Voici mes voisins.   Je ne **leur** parle pas.

9  *Au téléphone*

PARLER Demandez à vos camarades s'ils téléphonent aux personnes suivantes.

▶ ta copine

Tu téléphones à ta copine?

Oui, je lui téléphone.
(Non, je ne lui téléphone pas.)

1. ton copain
2. tes cousins
3. ta grand-mère
4. ton prof de français
5. tes voisins
6. ta tante favorite

VOCABULAIRE Verbes suivis *(followed)* d'un complément indirect

parler à	*to speak, talk (to)*	Je **parle à** mon copain.
rendre visite à	*to visit*	Nous **rendons visite à** nos voisins.
répondre à	*to answer*	Tu **réponds au** professeur.
téléphoner à	*to phone, call*	Jérôme **téléphone à** Juliette.
demander à	*to ask*	Je ne **demande** pas d'argent **à** mes frères.
donner à	*to give (to)*	Tu **donnes** ton adresse **à** ta copine.
montrer à	*to show (to)*	Nous **montrons** nos photos **à** nos amis.
prêter à	*to lend, loan (to)*	Je ne **prête** pas mon baladeur **à** ma soeur.

→ **Répondre** is a regular **-re** verb.
  Je réponds à François. **J'ai répondu** à Catherine.

→ The verbs **téléphoner**, **répondre**, and **demander** take indirect objects in French, but not in English. Compare:

téléphoner	Nous **téléphonons**	à	Paul.	Nous **lui téléphonons.**
	*We **are calling***	…	*Paul.*	*We **are calling him.***

répondre	Tu **réponds**	à	tes parents.	Tu **leur réponds.**
	*You **answer***	…	*your parents.*	*You **answer them.***

demander	Je **demande**	à	Sylvie	…	son stylo.	Je **lui demande** son stylo.
	*I **am asking***	…	*Sylvie*	*for*	*her pen.*	*I **am asking her** for her pen.*

10 Les copains de Léa

PARLER/ÉCRIRE Léa a beaucoup de copains. Décrivez ce que chacun fait pour elle. Complétez les phrases avec **Léa** ou **à Léa.**

▶ Françoise invite <u>Léa</u>.
  Patrick rend visite <u>à Léa</u>.

1. Marc téléphone …
2. Jean-Paul voit … samedi prochain.
3. Sophie prête son vélo …
4. Mélanie écoute …
5. François donne son adresse …
6. Philippe regarde … pendant la classe.
7. Antoine attend … après la classe.
8. Nathalie parle …
9. Pauline invite … au concert.
10. Pierre répond …
11. Céline montre ses photos …
12. Thomas demande … son numéro de téléphone.
13. Éric rend visite …

⓫ Joyeux anniversaire!

PARLER Choisissez un cadeau d'anniversaire pour les personnes suivantes. Un(e) camarade va vous demander ce que vous donnez à chaque personne.

▶ à ton copain

Qu'est-ce que tu donnes à ton copain?

Je lui donne un livre.

1. à ton petit frère
2. à ta mère
3. à ta grand-mère
4. à ta copine
5. à tes cousins
6. à ton (ta) prof
7. à tes copains

Cadeaux

un pull
un jeu vidéo
une cravate
un livre
des billets *(tickets)* de théâtre
un magazine
ma photo
une boîte *(box)* de chocolats
un gâteau
??

⓬ *Questions personnelles*

PARLER/ÉCRIRE Réponds aux questions suivantes. Utilise **lui** ou **leur** dans tes réponses.

1. Le week-end, est-ce que tu rends visite à tes copains? à ton oncle?
2. Est-ce que tu prêtes tes CD à ta soeur? à ton frère? à tes copains?
3. Est-ce que tu demandes de l'argent à ton père? à ta mère?
4. Est-ce que tu demandes des conseils *(advice)* à tes parents? à tes professeurs?
5. Est-ce que tu donnes de bons conseils à tes copains?
6. Est-ce que tu montres tes photos à ton frère? à ta soeur? à ta copine? à ton copain? à tes cousins?
7. En classe, est-ce que tu réponds en français à ton professeur?
8. Quand tu as un problème, est-ce que tu parles à tes copains? à ton professeur? à tes grands-parents? à tes parents?

Ⓔ **Les verbes** *dire* **et** *écrire*

Note the forms of the irregular verbs **dire** *(to say, tell)* and **écrire** *(to write)*.

INFINITIVE	dire	écrire
PRESENT	je **dis** tu **dis** il/elle/on **dit** nous **disons** vous **dites** ils/elles **disent**	j' **écris** tu **écris** il/elle/on **écrit** nous **écrivons** vous **écrivez** ils/elles **écrivent**
PASSÉ COMPOSÉ	j'**ai dit**	j'**ai écrit**

➜ Note the use of **que/qu'** *(that)* after **dire** and **écrire**.

Florence **dit que** Frédéric est sympathique.   *Florence **says (that)** Frédéric is nice.*
Alain **écrit qu'**il est allé à un pique-nique.   *Alain **writes (that)** he went on a picnic.*

➜ **Décrire** *(to describe)* follows the same pattern as **écrire**.

13 *Correspondance*

PARLER/ÉCRIRE Pendant les vacances, on écrit beaucoup de lettres. Dites à qui les personnes suivantes écrivent.

▶ Juliette/à Marc
  Juliette écrit à Marc.

1. nous/à nos copains
2. toi/à ta cousine
3. moi/à ma grand-mère

4. Nicolas/à ses voisins
5. vous/à vos parents
6. les élèves/au professeur

14 *La boum*

PARLER/ÉCRIRE Des amis sont à une boum. Décrivez ce que chacun dit.

▶ toi/la musique est super
  Tu dis que la musique est super.

1. Nicole/les sandwichs sont délicieux
2. nous/les invités *(guests)* sont sympathiques
3. Pauline/Jérôme danse bien
4. moi/ces garçons dansent mal
5. vous/vous n'aimez pas ce CD
6. mes copains/ils vont organiser une soirée le week-end prochain

15 *Questions personnelles* **PARLER/ÉCRIRE**

1. Est-ce que tu aimes écrire?
2. Pendant les vacances, est-ce que tu écris à tes copains? à tes voisins? à ton(ta) meilleur(e) *(best)* ami(e)?
3. À Noël, est-ce que tu écris des cartes *(cards)*? À qui?
4. À qui as-tu écrit un mail récemment *(recently)*?
5. Est-ce que tu dis toujours la vérité *(truth)*?
6. À ton avis, est-ce que les journalistes disent toujours la vérité? Et les politiciens?

PRONONCIATION   **on = /ɔ̃/**   **on(n)e = /ɔ/**

Les lettres «on» et «om»

Be sure to distinguish between the nasal and non-nasal vowel sounds.

REMEMBER: Do not pronounce an /n/ or /m/ after the nasal vowel /ɔ̃/.

lion

lionne

Répétez:

/ɔ̃/ **m<u>on</u> t<u>on</u> s<u>on</u> b<u>on</u> avi<u>on</u> m<u>on</u>trer rép<u>on</u>dre invit<u>on</u>s blous<u>on</u>**

/ɔn/ **téléph<u>one</u> Sim<u>one</u> d<u>onn</u>er c<u>onn</u>ais may<u>onn</u>aise pers<u>onne</u> b<u>onne</u>**

/ɔm/ **fr<u>om</u>age pr<u>om</u>enade t<u>om</u>ate p<u>omme</u> d<u>omm</u>age c<u>omm</u>ent**

/ɔ̃/–/ɔn/ **li<u>on</u>–li<u>onne</u> b<u>on</u>–b<u>onne</u> Sim<u>on</u>–Sim<u>one</u> Yv<u>on</u>–Yv<u>onne</u>**

M<u>on</u>ique d<u>onne</u> une p<u>omme</u> à Raym<u>on</u>d.
Sim<u>one</u> c<u>onn</u>aît m<u>on</u> <u>on</u>cle Lé<u>on</u>.

À votre tour!

OBJECTIFS

Now you can …
• talk about people you know and don't know
• use pronouns to refer to people and things

1 Allô!

PARLER Reconstituez la conversation entre Olivier et Sophie. Pour cela, faites correspondre les réponses de Sophie avec les questions d'Olivier.

1. Qu'est-ce que tu fais ce week-end?

2. Tu m'invites?

3. Et Catherine? Tu l'invites aussi?

4. C'est ma nouvelle copine.

5. Tu veux son numéro de téléphone?

6. C'est le 01.44.32.28.50.

a. Je lui téléphone tout de suite *(right away)*.
b. Oui, je ne l'ai pas.
c. Bien sûr, je t'invite.
d. J'organise une fête.
e. Catherine? Je ne la connais pas. Qui est-ce?
f. Ah oui, je vois qui c'est maintenant. Eh bien, d'accord! Je l'invite.

2 Créa-dialogue

PARLER Avec vos camarades, discutez de certaines choses que vous faites. Posez plusieurs questions sur chaque activité.

Tu regardes la télé?

Oui je la regarde.

À quelle heure est-ce que tu la regardes?

À huit heures.

▶ regarder la télé?	1. inviter tes amis?	2. voir tes cousins?
à quelle heure?	quand? à quelle occasion?	quand? où?

3. faire les courses?	4. aider ta mère?	5. faire tes devoirs?	6. téléphoner à tes copains?	7. rendre visite à ta grand-mère?	8. écrire à ton cousin?
quand? où?	quand? comment?	quand? où?	quand? pourquoi?	quand? pourquoi?	pourquoi?

③ ✎ Composition: Les personnes dans ma vie (life) ------------------------------------

Select three people from the list and write a short paragraph about each one. Give their names, say when you see them, and describe several things you do for them as well as one thing that you can't do. In your descriptions use the suggested verbs … and your imagination!

- un cousin/une cousine
- un frère/une soeur
- un copain/une copine
- un voisin/une voisine
- mon meilleur *(best)* ami
- ma meilleure amie
- un professeur de français (d'anglais, de maths, d'histoire)

téléphoner	voir	prêter	inviter
écrire	connaître	donner	rendre visite
répondre	parler	aider	

▶

Ma cousine s'appelle Denise. Je la vois pendant les vacances de Noël. Je lui écris des mails et elle me répond toujours. …

COMMENT DIT-ON …?

How to tell someone to leave you alone:

Laisse-moi tranquille!

Fiche-moi la paix!

LESSON REVIEW
CLASSZONE.COM

Tests de contrôle

By taking the following tests, you can check your progress in French and also prepare for the unit test. Write your answers on a separate sheet of paper.

Review...
• foods and beverages:
  pp. 366-367
• partitive article:
  pp. 378-379

1 Foods and beverages

Give the names of the foods and beverages you see on the table. With each one, be sure to use the appropriate partitive article: **du, de la,** or **de l'.**

Sur la table, il y a ...

1. —	3. —	5. —	7. —	9. —
2. —	4. —	6. —	8. —	10. —

2 The right choice

Review...
• new verbs:
  pp. 364, 370, 377,
  383, 389, and 404

Complete each of the following sentences with the appropriate forms of the verbs in the box. Be logical in your choice of verbs and do not use the same word more than once.

1. Caroline — ses photos de vacances à sa copine.
2. Madame Durand — au restaurant La Marmite.
3. Monsieur Lemaire — les courses au supermarché Prisunic.
4. À la piscine, mon petit frère — à nager.
5. Les gens généreux — de l'argent aux pauvres *(poor people)*.
6. Nicolas — un mail à sa cousine.
7. Est-ce que tu — bien quand le professeur parle français?
8. Au petit déjeuner, je — du jus d'orange.
9. Pauline — des photos avec son nouvel appareil-photo.
10. Catherine — souvent son vélo à sa soeur.

apprendre
boire
comprendre
déjeuner
donner
écrire
faire
montrer
prendre
prêter

3 The right verb

Complete the following sentences with the appropriate forms of the present tense of the verb in parentheses.

Review...
• irregular verbs:
  pp. 376, 377, 383, 392, 398, and 404

(vouloir)   **1.** Cécile — voyager. Ses copines — visiter Paris.

(prendre)   **2.** Les touristes — le train. Nous — le bus.

(apprendre) **3.** Élodie — l'anglais. Ses copains — l'espagnol.

(boire)   **4.** Nous — du thé. Les enfants — du lait.

(pouvoir)   **5.** Mes amis — venir à la boum. Est-ce que vous — rester?

(devoir)   **6.** Éric — étudier. Nous — aider nos parents.

(connaître) **7.** Isabelle — Céline. Nous — ses copains.

(écrire)   **8.** Tu — une lettre. Mes cousins — un mail.

(dire)   **9.** Je — «oui». Mais vous, vous — «non».

4 The right pronoun

Complete the following sentences with the appropriate pronoun in parentheses that replaces the underlined words.

Review...
• object pronouns:
  pp. 399 and 402

▶ Je connais <u>Céline</u>.   Je **la** connais. **(le, la)**

1. Nous invitons <u>Pierre</u>.   Nous — invitons à la boum. **(l', le)**
2. Tu écris <u>à Charlotte</u>.   Tu — écris. **(la, lui)**
3. J'aide <u>mes parents</u>.   Je — aide. **(l', les)**
4. Vous téléphonez <u>à Mathieu</u>.   Vous — téléphonez souvent. **(le, lui)**
5. J'écoute <u>mes CD</u>.   Je — écoute. **(les, leur)**
6. Nous parlons <u>à nos amis</u>.   Nous — parlons. **(les, leur)**
7. Tu regardes <u>ces photos</u>.   Tu — regardes avec Léa. **(les, leur)**
8. Vous lavez <u>la voiture</u>.   Vous — lavez. **(la, lui)**

5 Composition: Mon repas d'anniversaire

Write a short paragraph of five or six sentences describing what you would like for a special birthday dinner. Use only vocabulary and expressions that you know in French.

STRATEGY Writing

a First write out your menu.

b Then plan your paragraph, perhaps explaining why you are choosing certain items.

c Read over your composition to check that you are using the correct article with each food item.

hors d'oeuvre: _____

viande ou poisson: _____

autres plats: _____

_____

dessert: _____

boissons: _____

Vocabulaire

POUR COMMUNIQUER

Saying where you will eat

Je vais déjeuner	à la maison.		I will have lunch	at home.
	à la cantine (de l'école)			at the (school) cafeteria
	au restaurant			at the restaurant

Planning a meal

Il faut ...		
aller au marché	go to the market
faire les courses	do the food shopping
acheter la nourriture	buy the food
choisir les boissons	choose the beverages
préparer le repas	fix the meal
faire la cuisine	do the cooking
mettre le couvert	set the table

Saying what foods you like and dislike

J'aime [le rosbif].	I like roast beef.
Je préfère [la glace].	I prefer ice cream.
Je déteste [les frites].	I detest French fries.

Shopping for food, asking for certain quantities

Je voudrais ...			une livre de beurre	a pound of butter
du beurre	(some) butter		un kilo de sole	a kilo (2.2 pounds) of sole
de la sole	(some) sole		une douzaine d'oeufs	a dozen eggs
des oeufs	(some) eggs			

MOTS ET EXPRESSIONS

Les repas (Meals)

le petit déjeuner	breakfast		prendre le petit déjeuner	to have breakfast
le déjeuner	lunch		déjeuner	to have lunch
le dîner	dinner		dîner	to have dinner

Le couvert (Place settings)

un couteau	knife		une assiette	plate
un verre	glass		une cuillère	spoon
			une fourchette	fork
			une serviette	napkin
			une tasse	cup

La nourriture et les plats

un dessert	dessert	le poulet	chicken	les céréales	cereal
le fromage	cheese	le riz	rice	les frites	French fries
le gâteau	cake	le rosbif	roast beef	la glace	ice cream
un hors-d'oeuvre	appetizer	le saucisson	salami	la nourriture	food
le jambon	ham	les spaghetti	spaghetti	la salade	salad
le pain	bread	le thon	tuna	la sole	sole
un plat	dish	le veau	veal	la soupe	soup
le poisson	fish	le yaourt	yogurt	la tarte	pie
				la viande	meat

Les fruits et les légumes

un fruit	fruit	une banane	banana	une poire	pear
des haricots verts	green beans	une carotte	carrot	une pomme	apple
un légume	vegetable	une cerise	cherry	une pomme de terre	potato
un pamplemousse	grapefruit	une fraise	strawberry	une salade	(head of) lettuce
des petits pois	peas	une orange	orange	une tomate	tomato

Les ingrédients

le beurre	butter	la confiture	jam
le ketchup	ketchup	la mayonnaise	mayonnaise
un oeuf	egg		
le sel	salt		
le sucre	sugar		

Les boissons

le jus d'orange	orange juice	une boisson	beverage
le jus de pomme	apple juice	l'eau	water
le lait	milk	l'eau minérale	mineral water
le thé glacé	iced tea		

Interacting with others

Est-ce que Paul	me te nous vous le la les	connaît?	Does Paul know	me ? you? us? you? him? her? them?
Est-ce que Sophie	me te nous vous lui leur	parle?	Is Sophie talking	to me? to you? to us? to you? to him/her? to them?

Verbes réguliers

aider	to help
amener	to bring (people)
apporter	to bring (things)
demander (à)	to ask
donner (à)	to give (to)
montrer (à)	to show (to)
prêter (à)	to lend, to loan (to)
répondre (à)	to answer

Verbes irréguliers

apprendre	to learn
apprendre à + *infinitive*	to learn how to
boire	to drink
comprendre	to understand
connaître	to know
décrire	to describe
devoir	must, to have to
dire	to say, to tell
écrire (à)	to write (to)
pouvoir	can, may, to be able
prendre	to take, to have (a meal)
vouloir	to want

TEST PREP
CLASSZONE.COM

FLASHCARDS
AND MORE!

Bon appétit, Aurélie!

Nous avons demandé à Aurélie de décrire ses repas. Voici sa réponse.

À midi, je mange à la cantine de l'école et le soir à la maison. C'est ma mère qui fait les courses et c'est mon père qui prépare le dîner. J'adore ça! Il fait une cuisine assez traditionnelle, mais bien équilibrée. En général, on commence par une salade de concombres ou de tomates. Ensuite, il y a de la viande, par exemple, un bifteck ou du poulet, avec des haricots verts ou des pommes de terre. Parfois, on mange du cassoulet en boîte. Après, il y a une salade verte et des fromages divers. Comme dessert, il y a du yaourt ou un fruit. Avec le repas, on boit de l'eau minérale.

Quand mon père n'a pas envie de faire la cuisine, on va au restaurant. Dans notre quartier, il y a un restaurant vietnamien que nous aimons bien. Mon plat préféré, c'est le riz avec des crevettes et des petits pois.

Quand je sors avec mes copains, on va dans les fast food. J'aime bien aller dans les pizzerias parce qu'on peut choisir ses ingrédients. En général, je prends une pizza avec du fromage, des olives et des anchois. Avec la pizza, je bois souvent un soda.

équilibrée *balanced*
cassoulet *bean stew with pork or duck*
en boîte *canned*   **crevettes** *shrimp*

COMPARAISONS CULTURELLES

Comparez les repas d'Aurélie avec vos repas. Qu'est-ce que vous mangez pour le dîner? Faites une liste des similarités et des différences.

	AURÉLIE	LES SIMILARITÉS AVEC MOI	LES DIFFÉRENCES AVEC MOI
À la maison	_____	_____	_____
Au restaurant avec la famille	_____	_____	_____
Au restaurant avec les copains	_____	_____	_____

ALLO*pizza*

MENU

		26 cm. 1 pers.	31 cm. 2/3 pers.	40 cm. 3/4 pers.
ITALIENNE	sauce tomate, origan, mozzarella, anchois, olives	7,50 €	12 €	15 €
4 SAISONS	sauce tomate, mozzarella, crème, olives, tomates fraîches, champignons	7,50 €	12 €	15 €
3 FROMAGES	sauce tomate, mozzarella, origan, chèvre, Roquefort	8 €	13 €	17 €
PESCATORE	sauce tomate, mozzarella, origan, oignons, saumon, champignons	8 €	13 €	17 €
ANGLAISE	sauce tomate, mozzarella, origan, bacon, oeuf, pommes de terre	9 €	14 €	20 €
TEXANE	sauce tomate, mozzarella, origan, boeuf épicé, pepperoni, oignons	9 €	14 €	20 €

02-47-66-89-89

Petit dictionnaire

anchois	*anchovies*
frais/fraîche	*fresh*
boeuf épicé	*spicy beef*
oignon	*onion*
champignon	*mushroom*
origan	*oregano*
chèvre	*goat cheese*
saumon	*salmon*

Et vous?

Formez un groupe de 4 à 5 personnes. Imaginez que vous êtes en France. Vous voulez dîner et vous avez décidé de commander des pizzas. Faites une liste de ce que chacun veut commander.

NOM	TYPE DE PIZZA	DIMENSION	PRIX
John	Texane	31 cm.	14 €
•			
•			
•			
•			
•			

Le petit déjeuner *en France*

«Qu'est-ce que vous prenez au petit déjeuner?» Aux États-Unis, le petit déjeuner est généralement un repas abondant.° En France, c'est un repas simple.

Fabrice (13 ans)

Chez nous, nous sommes très traditionnels. Je mange du pain avec du beurre et de la confiture. Je bois un grand bol° de café au lait.

Mathieu (16 ans)

Chez nous, on prend le petit déjeuner «à l'américaine». Je mange des céréales et je bois du jus d'orange.

Sandrine (16 ans)

Je mange des tartines de pain° grillé° et je bois du lait chaud ou du chocolat avec beaucoup de sucre. Le dimanche, il y a parfois° des croissants. (Ça dépend si quelqu'un veut faire les courses!)

Sylvie (15 ans)

Le matin, je n'ai pas très faim. En général, je mange une tartine, c'est tout.° Je prends avec moi une barre de céréales ou une barre chocolatée que je mange avant° la première classe.

---

abondant *abundant, copious*   **bol** *deep bowl*   **tartines de pain** *slices of bread*   **grillé** *toasted*   **parfois** *sometimes*   **tout** *all*   **avant** *before*

COMPARAISONS CULTURELLES

Comparez le petit déjeuner des cinq jeunes Français avec votre petit déjeuner.

• Qui a le petit déjeuner le plus semblable *(most similar)*? Expliquez.

• Qui a le petit déjeuner le plus différent? Expliquez.

Activité écrite

Décrivez le petit déjeuner chez vous:

• pendant la semaine

• le dimanche matin

Stéphanie (13 ans)

Je suis martiniquaise. En général, je mange du pain et de la confiture comme° tout le monde.° Parfois ma mère prépare un petit déjeuner martiniquais typique. On mange du blaff de poisson° et des bananes vertes cuites.° On mange aussi des ananas,° des papayes et de la gelée de goyave.° C'est délicieux!

comme *like* **tout le monde** *everyone* **blaff de poisson** *fish stew* **cuites** *cooked* **ananas** *pineapple* **gelée de goyave** *guava jelly*

NOTE **culturelle**

La cuisine créole

La cuisine créole est une cuisine régionale typique de la Martinique et de la Guadeloupe. C'est une cuisine assez épicée° qui utilise les produits locaux,° principalement les produits de la mer° et les fruits exotiques.

Voici certaines spécialités:

boudin créole	*spicy sausage*
colombo	*rice with spicy meat sauce*
blaff de poisson	*fish stew*
matoutou crabes	*stewed crabs served with rice*
crabes farcis	*stuffed crabs*
langoustes grillées	*(small) lobsters, broiled*

épicée *hot (spicy)* **locaux** *local* **mer** *sea*

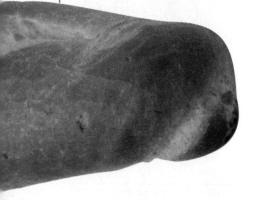

DÉCOUVREZ LA MARTINIQUE

au

TYPIC BELLEVUE

LE PLUS TYPIQUE DES RESTAURANTS

UN CHOIX UNIQUE DE SPÉCIALITÉS CRÉOLES

Boulevard de la Marne Tél. 05.96.71.68.87
FORT-DE-FRANCE
Parking Boulevard de Verdun

✱ ✱ **RELAIS CRÉOLE** ✱ ✱

Menu du jour et à la carte

Ouvert midi et soir sauf dimanche

LA VILLA CRÉOLE

La Bonne Cuisine Française et Créole

ANSE-MITAN
TROIS-ILETS
☎ 66.05.53

CONNEXIONS

Haitian people have their own creole cuisine which is somewhat different from that of Martinique. Find out about Haitian cuisine by visiting a local Haitian restaurant or by surfing the Internet.

• What products do Haitians use in their cooking?

• What are some typical dishes?

Les crêpes

Les crêpes sont d'origine bretonne.° Aujourd'hui, on vend les crêpes dans les «crêperies». On peut aussi faire des crêpes à la maison. Voici une recette° très simple.

les ingrédients

3 oeufs
3 cuillères à soupe de sucre
une pincée° de sel
2 tasses de lait
1 tasse de farine°
1 cuillère à soupe d'huile°
du beurre

les ustensiles

un petit bol   un grand bol

un fouet   une poêle

STRATEGY Reading

Using illustrations When you are reading, the context is not only the printed word. Sometimes the illustrations can help you understand the text. As you read the recipe, try guessing the meanings of the new words by studying the pictures.

D'abord: Pour faire la pâte°

Mettez les oeufs dans le petit bol. Battez-les° bien avec le fouet.

Ajoutez° le sucre, le sel et un peu de lait.

Mettez la farine dans le grand bol. Versez° le contenu° du petit bol dans le grand bol.

Ajoutez l'huile et le reste du lait. Mélangez° bien la pâte. Attendez deux heures.

---

bretonne *from Brittany* **recette** *recipe* **pincée** *pinch* **farine** *flour*
huile *oil* **pâte** *batter* **Battez-les** *Beat them* **Ajoutez** *Add* **Versez** *Pour*
contenu *contents* **Mélangez** *Mix, Stir*

Ensuite: Pour faire les crêpes

Chauffez° la poêle. Mettez
du beurre dans la poêle.

Mettez une cuillère de
pâte dans la poêle.

Agitez° la poêle pour
étendre° la pâte.

Retournez° la crêpe quand
elle est dorée.°

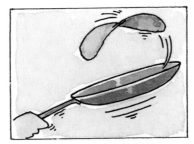

Si vous êtes adroit(e), faites
sauter° la crêpe en l'air.
Si vous n'êtes pas adroit(e),
abstenez-vous!°

Enfin: Pour servir les crêpes

Mettez la crêpe sur une
assiette chaude.
Faites les autres° crêpes.

Mettez du sucre ou de la
confiture sur chaque° crêpe.

Au choix, roulez-la° ou
pliez-la° en quatre.

Chauffez *Heat* **Agitez** *Shake* **étendre** *spread* **Retournez** *Turn over* **dorée** *golden brown* **faites sauter** *flip*
abstenez-vous *don't try* **autres** *other* **chaque** *each* **roulez-la** *roll it* **pliez-la** *fold it*

Reference Section

CONTENTS

APPENDIX 1   Maps   **R2**

APPENDIX 2   Sound/Spelling Correspondences   **R5**

APPENDIX 3   Numbers   **R7**

APPENDIX 4   Verbs   **R8**

French-English Vocabulary   **R13**

English-French Vocabulary   **R35**

Index   **R49**

Credits   **R52**

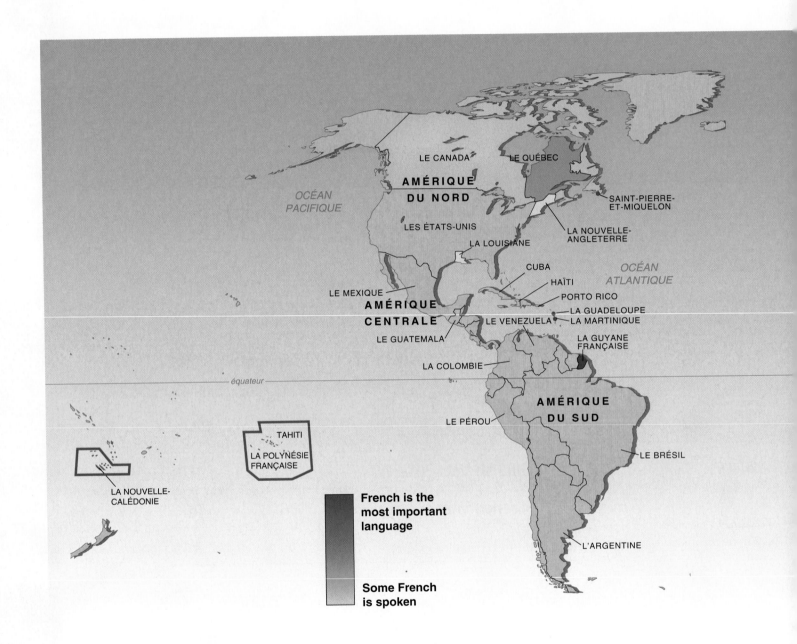

LE CANADA
LE QUÉBEC

AMÉRIQUE
DU NORD

OCÉAN
PACIFIQUE

SAINT-PIERRE-
ET-MIQUELON

LES ÉTATS-UNIS

LA NOUVELLE-
ANGLETERRE

LA LOUISIANE

CUBA

OCÉAN
ATLANTIQUE

HAÏTI

LE MEXIQUE

PORTO RICO

LA GUADELOUPE

AMÉRIQUE
CENTRALE

LE VENEZUELA

LA MARTINIQUE

LE GUATEMALA

LA GUYANE
FRANÇAISE

LA COLOMBIE

équateur

AMÉRIQUE
DU SUD

LE PÉROU

TAHITI
LA POLYNÉSIE
FRANÇAISE

LE BRÉSIL

LA NOUVELLE-
CALÉDONIE

**French is the
most important
language**

L'ARGENTINE

**Some French
is spoken**

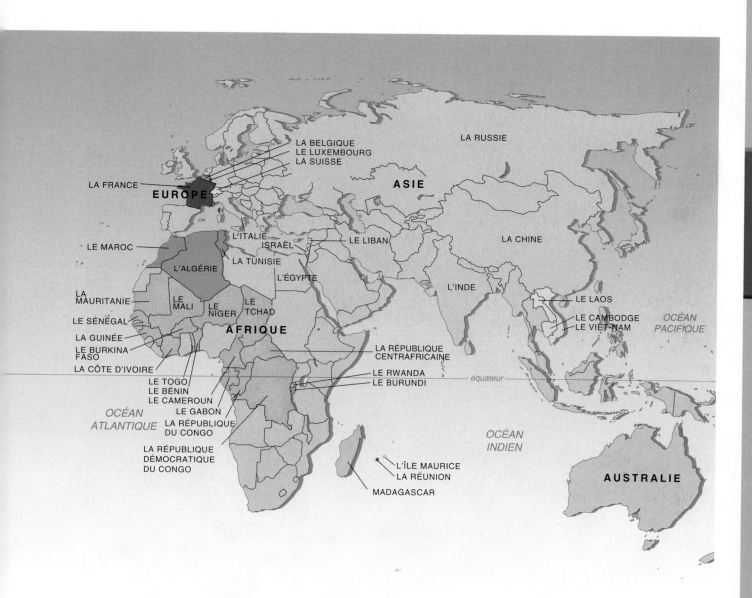

LA BELGIQUE
LE LUXEMBOURG
LA SUISSE

LA RUSSIE

LA FRANCE

EUROPE

ASIE

L'ITALIE
ISRAËL

LE LIBAN

LA CHINE

LE MAROC

L'ALGÉRIE

LA TUNISIE

L'ÉGYPTE

L'INDE

LE LAOS

LA MAURITANIE

LE MALI

LE NIGER

LE TCHAD

LE CAMBODGE
LE VIÊT-NAM

OCÉAN
PACIFIQUE

LE SÉNÉGAL

LA GUINÉE

AFRIQUE

LE BURKINA
FASO

LA CÔTE D'IVOIRE

LA RÉPUBLIQUE
CENTRAFRICAINE

LE TOGO
LE BÉNIN
LE CAMEROUN

LE RWANDA
LE BURUNDI

équateur

LE GABON

OCÉAN
ATLANTIQUE

LA RÉPUBLIQUE
DU CONGO

OCÉAN
INDIEN

LA RÉPUBLIQUE
DÉMOCRATIQUE
DU CONGO

L'ÎLE MAURICE
LA RÉUNION

AUSTRALIE

MADAGASCAR

Map France

- L'ANGLETERRE
- LA BELGIQUE
- L'ALLEMAGNE
- LA MANCHE
- Lille
- NORD [2]
- LE LUXEMBOURG
- HAUTE-NORMANDIE
- PICARDIE
- Le Havre
- Rouen
- Caen
- LORRAINE
- LES VOSGES
- ALSACE
- Versailles
- Paris
- Nancy
- Strasbourg
- RÉGION PARISIENNE [1]
- CHAMPAGNE-ARDENNE
- Colmar
- BRETAGNE
- Rennes
- PAYS DE LA LOIRE
- Loire
- CENTRE
- Seine
- Dijon
- FRANCHE-COMTÉ
- Meuse
- Rhin
- Tours
- BOURGOGNE
- LA SUISSE
- Nantes
- OCÉAN ATLANTIQUE
- POITOU-CHARENTES
- AUVERGNE
- Vichy
- Annecy
- Saône
- LIMOUSIN
- Clermont-Ferrand
- Lyon
- RHÔNE-ALPES
- Bordeaux
- LE MASSIF
- Grenoble
- LES ALPES
- L'ITALIE
- Garonne
- CENTRAL
- Rhône
- AQUITAINE
- Albi
- Nîmes
- Avignon
- PROVENCE-CÔTE D'AZUR [3]
- MONACO
- MIDI-PYRÉNÉES
- Montpellier
- Nice
- Toulouse
- Cannes
- LANGUEDOC-ROUSSILLON
- Marseille
- Saint-Tropez
- LES PYRÉNÉES
- Toulon
- L'ESPAGNE
- MER MÉDITERRANÉE
- LA CORSE

[1] Also known as Île-de-France
[2] Also known as Nord-Pas-de-Calais
[3] Also known as Provence-Alpes-Côte d'Azur *(Bottin 1989)*

VOWELS

SOUND	SPELLING	EXAMPLES
/a/	a, à, â	Madame, là-bas, théâtre
/i/	i, î	visite, Nice, dîne
	y (initial, final, or between consonants)	Yves, Guy, style
/u/	ou, où, oû	Toulouse, où, août
/y/	u, û	tu, Luc, sûr
/o/	o (final or before silent consonant)	piano, idiot, Margot
	au, eau	jaune, Claude, beau
	ô	hôtel, drôle, Côte d'Ivoire
/ɔ/	o	Monique, Noël, jolie
	au	Paul, restaurant, Laure
/e/	é	Dédé, Québec, télé
	e (before silent final z, t, r)	chez, et, Roger
	ai (final or before final silent consonant)	j'ai, mai, japonais
/ɛ/	è	Michèle, Ève, père
	ei	seize, neige, tour Eiffel
	ê	tête, être, Viêt-nam
	e (before two consonants)	elle, Pierre, Annette
	e (before pronounced final consonant)	Michel, avec, cher
	ai (before pronounced final consonant)	française, aime, Maine
/ə/	e (final or before single consonant)	je, Denise, venir
/φ/	eu, oeu	deux, Mathieu, euro, oeufs
	eu (before final se)	nerveuse, généreuse, sérieuse
/œ/	eu (before final pronounced consonant except /z/)	heure, neuf, Lesieur
	oeu	soeur, coeur, oeuf
	oe	oeil

NASAL VOWELS

SOUND	SPELLING	EXAMPLES
/ã/	an, am	France, quand, lampe
	en, em	Henri, pendant, décembre
/ɔ̃/	on, om	non, Simon, bombe
/ɛ̃/	in, im	Martin, invite, impossible
	yn, ym	syndicat, sympathique, Olympique
	ain, aim	Alain, américain, faim
	(o) + in	loin, moins, point
	(i) + en	bien, Julien, viens
	un, um	un, Lebrun, parfum
[/œ̃/	un, um	un, Lebrun, parfum]

Sound-Spelling Correspondences *continued*

SEMI-VOWELS

SOUND	SPELLING	EXAMPLES
/j/	i, y (before vowel sound)	bien, piano, Lyon
	-il, -ill (after vowel sound)	oeil, travaille, Marseille, fille
/ɥ/	u (before vowel sound)	lui, Suisse, juillet
/w/	ou (before vowel sound)	oui, Louis, jouer
/wa/	oi, oî	voici, Benoît
	oy (before vowel)	voyage

CONSONANTS

SOUND	SPELLING	EXAMPLES
/b/	b	Barbara, banane, Belgique
/k/	c (before a, o, u, or consonant)	casque, cuisine, classe
	ch(r)	Christine, Christian, Christophe
	qu, q (final)	Québec, qu'est-ce que, cinq
	k	kilo, Kiki, ketchup
/ʃ/	ch	Charles, blanche, chez
/d/	d	Didier, dans, médecin
/f/	f	Félix, franc, neuf
	ph	Philippe, téléphone, photo
/g/	g (before a, o, u, or consonant)	Gabriel, gorge, légumes, gris
	gu (before e, i, y)	vague, Guillaume, Guy
/ɲ/	gn	mignon, champagne, Allemagne
/ʒ/	j	je, Jérôme, jaune
	g (before e, i, y)	rouge, Gigi, gymnastique
	ge (before a, o, u)	orangeade, Georges, nageur
/l/	l, ll	Lise, elle, cheval
/m/	m	Maman, moi, tomate
/n/	n	banane, Nancy, nous
/p/	p	peu, Papa, Pierre
/r/	r, rr	arrive, rentre, Paris
/s/	c (before e, i, y)	ce, Cécile, Nancy
	ç (before a, o, u)	ça, garçon, déçu
	s (initial or before consonant)	sac, Sophie, reste
	ss (between vowels)	boisson, dessert, Suisse
	t (before i + vowel)	attention, Nations Unies, natation
	x	dix, six, soixante
/t/	t	trop, télé, Tours
	th	Thérèse, thé, Marthe
/v/	v	Viviane, vous, nouveau
/gz/	x	examen, exemple, exact
/ks/	x	Max, Mexique, excellent
/z/	s (between vowels)	désert, Louise, télévision
	z	Suzanne, zut, zéro

A. CARDINAL NUMBERS

0	zéro	18	dix-huit	82	quatre-vingt-deux
1	un (une)	19	dix-neuf	90	quatre-vingt-dix
2	deux	20	vingt	91	quatre-vingt-onze
3	trois	21	vingt et un (une)	100	cent
4	quatre	22	vingt-deux	101	cent un (une)
5	cinq	23	vingt-trois	102	cent deux
6	six	30	trente	200	deux cents
7	sept	31	trente et un (une)	201	deux cent un
8	huit	32	trente-deux	300	trois cents
9	neuf	40	quarante	400	quatre cents
10	dix	41	quarante et un (une)	500	cinq cents
11	onze	50	cinquante	600	six cents
12	douze	60	soixante	700	sept cents
13	treize	70	soixante-dix	800	huit cents
14	quatorze	71	soixante et onze	900	neuf cents
15	quinze	72	soixante-douze	1 000	mille
16	seize	80	quatre-vingts	2 000	deux mille
17	dix-sept	81	quatre-vingt-un (une)	1 000 000	un million

Notes:
1. The word **et** occurs only in the numbers 21, 31, 41, 51, 61, and 71:   **vingt et un** / **soixante et onze**
2. **Un** becomes **une** before a feminine noun: **trente et une filles**
3. **Quatre-vingts** becomes **quatre-vingt** before another number: **quatre-vingt-cinq**
4. **Cents** becomes **cent** before another number: **trois cent vingt**
5. **Mille** never adds an -**s**:   **quatre mille**

B. ORDINAL NUMBERS

1$^{er\ (ère)}$	**premier (première)**	5^e	**cinquième**	9^e	**neuvième**
2^e	**deuxième**	6^e	**sixième**	10^e	**dixième**
3^e	**troisième**	7^e	**septième**	11^e	**onzième**
4^e	**quatrième**	8^e	**huitième**	12^e	**douzième**

Note: **Premier** becomes **première** before a feminine noun: **la première histoire**

C. METRIC EQUIVALENTS

1 gramme	= 0.035 ounces		**1 ounce**	=	**28,349 grammes**
1 kilogramme	= 2.205 pounds		**1 pound**	=	**0,453 kilogrammes**
1 litre	= 1.057 quarts		**1 quart**	=	**0,946 litres**
1 mètre	= 39.37 inches		**1 foot**	=	**30,480 centimètres**
1 kilomètre	= 0.62 miles		**1 mile**	=	**1,609 kilomètres**

APPENDIX 4

A. REGULAR VERBS

INFINITIVE	PRESENT		PASSÉ COMPOSÉ	
parler *(to talk, speak)*	je **parle**	nous **parlons**	j'ai **parlé**	nous **avons parlé**
	tu **parles**	vous **parlez**	tu **as parlé**	vous **avez parlé**
	il **parle**	ils **parlent**	il **a parlé**	ils **ont parlé**

IMPERATIVE: **parle, parlons, parlez**

INFINITIVE	PRESENT		PASSÉ COMPOSÉ	
finir *(to finish)*	je **finis**	nous **finissons**	j'ai **fini**	nous **avons fini**
	tu **finis**	vous **finissez**	tu **as fini**	vous **avez fini**
	il **finit**	ils **finissent**	il **a fini**	ils **ont fini**

IMPERATIVE: **finis, finissons, finissez**

INFINITIVE	PRESENT		PASSÉ COMPOSÉ	
vendre *(to sell)*	je **vends**	nous **vendons**	j'ai **vendu**	nous **avons vendu**
	tu **vends**	vous **vendez**	tu **as vendu**	vous **avez vendu**
	il **vend**	ils **vendent**	il **a vendu**	ils **ont vendu**

IMPERATIVE: **vends, vendons, vendez**

B. -er VERBS WITH SPELLING CHANGES

INFINITIVE	PRESENT		PASSÉ COMPOSÉ
acheter *(to buy)*	j'**achète**	nous **achetons**	j'ai **acheté**
	tu **achètes**	vous **achetez**	
	il **achète**	ils **achètent**	

Verb like **acheter:** amener *(to bring, take along)*

INFINITIVE	PRESENT		PASSÉ COMPOSÉ
espérer *(to hope)*	j'**espère**	nous **espérons**	j'ai **espéré**
	tu **espères**	vous **espérez**	
	il **espère**	ils **espèrent**	

Verbs like **espérer:** célébrer *(to celebrate)*, préférer *(to prefer)*

INFINITIVE	PRESENT		PASSÉ COMPOSÉ
commencer *(to begin, start)*	je **commence**	nous **commençons**	j'ai **commencé**
	tu **commences**	vous **commencez**	
	il **commence**	ils **commencent**	

INFINITIVE	PRESENT		PASSÉ COMPOSÉ
manger *(to eat)*	je **mange**	nous **mangeons**	j'ai **mangé**
	tu **manges**	vous **mangez**	
	il **mange**	ils **mangent**	

Verbs like **manger:** nager *(to swim)*, voyager *(to travel)*

INFINITIVE	PRESENT		PASSÉ COMPOSÉ
payer *(to pay, pay for)*	je **paie**	nous **payons**	j'ai **payé**
	tu **paies**	vous **payez**	
	il **paie**	ils **paient**	

Verbs like **payer:** nettoyer *(to clean)*

C. IRREGULAR VERBS

INFINITIVE	*PRESENT*		*PASSÉ COMPOSÉ*
avoir *(to have, own)*	j'**ai** tu **as** il **a**	nous **avons** vous **avez** ils **ont**	j'ai **eu**
	IMPERATIVE: **aie, ayons, ayez**		
être *(to be)*	je **suis** tu **es** il **est**	nous **sommes** vous **êtes** ils **sont**	j'ai **été**
	IMPERATIVE: **sois, soyons, soyez**		
aller *(to go)*	je **vais** tu **vas** il **va**	nous **allons** vous **allez** ils **vont**	je **suis allé(e)**
	IMPERATIVE: **va, allons, allez**		
boire *(to drink)*	je **bois** tu **bois** il **boit**	nous **buvons** vous **buvez** ils **boivent**	j'ai **bu**
connaître *(to know)*	je **connais** tu **connais** il **connaît**	nous **connaissons** vous **connaissez** ils **connaissent**	j'ai **connu**
devoir *(to have to, should, must)*	je **dois** tu **dois** il **doit**	nous **devons** vous **devez** ils **doivent**	j'ai **dû**
dire *(to say, tell)*	je **dis** tu **dis** il **dit**	nous **disons** vous **dites** ils **disent**	j'ai **dit**
dormir *(to sleep)*	je **dors** tu **dors** il **dort**	nous **dormons** vous **dormez** ils **dorment**	j'ai **dormi**
écrire *(to write)*	j'**écris** tu **écris** il **écrit**	nous **écrivons** vous **écrivez** ils **écrivent**	j'ai **écrit**
	Verb like **écrire**: décrire *(to describe)*		
faire *(to make, do)*	je **fais** tu **fais** il **fait**	nous **faisons** vous **faites** ils **font**	j'ai **fait**

Verbs *continued*

INFINITIVE	*PRESENT*		*PASSÉ COMPOSÉ*
lire *(to read)*	je **lis** tu **lis** il **lit**	nous **lisons** vous **lisez** ils **lisent**	j'ai **lu**
mettre *(to put, place)*	je **mets** tu **mets** il **met**	nous **mettons** vous **mettez** ils **mettent**	j'ai **mis**

Verb like **mettre:** promettre *(to promise)*

INFINITIVE	*PRESENT*		*PASSÉ COMPOSÉ*
ouvrir *(to open)*	j'**ouvre** tu **ouvres** il **ouvre**	nous **ouvrons** vous **ouvrez** ils **ouvrent**	j'ai **ouvert**

Verbs like **ouvrir:** découvrir *(to discover)*, offrir *(to offer)*

INFINITIVE	*PRESENT*		*PASSÉ COMPOSÉ*
partir *(to leave)*	je **pars** tu **pars** il **part**	nous **partons** vous **partez** ils **partent**	je **suis parti(e)**
pouvoir *(to be able, can)*	je **peux** tu **peux** il **peut**	nous **pouvons** vous **pouvez** ils **peuvent**	j'ai **pu**
prendre *(to take)*	je **prends** tu **prends** il **prend**	nous **prenons** vous **prenez** ils **prennent**	j'ai **pris**

Verbs like **prendre:** apprendre *(to learn)*, comprendre *(to understand)*

INFINITIVE	*PRESENT*		*PASSÉ COMPOSÉ*
savoir *(to know)*	je **sais** tu **sais** il **sait**	nous **savons** vous **savez** ils **savent**	j'ai **su**
sortir *(to go out, get out)*	je **sors** tu **sors** il **sort**	nous **sortons** vous **sortez** ils **sortent**	je **suis sorti(e)**
venir *(to come)*	je **viens** tu **viens** il **vient**	nous **venons** vous **venez** ils **viennent**	je **suis venu(e)**

Verb like **venir:** revenir *(to come back)*

INFINITIVE	*PRESENT*		*PASSÉ COMPOSÉ*
voir *(to see)*	je **vois** tu **vois** il **voit**	nous **voyons** vous **voyez** ils **voient**	j'ai **vu**

C. IRREGULAR VERBS *continued*

INFINITIVE	*PRESENT*		*PASSÉ COMPOSÉ*
vouloir	je **veux**	nous **voulons**	j'ai voulu
(to want)	tu **veux**	vous **voulez**	
	il **veut**	ils **veulent**	

D. VERBS WITH *ÊTRE* IN THE *PASSÉ COMPOSÉ*

aller *(to go)*	je **suis allé(e)**	**passer** *(to go by, through)*	je **suis passé(e)**
arriver *(to arrive, come)*	je **suis arrivé(e)**	**rentrer** *(to go home)*	je **suis rentré(e)**
descendre *(to go down)*	je **suis descendu(e)**	**rester** *(to stay)*	je **suis resté(e)**
entrer *(to enter, go in)*	je **suis entré(e)**	**revenir** *(to come back)*	je **suis revenu(e)**
monter *(to go up)*	je **suis monté(e)**	**sortir** *(to go out, get out)*	je **suis sorti(e)**
mourir *(to die)*	il/elle **est mort(e)**	**tomber** *(to fall)*	je **suis tombé(e)**
naître *(to be born)*	je **suis né(e)**	**venir** *(to come)*	je **suis venu(e)**
partir *(to leave)*	je **suis parti(e)**		

FRENCH-ENGLISH VOCABULARY

French-English Vocabulary

The French-English vocabulary contains active and passive words from the text, as well as the important words of the illustrations used within the units. Obvious passive cognates have not been listed.

The numbers following an entry indicate the lesson in which the word or phrase is activated. (**I** stands for the list of classroom expressions at the end of the first **Images** section; **E** stands for **Entracte.**)

Nouns: If the article of a noun does not indicate gender, the noun is followed by *m.* (*masculine*) or *f.* (*feminine*). If the plural (*pl.*) is irregular, it is given in parentheses.

Adjectives: Adjectives are listed in the masculine form. If the feminine form is irregular, it is given in parentheses. Irregular plural forms (*pl.*) are also given in parentheses.

Verbs: Verbs are listed in the infinitive form. An asterisk (*) in front of an active verb means that it is irregular. (For forms, see the verb charts in Appendix 4C.) Irregular present tense forms are listed when they are used before the verb has been activated. Irregular past participle (*p.p.*) forms are listed separately.

Words beginning with an **h** are preceded by a bullet (•) if the **h** is aspirate; that is, if the word is treated as if it begins with a consonant sound.

A

a: il y a there is, there are **9**
à at, in, to **6, 14**
  à côté next door; next to
  à demain see you tomorrow **4B**
  à droite on (to) the right **13**
  à gauche on (to) the left **13**
  à la mode popular; in fashion; fashionable **17**
  à mon avis in my opinion **19**
  à partir de as of, beginning
  à pied on foot **14**
  à samedi! see you Saturday! **4B**
  à vélo by bicycle **14**
abolir to abolish
abondant plentiful, copious, large
  abord: d'abord (at) first **22**
un **abricot** apricot
absolument absolutely
un **accent** accent mark, stress
accepter to accept
des **accessoires** *m.* accessories **17**
un **accord** agreement
  d'accord okay, all right **5**
  être d'accord to agree **6**
un **achat** purchase
  faire des achats to go shopping **21**
  acheter to buy **17, 18**
    acheter + du, de la (*partitive*) to buy (some) **26**

un **acteur, une actrice** actor, actress
une **activité** activity
l' **addition** *f.* check
  adorer to love
une **adresse** address **13**
  quelle est ton adresse? what's your address? **13**
  adroit skilled, skillful
un(e) **adulte** adult
  aéronautique aeronautic, aeronautical
un **aéroport** airport
  affectueusement affectionately (*at the end of a letter*)
une **affiche** poster **9**
  affirmativement affirmatively
l' **Afrique** *f.* Africa
l' **âge** *m.* age
  quel âge a-t-il/elle? how old is he/she? **9**
  quel âge as-tu? how old are you? **2C**
  quel âge a ton père/ta mère? how old is your father/your mother? **2C**
  âgé old
une **agence** agency
  une agence de tourisme tourist office
  une agence de voyages travel agency
  agiter to shake
  agité agitated
  ah! ah!, oh!

  ah bon? oh? really? **8**
  ah non! ah, no!
  ai (*see* **avoir**): **j'ai** I have **9**
  j'ai... ans I'm ... (years old) **2C**
  aider to help **21, 27**
une **aile** wing
  aimer to like **7, 25**
    est-ce que tu aimes...? do you like ...? **5**
    j'aime... I like ... **5**
    j'aimerais I would like
    je n'aime pas... I don't like ... **5**
  ainsi thus
  aîné older
    un frère aîné older brother
    une soeur aînée older sister
  ajouter to add
l' **Algérie** *f.* Algeria (*country in North Africa*)
  algérien (algérienne) Algerian
l' **Allemagne** *f.* Germany
  allemand German
* **aller** to go **14**
  aller + inf. to be going to + *inf.* **14**
  allez (*see* **aller**): **allez-vous-en** go away!
  allez-y come on!, go ahead!, do it!
  comment allez-vous? how are you? **1C**
  allô! hello! (*on the telephone*)
  allons (*see* **aller**): **allons-y** let's go! **14**

alors so, then **11**

une **alouette** lark

les **Alpes** *f.* (the) Alps

l' **alphabet** *m.* alphabet

l' **Alsace** *f.* Alsace *(province in eastern France)*

amener to bring *(a person)* **18, 27**

américain American **1B, 11**

à l'américaine American-style

un **Américain, une Américaine** American person

l' **Amérique** *f.* America

un **ami, une amie** *(close)* friend **2A**

amicalement love *(at the end of a letter)*

l' **amitié** *f.* friendship

amitiés best regards *(at the end of a letter)*

amusant funny, amusing **11**

amuser to amuse

s'amuser to have fun

on s'est bien amusé! we had a good time!

un **an** year

avoir... ans to be ... (years old) **10**

il/elle a... ans he/she is ... (years old) **2C**

j'ai... ans I'm ... (years old) **2C**

l'an dernier last year

par an per year

un **ananas** pineapple

ancien (ancienne) former, old, ancient

un **âne** donkey

un **ange** angel

anglais English **1B, 11**

un **Anglais, une Anglaise** English person

un **animal** *(pl.* **animaux)** animal

une **animation** live entertainment

animé animated, lively

une **année** year **4B**

Bonne année! Happy New Year! **24**

toute l'année all year long

un **anniversaire** birthday **4B**

bon anniversaire! happy birthday! **24**

c'est quand, ton anniversaire? when is your birthday? **4B**

mon anniversaire est le (2 mars) my birthday is (March 2nd) **4B**

un **annuaire** telephone directory

un **anorak** ski jacket

les **antiquités** *f.* antiquities, antiques

août *m.* August **4B**

un **appareil-photo** *(pl.* **appareils-photo)** (still) camera **9**

un **appartement** apartment **13**

s' **appeler** to be named, called

comment s'appelle...? what's ...'s name? **2B**

comment s'appelle-t-il/elle? what's his/her name? **9**

comment t'appelles-tu? what's your name? **1A**

il/elle s'appelle... his/her name is ... **2B**

je m'appelle... my name is ... **1A**

apporter to bring *(things)* **18**

apporter quelque chose à quelqu'un to bring something to someone **27**

apporte-moi (apportez-moi) bring me **I**

* **apprendre (à)** + *inf.* to learn (to) **26**

apprécier to appreciate

approprié appropriate

après after **21;** after, afterwards **22, 23**

d'après according to

l' **après-midi** *m.* afternoon **21**

cet après-midi this afternoon **23**

de l'après-midi in the afternoon, P.M. **4A**

demain après-midi tomorrow afternoon **23**

hier après-midi yesterday afternoon **23**

l' **arabe** *m.* Arabic *(language)*

un **arbre** tree

un arbre généalogique family tree

l' **arche** *f.* **de Noé** Noah's Ark

l' **argent** *m.* money **20**

l' **argent de poche** allowance, pocket money

arrêter to arrest; to stop

arriver to arrive, come **14**

j'arrive! I'm coming!

une **arrivée** arrival

un **arrondissement** district

un **artifice: le feu d'artifice** fireworks

un **artiste, une artiste** artist

as *(see* **avoir): est-ce que tu as...?** do you have ...? **9**

un **ascenseur** elevator

un **aspirateur** vacuum cleaner

asseyez-vous! sit down! **I**

assez rather **11;** enough

assieds-toi! sit down! **I**

une **assiette** plate **25**

assister à to go to, attend **21**

associer to associate

l' **Atlantique** *m.* Atlantic Ocean

attendre to wait, wait for **20**

attention *f.:* **faire attention** to be careful, pay attention **8**

attentivement carefully

au (à + le) to (the), at (the), in (the) **6, 14**

au revoir! good-bye! **1C**

une **auberge** inn

une auberge de campagne country inn **27**

aucun: ne... aucun none, not any

aujourd'hui today **4B, 23**

aujourd'hui, c'est... today is ... **4B**

aussi also, too **1B, 7**

aussi... que as ... as **19**

une **auto (automobile)** car, automobile **9**

une auto-école driving school

un **autobus** bus

un **autocar** touring bus **21**

l' **automne** *m.* autumn, fall

en automne in (the) autumn, fall **4C**

autre other **25**

d'autres others

un(e) autre another

aux (à + les) to (the), at (the), in (the) **14**

avant before **21**

avant hier the day before yesterday

en avant let's begin

avantageux (avantageuse) reasonable, advantageous

avec with **6**

avec moi, avec toi with me, with you 5

avec qui? with who(m)? 8

une avenue avenue 13

un avion airplane, plane 21

en avion by airplane 21

un avis opinion

avis de recherche missing person's bulletin

à mon avis in my opinion 19

à votre avis in your opinion

* avoir to have 10

avoir… ans to be … (years old) 10

avoir besoin de to need 20

avoir chaud to be warm, hot 22

avoir de la chance to be lucky 22

avoir envie de to feel like, want 20

avoir faim to be hungry 10

avoir froid to be cold 22

avoir lieu to take place

avoir raison to be right 22

avoir soif to be thirsty 10, 22

avoir tort to be wrong 22

avril *m.* April 4B

B

le babyfoot tabletop soccer game

le babysitting: faire du babysitting to baby-sit

les bagages *m.* bags, baggage

bain: un maillot de bain bathing suit 17

un baladeur portable player 9

une banane banana 25

une bande dessinée comic strip

des bandes dessinées comics

la Bannière étoilée Star-Spangled Banner

une banque bank

une barbe: quelle barbe! what a pain! *(colloq.)*

bas: en bas downstairs 13

au bas at the bottom

le baseball baseball 15

basé based

le basket (basketball) basketball 15

jouer au basket to play basketball 5

des baskets *m.* hightops (sneakers) 17

un bateau boat, ship 21

un bateau-mouche sightseeing boat

la batterie drums 15

battre to beat

bavard talkative

beau (bel, belle; *m.pl.* beaux) handsome, good-looking, beautiful 9, 12, 19

il est beau he is good-looking, handsome 9

il fait beau it's beautiful (nice) out 4C

un beau-frère stepbrother, brother-in-law

un beau-père stepfather, father-in-law

beaucoup (de) much, very much, many, a lot 7

la beauté beauty

un bec beak

bel (*see* beau) beautiful, handsome 19

belge Belgian

la Belgique Belgium

belle (*see* beau) beautiful 9, 12, 19

elle est belle she is beautiful 9

une belle-mère stepmother, mother-in-law

une belle-sœur stepsister, sister-in-law

les Bermudes *f.* Bermuda

le besoin need

avoir besoin de to need, to have to 20

des besoins d'argent money needs

bête dumb, silly 11

le beurre butter 25

une bibliothèque library 13

une bicyclette bicycle 9

bien well, very well, carefully 7

bien sûr of course 5

ça va bien everything's fine (going well) 1C

ça va très bien I'm (everything's) very well 1C

c'est bien that's good (fine) 12

eh bien! well! 18

je veux bien (…) I'd love to (…), I do, I want to 5, 26

oui, bien sûr… yes, of course … 5

très bien very well 7

bientôt: à bientôt! see you soon!

bienvenue welcome

le bifteck steak

un bifteck de tortue turtle steak

bilingue bilingual

un billet bill, paper money 20; ticket

la biologie biology

une biscotte dry toast

blaff de poisson *m.* fish stew

blanc (blanche) white E1, 12

Blanche-Neige Snow White

blanchir to blanch, turn white

bleu blue E1, 12

blond blonde 9

il/elle est blond(e) he/she is blond 9

un blouson jacket 17

* boire to drink 26

une boisson drink, beverage 3B, 25

une boîte box

un bol deep bowl

bon (bonne) good 12

bon marché *(inv.)* inexpensive 17

ah bon? oh, really? 8

de bonne humeur in a good mood

il fait bon the weather's good (pleasant) 4C

le bonheur happiness

bonjour hello 1A, 1C

une botte boot 17

une bouche mouth E2

une boucherie butcher shop

le boudin sausage

une boulangerie bakery

un boulevard boulevard 13

une boum party *(colloq.)* 14

une boutique boutique, shop 17

boxe: un match de boxe boxing match

un bras arm E2

brésilien (brésilienne) Brazilian

la Bretagne Brittany *(province in northwestern France)*

bricoler to do things around the house

broche: à la broche on the spit

bronzé tan

un **bruit** noise
brun brown, dark-haired **9**
il/elle est brun(e) he/she has dark hair **9**
brunir to turn brown
Bruxelles Brussels
le **bulletin de notes** report card
un **bureau** desk **I, 9**; office
un **bus** bus
en bus by bus **14**
un **but** goal; end

C

ça that, it
ça fait combien? ça fait… how much is that (it)? that (it) is … **3C**
ça, là-bas that (one), over there **9**
ça va? how's everything? how are you? **1C**
ça va everything's fine, I'm OK **1C**
ça va (très) bien, ça va bien everything's going very well, everything's fine (going well) **1C**
ça va comme ci, comme ça everything's (going) so-so **1C**
ça va (très) mal things are going (very) badly **1C**
regarde ça look at that **9**
une **cabine d'essayage** fitting room
les **cabinets** *m.* toilet
un **cadeau** (*pl.* **cadeaux**) gift, present
cadet (cadette) younger
un frère cadet (a) younger brother
une soeur cadette (a) younger sister
le **café** coffee **3B**
un café au lait coffee with hot milk
un **café** café (*French coffee shop*) **6**
au café to (at) the café **6**
un **cahier** notebook **I, 9**
une **calculatrice** calculator **9**
un **calendrier** calendar
un **camarade, une camarade** classmate **9**

le **Cambodge** Cambodia (*country in Asia*)
un **cambriolage** burglary
un **cambrioleur** burglar
une **caméra** movie camera
la **campagne** countryside **21**
à la campagne to (in) the countryside **21**
une auberge de campagne country inn
le **Canada** Canada
canadien (canadienne) Canadian **1B, 11**
un **Canadien, une Canadienne** Canadian person
un **canard** duck
la **cantine de l'école** school cafeteria **25**
un **car** touring bus **21**
un car scolaire school bus
une **carotte** carrot **25**
des carottes râpées grated carrots
un **carré** square
le Vieux Carré *the French Quarter in New Orleans*
une **carte** map **I**; card
une carte postale postcard
les cartes *f.* (playing) cards **15**
jouer aux cartes to play cards **15**
un **cas** case
en cas de in case of
une **casquette** (baseball) cap **17**
une **cassette** cassette tape
une **cassette vidéo** videotape **9**
le **catch** wrestling
une **cathédrale** cathedral
une **cave** cellar
un **CD** CD, compact disc **9**
ce (c') this, that, it
ce n'est pas that's/it's not **12**
ce que what
ce sont these are, those are, they are **12**
c'est it's, that's **2A, 9, 12**
c'est + *day of the week* it's … **4B**
c'est + *name or noun* it's … **2A**
c'est bien/mal that's good/bad **12**
c'est combien? how much is that/it? **3C**
c'est le (12 octobre) it's (October 12) **4B**

qu'est-ce que c'est? what is it? what's that? **9**
qui est-ce? who's that/this? **9**
ce (cet, cette; ces) this, that, these, those **18**
ce… -ci this… (over here) **18**
ce mois-ci this month **23**
ce n'est pas it's (that's) not **12**
ce soir this evening, tonight **23**
un **cédérom (un CD-ROM)** CD-ROM
une **cédille** cedilla
une **ceinture** belt **17**
cela that
célèbre famous
cent one hundred **2B, 17**
cent un, cent deux 101, 102 **17**
deux cents, trois cents, … neuf cents 200, 300, … 900 **17**
une **centaine** about a hundred
un **centime** centime (*1/100 of a euro*)
un **centre** center
un centre commercial shopping center **13**
les **céréales** *f.* cereal **25**
une **cerise** cherry **25**
certain certain
certains some of them
ces (*see* **ce**) these, those **18**
c'est (*see* **ce**)
cet (*see* **ce**) this, that **18**
cette (*see* **ce**) this, that **18**
chacun each one, each person
une **chaise** chair **I, 9**
une **chaîne** (TV) channel
une **chaîne hi-fi** stereo set **9**
une mini-chaîne compact stereo
la **chaleur** heat, warmth
une **chambre** bedroom **9, 13**
un **champion, une championne** champion
la **chance** luck
avoir de la chance to be lucky **22**
bonne chance! good luck! **23**
une **chanson** song
chanter to sing **5, 7**
un **chanteur, une chanteuse** singer

un **chapeau** (*pl.* **chapeaux**) hat **17**
chaque each, every
charmant charming
un **chat** cat **2C, E4**
un **château** (*pl.* **châteaux**) castle
chatter to chat (online)
chaud warm, hot
  avoir chaud to be warm (hot) (*people*) **22**
  il fait chaud it's warm (hot) (*weather*) **4C**
chauffer to warm, heat up
un **chauffeur** driver
une **chaussette** sock **17**
une **chaussure** shoe **17**
un **chef** boss; chef
une **chemise** shirt **17**
un **chemisier** blouse **17**
cher (chère) expensive; dear **17**
chercher to look for, to get, to find **17**
  je cherche… I'm looking for… **17**
un **cheval** (*pl.* **chevaux**) horse **E4**
les **cheveux** *m.* hair **E2**
chez + *person* at (to) someone's house **14**; at (to) the office of
  chez moi (toi, lui…) (at) home **15**
chic (*inv.*) nice; elegant, in style
  une chic fille a great girl
un **chien** dog **2C**
la **chimie** chemistry
chinois Chinese **11**
le **chinois** Chinese (*language*)
le **chocolat** hot chocolate, cocoa **3B**
  une glace au chocolat chocolate ice cream
choisir to choose **19**
un **choix** choice
  au choix choose one, your choice
une **chorale** choir
une **chose** thing **9**
  quelque chose something **24**
chouette great, terrific **12, 17**
le **cidre** cider
un **cinéaste, une cinéaste** film maker
un **cinéma** movie theater **13**
  le cinéma the movies
  au cinéma to (at) the movies, movie theater **6**

cinq five **1A**
cinquante fifty **1C**
cinquième fifth **16**
une **circonstance** circumstance
cité: la Cité Interdite Forbidden City
une **clarinette** clarinet **15**
une **classe** class
  en classe in class **6**
classique classical
un **clavier** keyboard **15**
un **client, une cliente** customer
un **clip** music video
un **cochon** pig
un **coiffeur, une coiffeuse** hairdresser
un **coin** spot
une **coïncidence** coincidence
le **Colisée** the Coliseum (*a large stadium built by the Romans*)
des **collants** *m.* (pair of) tights, pantyhose **17**
un **collège** junior high school
une **colonie** colony
une **colonne** column
combien how much **20**
  combien coûte…? how much does…cost? **3C, 17**
  combien de how much, how many **20**
  combien de temps? how long?
  combien d'heures? how many hours?
  ça fait combien? how much is this (it)? **3C**
  c'est combien? how much is this (it)? **3C**
combinaison spatiale space suit
commander to order
comme like, as, for
  comme ci, comme ça so-so
  ça va comme ci, comme ça everything's so-so **1C**
commencer to begin, start
comment? how? **8**; what?
  comment allez-vous? how are you? **1C**
  comment est-il/elle? what's he/she like? what does he/she look like? **9**
  comment dit-on… en français? how do you say … in French? **I**
  comment lire reading hints

  comment s'appelle…? what's…'s name? **2B**
  comment s'appelle-t-il/elle? what's his/her name? **9**
  comment t'appelles-tu? what's your name? **1A**
  comment trouves-tu…? what do you think of…? **17**
  comment vas-tu? how are you? **1C**
un **commentaire** comment, commentary
commercial: un centre commercial shopping center **13**
le **commérage** gossip
communiquer to communicate
un **compact (disc), un CD** compact disc, CD **9**
complément object
compléter to complete
* **comprendre** to understand **26**
  je (ne) comprends (pas) I (don't) understand **I**
compter to count (on); to expect, intend
concerne: en ce qui concerne as for
un **concert** concert **14**
un **concombre** cucumber
la **confiture** jam **25**
confortable comfortable **13**
une **connaissance** acquaintance
  faire connaissance (avec) to become acquainted (with)
* **connaître** to know, be acquainted with; (*in passé composé*) to meet for the first time **28**
  tu connais…? do you know…? are you acquainted with…? **2B**
connu (*p.p. of* **connaître**) knew, met **28**
un **conseil** piece of advice, counsel
  des conseils *m.* advice
un **conservatoire** conservatory
une **consonne** consonant
se **contenter** to limit oneself
le **contenu** contents
continuer to continue **13**
une **contradiction** disagreement
une **contravention** (traffic) ticket
cool cool, neat

un **copain, une copine** friend, pal
  2A
  **un petit copain, une petite
    copine** boyfriend,
    girlfriend
  copier to copy
une **copine** friend **2A**
  coréen (coréenne) Korean
un **corps** body
  correspondant corresponding
  correspondre to correspond,
    agree
la **Corse** Corsica *(French island off
    the Italian coast)*
un **costume** man's suit
la **Côte d'Azur** Riviera *(southern
    coast of France on the
    Mediterranean)*
la **Côte d'Ivoire** Ivory Coast
    *(French-speaking country in
    West Africa)*
  côté: à côté (de) next door;
    next to
une **côtelette de porc** pork chop
le **cou** neck **E2**
une **couleur** color **12**
  de quelle couleur …? what
    color …? **12**
un **couloir** hall, corridor
  coup: dans le coup with it
  courage: bon courage! good
    luck! **23**
  courageux (courageuse)
    courageous
le **courrier électronique** e-mail,
    electronic mail
une **course** race
  faire les courses to go
    shopping *(for food)* **25**
  court short **17**
un **cousin, une cousine** cousin **2C**,
    16
le **coût: le coût de la vie** cost of
    living
un **couteau** *(pl.* **couteaux)** knife
    25
  coûter to cost
  combien coûte…? how
    much does…cost? **3C, 17**
  il (elle) coûte… it costs…**3C**
un **couturier, une couturière**
    fashion designer
un **couvert** place setting **25**
un **crabe** crab

des **matoutou crabes** stewed
    crabs with rice
la **craie** chalk
  un morceau de craie piece of
    chalk **I**
une **cravate** tie **17**
un **crayon** pencil **I, 9**
  créer to create
un **crétin** idiot
une **crêpe** crepe (pancake) **3A**
une **crêperie** crepe restaurant
une **crevaison** flat tire
une **croisade** crusade
un **croissant** crescent (roll) **3A**
une **cuillère** spoon **25**
  une cuillère à soupe soup
    spoon
la **cuisine** cooking **25**
une **cuisine** kitchen **13**
  cuit cooked
  culturel (culturelle) cultural
  curieux (curieuse) curious,
    strange
la **curiosité** curiosity
le **cybercafé** internet café
un **cyclomoteur** moped

D

  d'abord (at) first **22**
  d'accord okay, all right
    être d'accord to agree **6**
    oui, d'accord yes, okay **5**
une **dame** lady, woman *(polite term)*
    2A
les **dames** *f.* checkers *(game)* **15**
  dangereux (dangereuse)
    dangerous
  dans in **9**
  danser to dance **5, 7**
la **date** date **4B**
  quelle est la date? what's the
    date? **4B**
  de (d') of, from, about **6, 15**
    de l'après-midi in the
      afternoon **4A**
    de quelle couleur…? what
      color …? **12**
    de qui? of whom? **8**
    de quoi? about what?
    de temps en temps from
      time to time
    pas de not any, no **10, 26**
  débarquer to land

  décembre *m.* December **4B**
  décider (de) to decide (to)
une **déclaration** statement
  décoré decorated
* **découvrir** to discover
* **décrire** to describe
    décrivez… describe…
un **défaut** shortcoming
un **défilé** parade
  dégoûtant: c'est dégoûtant! it's
    (that's) disgusting **27**
  dehors outside
    en dehors de outside of
  déjà already; ever
  déjeuner to eat (have) lunch **25**
le **déjeuner** lunch **25**
    le petit déjeuner breakfast **25**
  délicieux (délicieuse) delicious
    26
  demain tomorrow **4B**
    à demain! see you
      tomorrow! **4B**
    demain, c'est… (jeudi)
      tomorrow is … (Thursday)
      4B
  demander (à) to ask **28**
    demandez … ask …
un **demi-frère** half-brother
une **demi-soeur** half-sister
  demi: … heures et demie half
    past … **4A**
    midi et demi half past noon
      4A
    minuit et demi half past
      midnight **4A**
  démodé out of style,
    unfashionable **17**
un **démon** devil
une **dent** tooth
un **départ** departure
se **dépêcher: dépêchez-vous!**
    hurry up!
  dépend: ça dépend that
    depends
une **dépense** expense
  dépenser to spend (money) **20**
  dernier (dernière) last **23**
  derrière behind, in back of **9**
  des some, any **10;** of (the), from
    (the), about (the) **15**
le **désert** desert
  désirer to wish, want
    vous désirez? what would
      you like? may I help you?
      3B, 17

French-English Vocabulary · *continued*

désolé sorry
le **dessert** dessert **25**
le **dessin** art, drawing
   un **dessin animé** cartoon
détester to hate, detest **1C**
deux two **1A**
deuxième second **16**
   le **deuxième étage** third
      floor
devant in front of **9**
développer to develop
deviner to guess
* **devoir** to have to, should, must
   27
un **devoir** homework assignment **I**
les **devoirs** *m.* homework
   faire mes devoirs to do my
      homework **21**
d'habitude usually
différemment differently
différent different
difficile hard, difficult **12**
la **dignité** dignity
dimanche *m.* Sunday **4B**
dîner to have dinner **7, 25**
   dîner au restaurant to have
      dinner at a restaurant **5**
le **dîner** dinner, supper **25**
* **dire** to say, tell **28**
   que veut dire…? what
      does…mean? **I**
directement straight
un **directeur, une directrice**
   director, principal
dirigé directed, guided
dis! (*see* **dire**) say!, hey! **12**
   dis donc! say there!, hey
      there! **12**
discuter to discuss
une **dispute** quarrel, dispute
distrait absent-minded
dit (*p.p. of* **dire**) said
dit (*see* **dire**): **comment dit-**
   on… en français? how do
      you say…in French? **I**
dites… (*see* **dire**) say…, tell…
dix ten **1A, 1B**
dix-huit eighteen **1B**
dixième tenth **16**
dix-neuf nineteen **1B**
dix-sept seventeen **1B**
un **docteur** doctor
dois (*see* **devoir**): **je dois** I have
   to (must) **5**
domestique domestic

les **animaux** *m.* **domestiques**
   pets **2C**
dommage! too bad! **7**
donner (à) to give (to) **27, 28**
   donne-moi… give me… **3A, I**
   donnez-moi… give me **3B, I**
   s'il te plaît, donne-moi…
      please, give me… **3B**
doré golden brown
* **dormir** to sleep
le **dos** back **E2**
une **douzaine** dozen **25**
douze twelve **1B**
douzième twelfth **16**
droit: tout droit straight **13**
droite right
   à droite to (on) the right **13**
drôle funny **12**
du (de + le) of (the), from (the)
   15; some, any **26**
   du matin in the morning,
      A.M. **4A**
   du soir in the evening, P.M.
      4A
dû (*p.p. of* **devoir**) had to **27**
dur hard
   des oeufs (*m.*) **durs** hard-
      boiled eggs
durer to last
un **DVD** DVD **9**
dynamique dynamic

E

l' **eau** *f.* (*pl.* **eaux**) water **25**
   l'eau minérale mineral water
      25
un **échange** exchange
les **échecs** *m.* chess **15**
une **éclosion** hatching
une **école** school **13**
économiser to save money
écouter to listen to **I, 7**
   écouter la radio to listen to
      the radio **5**
   écouter des CD to listen to
      CDs **21**
l' **écran** *m.* screen (computer)
* **écrire** to write **28**
l' **éducation** *f.* education
   l'éducation civique civics
   l'éducation physique
      physical education
une **église** church **13**

égyptien (égyptienne)
   Egyptian
eh bien! well! **18**
   électronique: une guitare
      électrique electric guitar
élégant elegant **17**
un **éléphant** elephant **E4**
un **élève, une élève** pupil, student
   9
élevé high
elle she, it **3C, 6, 10;** her **15**
   elle coûte… it costs … **3C**
   elle est (canadienne) she's
      (Canadian) **2B**
   elle s'appelle… her name is
      … **2B**
embrasser: je t'embrasse love
   and kisses (*at the end of a*
   letter)
un **emploi du temps** time-table (*of*
   work)
emprunter à to borrow from
en in, on, to, by
   en avion by airplane, plane **21**
   en bas (haut) downstairs
      (upstairs) **13**
   en bus (métro, taxi, train,
      voiture) by bus (subway,
      taxi, train, car) **14**
   en ce qui concerne as for
   en face opposite, across (the
      street)
   en fait in fact
   en famille at home
   en plus in addition
   en scène on stage
   en solde on sale
   va-t'en! go away! **14**
un **endroit** place **14**
un **enfant, une enfant** child **16**
enfin at last **22**
ensuite then, after that **22**
entendre to hear **20**
entier (entière) entire
l' **entracte** *m.* interlude
entre between
une **entrée** entry (*of a house*)
un **entretien** discussion
envers toward
l' **envie** *f.* envy; feeling
   avoir envie de to want; to
      feel like, want to **20**
envoyer to send
   envoyer un mail to send an
      e-mail

épicé hot (spicy)

une épicerie grocery store

les épinards *m.* spinach

une équipe team

une erreur error, mistake

es *(see* être)

  tu es + *nationality* you are …
1B

  tu es + *nationality?* are you
…? 1B

  tu es de…? are you from …?
1B

l' escalade *f.* rock climbing 21

  faire de l'escalade to go rock
climbing 21

un escalier staircase

un escargot snail

l' Espagne *f.* Spain

espagnol Spanish 11

  parler espagnol to speak
Spanish 5

espérer to hope 18

un esprit spirit

essayer to try on, to try

l' essentiel *m.* the important
thing

est *(see* être)

  est-ce que (qu')…? *phrase
used to introduce a question*
6

  c'est… it's …, that's … 2A,
2C, 12

  c'est le + *date* it's … 4B

  il/elle est + nationality
he/she is … 2B

  n'est-ce pas…? isn't it? 6

  où est…? where is …? 6

  quel jour est-ce? what day is
it? 4B

  qui est-ce? who's that (this)?
2A, 9

l' est *m.* east

et and 1B, 6

  et demi(e), et quart half past,
quarter past 4A

  et toi? and you? 1A

établir to establish

un étage floor of a building, story

les États-Unis *m.* United States

été *(p.p. of* être) been, was 23

l' été *m.* summer

  en été in (the) summer 4C

  l'heure d'été daylight
savings time

étendre to spread

---

une étoile star

étrange strange

étranger (étrangère) foreign

* être to be 6

  être à to belong to

  être d'accord to agree 6

une étude study

un étudiant, une étudiant(e)
(college) student 9

étudier to study 5, 7

eu *(p.p. of* avoir) had 23

  il y a eu there was

euh… er …, uh …

  euh non… well, no

un euro euro; monetary unit of
Europe

européen (européenne)
European

eux they, them 15

  eux-mêmes themselves

un événement event 14

un examen exam, test

  réussir à un examen to pass
an exam, a test

excusez-moi excuse me 13

un exemple example

  par exemple for instance

un exercice exercise

  faire des exercices to
exercise

exiger to insist

expliquer to explain

  expliquez… explain …

exprimer to express

exquis: c'est exquis! it's
exquisite! 26

extérieur: à l'extérieur outside

extraordinaire extraordinary

  il a fait un temps
extraordinaire! the
weather was great!

F

face: en face (de) opposite,
across (the street) from

facile easy 12

faible weak

la faim hunger

  avoir faim to be hungry 22

  j'ai faim I'm hungry 3A

  tu as faim? are you hungry?
3A

* faire to do, make 8

---

faire attention to pay
attention, be careful 8

faire de + *activity* to do, play,
study, participate in 21

faire des achats to go
shopping 21

faire les courses to go
shopping 25

faire mes devoirs to do my
homework 21

faire les magasins to go
shopping (browsing from
store to store)

faire partie de to be a
member of

faire sauter to flip

faire un match to play a
game (match) 8

faire un pique-nique to have
a picnic 21

faire un voyage to take a trip
8

faire une promenade to take
a walk 8

faire une promenade à pied
(à vélo, en voiture) to take
a walk (a bicycle ride, a
drive) 14

fait *(p.p. of* faire) did, done,
made 23

fait: en fait in fact

fait *(see* faire): ça fait
  combien? how much is that
(it)? 3C

  ça fait… euros that's (it's) …
euros 3C

  il fait (beau, etc.) it's
(beautiful, etc.) *(weather)*
4C

  quel temps fait-il? what
(how) is the weather? 4C

fameux: c'est fameux! it's
superb! 26

familial with the family

une famille family 2C, 16

  en famille at home

un fana, une fana fan *(person)*

un fantôme ghost

la farine flour

fatigué tired

faux (fausse) false 12

favori (favorite) favorite

les félicitations *f.* congratulations

une femme woman 9; wife 16

une fenêtre window I, 9

une **fermer** to close **I**
une **fête** party, holiday
le **feu d'artifice** fireworks
une **feuille** sheet, leaf **I**
 une **feuille de papier** sheet of paper **I**
un **feuilleton** series, serial story *(in newspaper)*
février *m.* February **4B**
fiche-moi la paix! leave me alone! *(colloq.)* **28**
la **fièvre** fever
une **fille** girl **2A**; daughter **16**
un **film** movie **14, 21**
 un **film policier** detective movie
un **fils** son **16**
la **fin** end
finalement finally **22**
fini *(p.p. of finir)* over, finished **23**
finir to finish **19**
flamand Flemish
un **flamant** flamingo
une **fleur** flower
un **fleuve** river
un **flic** cop *(colloq.)*
une **flûte** flute **15**
une **fois** time
 à la fois at the same time
la **folie: à la folie** madly
folklorique: une chanson folklorique folksong
fonctionner to work, function
fondé founded
le **foot (football)** soccer **15**
 le **football américain** football
 jouer au foot to play soccer **5**
une **forêt** forest
formidable great!
fort strong
 plus fort louder **I**
un **fouet** whisk
une **fourchette** fork **25**
la **fourrure** fur
 un **manteau de fourrure** fur coat
frais: il fait frais it's cool *(weather)* **4C**
une **fraise** strawberry **25**
un **franc** franc *(former monetary unit of France)* **3C**
 ça fait... francs that's (it's) ... francs **3C**
français French **1B, 11**

comment dit-on... en français? how do you say... in French? **I**
parler français to speak French **5**
le **français** French *(language)*
un **Français, une Française** French person
la **France** France **6**
 en France in France **6**
francophone French-speaking
un **frère** brother **2C, 16**
des **frites** *f.* French fries **25**
 un **steak-frites** steak and French fries **3A**
froid cold
 avoir froid to be (feel) cold *(people)* **22**
 il fait froid it's cold out *(weather)* **4C**
le **fromage** cheese **25**
 un **sandwich au fromage** cheese sandwich
un **fruit** fruit **25**
furieux (furieuse) furious
une **fusée** rocket

gagner to earn, to win **20**
un **garage** garage **13**
un **garçon** boy **2A**; waiter
une **gare** train station
une **garniture** side dish
un **gâteau** *(pl. gâteaux)* cake **25**
gauche left
 à gauche to (on) the left **13**
une **gelée** jelly
généralement generally
généreux (généreuse) generous
la **générosité** generosity
génial brilliant; terrific **12**
des **gens** *m.* people **10**
gentil (gentille) nice, kind **11**; sweet
la **géographie** geography
une **girafe** giraffe **E4**
une **glace** ice cream **3A, 25**; mirror, ice
glacé iced
 un **thé glacé** iced tea **25**
un **goûter** afternoon snack
une **goyave** guava

grand tall **9**; big, large **12**; big *(size of clothing)* **17**
un **grand magasin** department store **17**
une **grande surface** big store, self-service store
grandir to get tall; to grow up
une **grand-mère** grandmother **2C, 16**
un **grand-père** grandfather **2C, 16**
les **grands-parents** *m.* grandparents **16**
grec (grecque) Greek
un **grenier** attic
une **grillade** grilled meat
une **grille** grid
grillé: le pain grillé toast
 une **tartine de pain grillé** buttered toast
la **grippe** flu
gris gray **12**
gros (grosse) fat, big
grossir to gain weight, get fat **19**
la **Guadeloupe** Guadeloupe *(French island in the West Indies)*
une **guerre** war
une **guitare** guitar **9, 15**
un **gymnase** gym

habillé dressed
habiter (à) to live (in + *city*) **7**
Haïti Haiti *(French- and Creole-speaking country in the West Indies)*
un • **hamburger** hamburger **3A**
les • **haricots** *m.* **verts** green beans **25**
la • **hâte** haste
 en hâte quickly
• **haut** high
 en haut upstairs **13**
 plus haut above
• **hélas!** too bad!
hésiter to hesitate
l' **heure** *f.* time, hour; o'clock **4A**
 ... heure(s) (dix) (ten) past ... **4A**
 ... heure(s) et demie half past ... **4A**
 ... heure(s) et quart quarter past ... **4A**

... heure(s) moins (dix) (ten) of ... **4A**

... heure(s) moins le quart quarter to ... **4A**

à... heures at ... o'clock **6**

à quelle heure...? at what time ...? **8**

à quelle heure est...? at what time is ...? **4A**

il est... heure(s) it's ... o'clock **4A**

par heure per hour, an hour

quelle heure est-il? what time is it? **4A**

heureux (heureuse) happy

hier yesterday **23**

avant-hier the day before yesterday

un **hippopotame** hippopotamus **E4**

une **histoire** story, history

l' **hiver** *m.* winter **4C**

en hiver in (the) winter **4C**

• **hollandais** Dutch

un **homme** man **9**

honnête honest

un **hôpital** (*pl.* **hôpitaux**) hospital **13**

une **horreur** horror

quelle horreur! what a scandal! how awful!

un • **hors-d'oeuvre** appetizer **25**

un • **hot dog** hot dog **3A**

un **hôte, une hôtesse** host, hostess

un **hôtel** hotel **13**

un hôtel de police police department

l' **huile** *f.* oil

• **huit** eight **1A**

huitième eighth **16**

l' **humeur** *f.* mood

de bonne humeur in a good mood

un **hypermarché** shopping center

ici here **6**

une **idée** idea

c'est une bonne idée! it's (that's) a good idea! **20**

ignorer to be unaware of

il he, it **3C, 6, 10**

il est it is **12**

il/elle est + *nationality* he/she is ... **2B**

il y a there is, there are **9**

il y a + du, de la (*partitive*) there is (some) **26**

il y a eu there was

il n'y a pas de... there is/are no ... **10**

est-ce qu'il y a...? is there, are there ...? **9**

qu'est-ce qu'il y a...? what is there ...? **9**

une **île** island

illustré illustrated

un **immeuble** apartment building **13**

un **imper (imperméable)** raincoat **17**

l' **impératif** *m.* imperative (command) mood

impoli impolite

l' **importance** *f.* importance

ça n'a pas d'importance it doesn't matter

importé imported

impressionnant impressive

l' **imprimante** *f.* printer

inactif (inactive) inactive

inclure to include

l' **indicatif** *m.* area code

indiquer to indicate, show

indiquez... indicate ...

infâme: c'est infâme! that's (it's) awful! **27**

infect: c'est infect! that's revolting! (*colloq.*) **27**

les **informations** *f.* news

l' **informatique** *f.* computer science

s' **informer (de)** to find out about

un **ingénieur** engineer

un **ingrédient** ingredient **25**

un **inspecteur, une inspectrice** police detective

un **instrument** instrument **15**

intelligent intelligent **11**

intéressant interesting **11**

l' **intérieur** *m.* interior, inside

l' **Internet** *m.* the Internet

surfer sur l'Internet (sur le Net) to surf the Internet

interroger to question

interviewer to interview

inutilement uselessly

un **inventaire** inventory

un **invité, une invitée** guest

inviter to invite **7**

israélien (israélienne) Israeli

italien (italienne) Italian **11**

un **Italien, une Italienne** Italian person

j' (*see* **je**)

jamais ever; never

jamais le dimanche! never on Sunday!

ne... jamais never **24**

la **Jamaïque** Jamaica

une **jambe** leg **E2**

un **jambon** ham **25**

janvier *m.* January **4B**

japonais Japanese **11**

un **jardin** garden **13**

jaune yellow **E1, 12**

jaunir to turn yellow

je I **6**

un **jean** pair of jeans **15**

un **jeu** (*pl.* **jeux**) game **17**

les jeux d'ordinateur computer games

les jeux télévisés TV game shows

les jeux vidéo video games

jeudi *m.* Thursday **4B**

jeune young **9**

les **jeunes** *m.* young people

un **job** (part-time) job

le **jogging** jogging **21**

faire du jogging to jog **21**

un **jogging** jogging suit **25**

joli pretty (*for girls, women* **17**; (*for clothing*) **17**

plus joli(e) que prettier than

jouer to play **7**

jouer à + *game, sport* to play a game, sport **15**

jouer aux jeux vidéo to play video games **5**

jouer au tennis (volley, basket, foot) to play tennis (volleyball, basketball, soccer) **5**

jouer de + *instrument* to play a musical instrument **15**

un **jour** day **4B, 21**

le Jour de l'An New Year's Day

par jour per week, a week

FRENCH-ENGLISH VOCABULARY

quel jour est-ce? what day is it? **8**

un **journal** (*pl.* **journaux**) newspaper

une **journée** day, whole day
  bonne journée! have a nice day!
joyeux (joyeuse) happy
juillet *m.* July **4B**
  le quatorze juillet Bastille Day *(French national holiday)*
juin *m.* June **4B**

un **jumeau** (*pl.* **jumeaux**), une **jumelle** twin

une **jupe** skirt **17**

le **jus** juice
  le jus d'orange orange juice **3B, 25**
  le jus de pomme apple juice **3B, 25**
  le jus de raisin grape juice **3B**
  le jus de tomate tomato juice **3B**
jusqu'à until
juste right, fair
  le mot juste the right word

un **kangourou** kangaroo **E4**
le **ketchup** ketchup **25**
un **kilo** kilogram
  un kilo (de) a kilogram (of) **25**

l' (*see* **le, la**)
la **the 2B, 10;** her, it **28**
là here, there **6**
  là-bas over there **6**
  ça, là-bas that (one), over there **9**
  ce... -là that ... (over there) **18**
  oh là là! uh, oh!; oh, dear!; wow!; oh, yes!
laid ugly
laisser (un message) to leave (a message)
  laisser: laisse-moi tranquille! leave me alone! **28**

le **lait** milk **25**
une **lampe** lamp **9**
une **langue** language
large wide
laver to wash **21**
  se laver to wash (oneself), wash up
le **the 2B, 10;** him, it **28**
  le + *number* + *month* the ... **4B**
  le (lundi) on (Mondays) **10**
une **leçon** lesson
un **légume** vegetable **25**
lent slow
les the **10;** them **28**
une **lettre** letter
leur(s) their **16**
leur (to) them **28**
se **lever: lève-toi!** stand up! **I**
  levez-vous! stand up! **I**
un **lézard** lizard **E4**
le **Liban** Lebanon *(country in the Middle East)*
libanais Lebanese
libéré liberated
une **librairie** bookstore
libre free
un **lieu** place, area
  avoir lieu to take place
une **ligne** line
limité limited
la **limonade** lemon soda **3B**
un **lion** lion **E4**
 * **lire** to read
  comment lire reading hints
  lisez... (*see* **lire**) read ... **I**
une **liste** list
  une liste des courses shopping list
un **lit** bed **9**
un **living** living room *(informal)*
un **livre** book **I, 9**
une **livre** metric pound **25**
local (*m.pl.* **locaux**) local
une **location** rental
logique logical
logiquement logically
loin far **13**
  loin d'ici far (from here)
le **loisir** leisure, free time
un **loisir** leisure-time activity
Londres London
long (longue) long **17**
longtemps (for) a long time

moins longtemps que for a shorter time
le **loto** lotto, lottery, bingo
louer to rent **21**
un **loup** wolf **E4**
lui him **15;** (to) him/her **28**
lui-même: en lui-même to himself
lundi *m.* Monday **4B**
des **lunettes** *f.* glasses **17**
  des lunettes de soleil sunglasses **17**
le **Luxembourg** Luxembourg
un **lycée** high school

m' (*see* **me**)
M. (monsieur) Mr. (Mister) **1C**
ma my **2C, 16**
  et voici ma mère and this is my mother **2C**
  ma chambre my bedroom **9**
une **machine** machine
  une machine à coudre sewing machine
Madagascar Madagascar *(French-speaking island off of East Africa)*
Madame (Mme) Mrs., ma'am **1C**
Mademoiselle (Mlle) Miss **1C**
un **magasin** store, shop **13, 17**
  faire les magasins to go shopping (browsing from store to store)
  un grand magasin department store **17**
magnétique magnetic
un **magnétophone** tape recorder
un **magnétoscope** VCR (videocassette recorder)
magnifique magnificent
mai *m.* May **4B**
maigre thin, skinny
maigrir to lose weight, get thin **19**
un **mail** e-mail
un **maillot de bain** bathing suit **17**
une **main** hand **E2**
maintenant now **7, 23**
mais but **6**
  j'aime..., mais je préfère... I like ..., but I prefer ... **5**

je regrette, mais je ne peux pas... I'm sorry, but I can't ... **5**

mais oui! sure! **6**

mais non! of course not! **6**

une **maison** house **13**

à la maison at home **6**

mal badly, poorly **1C, 7**

le **mal** evil

ça va mal things are going badly **1C**

ça va très mal things are going very badly **1C**

c'est mal that's bad **12**

malade sick

malheureusement unfortunately

malin clever

manger to eat **7**

j'aime manger I like to eat **5**

manger + du, de la *(partitive)* to eat (some) **26**

une salle à manger dining room **13**

un **manteau** *(pl.* **manteaux)** overcoat **17**

un manteau de fourrure fur coat

un **marchand, une marchande** merchant, shopkeeper, dealer

un **marché** open-air market **25**

un marché aux puces flea market

bon marché *(inv.)* inexpensive **17**

marcher to work, to run *(for objects)* **9;** to walk *(for people)* **9**

il/elle (ne) marche (pas) bien it (doesn't) work(s) well **9**

est-ce que la radio marche? does the radio work? **9**

mardi *m.* Tuesday **4B**

le **Mardi gras** Shrove Tuesday

un **mari** husband **16**

le **mariage** wedding, marriage

marié married

une **marmite** covered stew pot

le **Maroc** Morocco *(country in North Africa)*

une **marque** brand (name)

une **marraine** godmother

marrant fun

marron *(inv.)* brown **12**

mars *m.* March **4B**

martiniquais from Martinique

la **Martinique** Martinique *(French island in the West Indies)*

un **match** game, (sports) match **14**

faire un match to play a game, (sports) match **8**

les **maths** *f.* math

le **matin** morning **21**

ce matin this morning **23**

demain matin tomorrow morning **23**

du matin in the morning, A.M. **4A**

hier matin yesterday morning **23**

le matin in the morning

des **matoutou crabes** *m.* stewed crabs with rice

mauvais bad **12**

c'est une mauvaise idée that's a bad idea

il fait mauvais it's bad *(weather)* **4C**

la **mayonnaise** mayonnaise **25**

me (to) me **27**

méchant mean, nasty **11**

un **médecin** doctor

un médecin de nuit doctor on night duty

la **Méditerranée** Mediterranean Sea

meilleur(e) better, best **19**

un **mél** e-mail

mélanger to mix, stir

même same; even

eux-mêmes themselves

les mêmes choses the same things

une **mémoire** memory

mentionner to mention

la **mer** ocean, shore **21**

à la mer to (at) the sea **21**

merci thank you **1C**

oui, merci yes, thank you **5**

mercredi *m.* Wednesday **4B**

une **mère** mother **2C, 16**

mériter to deserve

mes my **16**

la **messagerie vocale** voice mail

le **métro** subway

en métro by subway **14**

* **mettre** to put on, to wear **17;** to put, to place, to turn on **18**

mettre la table to set the table **25**

mexicain Mexican **11**

midi *m.* noon **4A**

mieux better

mignon (mignonne) cute **11**

militaire military

mille one thousand **2B, 17**

minérale: l'eau *f.* **minérale** mineral water **25**

une **mini-chaîne** compact stereo **9**

minuit *m.* midnight **4A**

mis *(p.p. of* **mettre)** put, placed **23**

mixte mixed

Mlle Miss **1C**

Mme Mrs. **1C**

une **mob (mobylette)** motorbike, moped **9**

moche plain, ugly **17**

la **mode** fashion

à la mode popular; in fashion; fashionable **17**

moderne modern **13**

moi me **1A, 15;** (to) me **27**

moi, je m'appelle (Marc) me, my name is (Marc) **1A**

avec moi with me **5**

donne-moi give me **3A**

donnez-moi give me **3B**

excusez-moi... excuse me ... **13**

prête-moi... lend me ... **3C**

s'il te plaît, donne-moi... please give me ... **3B**

un **moine** monk

moins less

moins de less than

moins... que less ... than **19**

... heure(s) moins (dix) (ten) of ... **4A**

... heure(s) moins le quart quarter of ... **4A**

un **mois** month **4B, 21**

ce mois-ci this month **23**

le mois dernier last month **23**

le mois prochain next month **23**

par mois per month, a month

mon (ma; mes) my **2C, 16**

mon anniversaire est le... my birthday is the ... **4B**

voici mon père this is my father **2C**

French-English Vocabulary   *continued*

le **monde** world
　du monde in the world
　tout le monde everyone
la **monnaie** money; change
Monsieur (M.) Mr., sir **1C**
un **monsieur** (*pl.* **messieurs**)
　gentleman, man (*polite term*) **2A**
une **montagne** mountain **21**
　à la montagne to (at) the mountains **21**
une **montre** watch **9**
　montrer à to show … to **27, 28**
　montre-moi (montrez-moi) show me **I**
un **morceau** piece
　un morceau de craie piece of chalk **I**
un **mot** word
une **moto** motorcycle **9**
la **moutarde** mustard
un **mouton** sheep
　moyen (moyenne) average, medium
　en moyenne on the average
un **moyen** means
　muet (muette) silent
le **multimédia** multimedia
un **musée** museum **13**
la **musique** music **15**

n' (*see* **ne**)
nager to swim **7**
　j'aime nager I like to swim **5**
une **nationalité** nationality **1B**
nautique: le ski nautique water-skiing **21**
ne (n')
　ne… aucun none, not any
　ne… jamais never **24**
　ne… pas not **6**
　ne… personne nobody **24**
　ne… plus no longer
　ne… rien nothing **24**
　n'est-ce pas? right?, no?, isn't it (so)?, don't you?, aren't you? **6**
né born
nécessaire necessary
négatif (négative) negative
　négativement negatively
la **neige** snow

neiger to snow
　il neige it's snowing **4C**
le **Net** the Internet
nettoyer to clean **21**
neuf nine **1A**
neuvième ninth **16**
un **neveu** (*pl.* **neveux**) nephew
un **nez** nose **E2**
une **nièce** niece
un **niveau** (*pl.* **niveaux**) level
Noël *m.* Christmas
　à Noël at Christmas **21**
noir black **E1, 12**
un **nom** name; noun
un **nombre** number
　nombreux (nombreuses) numerous
　nommé named
non no **1B, 6**
　non plus neither
　mais non! of course not! **6**
le **nord** north
　le nord-est northeast
normalement normally
nos our **16**
une **note** grade
notre (*pl.* **nos**) our **16**
la **nourriture** food **25**
nous we **6**; us **15**; (to) us **27**
nouveau (nouvel, nouvelle; *m.pl.* **nouveaux)** new **19**
la **Nouvelle-Angleterre** New England
la **Nouvelle-Calédonie** New Caledonia (*French island in the South Pacific*)
novembre *m.* November **4B**
　le onze novembre Armistice Day
la **nuit** night
un **numéro** number

objectif (objective) objective
un **objet** object **9**
une **occasion** occasion; opportunity
occupé occupied
un **océan** ocean
octobre *m.* October **4B**
une **odeur** odor
un **oeil** (*pl.* **yeux**) eye **E2**
un **oeuf** egg **25**

officiel (officielle) official
offert (*p.p. of* **offrir**) offered
* **offrir** to offer, to give
oh là là! uh,oh!, oh, dear!, wow!, oh, yes!
un **oiseau** (*pl.* **oiseaux**) bird
une **omelette** omelet **3A**
on one, they, you, people **20**
　on est… today is …
　on va dans un café? shall we go to a café?
　on y va let's go
　comment dit-on… en français? how do you say … in French? **I**
un **oncle** uncle **2C, 16**
onze eleven **1B**
opérer to operate
l' **or** *m.* gold
orange (*inv.*) orange (*color*) **E1, 12**
une **orange** orange (*fruit*)
　le jus d'orange orange juice **3B, 25**
un **ordinateur** computer **9**
　un ordinateur portable laptop computer
une **oreille** ear **E2**
organiser to organize **7**
originairement originally
l' **origine** *f.* origin, beginning
　d'origine bretonne from Brittany
orthographiques: les signes *m.* **orthographiques** spelling marks
ou or **1B, 6**
où where **6, 8**
　où est…? where is …? **6**
　où est-ce? where is it? **13**
　d'où? from where? **15**
oublier to forget
l' **ouest** *m.* west
oui yes **1B, 6**
　oui, bien sûr… yes, of course … **5**
　oui, d'accord… yes, okay … **5**
　oui, j'ai… yes, I have … **9**
　oui, merci… yes, thank you … **5**
　mais oui! sure! **6**
un **ouragan** hurricane
un **ours** bear **E4**
ouvert open

* **ouvrir** to open
    ouvre… (ouvrez…) open … I

P

le **pain** bread **25**
  pâle pale
un **pamplemousse** grapefruit **25**
une **panne** breakdown
    une panne d'électricité power failure
un **pantalon** pants, trousers **17**
une **panthère** panther
une **papaye** papaya
le **papier** paper
    une feuille de papier a sheet (piece) of paper I
  Pâques *m.* Easter **21**
    à Pâques at Easter **21**
  par per
    par exemple for example
    par jour per day
un **parc** park **13**
    un parc public city park
  parce que (parce qu') because **8**
  pardon excuse me **13, 17**
les **parents** *m.* parents, relatives **16**
  paresseux (paresseuse) lazy
  parfait perfect
    rien n'est parfait nothing is perfect
  parfois sometimes
  parisien (parisienne) Parisian
  parler to speak, talk **I, 7**
    parler à to speak (talk) to **28**
    parler (français, anglais, espagnol) to speak (French, English, Spanish) **5**
un **parrain** godfather
une **partie** part
* **partir** to leave
    à partir de as of, beginning
  partitif (partitive) partitive
  pas not
    ne… pas not **6**
    pas de not a, no, not any **10, 26**
    pas du tout not at all, definitely not **15**
    pas possible not possible
    pas toujours not always **5**
    pas très bien not very well

le **passé composé** compound past tense
  passer to spend (time) **21**; to pass by
  passionnément passionately
une **pâte** dough
  patient patient
le **patinage** ice skating, roller skating
une **patinoire** skating rink
une **pâtisserie** pastry, pastry shop
une **patte** foot, paw *(of bird or animal)*
  pauvre poor **20**
  payer to pay, pay for **20**
un **pays** country
un **PC portable** laptop computer
la **peau** skin, hide
* **peindre** to paint
  peint painted
une **pellicule** film (camera)
  pendant during **21**
  pénétrer to enter
  pénible bothersome, a pain **12**
  penser to think **17**
    penser de to think of **17**
    penser que to think that **17**
    qu'est-ce que tu penses de…? what do you think of …? **17**
une **pension** inn, boarding house
  Pentecôte *f.* Pentecost
  perdre to lose, to waste **20**
  perdu *(p.p. of* **perdre***)* lost
un **père** father **2C, 16**
* **permettre** to permit
un **perroquet** parrot
  personne (de) nobody **24**
    ne… personne nobody, not anybody, not anyone **24**
une **personne** person **2A**
  personnel (personnelle) personal
  personnellement personally
  péruvien (péruvienne) Peruvian
  petit small, short **9, 12, 17**
    il/elle est petit(e) he/she is short **9**
    un petit copain, une petite copine boyfriend, girlfriend
    plus petit(e) smaller
le **petit déjeuner** breakfast **25**

  prendre le petit déjeuner to have breakfast **25**
le **petit-fils, la petite-fille** grandson, granddaughter
les **petits pois** *m.* peas **25**
  peu little, not much
    un peu a little, a little bit **7**
    un peu de a few
  peut *(see* **pouvoir***)*
  peut-être perhaps, maybe **6**
  peux *(see* **pouvoir***)*
    est-ce que tu peux…? can you …? **5**
    je regrette, mais je ne peux pas… I'm sorry, but I can't … **5**
la **photo** photography
une **phrase** sentence I
la **physique** physics
un **piano** piano **15**
une **pie** magpie **E4**
une **pièce** coin **20**; room
un **pied** foot **E2**
    à pied on foot **14**
    faire une promenade à pied to take a walk **14**
  piloter to pilot (a plane)
une **pincée** pinch
le **ping-pong** Ping-Pong **15**
un **pique-nique** picnic **14**
    faire un pique-nique to have a picnic **21**
une **piscine** swimming pool **13**
une **pizza** pizza **3A**
un **placard** closet
une **plage** beach **13**
  plaît: s'il te plaît please (informal) **3A**; excuse me (please)
    s'il te plaît, donne-moi… please, give me … **3B**
    s'il vous plaît please (formal) **3B**; excuse me (please)
un **plan** map
la **planche à voile** windsurfing **21**
    faire de la planche à voile to windsurf **21**
une **plante** plant
un **plat** dish, course (of a meal) **25**
    le plat principal main course
un **plateau** tray
  pleut: il pleut it's raining **4C**
  plier to fold

French-English Vocabulary *continued*

plumer to pluck
plus more
  plus de more than
  plus joli que prettier than
  plus... que more ... than, ...
    -er than **19**
  en plus in addition
  le plus the most
  ne... plus no longer, no
    more
  non plus neither
plusieurs several
une **poche** pocket
  l'argent *m.* **de poche**
    allowance, pocket money
une **poêle** frying pan
un **point de vue** point of view
une **poire** pear **25**
  pois: les petits pois *m.* peas **25**
un **poisson** fish **E4, 25**
  un poisson rouge goldfish
  blaff de poisson fish stew
  poli polite
un **politicien, une politicienne**
    politician
un **polo** polo shirt **17**
une **pomme** apple
  le jus de pomme apple juice
    3B, 25
une **pomme de terre** potato **25**
  une purée de pommes de
    terre mashed potatoes
le **porc: une côtelette de porc**
    pork chop
un **portable** cell phone **9**
une **porte** door **I, 9**
un **porte-monnaie** change purse,
    wallet
  porter to wear **17**
  portugais Portuguese
  poser: poser une question to
    ask a question
une **possibilité** possibility
la **poste** post office
  pouah! yuck! yech!
une **poule** hen **E4**
le **poulet** chicken **25**
  pour for **6**; in order to **21**
    pour que so that
    pour qui? for whom? **8**
le **pourcentage** percentage
  pourquoi why **8**
* **pouvoir** to be able, can, may
    27
  pratique practical

pratiquer to participate in
des **précisions** *f.* details
  préféré favorite
  préférer to prefer **18**; to like (in
    general)
  je préfère I prefer **5**
  tu préférerais? would you
    prefer?
  premier (première) first **16**
  le premier de l'an New
    Year's Day
  le premier étage second
    floor
  le premier mai Labor Day *(in*
    France)
  c'est le premier juin it's June
    first **4B**
* **prendre** to take, to have *(food)*
    I, 26
  prendre + du, de la *(partitive)*
    to have (some) **26**
  prendre le petit déjeuner
    to have breakfast **25**
un **prénom** first name
  préparer to prepare;
    to prepare for **21**
  près nearby **13**
  près d'ici nearby, near here
  tout près very close
une **présentation** appearance
  la présentation extérieure
    outward appearance
des **présentations** *f.* introductions
  presque almost
  pressé in a hurry
  prêt ready
un **prêt** loan
  prêter à to lend to, to loan **27,**
    28
    prête-moi... lend me... **3C**
  principalement mainly
le **printemps** spring **4C**
  au printemps in the spring
    4C
  pris *(p.p. of* **prendre***)* took **26**
un **prix** price
  quel est le prix ...? what's
    the price ...? **17**
un **problème** problem
  prochain next **21, 23**
  le week-end prochain next
    weekend **21**
un **produit** product
un **prof, une prof** teacher
    (informal) **2A, 9**

un **professeur** teacher **9**
  professionnel (professionnelle)
    professional
un **programme** program
un **projet** plan
une **promenade** walk
  faire une promenade à pied
    to go for a walk **8, 14**
  faire une promenade à vélo
    to go for a ride (by bike) **14**
  faire une promenade en
    voiture to go for a drive
    (by car) **14**
* **promettre** to promise
une **promo** special sale
  proposer to suggest
  propre own
un **propriétaire, une propriétaire**
    landlord/landlady, owner
la **Provence** Provence *(province in*
    southern France)
  pu *(p.p. of* **pouvoir***)* could, was
    able to **27**
  n'a pas pu was not able to
  public: un parc public city park
  un jardin public public
    garden
la **publicité** commercials,
    advertising, publicity
une **puce** flea
  un marché aux puces flea
    market
  puis then, also
  puisque since
un **pull** sweater, pullover **17**
les **Pyrénées** (the) Pyrenees
    (mountains between France
    and Spain)

  qu' *(see* **que***)*
une **qualité** quality
  quand when **8**
  c'est quand, ton
    anniversaire? when is
    your birthday? **4B**
une **quantité** quantity **25**
  quarante forty **1C**
un **quart** one quarter
  ... heure(s) et quart quarter
    past ... **4A**
  ... heure(s) moins le quart
    quarter of ... **4A**

un quartier district, neighborhood **13**
  un joli quartier a nice neighborhood **13**
quatorze fourteen **1B**
quatre four **1A**
quatre-vingt-dix ninety **2B**
quatre-vingts eighty **2B**
quatrième fourth **16**
que that, which
  que veut dire…? what does … mean? **I**
  qu'est-ce que (qu') what (*phrase used to introduce a question*) **8**
  qu'est-ce que c'est? what is it? what's that? **9**
  qu'est-ce que tu penses de…? what do you think of …? **17**
  qu'est-ce que tu veux? what do you want? **3A**
  qu'est-ce qu'il y a? what is there? **9**; what's the matter?
  qu'est-ce qui ne va pas? what's wrong?
un Québécois, une Québécoise person from Quebec
québécois from Quebec
quel (quelle) what, which, what a **18**
  quel (quelle)…! what a…!
  quel âge a ta mère/ton père? how old is your mother/your father? **2C**
  quel âge a-t-il/elle? how old is he/she? **9**
  quel âge as-tu? how old are you? **2C**
  quel est le prix…? what is the price …? **17**
  quel jour est-ce? what day is it? **4B**
  quel temps fait-il? what's (how's) the weather? **4C**
  quelle est la date? what's the date? **4B**
  quelle est ton adresse? what's your address? **13**
  quelle heure est-il? what time is it? **4A**
  à quelle heure? at what time? **4A**

à quelle heure est…? at what time is …? **4A**
de quelle couleur…? what color is …? **12**
quelqu'un someone **24**
quelque chose something **24**
quelques some, a few **9**
une question question
une queue tail
qui who, whom **8**
  qui est-ce? who's that (this)? **2A, 9**
  qui se ressemble… birds of a feather …
  à qui? to whom? **8**
  avec qui? with who(m)? **8**
  c'est qui? who's that? (*casual speech*)
  de qui? about who(m)? **8**
  pour qui? for who(m)? **8**
quinze fifteen **1B**
quoi? what? **9**
quotidien (quotidienne) daily
la vie quotidienne daily life

raconter to tell about
une radio radio **9**
  écouter la radio to listen to the radio **5**
  une radiocassette boom box **9**
  une radiocassette/CD boom box with CD
raisin: le jus de raisin grape juice **3B**
une raison reason
  avoir raison to be right **22**
ranger to pick up **21**
rapidement rapidly
un rapport relationship
une raquette racket **9**
  une raquette de tennis tennis racket **15**
rarement rarely, seldom **7**
un rayon department (*in a store*)
réalisé made, directed
récemment recently
une recette recipe
  recherche: un avis de recherche missing person's bulletin

un récital (*pl.* **récitals**) (musical) recital
reconstituer to reconstruct
un réfrigérateur refrigerator
refuser to refuse
regarder to look at, watch **I, 7**
  regarde ça look at that **9**
  regarder la télé to watch TV **5**
un régime diet
  être au régime to be on a diet
régional (*m.pl.* **régionaux**) regional
regretter to be sorry
  je regrette, mais… I'm sorry, but … **5**
régulier (régulière) regular
une reine queen
rencontrer to meet **21**
une rencontre meeting, encounter
un rendez-vous date, appointment **14**
  j'ai un rendez-vous à… I have a date, appointment at … **4A**
  rendre visite à to visit, come to visit **20, 28**
la rentrée first day back at school in fall
rentrer to go back, come back **14**; to return, go back, come back **24**
réparer to fix, repair **21**
un repas meal **25**
* **repeindre** to repaint
répéter to repeat **I**
répondre (à) to answer, respond (to) **I, 28**
  répondez-lui (moi) answer him (me)
  répondre que oui to answer yes
une réponse answer
un reportage documentary
représenter to represent
réservé reserved
une résolution resolution
un restaurant restaurant **13**
  au restaurant to (at) the restaurant **6**
  dîner au restaurant to have dinner at a restaurant **5**
  un restaurant trois étoiles three star restaurant

rester to stay **14, 24**

retard: un jour de retard one day behind

en retard late

retourner to return; to turn over

réussir to succeed **19**

réussir à un examen to pass an exam **19**

* **revenir** to come back **15**

revoir: au revoir! good-bye! **1C**

le **rez-de-chaussée** ground floor

un **rhinocéros** rhinoceros **E4**

riche rich **20**

rien (de) nothing **24**

rien n'est parfait nothing is perfect

ne… rien nothing **24**

une **rive** (river) bank

une **rivière** river, stream

le **riz** rice **25**

une **robe** dress **17**

le **roller** in-line skating **21**

faire du roller to go in-line skating **21**

des **rollers** in-line skates **21**

romain Roman

le **rosbif** roast beef **25**

rose pink **12**

rosse nasty *(colloq.)*

une **rôtie** toast *(Canadian)*

rôtir to roast

une **roue** wheel

rouge red **E1, 12**

rougir to turn red

rouler to roll

roux (rousse) red-head

une **rue** street **13**

dans la rue (Victor Hugo) on (Victor Hugo) street **13**

russe Russian

S

sa his, her **16**

un **sac** book bag, bag **I**; bag, handbag **9**

sais *(see* **savoir***)*

je sais I know **I, 9, 28**

je ne sais pas I don't know **I, 9**

tu sais you know **28**

une **saison** season **4C**

toute saison all year round (any season)

une **salade** salad **3A, 25**; lettuce **25**

un **salaire** salary

une **salle** hall, large room

une salle à manger dining room **13**

une salle de bains bathroom **13**

une salle de séjour informal living room

un **salon** formal living room **13**

salut hi!, good-bye! **1C**

une **salutation** greeting

samedi Saturday **4B, 23**

samedi soir Saturday night

à samedi! see you Saturday! **4B**

le samedi on Saturdays **10**

une **sandale** sandal **17**

un **sandwich** sandwich **3A**

sans without

des **saucisses** *f.* sausages

le **saucisson** salami **25**

* **savoir** to know *(information)*

je sais I know **I, 9, 28**

je ne sais pas I don't know **I, 9**

tu sais you know **28**

un **saxo (saxophone)** saxophone **15**

une **scène** scene, stage

les **sciences** *f.* **économiques** economics

les **sciences** *f.* **naturelles** natural science

un **scooter** motor scooter **9**

second second

seize sixteen **1B**

un **séjour** stay; informal living room

le **sel** salt **25**

selon according to

selon toi in your opinion

une **semaine** week **4B, 21**

cette semaine this week **23**

la semaine dernière last week **23**

la semaine prochaine next week **23**

par semaine per week, a week

semblable similar

le **Sénégal** Senegal *(French-speaking country in Africa)*

sensationnel (sensationnelle) sensational

séparer to separate

sept seven **1A**

septembre *m.* September **4B**

septième seventh **16**

une **série** series

sérieux (sérieuse) serious

un **serveur, une serveuse** waiter, waitress

servi served

une **serviette** napkin **25**

ses his, her **16**

seul alone, only; by oneself **21**

seulement only, just

un **short** shorts **17**

si if, whether

si! so, yes! *(to a negative question)* **10**

un **signal** *(pl.* **signaux***)* signal

un **signe** sign

un signe orthographique spelling mark

un **singe** monkey **E4**

situé situated

six six **1A**

sixième sixth **16**

le **skate** skateboarding **21**

un **skate** skateboard **21**

faire du skate to go skateboarding **21**

le **ski** skiing

le ski nautique water-skiing **21**

faire du ski to ski **21**

faire du ski nautique to go water-skiing **21**

skier to ski

snob snobbish

le **snowboard** snowboarding **21**

faire du snowboard to go snowboarding **21**

un **snowboard** snowboard **21**

la **Société Nationale des Chemins de Fer (SNCF)** *French railroad system*

une **société** society

un **soda** soda **3B**

une **soeur** sister **2C, 16**

la **soie** silk

la **soif** thirst

avoir soif to be thirsty **22**

j'ai soif I'm thirsty **3B**

tu as soif? are you thirsty? **3B**

un **soir** evening **21**
    ce soir this evening, tonight **23**
    demain soir tomorrow night (evening) **21, 23**
    du soir in the evening, P.M. **4A**
    hier soir last night **23**
    le soir in the evening
une **soirée** (whole) evening; (evening) party
    soixante sixty **1C, 2A**
    soixante-dix seventy **2A**
un **soldat** soldier
un **solde** (clearance) sale
    en solde on sale
la **sole** sole (fish) **25**
le **soleil** sun
    les lunettes f. **de soleil** sunglasses **17**
    sommes (see **être**)
    nous sommes... it is, today is ... (date)
    son (sa; ses) his, her **16**
un **sondage** poll
une **sorte** sort, type, kind
* **sortir** to leave, come out
un **souhait** wish
la **soupe** soup **25**
une **souris** mouse (computer)
    sous under **9**
le **sous-sol** basement
    souvent often **7**
    soyez (see **être**): **soyez logique** be logical
les **spaghetti** m. spaghetti **25**
    spécialement especially
    spécialisé specialized
une **spécialité** specialty
le **sport** sports **15, 21**
    faire du sport to play sports **21**
    des vêtements m. **de sport** sports clothing **17**
    une voiture de sport sports car **15**
    sportif (sportive) athletic **11**
un **stade** stadium **13**
un **stage** sports training camp; internship
une **station-service** gas station
un **steak** steak **3A**
un **steak-frites** steak and French fries **3A**
un **stylo** pen **I, 9**

le **sucre** sugar **25**
le **sud** south
    suggérer to suggest
    suis (see **être**)
    je suis + nationality I'm ... **1B**
    je suis de... I'm from ... **1B**
    suisse Swiss **11**
la **Suisse** Switzerland
    suivant following
    suivi followed
un **sujet** subject, topic
    super terrific **7**; great **12, 17**
un **supermarché** supermarket **13**
    supersonique supersonic
    supérieur superior
    supplémentaire supplementary, extra
    sur on **9**; about
    sûr sure, certain
    bien sûr! of course! **6**
    oui, bien sûr... yes, of course ...! **5**
    tu es sûr(e)? are you sure? **16**
    sûrement surely
la **surface: une grande surface** big store, self-service store
    surfer to go snowboarding
    surfer sur l'Internet (sur le Net) to surf the Internet
    surtout especially
un **survêtement** jogging or track suit **17**
un **sweat** sweatshirt **17**
une **sweaterie** shop specializing in sweatshirts and sportswear
    sympa nice, pleasant (colloq.)
    sympathique nice, pleasant **11**
une **synagogue** Jewish temple or synagogue
un **synthétiseur** electronic keyboard, synthesizer

T

    t' (see **te**)
    ta your **2C, 16**
une **table** table **I, 9**
    mettre la table to set the table **25**
un **tableau** (pl. **tableaux**) chalkboard **I**

    Tahiti Tahiti (French island in the South Pacific)
une **taille** size
    de taille moyenne of medium height or size
un **tailleur** woman's suit
se **taire: tais-toi!** be quiet!
une **tante** aunt **2C, 16**
la **tarte** pie **25**
une **tasse** cup **25**
un **taxi** taxi
    en taxi by taxi **14**
    te (to) you **27**
un **tee-shirt** T-shirt **17**
la **télé** TV **9**
    à la télé on TV
    regarder la télé TV **5**
    télécharger to download
un **téléphone** telephone **9**
    téléphoner (à) to call, phone **5, 7, 28**
    télévisé: des jeux m. **télévisés** TV game shows
un **temple** Protestant church
le **temps** time; weather
    combien de temps? how long?
    de temps en temps from time to time
    quel temps fait-il? what's (how's) the weather? **4C**
    tout le temps all the time
le **tennis** tennis **15**
    jouer au tennis to play tennis **5**
des **tennis** m. tennis shoes, sneakers **17**
un **terrain de sport** (playing) field
une **terrasse** outdoor section of a café, terrace
la **terre** earth
    une pomme de terre potato **25**
    terrifiant terrifying
    tes your **16**
la **tête** head **E2**
le **thé** tea **3B**
    un thé glacé iced tea **25**
un **théâtre** theater **13**
le **thon** tuna **25**
    tiens! look!, hey! **2A, 10**
un **tigre** tiger **E4**
    timide timid, shy **11**
le **tissu** fabric
un **titre** title

toi you **15**
    avec toi with you **5**
    et toi? and you? **1A**
les **toilettes** *f.* bathroom, toilet **13**
un **toit** roof
une **tomate** tomato **25**
    le jus de tomate tomato juice **3B**
un **tombeau** tomb
ton (ta; tes) your **2C, 16**
    c'est quand, ton anniversaire? when's your birthday? **4B**
tort: avoir tort to be wrong **22**
une **tortue** turtle **E4**
    un bifteck de tortue turtle steak
toujours always **7**
    je n'aime pas toujours… I don't always like … **5**
un **tour** turn
    à votre tour it's your turn
la **Touraine** Touraine *(province in central France)*
tourner to turn **13**
la **Toussaint** All Saints' Day *(November 1)*
tout (toute; tous, toutes) all, every, the whole
    tous les jours every day
    tout ça all that
    tout le monde everyone
    tout le temps all the time
    toutes sortes all sorts, kinds
tout completely, very
    tout droit straight **13**
    tout de suite right away
    tout près very close
tout all, everything
    pas du tout not at all **15**
un **train** train **21**
tranquille quiet
    laisse-moi tranquille! leave me alone! **28**
un **travail** *(pl.* **travaux***)* job
travailler to work **5, 7**
une **traversée** crossing
treize thirteen **1B**
trente thirty **1C**
un **tréma** diaeresis *(accent mark)*
très very **11**
    très bien very well **7**
    ça va très bien things are going very well **1C**

ça va très mal things are going very badly **1C**
trois three **1A**
troisième third **16**; *9th grade in France*
trop too, too much **17**
trouver to find, to think of **17**
    comment trouves-tu…? what do you think of …? how do you find …? **17**
    s'y trouve is there
tu you **6**
la **Tunisie** Tunisia *(country in North Africa)*

U

un, une one **1A**; a, an **2A, 10**
unique only
uniquement only
une **université** university, college
l' **usage** *m.* use
un **ustensile** utensil
utile useful
utiliser to use
    en utilisant (by) using
    utilisez… use …

V

va *(see* **aller***)*
    va-t'en! go away! **14**
    ça va? how are you? how's everything? **1C**
    ça va! everything's fine (going well); fine, I'm OK **1C**
    on va dans un café? shall we go to a café?
    on y va let's go
les **vacances** *f.* vacation
    bonnes vacances! have a nice vacation!
    en vacances on vacation **6**
    les grandes vacances summer vacation **21**
une **vache** cow
vais *(see* **aller***)*: **je vais** I'm going **14**
la **vaisselle** dishes
    faire la vaisselle to do the dishes
valable valid

une **valise** suitcase
vanille: une glace à la vanille vanilla ice cream
varié varied
les **variétés** *f.* variety show
vas *(see* **aller***)*
    comment vas-tu? how are you? **1C**
    vas-y! come on!, go ahead!, do it! **14**
le **veau** veal **25**
une **vedette** star
un **vélo** bicycle **9**
    à vélo by bicycle **14**
    faire une promenade à vélo to go for a bicycle ride **14**
un **vélo tout terrain (un VTT)** mountain bike
un **vendeur, une vendeuse** salesperson
vendre to sell **20**
vendredi *m.* Friday **4B**
vendu *(p.p. of* **vendre***)* sold **23**
* **venir** to come **15**
le **vent** wind
une **vente** sale
le **ventre** stomach **E2**
venu *(p.p. of* **venir***)* came, come **24**
vérifier to check
la **vérité** truth
un **verre** glass **25**
verser to pour
vert green **E1, 12**
    les • **haricots** *m.* **verts** green beans **25**
une **veste** jacket **17**
des **vêtements** *m.* clothing **17**
    des vêtements de sport sports clothing **17**
veut *(see* **vouloir***)*: **que veut dire…?** what does … mean? **I**
veux *(see* **vouloir***)*
    est-ce que tu veux…? do you want …? **5**
    je ne veux pas… I don't want … **5**
    je veux… I want … **5, 26**
    je veux bien… I'd love to, I do, I want to … **5, 26**
    qu'est-ce que tu veux? what do you want? **3A**
    tu veux…? do you want …? **3A**

la **viande** meat 25
la **vie** life
   la vie quotidienne daily life
  viens (*see* **venir**)
   viens… come … I
   oui, je viens yes, I'm coming along with you
  vieux (vieil, vieille; *m.pl.* **vieux)** old 19
   le Vieux Carré *the French Quarter in New Orleans*
le **Viêt-nam** Vietnam (*country in Southeast Asia*)
  vietnamien (vietnamienne) Vietnamese
une **vigne** vineyard
un **village** town, village 13
  un petit village small town 13
une **ville** city
  en ville in town 6
  une grande ville big city, town 13
le **vin** wine
  vingt twenty 1B, 1C
  violet (violette) purple, violet E1
un **violon** violin 15
une **visite** visit
  rendre visite à to visit (*a person*) 20, 28
  visiter to visit (*places*) 23, 20
  vite! fast!, quick!
  vive: vive les vacances! three cheers for vacation!
* **vivre** to live
le **vocabulaire** vocabulary
  voici… here is, this is…, here come(s) … 2A
   voici + du, de la (*partitive*) here's some 26
   voici mon père/ma mère here's my father/my mother 2C
  voilà… there is …, there come(s) … 2A

  voilà + du, de la (*partitive*) there's some 26
la **voile** sailing 21
  faire de la voile to sail 21
  la planche à voile windsurfing 21
* **voir** to see 21, 23
  voir un film to see a movie 21
un **voisin, une voisine** neighbor 9
une **voiture** car 9
  une voiture de sport sports car 15
  en voiture by car 14
  faire une promenade en voiture to go for a drive by car 14
une **voix** voice
le **volley (volleyball)** volleyball 15
un **volontaire, une volontaire** volunteer
  comme volontaire as a volunteer
  vos your 16
  votre (*pl.* **vos**) your 16
  voudrais (*see* **vouloir**): **je voudrais** I'd like 3A, 3B, 5, 26
* **vouloir** to want 26
  vouloir + du, de la (*partitive*) to want some (of something) 26
  vouloir dire to mean 26
  voulu (*p.p. of* **vouloir**) wanted 26
  vous you 6; (to) you 27
  vous désirez? what would you like? may I help you? 3B, 17
  s'il vous plaît please 3B
un **voyage** trip
  bon voyage! have a nice trip!
  faire un voyage to take a trip 8
  voyager to travel 5, 7

  vrai true, right, real 12
  vraiment really 15
le **VTT** mountain biking 21
  faire du VTT to go mountain biking 21
un **VTT** mountain bike 21
  vu (*p.p. of* **voir**) saw, seen 23
une **vue** view
  un point de vue point of view

les **WC** *m.* toilet
un **week-end** weekend 21, 23
  bon week-end! have a nice weekend!
  ce week-end this weekend 21, 23
  le week-end on weekends
  le week-end dernier last weekend 23
  le week-end prochain next weekend 21, 23

  y there
  il y a there is, there are 9
  est-ce qu'il y a…? is there …?, are there …? 9
  qu'est-ce qu'il y a? what is there? 9
  allons-y! let's go! 14
  vas-y! come on!, go ahead!, do it! 14
le **yaourt** yogurt 25
des **yeux** *m.* (*sg.* **oeil**) eyes E2

---Z---

un **zèbre** zebra
  zéro zero 1A
  zut! darn! 1C

ENGLISH-FRENCH VOCABULARY

English-French Vocabulary

The English-French vocabulary contains only active vocabulary.

The numbers following an entry indicate the lesson in which the word or phrase is activated. (**I** stands for the list of classroom expressions at the end of the first **Images** section; **E** stands for **Entracte.**)

Nouns: If the article of a noun does not indicate gender, the noun is followed by *m.* (*masculine*) or *f.* (*feminine*). If the plural (*pl.*) is irregular, it is given in parentheses.

Verbs: Verbs are listed in the infinitive form. An asterisk (') in front of an active verb means that it is irregular. (For forms, see the verb charts in Appendix 4C.)

Words beginning with an **h** are preceded by a bullet (•) if the **h** is aspirate; that is, if the word is treated as if it begins with a consonant sound.

a, an un, une **2A, 10**
  a few quelques **25**
  a little (bit) un peu **7**
  a lot beaucoup **7**
able: to be able (to) *pouvoir **27**
about de **15**
  about whom? de qui? **8**
accessories des accessoires *m.* **17**
acquainted: to be acquainted with *connaître **28**
  are you acquainted with …? tu connais…? **2B**
address une adresse **13**
  what's your address? quelle est ton adresse? **13**
after après **21, 22**
  after that ensuite **22**
afternoon l'après-midi *m.* **21**
  in the afternoon de l'après-midi **4A**
  this afternoon cet après-midi **23**
  tomorrow afternoon demain après-midi **23**
  yesterday afternoon hier après-midi **23**
afterwards après **22**
to agree *être d'accord **6**
airplane un avion **21**
  by airplane en avion **21**
all tout
  all right d'accord **5**
  not at all pas du tout **15**
alone seul **21**
  leave me alone! laisse-moi tranquille! **28**
also aussi **1B, 7**

always toujours **7**
  not always pas toujours **5**
A.M. du matin **4A**
am (*see* **to be**)
  I am … je suis + *nationality* **1B**
American américain **1B, 11**
  I'm American je suis américain(e) **1B**
amusing amusant **11**
an un, une **2A, 10**
and et **1B, 6**
  and you? et toi? **1A**
annoying pénible **12**
another un(e) autre
to answer répondre (à) **28**
any des **10**; du, de la, de l', de **26**
  not any pas de **10, 26**
anybody: not anybody ne… personne **24**
anyone quelqu'un **24**
anything quelque chose **24**
  not anything ne… rien **24**
apartment un appartement **13**
  apartment building un immeuble **13**
appetizer un • hors-d'oeuvre **25**
apple une pomme
  apple juice le jus de pomme **3B, 25**
appointment un rendez-vous **14**
  I have an appointment at… j'ai un rendez-vous à… **4A**
April avril *m.* **4B**
are (*see* **to be**)
  are there? est-ce qu'il y a? **9**
  are you…? tu es + *nationality?* **1B**

  there are il y a **9**
  these/those/they are ce sont **12**
arm un bras **E2**
to arrive arriver **14**
  as … as aussi… que **19**
to ask demander (à) **28**
  at à **6**; chez **14**
  at (the) au, à la, à l', aux **14**
  at …'s house chez … **14**
  at … o'clock à … heure(s) **6**
  at home à la maison **6**
  at last enfin **22**
  at the restaurant au restaurant **6**
  at what time? à quelle heure? **4A, 8**
  at what time is …? à quelle heure est …? **4A**
athletic sportif (sportive) **11**
to attend assister à **21**
  attention: to pay attention *faire attention **8**
August août *m.* **4B**
aunt une tante **2C, 16**
automobile une auto, une voiture **9**
autumn l'automne *m.* **4C**
  in (the) autumn en automne **4C**
avenue une avenue **13**
away: go away! va-t'en! **14**

back le dos **E2**
back: to come back rentrer **14, 24**; *revenir **15**
  to go back rentrer **14, 24**
  in back of derrière **9**

bad mauvais **12**
 I'm/everything's (very) bad ça va (très) mal **1C**
 it's bad (weather) il fait mauvais **4C**
 that's bad c'est mal **12**
 too bad! dommage! **7**
badly mal **1C**
 things are going (very) badly ça va (très) mal **1C**
bag un sac **I, 9**
banana une banane **25**
banknote un billet **20**
baseball le baseball **15**
basketball le basket (basketball) **15**
bathing suit un maillot de bain **17**
bathroom une salle de bains **13**
to **be** *être **6**
 to be … (years old) *avoir… ans **10**
 to be able (to) *pouvoir **27**
 to be acquainted with *connaître **28**
 to be active in *faire de + *activity* **21**
 to be careful *faire attention **8**
 to be cold (*people*) *avoir froid **22**; (*weather*) il fait froid **4C**
 to be going to (*do something*) *aller + *inf.* **14**
 to be hot (*people*) *avoir chaud **22**
 to be hungry *avoir faim **10, 22**
 to be lucky *avoir de la chance **22**
 to be present at assister à **21**
 to be right *avoir raison **22**
 to be supposed to *devoir **27**
 to be thirsty *avoir soif **10, 22**
 to be warm (*people*) *avoir chaud **22, 23**
 to be wrong *avoir tort **22**
beach une plage **13**
beans: green beans les •haricots *m.* verts **25**
beautiful beau (bel, belle; *m.pl.* beaux) **9**
 it's beautiful (nice) weather il fait beau **4C**

because parce que (qu') **8**
bed un lit **9**
bedroom une chambre **9, 13**
been été (*p.p. of* *être) **23**
before avant **21, 23**
behind derrière **9**
below en bas **13**
belt une ceinture **17**
best meilleur **19**
better meilleur **19**
beverage une boisson **3B, 25**
bicycle un vélo, une bicyclette **9**
 by bicycle à vélo **14**
 take a bicycle ride *faire une promenade à vélo **14**
big grand **9, 12**
bill (*money*) un billet **20**
birthday un anniversaire **4B**
 my birthday is (March 2) mon anniversaire est le (2 mars) **4B**
 when is your birthday? c'est quand, ton anniversaire? **4B**
bit: a little bit un peu **7**
black noir **E1, 12**
blond blond **9**
blouse un chemisier **17**
blue bleu **E1, 12**
boat un bateau (*pl.* bateaux) **21**
book un livre **I1, 9**
boom box une radiocassette **9**
boots des bottes *f.* **17**
bothersome pénible **12**
boulevard un boulevard **13**
boutique une boutique **17**
boy le garçon **2A, 2B**
boyfriend un petit copain
bread le pain **25**
breakfast le petit déjeuner **25**
 to have breakfast prendre le petit déjeuner **25**
to **bring** (*a person*) amener **18**; (*things*) apporter **27**
 to bring something to someone apporter quelque chose à quelqu'un **27**
brother un frère **2C, 16**
brown brun **9**; marron (*inv.*) **12**
building: apartment building un immeuble **13**
bus un bus
 by bus en bus **14**

touring bus un autocar, un car **21**
but mais **5**
butter le beurre **25**
to **buy** acheter **33, 34**
 to buy (some) acheter + du, de la (*partitive*) **26**
by: by airplane, plane en avion **21**
 by bicycle à vélo **14**
 by bus en bus **14**
 by car en voiture **14**
 by oneself seul(e) **21**
 by subway en métro **14**
 by taxi en taxi **14**
 by train en train **14**

café un café **6**
 at (to) the café au café **6**
cafeteria: school cafeteria la cantine de l'école **25**
cake un gâteau (*pl.* gâteaux) **25**
calculator une calculatrice **9**
to **call** téléphoner **7**
came venu (*p.p. of* *venir) **23**
camera un appareil-photo (*pl.* appareils-photo) **9**
can *pouvoir **27**
 can you …? est-ce que tu peux…? **5**
 I can't je ne peux pas **5**
Canada le Canada
Canadian canadien (canadienne) **1B, 11**
 he's/she's (Canadian) il/elle est (canadien/canadienne) **2B**
cannot: I cannot je ne peux pas **5**
 I'm sorry, but I cannot je regrette, mais je ne peux pas **5**
cap (*baseball*) une casquette **17**
car une auto, une voiture **9**
 by car en voiture **14**
card une carte **(playing) cards** des cartes *f.* **15**
careful: to be careful *faire attention **8**
carrot une carotte **25**
cassette tape une cassette
cat un chat **2C**

CD un CD, un compact (disc) **9**
CD-ROM un cédérom (un CD-ROM)
cell phone un portable **9**
cereal les céréales *f.* **25**
chair une chaise **I, 9**
chalk la craie **I**
  piece of chalk un morceau de craie **I**
chalkboard un tableau (*pl.* tableaux) **I**
to **chat (online)** chatter
checkers les dames *f.* **15**
cheese le fromage **25**
cherry une cerise **25**
chess les échecs *m.* **15**
chicken le poulet **25**
child un (une) enfant **16**
  children des enfants *m.* **16**
Chinese chinois **11**
chocolate: hot chocolate un chocolat **3B**
to **choose** choisir **19**
chose, chosen choisi (*p.p. of* choisir) **23**
Christmas Noël **21**
  at Christmas à Noël **21**
church une église **13**
cinema le cinéma **6**
  to the cinema au cinéma **6**
city une ville **13**
  in the city en ville **6**
clarinet une clarinette **15**
class une classe **6**
  in class en classe **6**
classmate un (une) camarade **9**
to **clean** nettoyer **21**
clothing des vêtements *m.* **17**
  sports clothing des vêtements *m.* de sport **17**
coffee le café **3B, 13**
coin une pièce **20**
cold le froid
  to be (feel) cold *avoir froid **22**
  it's cold (*weather*) il fait froid **4C**
college student un étudiant, une étudiante **9**
color une couleur **12**
  what color? de quelle couleur? **12**
to **come** arriver **14**; *venir **15**
  come on! vas-y! **14**
  here comes ... voici... **2A**

to **come back** rentrer **14, 24**; *revenir **15**
to **come to visit** rendre visite à **20, 28**
comfortable confortable **13**
compact disc un compact (disc), un CD **9**
computer un ordinateur, un PC **9**
  computer game un jeu d'ordinateur (*pl.* les jeux d'ordinateur)
concert un concert **14**
to **continue** continuer **13**
cooking la cuisine **25**
cool: it's cool (*weather*) il fait frais **4C**
cost le coût **17**
to **cost** coûter
  how much does ... cost? combien coûte...? **3C, 17**
  it costs ... il/elle coûte... **3C**
country(side) la campagne **21**
  to (in) the country(side) à la campagne **21**
course: of course! bien sûr! **5**; mais oui! **6**
  of course not! mais non! **6**
cousin un cousin, une cousine **2C, 16**
crepe une crêpe **3A**
croissant un croissant **3A**
cuisine la cuisine **25**
cup une tasse **25**
cute mignon (mignonne) **11**

to **dance** danser **5, 7**
dark-haired brun **9**
darn! zut! **1C**
date la date **4B**; un rendez-vous **14**
  I have a date at ... j'ai un rendez-vous à... **4A**
  what's the date? quelle est la date? **4B**
daughter une fille **16**
day un jour **4B, 21**
  what day is it? quel jour est-ce? **4B**
  whole day une journée
dear cher (chère) **17**
December décembre *m.* **4B**

department store un grand magasin **17**
to **describe** *décrire
  describe ... décrivez...
desk un bureau **I, 9**
dessert le dessert **25**
to **detest** détester **25**
did fait (*p.p. of* *faire) **23**
difficult difficile **12**
dining room une salle à manger **13**
dinner le dîner **25**
  to have (eat) dinner dîner **7, 25**
  to have dinner at a restaurant dîner au restaurant **5**
dish (*course of a meal*) un plat **25**
to **do** *faire **8**
  do it! vas-y! **14**
  I do je veux bien **26**
  to do + *activity* *faire de + *activity* **21**
  to do my homework *faire mes devoirs **21**
dog un chien **2C**
door une porte **I, 9**
done fait (*p.p. of* *faire) **23**
to **download** télécharger
downstairs en bas **13**
downtown en ville **6**
dozen une douzaine **25**
dress une robe **17**
drink une boisson **3B, 25**
to **drink** *boire **26**
drive: to take a drive *faire une promenade en voiture **14**
drums une batterie **15**
dumb bête **11**
during pendant **21**
DVD un DVD **9**

e-mail un mail, un mél
ear une oreille **E2**
to **earn** gagner **20**
Easter Pâques *m.* **21**
  at Easter à Pâques **21**
easy facile **12**
to **eat** manger **7**
  I like to eat j'aime manger **5**

to eat breakfast *prendre le petit déjeuner **25**

to eat dinner dîner **7, 25**

to eat lunch déjeuner **25**

to eat (some) manger + du, de la *(partitive)* **26**

egg un oeuf **25**

eight •huit **1A**

eighteen dix-huit **1B**

eighth •huitième **16**

eighty quatre-vingts **2B**

elegant élégant **17**

elephant un éléphant **E4**

eleven onze **1B, 3C**

eleventh onzième **16**

England l'Angleterre *f.*

English anglais(e) **1B, 11**

errand: to run errands *faire les courses **25**

euro un euro

evening un soir **21**

in the evening du soir **4A**

this evening ce soir **23**

tomorrow evening demain soir **21, 23**

event un événement **14**

everything tout

everything's going (very) well ça va (très) bien **1C**

everything's (going) so-so ça va comme ci, comme ça **1C**

how's everything? ça va? **1C**

exam un examen

to pass an exam réussir à un examen **19**

excuse me excusez-moi **13**

expensive cher (chère) **17**

to explain expliquer

eye un oeil *(pl.* yeux) **E2**

fall l'automne **4C**

in (the) fall en automne **4C**

false faux (fausse) **12**

family une famille **2C, 16**

far (from) loin (de) **13**

fashion la mode

in fashion (fashionable) à la mode **17**

fat: to get fat grossir **19**

father un père **16**

this is my father voici mon père **2C**

February février *m.* **4B**

to feel like *avoir envie de + *inf.* **20**

few: a few quelques **9**

fifteen quinze **1B**

fifth cinquième **16**

fifty cinquante **1C**

film un film **14, 21**

finally finalement **22**

to find trouver **17**

fine ça va **1C**

fine! d'accord **5**

everything's fine ça va bien **1C**

that's fine c'est bien **12**

to finish finir **19**

finished fini *(p.p. of* finir) **23**

first d'abord **22**; premier (première) **16**

it's (June) first c'est le premier (juin) **4B**

fish un poisson **25**

five cinq **1A**

to fix réparer **21**

flute une flûte **15**

food la nourriture **25**

foot un pied **E2**

on foot à pied **14**

for pour **6**

for whom? pour qui? **8**

fork une fourchette **25**

forty quarante **1C**

four quatre **1A**

fourteen quatorze **1B**

fourth quatrième **16**

franc *(former monetary unit of France)* un franc **3C**

that's (it's) ... francs ça fait...francs **3C**

France la France **6**

in France en France **6**

French français(e) **1B, 11**

how do you say ... in French? comment dit-on... en français? **I**

French fries des frites *f.* **25**

steak and French fries un steak-frites **3A**

Friday vendredi *m.* **4B**

friend un ami, une amie **2A**; un copain, une copine **2A**

boyfriend, girlfriend un petit copain, une petite copine

school friend un (une) camarade **9**

---

from de **22**

from (the) du, de la, de l', des **15**

from where? d'où? **15**

are you from ...? tu es de...? **1B**

I'm from ... je suis de... **1B**

front: in front of devant **9**

fruit(s) des fruits *m.* **25**

funny amusant **11**; drôle **12**

to gain weight grossir **19**

game un jeu *(pl.* jeux) **15**; un match **14**

to play a game (match) *faire un match **8**

to play a game jouer à + *game* **15**

garage un garage **13**

garden un jardin **13**

gentleman un monsieur *(pl.* messieurs) **2A**

to get: to get fat grossir **19**

to get thin maigrir **19**

girl une fille **2A**

girlfriend une petite copine

to give (to) donner (à) **27, 28**

give me donne-moi, donnez-moi **3A, 3B**

please give me s'il te plaît donne-moi **3B**

glass un verre **25**

glasses des lunettes *f.* **17**

sunglasses des lunettes *f.* de soleil **17**

to go *aller **14**

go ahead! vas-y! **14**

go away! va-t'en! **14**

to go (come) back rentrer **14, 24**; *revenir **15**

to go by bicycle *aller en vélo **14**

to go by car, by train ... *aller en auto, en train... **14**

to go food shopping *faire les courses **25**

to go rock climbing *faire de l'escalade **21**

to go shopping *faire des achats **21**

to go to assister à **21**

English-French Vocabulary *continued*

gone allé(e) (*p.p. of* *aller) 24
good bon (bonne) 12
   good morning (afternoon)
      bonjour 1A
   that's good c'est bien 12
   the weather's good
      (pleasant) il fait bon 4C
good-bye! au revoir!, salut! 1C
good-looking beau (bel, belle;
   m.pl. beaux) 9, 12, 19
grandfather un grand-père 2C,
   16
grandmother une grand-mère
   2C, 16
grandparents
   les grandsparents *m.* 16
grape juice le jus de raisin 3B
grapefruit un pamplemousse 25
gray gris 12
great super 12, 17
green vert E1, 12
   green beans les •haricots *m.*
      verts 25
guitar une guitare 9, 15

had eu (*p.p. of* *avoir) 23
hair les cheveux *m.* E2, 15
   he/she has dark hair il/elle
      est brun(e) 9
half: half past ... ... heure(s) et
      demie 4A
   half past midnight minuit et
      demi 4A
   half past noon midi et demi
      4A
ham le jambon 25
hamburger un hamburger 3A
hand une main E2
handbag un sac 9
handsome beau (bel, belle;
   m.pl. beaux) 9, 12, 19
hard difficile 12
hat un chapeau (*pl.* chapeaux)
   17
to hate détester 25
to have *avoir 10; (*food*) *prendre
   26
   do you have ...? est-ce que
      tu as...? 9
   I have j'ai 9
   I have to (must) je dois 5
   to have (some) *avoir + du,

de la (*partitive*); *prendre +
   du, de la (*partitive*) 26
to have a picnic *faire
   un pique-nique 21
to have breakfast *prendre
   le petit déjeuner 25
to have dinner dîner 25
to have dinner at a
   restaurant dîner au
   restaurant 5
to have to *avoir besoin de +
   inf. 20; *devoir 27
he il 3C, 6, 10; lui 15
   he/she is ... il/elle est +
      nationality 2B
head la tête E2
to hear entendre 20
hello bonjour 1A, 1C
to help aider 21, 27
   may I help you? vous
      désirez? 3B, 17
her elle 15; son, sa; ses 16; la 28
   (to) her lui 28
   her name is ... elle
      s'appelle... 2B
   what's her name? comment
      s'appelle-t-elle? 9
here ici 6
   here comes, here is voici 2A
   here's my mother/father
      voici ma mère/mon père
      2C
   here's some voici + du, de la
      (*partitive*) 26
   this ... (over here) ce... -ci 18
hey! dis! 12; tiens! 2A, 10
   hey there! dis donc! 12
hi! salut! 1C
high school student un (une)
      élève 9
him lui 15; le 28
   (to) him lui 28
his son, sa; ses 16
   his name is ... il s'appelle...
      2B
   what's his name? comment
      s'appelle-t-il? 9
home, at home à la maison 6;
      chez (moi, toi...) 15
   to go home rentrer 14, 24
homework les devoirs *m.* 21
   homework assignment
      un devoir I
   to do my homework *faire
      mes devoirs 21

to hope espérer 18
   horse un cheval (*pl.* chevaux)
      E4
hospital un hôpital 13
hot chaud 4C, 23
   hot chocolate un chocolat
      3B
   hot dog un •hot dog 3A
   to be hot (*people*) *avoir
      chaud 22
   it's hot (*weather*) il fait chaud
      4C
hotel un hôtel 13
house une maison 13
   at someone's house chez +
      person 14
how? comment? 8
   how are you? comment
      allez-vous?, comment
      vas-tu?, ça va? 1C
   how do you find ...?
      comment trouves-tu...? 17
   how do you say ... in
      French? comment dit-on...
      en français? I
   how much? combien (de)?
      20
   how much does ... cost?
      combien coûte...? 3C, 17
   how much is that/this/it?
      c'est combien?, ça fait
      combien? 3C
   how old are you? quel âge
      as-tu? 2C
   how old is he/she? quel âge
      a-t-il/elle? 9
   how old is your
      father/mother? quel âge a
      ton père/ta mère? 2C
   how's everything? ça va? 1C
   how's the weather? quel
      temps fait-il? 4C
   to learn how to *apprendre à
      26
hundred cent 2B, 17
hungry avoir faim 3A
   are you hungry? tu as faim?
      3A
   I'm hungry j'ai faim 3A
   to be hungry avoir faim 10,
      22
husband un mari 16

I je **6**, moi **15**
 I don't know je ne sais pas **I, 9**
 I have a date/appointment at … j'ai un rendez-vous à… **4A**
 I know je sais **I, 9, 28**
 I'm fine/okay ça va **1C**
 I'm (very) well/so-so/(very) bad ça va (très) bien/comme ci, comme ça/(très) mal **1C**
ice la glace **3A, 25**
 ice cream une glace **3A, 25**
iced tea un thé glacé **25**
idea une idée **20**
 it's (that's) a good idea c'est une bonne idée **20**
if si
in à **6, 14**; dans **9**
 in (Boston) à (Boston) **6**
 in class en classe **6**
 in front of devant **9**
 in order to pour **21**
 in the afternoon de l'après-midi **4A**
 in the morning/evening du matin/soir **4A**
 in town en ville **6**
 in (the) au, à la, à l', aux **14**
to **indicate** indiquer
inexpensive bon marché (*inv.*) **17**
ingredient un ingrédient **25**
in-line skating le roller **21**
 in-line skates des rollers **21**
 to go in-line skating faire du roller **21**
instrument un instrument **15**
to **play a musical instrument** jouer de + *instrument* **15**
intelligent intelligent **25**
interesting intéressant **11**
to **invite** inviter **7**
is (*see* **to be**)
 is there? est-ce qu'il y a? **9**
 isn't it (so)? n'est-ce pas? **6**
 there is il y a **9**
 there is (some) il y a + du, de la (*partitive*) **26**
 it il, elle **6, 10**; le, la **28**
 it's … c'est… **2A**

it's … (o'clock) il est… heure(s) **4A**
it's … euros ça fait… euros **3C**
it's fine/nice/hot/cool/cold/bad (*weather*) il fait beau/bon/chaud/frais/froid/mauvais **4C**
it's (June) first c'est le premier (juin) **4B**
it's not ce n'est pas **12**
it's raining il pleut **4C**
it's snowing il neige **4C**
what time is it? quelle heure est-il? **4A**
who is it? qui est-ce? **2A, 9**
its son, sa; ses **16**
Italian italien, italienne **11**

jacket un blouson, une veste **17**
jam la confiture **25**
January janvier *m.* **4B**
Japanese japonais(e) **1**
jeans: pair of jeans un jean **17**
to **jog** *faire du jogging **21**
jogging le jogging **21**
 jogging suit un jogging, un survêtement **17**
juice le jus
 apple juice le jus de pomme **3B, 25**
 grape juice le jus de raisin **3B**
 orange juice le jus d'orange **3B, 25**
 tomato juice le jus de tomate **3B**
July juillet *m.* **4B**
June juin *m.* **4B**

K

ketchup le ketchup **25**
keyboard un clavier **15**
kilogram un kilo (de) **25**
kind gentil (gentille) **11**
kitchen une cuisine **13**
knife un couteau **25**

to **know** *connaître **36**
 do you know …? tu connais…? **2B**
 I (don't) know je (ne) sais (pas) **I, 9, 28**
 you know tu sais **28**

lady une dame **2A**
lamp une lampe **9**
laptop computer un ordinateur portable
large grand **9, 12**
last dernier (dernière) **23**
 last month le mois dernier **23**
 last night hier soir **23**
 last Saturday samedi dernier **23**
 at last enfin **22**
to **learn (how to)** *apprendre (à) + *inf.* **26**
left gauche
 on (to) the left à gauche **13**
leg une jambe **E2**
lemon soda la limonade **3B**
to **lend** prêter (à) **27, 28**
 lend me prête-moi **3C**
less … than moins… que **19**
let's go! allons-y! **14**
lettuce la salade **25**
library une bibliothèque **13**
like: what does he/she look like? comment est-il/elle? **9**
 what's he/she like? comment est-il/elle? **9**
to **like** aimer **7**
 do you like? est-ce que tu aimes? **5**
 I also like j'aime aussi **5**
 I don't always like je n'aime pas toujours **5**
 I don't like je n'aime pas **5**
 I like j'aime **5**
 I like …, but I prefer … j'aime…, mais je préfère… **5**
 I'd like je voudrais **3A, 3B, 5**
 what would you like? vous désirez? **3B, 17**
to **listen** écouter **7**
 to listen to CDs écouter des CD **21**

to listen to the radio écouter la radio **5**

little petit **9, 12, 17**

  a little (bit) un peu **7**

to live habiter **7**

living room (*formal*) un salon **13**

to loan prêter (à) **27, 28**

long long (longue) **17**

to look (at) regarder **7**

  look! tiens! **2A, 10**

  look at that regarde ça **9**

  I'm looking for … je cherche… **17**

  to look for chercher **17**

  what does he/she look like? comment est-il/elle? **9**

to lose perdre **20**

  to lose weight maigrir **19**

lot: a lot beaucoup **7**

to love: I'd love to je veux bien **5**

luck la chance **22**

  to be lucky *avoir de la chance **22**

lunch le déjeuner **25**

  to have (eat) lunch déjeuner **25**

made fait (*p.p. of* *faire) **23**

to make *faire **8**

man un homme **9**; un monsieur (*polite term*) **2A**

many beaucoup (de) **7**

  how many combien de **20**

map une carte **I**

March mars *m.* **4B**

match un match **8**

  to play a match *faire un match **8**

May mai *m.* **4B**

may *pouvoir **27**

maybe peut-être **6**

mayonnaise la mayonnaise **25**

me moi **1A, 27**

  excuse me pardon **13, 17**

  (to) me me, moi **27**

meal un repas **25**

mean méchant **11**

to mean *vouloir dire **26**

  what does … mean? que veut dire…? **I**

meat la viande **25**

to meet rencontrer **21**

to meet for the first time *connaître (*in passé composé*) **28**

Mexican mexicain(e) **11**

midnight minuit *m.* **4A**

milk le lait **25**

mineral water l'eau *f.* minérale **25**

Miss Mademoiselle (Mlle) **1C**

modern moderne **13**

Monday lundi *m.* **4B**

money l'argent *m.* **21**

month un mois **4B, 19**

  last month le mois dernier **23**

  next month le mois prochain **23**

  this month ce mois-ci **23**

moped une mob (mobylette) **9**

more … than plus… que **19**

morning le matin **21**

  good morning bonjour **1A**

  in the morning du matin **4A**

  this morning ce matin **21**

  tomorrow morning demain matin **23**

  yesterday morning hier matin **23**

mother une mère **2C, 16**

  this is my mother voici ma mère **2C**

motorbike une mob (mobylette) **9**

motorcycle une moto **9**

motorscooter un scooter **9**

mountain une montagne **21**

mountain bike un VTT **21**

  mountain biking le VTT **21**

  to do mountain biking faire du VTT **21**

  to (at/in) the mountain(s) à la montagne **21**

mouse une souris

mouth une bouche **E2**

movie un film **14, 21**

  movie theater un cinéma **6**

movies le cinéma **13**

  at (to) the movies au cinéma **6**

Mr. Monsieur (M.) **1C**

Mrs. Madame (Mme) **1C**

much, very much beaucoup **7**

  how much? combien? **20**

  how much does … cost? combien coûte…? **3C, 17**

  how much is it? ça fait combien?, c'est combien? **3C**

too much trop **17**

museum un musée **13**

music la musique **15**

must *devoir **27**

  I must je dois **5**

my mon, ma; mes **2C, 16**

  my birthday is (March 2) mon anniversaire est le (2 mars) **4B**

  my name is … je m'appelle… **1A**

name: his/her name is … il/elle s'appelle… **2B**

  my name is … je m'appelle… **1A**

  what's …'s name? comment s'appelle…? **2B**

  what's his/her name? comment s'appelle-t-il/elle? **9**

  what's your name? comment t'appelles-tu? **1A**

napkin une serviette **25**

nasty méchant **11**

nationality la nationalité **1B**

nearby près **13**

neat chouette **12**

neck le cou **E2**

to need *avoir besoin de **20**

neighbor un voisin, une voisine **9**

neighborhood un quartier **13**

  a nice neighborhood un joli quartier **13**

never ne… jamais **24**

new nouveau (nouvel, nouvelle; *m.pl.* nouveaux) **19**

next prochain **21, 23**

  next week la semaine prochaine **23**

nice gentil (gentille), sympathique **11**

  it's nice (beautiful) weather il fait beau **4C**

night: tomorrow night demain soir **4A**

last night hier soir **23**
nine neuf **1A**
nineteen dix-neuf **1B**
ninety quatre-vingt-dix **2B**
ninth neuvième **16**
no non **1B, 6**
  no … pas de **10, 26**
  no? n'est-ce pas? **6**
nobody ne… personne,
  personne **24**
noon midi *m.* **4A**
nose le nez **E2**
not ne… pas **6**
  not a, not any pas de **10, 26**
  not always pas toujours **5**
  not anybody ne… personne
  24
  not anything ne… rien **24**
  not at all pas du tout **15**
  it's (that's) not ce n'est pas **12**
  of course not! mais non! **6**
notebook un cahier **I, 9**
nothing ne… rien, rien **24**
November novembre *m.* **4B**
now maintenant **7, 23**

o'clock heure(s)
  at … o'clock à… heures **4A**
  it's … o'clock il est… heure(s)
  4A
object un objet **9**
ocean la mer **21**; l'océan *m.*
  to (at) the oceanside à la mer
  21
October octobre *m.* **4B**
of de **6**
  of (the) du, de la, de l', des **15**
  of course not! mais non! **6**
  of course! bien sûr! **5**
  of whom de qui **8**
often souvent **7**
oh: oh, really? ah, bon? **8**
okay d'accord **5**
  I'm okay ça va **1C**
old vieux (vieil, vieille; *m.pl.*
  vieux) **19**
  he/she is … (years old) il/elle
  a… ans **2C**
  how old are you? quel âge
  as-tu? **2C**
  how old is he/she? quel âge
  a-t-il/elle? **9**

how old is your father/
  mother? quel âge a ton
  père/ta mère? **2C**
I'm … (years old) j'ai… ans **2C**
to be … (years old) *avoir …
  ans **10**
omelet une omelette **3A**
on sur **9**
  on foot à pied **14**
  on Monday lundi **10**
  on Mondays le lundi **10**
  on vacation en vacances **6**
one un, une **1**; *(we, they, people)*
  on **20**
oneself: by oneself seul **21**
only seul **21**
open *ouvrir
  open … ouvre… (ouvrez…) **I**
opinion: in my opinion à mon
  avis **19**
or ou **1B, 6**
orange *(color)* orange *(inv.)* **E1,**
  12
orange *(fruit)* une orange **25**
  orange juice le jus d'orange
  3B, 25
order: in order to pour **21**
to **organize** organiser **7**
other autre **25**
our notre; nos **16**
out of style démodé **17**
over: over (at) …'s house
  chez… **15**
  over there là-bas **6**
  that (one), over there ça,
  là-bas **9**
overcoat un manteau
  (pl. manteaux) **17**
to **own** *avoir **10**

P

P.M. du soir **4A**
pain: a pain pénible **12**
pants un pantalon **17**
pantyhose des collants *m.* **17**
paper le papier **I**
  sheet of paper une feuille
  de papier **I**
parents les parents *m.* **16**
park un parc **13**
party *(informal)* une fête, une
  soirée, une boum **14**

to **pass a test (an exam)** réussir à
  un examen **19**
past: half past … … heure(s) et
  demie **4A**
  quarter past … … heure(s) et
  quart **4A**
to **pay (for)** payer **20**
  to pay attention *faire
  attention **8**
pear une poire **25**
peas les petits pois *m.* **25**
pen un stylo **I, 9**
pencil un crayon **I, 9**
people des gens *m.* **10**; on **20**
perhaps peut-être **6**
person une personne **2A, 9**
pet un animal *(pl.* animaux)
  domestique **2C**
to **phone** téléphoner **7**
piano un piano **15**
to **pick up** ranger **21**
picnic un pique-nique **14**
  to have a picnic *faire
  un pique-nique **21**
pie une tarte **25**
piece: piece of chalk
  un morceau de craie **I**
ping-pong le Ping-Pong **15**
pink rose **12**
pizza une pizza **3A**
place un endroit **14**
  place setting un couvert **25**
to **place** *mettre **18**
placed mis *(p.p. of* *mettre) **23**
plain moche **17**
plane un avion **21**
  by plane en avion **21**
plate une assiette **25**
to **play** jouer **7**
  to play a game jouer à +
  game **15**
  to play a game (match) *faire
  un match **8**
  to play a musical instrument
  jouer de + *instrument* **15**
  to play basketball (soccer,
  tennis) jouer au basket (au
  foot, au tennis) **5**
pleasant sympathique **11**
  it's pleasant (good) weather
  il fait bon **4C**
please s'il vous plaît *(formal)*
  3B; s'il te plaît *(informal)* **3A**
  please give me … s'il te plaît,
  donne-moi… **3B**

polo shirt un polo **17**
pool: swimming pool
  une piscine **13**
poor pauvre **20**
poorly mal **1C**
popular à la mode **17**
poster une affiche **9**
potato une pomme de terre **25**
pound une livre (de) **25**
to **prefer** préférer **18, 25**
  I prefer je préfère + *inf.* **5**
  I like …, but I prefer …
    j'aime…, mais je préfère… **5**
to **prepare** préparer **21**
pretty joli **9, 17**
price un prix **17**
  what's the price? quel est
    le prix? **17**
printer une imprimante
pullover un pull **17**
pupil un (une) élève **9**
to **purchase** acheter **21**
purple violet (violette) **E1**
to **put** *mettre **18**
  to put on *mettre **18**

quantity une quantité **25**
quarter un quart
  quarter of … … heure(s)
    moins le quart **4A**
  quarter past … … heure(s) et
    quart **4A**

racket une raquette **9**
radio une radio **9**
  to listen to the radio écouter
    la radio **5**
rain: it's raining il pleut **4C**
raincoat un imper
    (imperméable) **17**
rarely rarement **7**
rather assez **11**
really: oh, really? ah, bon? **8**
  really?! vraiment?! **15**
red rouge **E1, 12**
relatives les parents *m.* **16**
to **rent** louer **21**
to **repair** réparer **21**
to **respond** répondre **28**

restaurant un restaurant **13**
  at (to) the restaurant au
    restaurant **6**
  have dinner at a restaurant
    dîner au restaurant **5**
to **return** rentrer **24**; *revenir **15**
rice le riz **25**
rich riche **20**
ride: to take a bicycle ride
    *faire une promenade à
    vélo **14**
right vrai **12**; droite
  right? n'est-ce pas? **6**
  all right d'accord **5**
  to be right *avoir raison **22**
  to (on) the right à droite **13**
roast beef le rosbif **25**
rock climbing l'escalade *f.* **21**
  to do rock climbing *faire de
    l'escalade **21**
room une chambre **9**; une salle
    13
  bathroom une salle de bains
    13
  dining room une salle à
    manger **13**
  formal living room un salon
    13
to **run** *(referring to objects)* marcher **9**

sailing la voile **21**
salad une salade **3A, 25**
salami le saucisson **25**
salt le sel **25**
sandal une sandale **17**
sandwich un sandwich **3A**
Saturday samedi *m.* **4B, 23**
  see you Saturday! à samedi!
    4B
  last Saturday samedi dernier
    23
  next Saturday samedi
    prochain **23**
saw vu *(p.p. of* *voir) **23**
saxophone un saxo
    (saxophone) **15**
say *dire **28**
  say … dites…
  say! dis (donc)! **12**
  **how do you say … in
    French?** comment dit-on…
    en français? **I**

school une école **13**
  school cafeteria la cantine
    de l'école **25**
  school friend un (une)
    camarade **9**
screen *(computer)* un écran
sea la mer **21**
  to (at) the sea à la mer **21**
season une saison **4C**
second deuxième **16**
to **see** *voir **21**
  see you tomorrow! à
    demain! **4B, 21**
seen vu *(p.p. of* *voir) **23**
seldom rarement **7**
to **sell** vendre **20**
to **send** envoyer
  to send an e-mail envoyer
    un mail
September septembre *m.* **4B**
to **set the table** *mettre la table
    25
seven sept **1A**
seventeen dix-sept **1B**
seventh septième **16**
seventy soixante-dix **2A**
she elle **6, 10, 15**
sheet of paper une feuille de
    papier **I**
ship un bateau *(pl.* bateaux) **21**
shirt une chemise **17**
shoe une chaussure **17**
  tennis shoes des tennis *m.* **17**
shop une boutique **17**
shopping: shopping center
    un centre commercial **13**
  to go food shopping *faire
    les courses **25**
  to go shopping *faire des
    achats **21**
shore la mer **21**
short court **17**; petit **9, 12, 17**
  he/she is short il/elle est
    petit(e) **9**
shorts un short **17**
should *devoir **27**
to **show** indiquer; montrer à **27,
    28**
to **shut** fermer **I**
shy timide **11**
silly bête **11**
to **sing** chanter **5, 7**
sir Monsieur (M.) **1C**
sister une soeur **2C, 16**
six six **1A**

sixteen seize **1B**
sixth sixième **16**
sixty soixante **1C, 2A**
skateboard un skate
   skateboarding le skate **21**
   to go skateboarding faire du skate **21**
to **ski** *faire du ski **21**
   skiing le ski **21**
skirt une jupe **17**
small petit **9, 12, 17**
sneakers des tennis *m.* **17**
   hightop sneakers des baskets *m.* **17**
snow: it's snowing il neige **4C**
snowboard un snowboard, un surf (des neiges) **21**
   snowboarding le snowboard, le surf (des neiges) **21**
   to go snowboarding faire du snowboard **21**
so alors **7**
   so-so comme ci, comme ça **1C**
   everything's (going) so-so ça va comme ci, comme ça **1C**
soccer le foot (football) **15**
sock une chaussette **17**
soda un soda **3B**
   lemon soda une limonade **3B**
sold vendu (*p.p. of* vendre) **23**
sole (*fish*) la sole **25**
some des **10**; du, de la, de l' **26**; quelques **9**
somebody quelqu'un **24**
someone quelqu'un **24**
something quelque chose **24**
son un fils **16**
sorry: to be sorry regretter
   I'm sorry, but (I cannot) je regrette, mais (je ne peux pas) **5**
soup la soupe **25**
spaghetti les spaghetti *m.* **25**
Spanish espagnol(e) **11**
to **speak** parler **7**
   to speak (French, English, Spanish) parler (français, anglais, espagnol) **5**
   to speak to parler à **28**
to **spend** (*money*) dépenser **20**; (*time*) passer **21**

spoon une cuillère **25**
sports le sport **21**
   to play a sport *faire du sport **21**; jouer à + *sport* **15**
   sports clothing des vêtements *m.* de sport **17**
spring le printemps **4C**
   in the spring au printemps **4C**
stadium un stade **13**
to **stay** rester **14**
steak un steak **3A**
   steak and French fries un steak-frites **3A**
stereo set une chaîne hi-fi **9**
stomach le ventre **E2**
store un magasin **13, 17**
   department store un grand magasin **17**
straight tout droit **13**
strawberry une fraise **25**
street une rue **13**
student (*high school*) un (une) élève **9**; (*college*) un étudiant, une étudiante **9**
to **study** étudier **5, 7**
stupid bête **11**
style: in style à la mode **17**
   out of style démodé **17**
subway le métro **14**
   by subway en métro **14**
to **succeed** réussir **19**
sugar le sucre **25**
summer l'été *m.* **4C**
   summer vacation les grandes vacances **21**
   in the summer en été **4C**
sun le soleil **17**
Sunday dimanche *m.* **4B**
sunglasses des lunettes *f.* de soleil **17**
supermarket un supermarché **13**
supper le dîner **25**
   to have (eat) supper dîner **7, 25**
sure bien sûr **5**
   sure! mais oui! **6**
   are you sure? tu es sûr(e)? **16**
to **surf the Internet** surfer sur l'Internet
sweater un pull **17**
sweatshirt un sweat **17**
to **swim** nager **7**
   I like to swim j'aime nager **5**
swimming pool une piscine **13**

swimsuit un maillot de bain **17**
Swiss suisse **11**

table une table **I, 9**
   to set the table *mettre la table **25**
to **take** *prendre **I, 26**
   to take along amener **18, 27**
   to take a bicycle ride *faire une promenade à vélo **14**
   to take a drive *faire une promenade en voiture **14**
   to take a trip *faire un voyage **8**
   to take a walk *faire une promenade à pied **14**
to **talk** parler **7**
   to talk to parler à **28**
tall grand **9, 12**
tape: cassette tape une cassette
taxi un taxi **14**
   by taxi en taxi **14**
tea le thé **3B**
   iced tea un thé glacé **25**
teacher un (une) prof **2A, 9**; un professeur **9**
telephone un téléphone **9**
to **telephone** téléphoner **7**
television la télé **9**
   to watch television regarder la télé **5**
to **tell** *dire **28**
ten dix **1A, 1B**
tennis le tennis **15**
   tennis racket une raquette de tennis **15**
   tennis shoes des tennis *m.* **17**
   to play tennis jouer au tennis **5**
tenth dixième **16**
terrific génial **12**; super **12, 17**
test un examen
   to pass a test réussir à un examen **19**
than que **19**
thank you merci **1C**
that que **17**; ce, cet, cette **18**
   that is … c'est… **9, 12**
   that (one), over there ça, là-bas **9**

English-French Vocabulary *continued*

that's ... c'est... **2A, 9, 12;**
   voilà **2A**
that's ... euros ça fait...
   euros **3C**
that's bad c'est mal **12**
that's a good idea! c'est
   une bonne idée! **20**
that's good (fine) c'est bien
   12
that's not ... ce n'est pas... **12**
what's that? qu'est-ce que
   c'est? **9**
the le, la, l' **2B, 10;** les **10**
theater un théâtre **13**
   movie theater un cinéma **13**
their leur, leurs **16**
them eux, elles **15;** les **28**
   (to) them leur **28**
   themselves eux-mêmes
then alors **11;** ensuite **22**
there là **6**
   there is (are) il y a **9**
   **there is (here comes
      someone)** voilà **2A**
   there is (some) il y a + du, de
      la (*partitive*) **26**
   there's some voilà + du, de
      la (*partitive*) **26**
   over there là-bas **6**
   that (one), over there ça,
      là-bas **9;** ce...-là **18**
   what is there? qu'est-ce qu'il
      y a? **9**
these ces **18**
   these are ce sont **12**
they ils, elles **6;** eux **15;** on **20**
   they are ce sont **12**
thin: to get thin maigrir **19**
thing une chose
   things are going (very) badly
      ça va (très) mal **1C**
to **think** penser **17**
   to think of penser de,
      trouver **17**
   to think that penser que **17**
   what do you think of ...?
      comment trouves-tu...?,
      qu'est-ce que tu penses
      de...? **17**
third troisième **16**
thirsty: to be thirsty *avoir soif
   22
   are you thirsty? tu as soif?
      3B
   I'm thirsty j'ai soif **3B**

thirteen treize **1B**
thirty trente **1C**
   3:30 trois heures et demie
      4A
this ce, cet, cette **18**
   this is ... voici... **2A**
those ces **18**
   those are ce sont **12**
thousand mille **2B, 17**
three trois **1A**
Thursday jeudi *m.* **4B**
tie une cravate **17**
tights des collants *m.* **17**
time: at what time is ...? à
      quelle heure est...? **4A**
   at what time? à quelle
      heure? **4A**
   what time is it? quelle heure
      est-il? **4A**
to **à 6, 14;** chez **14, 15**
   to (the) au, à la, à l', aux **14**
   in order to pour **21**
   to class en classe **6**
   to someone's house chez +
      person **14**
   to whom à qui **8**
today aujourd'hui **4B, 23**
   today is (Wednesday)
      aujourd'hui, c'est
      (mercredi) **4B**
toilet les toilettes **13**
tomato une tomate
   tomato juice le jus de
      tomate **3B**
tomorrow demain **4B**
   tomorrow afternoon
      demain après-midi **23**
   tomorrow is (Thursday)
      demain, c'est (jeudi) **4B**
   tomorrow morning demain
      matin **23**
   tomorrow night (evening)
      demain soir **23**
   see you tomorrow!
      à demain! **4B, 21**
tonight ce soir **23**
too aussi **1B, 7;** trop **17**
   too bad! dommage! **7**
touring bus un autocar, un car
   21
tourist: tourist office office (*m.*)
   de tourisme
town un village **13**
   in town en ville **6**
track suit un survêtement **17**

train un train **21**
   by train en train **14, 21**
to **travel** voyager **5, 7**
   trip: to take a trip *faire
      un voyage **8**
trousers un pantalon **17**
true vrai **12**
T-shirt un tee-shirt **17**
Tuesday mardi *m.* **4B**
tuna le thon **25**
to **turn** tourner **13**
   to turn on *mettre **18**
TV la télé **9**
   to watch TV regarder la télé
      5
twelfth douzième **16**
twelve douze **1B**
twenty vingt **1B, 1C**
two deux **1A**

ugly moche **17**
uncle un oncle **2C, 16**
under sous **9**
to **understand** *comprendre **26**
   I (don't) understand je (ne)
      comprends (pas) **I**
unfashionable démodé **17**
United States les États-Unis *m.*
upstairs en • haut **13**
us nous **15**
   (to) us nous **27**
to **use** utiliser

vacation les vacances *f.* **21**
   on vacation en vacances **6**
   summer vacation les
      grandes vacances **21**
VCR (videocassette recorder)
   un magnétoscope
veal le veau **25**
vegetable un légume **25**
very très **11**
   very well très bien **7**
   very much beaucoup **7**
video game un jeu vidéo (*pl.*
   des jeux vidéo)
videotape une cassette vidéo **9**
violin un violon **15**

to visit (*place*) visiter **7, 20;** (*people*) rendre visite à **20, 28**
volleyball le volley (volleyball) **15**

to wait (for) attendre **20**
walk une promenade **14**
  to take (go for) a walk *faire une promenade à pied **8, 14**
  to walk *aller à pied **14;** marcher **9**
to want *avoir envie de **20;** *vouloir **26**
  do you want …? tu veux…? **3A**
  do you want to …? est-ce que tu veux…? **5**
  I don't want … je ne veux pas… **5**
  I want … je veux… **5, 26**
  I want to je veux bien **26**
  what do you want? qu'est-ce que tu veux? **3A;** vous désirez? **3B, 17**
wanted voulu (*p.p. of* *vouloir) **26**
warm chaud **4C, 23**
  to be warm (*people*) *avoir chaud **22**
  it's warm (*weather*) il fait chaud **4C**
was été (*p.p. of* *être) **23**
to wash laver **21**
to waste perdre **20**
watch une montre **9**
to watch regarder **7**
  to watch TV regarder la télé **5**
water l'eau *f.* **25**
  mineral water l'eau minérale **25**
to water-ski *faire du ski nautique **21**
  water-skiing le ski nautique **21**
we nous **6, 15;** on **20**
to wear *mettre **18;** porter **17**
weather: how's (what's) the weather? quel temps fait-il? **4C**
  it's … weather il fait… **4C**
Wednesday mercredi *m.* **4B**

week une semaine **4B, 21**
  last week la semaine dernière **23**
  next week la semaine prochaine **23**
  this week cette semaine **23**
weekend un week-end **21**
  last weekend le week-end dernier **23**
  next weekend le week-end prochain **21, 23**
  this weekend ce week-end **23**
weight: to gain weight grossir **19**
well bien **7**
  well! eh bien! **18**
  well then alors **11**
  everything's going (very) well ça va (très) bien **1C**
went allé (*p.p. of* *aller) **24**
what comment? quoi? **17;** qu'est-ce que **8**
  what color? de quelle couleur? **12**
  what day is it? quel jour est-ce? **4B**
  what do you think of …? comment trouves-tu…?, qu'est-ce que tu penses de…? **17**
  what do you want? qu'est-ce que tu veux? **3A;** vous désirez? **3B, 17**
  what does … mean? que veut dire…? **I**
  what does he/she look like? comment est-il/elle? **9**
  what is it? qu'est-ce que c'est? **9**
  what is there? qu'est-ce qu'il y a? **9**
  what time is it? quelle heure est-il? **4A**
  what would you like? vous désirez? **3B, 17**
  what's …'s name? comment s'appelle…? **2B**
  what's he/she like? comment est-il/elle? **9**
  what's his/her name? comment s'appelle-t-il/elle? **9**
  what's that? qu'est-ce que c'est? **9**

  what's the date? quelle est la date? **4B**
  what's the price? quel est le prix? **17**
  what's the weather? quel temps fait-il? **4C**
  what's your address? quelle est ton adresse? **13**
  what's your name? comment t'appelles-tu? **1A**
  at what time is …? à quelle heure est…? **4A**
  at what time? à quelle heure? **4A, 8**
when quand **8**
  when is your birthday? c'est quand, ton anniversaire? **4B**
where où **6, 8**
  where is …? où est…? **6**
  where is it? où est-ce? **13**
  from where? d'où? **15**
whether si
which quel (quelle) **18**
white blanc (blanche) **E1,12**
who qui **8**
  who's that/this? qui est-ce? **2A, 9**
  about whom? de qui? **8**
  for whom? pour qui? **8**
  of whom? de qui? **8**
  to whom? à qui? **8**
  with whom? avec qui? **8**
why pourquoi **8**
wife une femme **16**
to win gagner **20**
window une fenêtre **I, 9**
to windsurf *faire de la planche à voile **21**
  windsurfing la planche à voile **21**
winter l'hiver *m.* **4C**
  in the winter en hiver **4C**
with avec **6**
  with me avec moi **5**
  with you avec toi **5**
  with whom? avec qui? **8**
woman une dame (*polite term*) **2A;** une femme **9**
to work travailler **5, 7;** (*referring to objects*) marcher **9**
  does the radio work? est-ce que la radio marche? **9**
  it (doesn't) work(s) well il/elle (ne) marche (pas) bien **9**

would: I'd like je voudrais **3A, 3B, 5**
to **write** *écrire **28**
wrong faux (fausse) **12**
   to be wrong *avoir tort **22**

year un an, une année **4B**
   he/she is ... (years old) il/elle a... ans **2C**
   I'm ... (years old) j'ai... ans **2C**
   to be ... (years old) *avoir... ans **10**

yellow jaune **E1, 12**
yes oui **1B, 6;** *(to a negative question)* si! **10**
   yes, of course oui, bien sûr **5**
   yes, okay (all right) oui, d'accord **5**
   yes, thank you oui, merci **5**
yesterday hier **23**
   yesterday afternoon hier après-midi **23**
   yesterday morning hier matin **23**
yogurt le yaourt **25**
you tu, vous **6, 15;** on **20**

you are ... tu es + *nationality* **1B**
and you? et toi? **1A**
(to) you te, vous **27**
your ton, ta; tes **2C;** votre; vos **16**
   what's your name? comment t'appelles-tu? **1A**
young jeune **9**

zero zéro **1A**

Index

A

à 89, 208; + definite article 208; vs. **chez** 211; **à demain** 61; **à samedi** 61
acheter, and verbs like 268-269
activities, talking about daily 72
adjectives agreement and formation 20, 138-139, 164-165, 166; **beau, nouveau, vieux** 279; **bon/meilleur** 262, 280; comparison with 280; demonstrative 270; interrogative 271; invariable 174, 262; of nationality 19, 167; ordinal numbers as 233; position before and after the noun 168, 175; possessive 230, 232
adverbs ending in **-ment** 357; in impersonal expressions 178; of quantity 165; position of 100
age talking about your age and asking others 37
agreement noun-adjective 166; subject-past participle 342; subject-verb 84, 94, 96, 98, 278, 288, 290, 342
Algeria 305
aller in **passé composé** 342; present 24, 206; to express near future 212; expressions 206
alphabet 17
approval, expressing 100, 289
articles see definite article; indefinite article; partitive article
attention, how to get someone's 176
avoir expressions with 45, 152, 286, 320; **passé composé** formed with 321; past participle 335; present 152; to tell age 37

B

beau, belle 279
Belgium 242
body, identifying head, neck, etc. 68
boire past participle 383; present 383

C

ça va (bien; comme çi, comme ça; mal) 24
celebrating, how to celebrate a happy occasion 349
ce, cet, cette, ces 270
c'est 27, 53, 61, 62, 140; in impersonal expressions 178; vs. **il est** 31, 177; with stress pronouns 221
chez 211, 221
clothing, talking about 258, 260, 262
combien 53; **combien de** 286
cognates 122, 243, 357
colors, talking about 40-41, 174
commands see imperative
compliments, expressing 186
comparison with adjectives 280
conclusion, how to introduce 167
connaître 398; **tu connais** 31; vs. **savoir** 398
contractions **à** with **le, les** 208; **de** with **le, les** 219, 228
contradict, how to contradict negative statements or questions 157; how to contradict someone 222

D

danser 74
dates talking about the day and date 62, 63
days of week 61; with definite article 63, 159
de 89; + definite article 219; in expressions of quantity 378; in negative sentences 156; in noun + **de** + noun 223; indicating possession 228
definite article 32, 46, 153, 155; contractions with **à** 208; contractions with **de** 219; in general sense 158; with days of week 63, 159
demonstrative adjectives 270
devoir 78, 392
dire 404
direct object pronouns **le, la, les** 399; **me, te, nous, vous** 388; position in present tense 399;

with commands 390, 401
directions asking for information/directions 199

E

écrire 404
encourage, how to wish someone luck or encourage 339
elision 32, 89, 106
emphasize how to emphasize a question/remark 270
-er verbs imperative 291; past participle 321; present 95, 98
espérer, and verbs like 269
est-ce que in information questions 106; in **passé composé** 326; in "yes-no" questions 86-87
être **être de** 19; in descriptions 177; **passé composé** formed with 342, 344; past participle 335; present 84

F

faire expressions with 53, 65, 110, 313; past participle 335; present 110
familiar vs. formal 23, 84
family members, talking about 35, 229
food and meals, talking about 45, 49, 364, 366, 370, 376, 377, 378, 383, 384, 395
future expressed with **aller** 212

G

games, talking about 220
gender 20, 27, 28, 46
geographical names prepositions with 19

H

Haiti 151

il est 31; vs. **c'est** 177
il y a 144, 379
imperative 45, 53; forms and uses 291; position of object pronouns with 390; summary charts R8-R11
indefinite article 27, 28, 153, 155; in negative sentences 156
indirect object pronouns **lui, leur** 402; **me, te, nous, vous 388** position in present tense 402; with commands 390, 402
infinitive 94; after certain verbs 74, 75, 101; in **aller** + infinitive 212
interrogative constructions **combien, combien de** 262; **est-ce que** 86; in **passé composé** 326; information questions 106, 262; inversion 111; **quel, quelle** 271; **qu'est-ce que** 86, 109, 140, 262; **qui,** and expressions with 108; "yes-no" questions 86-87, 111; expressions 106
intonation 47, 51, 86-87, 106
invitations accepting, extending, rejecting 78
inversion in the **passé composé** 326, 342; in the present 111
-ir verbs imperative 291; past participle 333; present 278

jouer à 75; **jouer de** 220

leisure time, talking about 308
liaison 29, 32, 36, 57, 63, 84, 89, 94, 96, 152, 153, 155, 156, 175, 206, 208, 219, 223, 228, 230, 232, 268, 270, 271, 279, 280, 388, 399
live, describing where you live 196

maps 4, 8-9, R2, R4
Martinique 19
mettre 259; past participle 335;

present 272, 364
money (French) talking about how much things cost; borrowing money 52, 53, 285; expressions 53
months of the year 62
Morocco 357
music, talking about 220

nager 74
names giving your name; asking others 11, 15, 31
nationalities, talking about 19, 167
negation followed by **de** 381; how to answer yes/no questions 87; in the **passé composé** 324, 342; **ne...jamais** 346; **ne...pas** 74, 77, 78, 88, 98; **ne...personne** 347; **ne...rien** 347; position 212, 381; **si** 157
nouns abbreviations 23; gender: masculine/feminine 27, 28, 46, 138, 153; irregular plurals 258; noun + **de** + noun 223; number: singular/plural 154, 258; replaced by subject pronouns 53, 142; shortened forms 75
nouveau, nouvelle 279
numbers cardinal 17, 21, 25, 29, 33, 262; in dates 63; ordinal 62, 233; pronunciation of 33; summary chart R7

on 288
opinions, expressing 178; introducing personal opinions 281
ouvrir 132

parce que 106
partitive article 378-379; in negative phrases 381
parts of the body 68
passé composé 333; **-er** verbs 152 (TE); **-ir** verbs 278 (TE); **-re** verbs 290 (TE); **acheter (préférer)** 268-

269 (TE); **aller** 206-207 (TE); **mettre** 272 (TE); **venir** 218 (TE); formed with **avoir** 321; formed with **être** 342, 344; in negative sentences 324; in questions 326; summary charts R8-R11
past events, talking about 321, 333, 335, 340
past participle agreement with subject 342; irregular verbs 335; regular verbs 321, 333
people, talking about and describing 27, 138
plural adjectives 166, 230, 232, 270-271; articles 154-155; nouns 154-155
possession possessive adjectives 36, 230; with **de** 228
possessions, talking about 142, 144, 147
preferences expressing 268, 367; **j'aime, je n'aime pas, je préfère** 74; telling someone to leave you alone 391
pouvoir 78, 392
préférer 268
prendre past participle 377; present 364, 377, 379
prepositions 85, 89; with cities, countries 19; with stress pronouns 221
present tense 94-95; of regular verbs: *see* **-er, -ir, -re** verbs; summary charts R8; of irregular verbs: *see* individual verb listings; summary charts R9
pronouns direct object 388, 390; indirect object 402; stress 15, 221; subject 53, 84-85, 142, 153, 288
pronunciation 17, 21, 25, 29, 33, 37, 47, 51, 55, 57, 84, 89, 94, 96, 101, 111, 153, 154, 155, 159, 164, 166, 169, 175, 179, 208, 213, 219, 223, 228, 232, 233, 270, 271, 272, 273, 279, 280, 281, 290, 293, 327, 337, 347, 378, 383, 393, 405; summary chart R5

quantity expressions of 370, 371; partitive article to express 378-379

quand 62, 336
Quebec 31
quel, quelle 271; **quel âge...** 37
quelqu'un, quelque chose 347
qu'est-ce que 109
questions information 326; inversion 111; "yes-no" 87, 326
qui 108; qui **est-ce** 27, 138; expressions with 108

regret, expressing 100
-re verbs imperative 291; past participle 333; present 290, 403

salutations, asking how someone is doing 23
salut vs. **bonjour** 23
savoir 140; vs. **connaître** 398
seasons 65

sequence, how to talk about the order in which things take place 323
Senegal 105
sound-spelling correspondence summary chart R5
spelling marks 17
sports, talking about 220
stress pronouns 15, 221
subject pronouns 53, 84-85, 142, 153, 288
surprise, mild doubt, expressing 107, 222, 231

time, how to tell 56-58; at what time? 58
tu vs. **vous** 49, 84

vacation, talking about 312
venir in **passé composé** 344; present 218

verbs regular **-er** singular 94; plural 94; negative 98: see **-er, -ir, -re** verbs; irregular: see individual verb listings; summary charts R8-R11; followed by indirect objects 403; followed by infinitive 74-75, 77, 101; stem-changing 218, 268, 286, 310
vieux, vieille 279
voici 27, 379
voilà 27, 379
voir past participle 335; present 332
vouloir 376; **je veux/ne veux pas, je voudrais** 77, 78, 376, 379; **tu veux** 45
vous vs. **tu** 49, 84

weather expressions, talking about the seasons and weather 65
weekend, talking about 310
wishes, expressing 77

Credits